Travels in Another Country

A Guide to Gaelic Scotland

TRAVELS IN ANOTHER COUNTRY

A Guide to Gaelic Scotland

COINNEACH MACLEAN

acair

Gu Jo

Gun i a bhith ann, cha bhiodh seo ann.

Coinneach Maclean is a Gaelic speaker from the island of South Uist. Although he initially trained as an archaeologist at Edinburgh and Cambridge Universities he has had a diverse career, including deer farming, rural development and working at a senior level in the heritage industry. After retirement he trained as a Blue Badge tourist guide which led to guiding work all over Scotland. He also successfully defended a doctoral thesis entitled 'The Tourist Gaze on Gaelic Scotland' at Glasgow University. He has been a Board Member of Historic Environment Scotland. Now living in the Isle of Skye, he gives talks to tourists, sharing his wide knowledge of Gaelic and Highland history with them.

Clàr-innse: *Contents*

Gaelic's Decline in Scotland

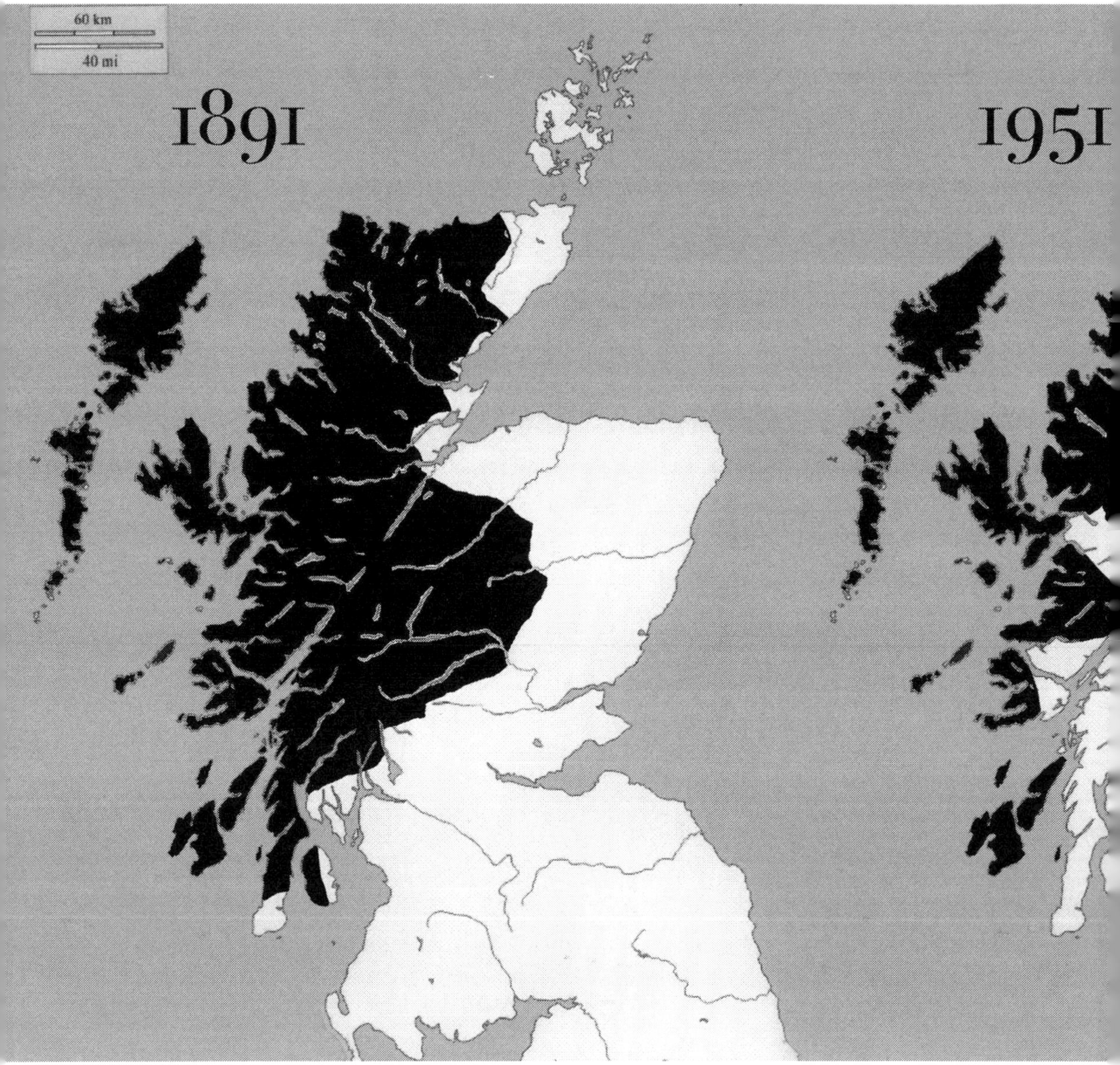

= Districts with over 50% Gaelic speakers

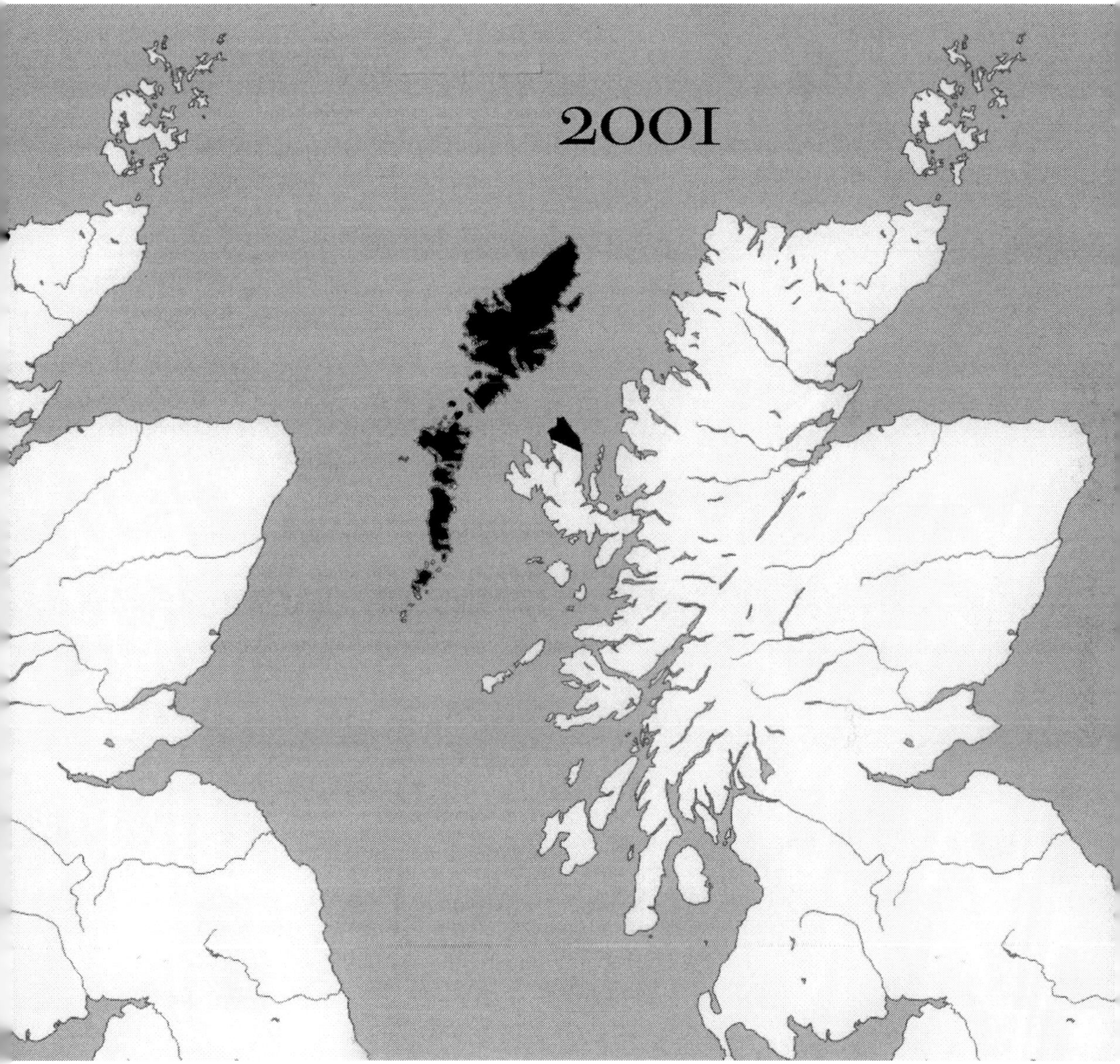

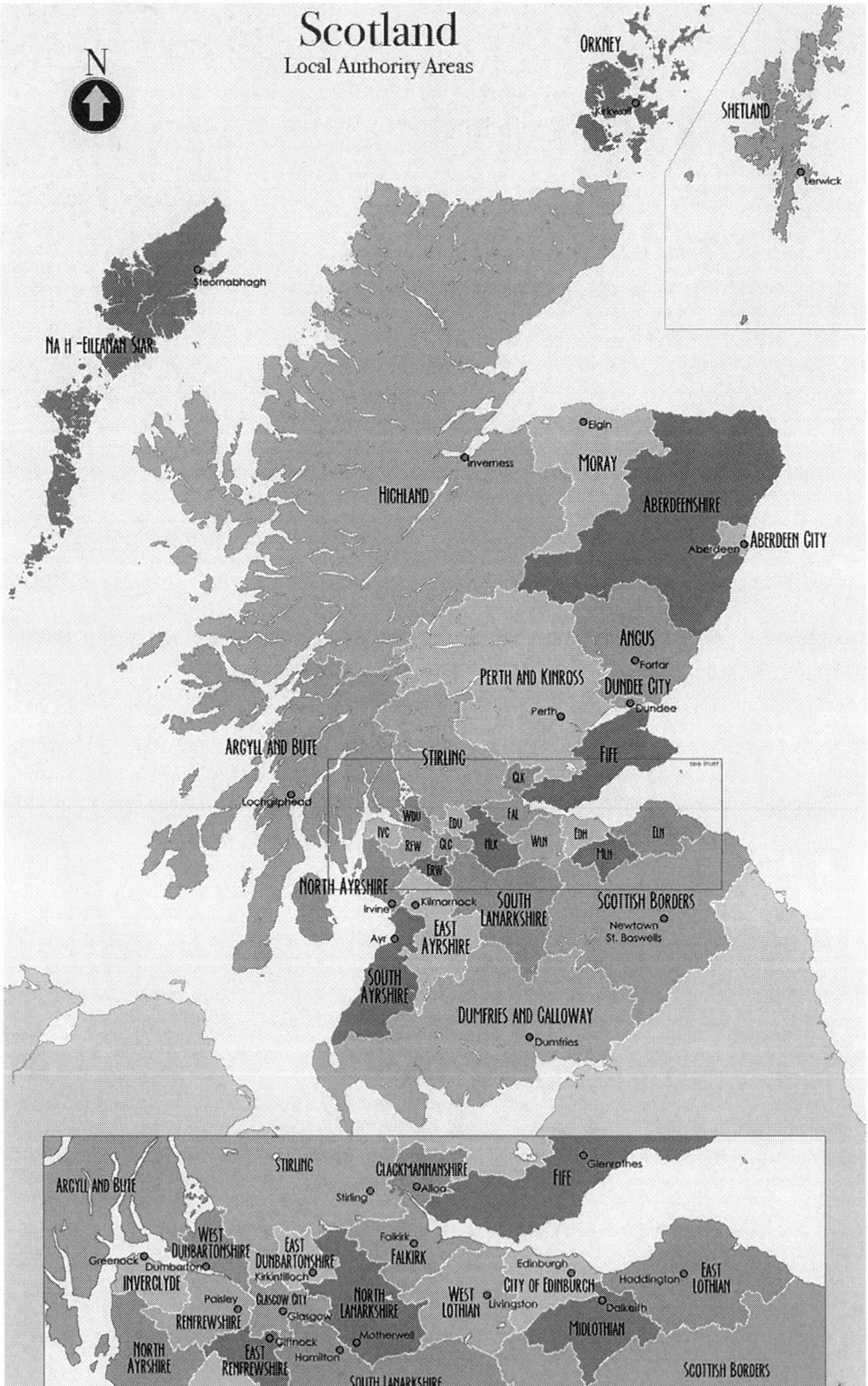
Scotland
Local Authority Areas
N
ORKNEY
Kirkwall
SHETLAND
Lerwick
Steornabhagh
NA H-EILEANAN SIAR
Elgin
Inverness
MORAY
HIGHLAND
ABERDEENSHIRE
Aberdeen
ABERDEEN CITY
ANGUS
Forfar
PERTH AND KINROSS
DUNDEE CITY
Dundee
Perth
ARGYLL AND BUTE
STIRLING
FIFE
CLK
Lochgilphead
WDU
EDU
FAL
IVC
RFW
GLC
NLK
WLN
EDH
ELN
MLN
ERW
NORTH AYRSHIRE
Kilmarnock
Irvine
SOUTH LANARKSHIRE
SCOTTISH BORDERS
Newtown St. Boswells
EAST AYRSHIRE
Ayr
SOUTH AYRSHIRE
DUMFRIES AND GALLOWAY
Dumfries
STIRLING
CLACKMANNANSHIRE
Glenrothes
ARGYLL AND BUTE
Alloa
FIFE
Stirling
WEST DUNBARTONSHIRE
EAST DUNBARTONSHIRE
Falkirk
FALKIRK
Greenock
Dumbarton
Kirkintilloch
Edinburgh
Haddington
EAST LOTHIAN
INVERCLYDE
CITY OF EDINBURGH
Paisley
GLASGOW CITY
NORTH LANARKSHIRE
WEST LOTHIAN
Livingston
Dalkeith
Glasgow
RENFREWSHIRE
MIDLOTHIAN
Giffnock
Motherwell
NORTH AYRSHIRE
EAST RENFREWSHIRE
Hamilton
SOUTH LANARKSHIRE
SCOTTISH BORDERS

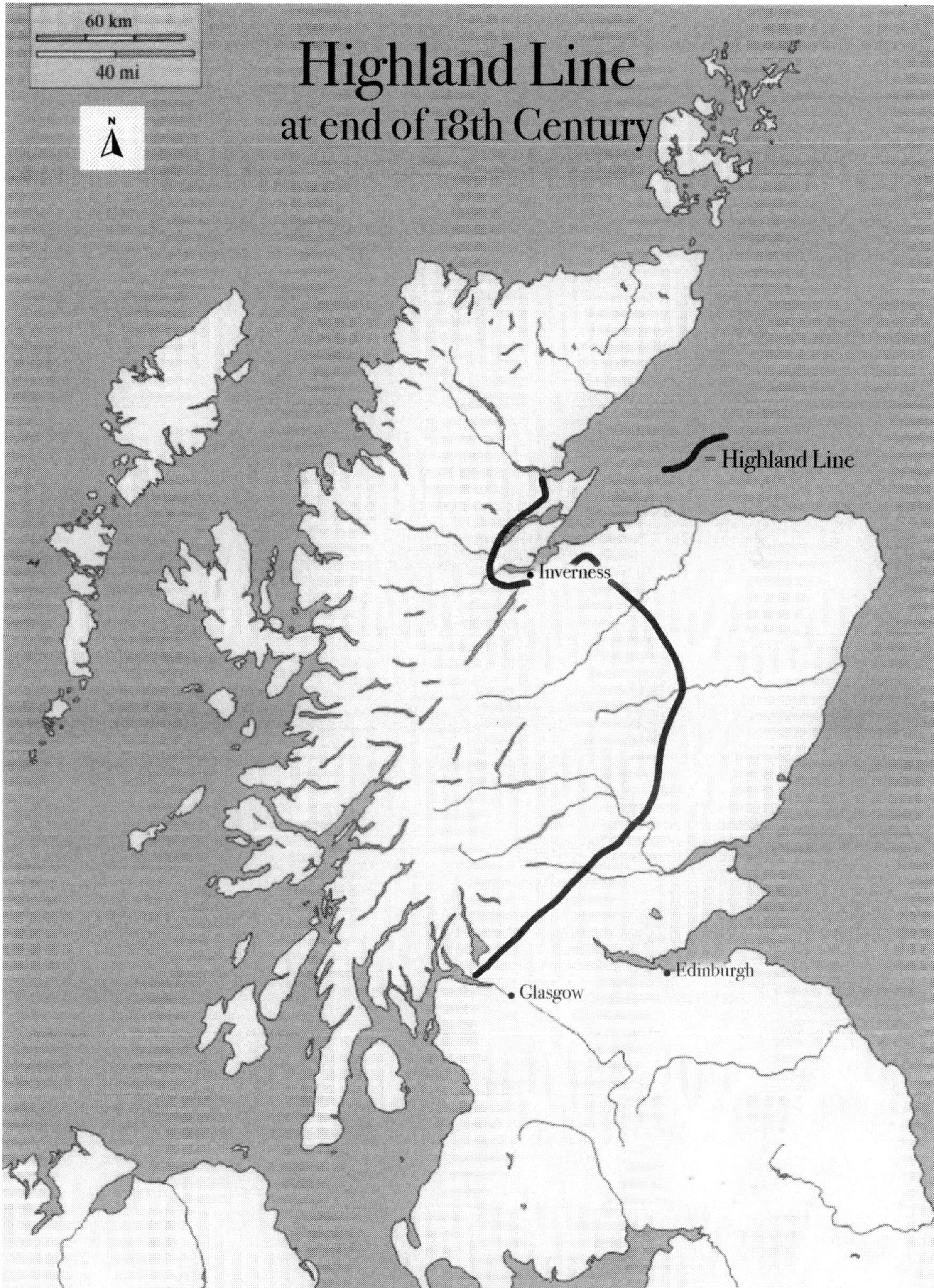
60 km
40 mi
N
Highland Line
at end of 18th Century
= Highland Line
Inverness
Edinburgh
Glasgow

Ro-ràdh: *Introduction*

Scotland is a Gaelic country. By that I mean that most of it was once inhabited and named by people who spoke Scottish Gaelic, a Celtic language which is still used today. This Gaelic is closely related to Irish Gaeilge. It also shares many common features with the other Celtic languages of the British Isles – Manx, Welsh and Cornish. It is now generally agreed that the people who spoke the language migrated from the northern part of Ireland into western Scotland almost 2000 years ago. Through a gradual process of conquest, diplomacy and marriage, they succeeded in dominating the country and displacing other languages, primarily Pictish. The term Gàidheal (Gael) is used for somebody who speaks the Gaelic language. The area where it is, or was recently, the language of everyday speech is known as the Gàidhealtachd.

Around 1000 years ago, Gaelic speakers lived in almost the whole of the area we now know as Scotland. After the invasion and conquest of Orkney and Shetland by Vikings, Scandinavian language and culture came to dominate these islands and so they are not included in this book. At the same time, however, the use of a form of northern English, known as 'Inglis', became an alternative means of communication, especially in the trading towns and at the courts of the monarchs and the great Anglo-Norman barons. The gradual spread of this new tongue, now referred to as 'Scots', has meant that in 2022, out of a population of 5.2 million, just some 70,000 people in Scotland could speak Gaelic, though hearteningly some 130,000 in all claim to have some ability in the language. There is a significant and increased interest and value associated with the Gaelic language and culture, as highlighted in the Scottish Social Attitudes Survey 2021, where more than three-quarters of the population thought that Gaelic was either important or very important to Scotland's cultural heritage.

Wilhelm von Humbolt stated that:

> Absolutely nothing is so important for a nation's culture as its language.

In this, he echoed Samuel Johnson, distinguished man of letters, who once observed:

> … languages are the pedigree of nations.

The use of a language denotes far more than a code of communication. This is true of Scotland, where Gaelic speech came to mark the people of the North and West of Scotland as distinct and separate from the English-speaking communities of the Lowlands and the towns. The imagined linguistic and cultural boundary between the two communities was known as The Highland Line. By about 700 years ago, these two language communities had become prejudiced towards each other and some of these misunderstandings are still with us.

Despite this, the Gaelic Highlands were one of the first, and sustained, destinations for modern mass tourism, partly through the efforts of the 19th-century package holiday pioneer, Thomas Cook. Inevitably, a mass of material has thus been written about Gaelic Scotland and its people, though many Gaels would not recognise in it the culture they live and breathe; most of it fails to give a clear and rounded picture of Gaeldom's history and culture. Sadly, this is not a new phenomenon. Allan Cameron of Erracht wrote in 1827:

> But it is to the long succession of southern travellers … that we chiefly owe those hordes of printed Highland anecdotes, which, like a rolling snowball, had been magnified wonderfully as they have passed from the earlier times to the more recent tourists' volumes… [so that] …Highlanders … have marvelled at … their simplicity and folly.

As a qualified tourist guide, I too have observed that the Gaels and their Gaelic culture suffer from a mixture of distortion and invention. Because there has been so much invention about Gaelic Scotland, it may be difficult for visitors to separate fact from fiction, and much invented narrative now stands as received wisdom. This process of invention has a long history. In introducing the British Museum exhibition on the Celts in 2016, the then director Neil MacGregor stated:

> The word 'Celtic' still resonates powerfully today … because it has been continually redefined to echo contemporary concerns over politics, religion and identity.

This perspective is borne out by a review of the Anglophone literature about Gaelic Scotland in which can be discerned a pattern of external representation of the Gael from 1428 to 1958 (and beyond) that matched MacGregor's contention. Much that has been said and written about the Gael is distorted by these forces and the accumulation of so-called 'facts'.

The 16th-century witnessed the delineation of a line that was closing around a self-contained Scottish polity, synonymous with the Lowlands, yet looking to the Highlands for legitimisation of origins and validation of progress. This 'Highland Line' distinguished the two Scottish cultures in terms of language: Scottish Gaelic in the Gàidhealtachd to the north and a form of English to the south. As has been pointed out by historians, the 'division' is, first and foremost, a function of the imagination of particular groups in particular contexts. Today, the demarcation is conflated with the hard geological junction of the Highland Boundary Fault where the bedrock changes along a fault line which spans Scotland from the island of Arran in the southwest to Stonehaven in the North-East; a break of 400 million years in duration.

Although much of this distortion is relatively harmless, its cumulative impact pushes the actual reality of Gaelic culture farther away from the notion of a normal society. Put bluntly, the Gaels are seen as a different people, in a different country, with a different history, culture and society, and with an ancient, impenetrable and difficult-to-learn language. In the words of one Scottish literary scholar, specialising in Scottish and modernist literature, Scotland is itself 'Out of History' and the Highlands even more so. To him the Highlands are:

> … entirely divorced from historical process, as yet untouched by narrative; a world whose existence has to be defined in terms of cycles and repetitions …

'The winner writes history' is a tired adage but it has resonance in Scotland. The Gaels have rarely been afforded the dignity of a narrative on Scotland from their perspective. Possibly the most coherent and comprehensive effort was last attempted in 1838 in Donald Gregory's *History of the Western Highlands and Islands of Scotland*, though academic efforts are now underway to rectify this state of affairs.

Just as the Gaels' history is not heard, visitors do not see much evidence of former settlement as they gaze upon an emptied landscape. Save for a few place-names which point to earlier human activity, the rupture in the historic record, caused by the clearance of the people, renders the landscape largely mute.

An effort to display Gaelic has been made at key entry points such as the Scottish-English border and major airports, and it is often through new road signs erected by local authorities, displaying the original Gaelic place-name alongside the English version, that most visitors to Scotland first encounter the language. The written Gaelic form of a place-name can often be startlingly different from its English name and, despite these efforts to reveal the original landscape meanings, it is quite common to hear people express the view that the language was never spoken in their area, often in direct response to the erection of a bilingual road sign. In one bizarre case, a resident took a pot-shot at such a sign. Single-interest 'astroturfing' groups periodically raise a hue and cry over the cost of such signs. In 2016, the Scottish Government responded to a Freedom of Information request, confirming that a mere £60,000 was spent on bilingual signage as part of the £5 million of expenditure on the Crianlarich Bypass project.

Yet a huge amount of material by the Gaels in their own voices survives, now mainly in archives of songs and stories. Using some of this material, this book seeks to provide an introduction to Gaelic Scotland and to address some of the misinformation often provided to visitors. It is impossible to cram almost 2000 years of Gaelic historical record in Scotland into a single book, so this is not a comprehensive description of Scotland's Gaelic culture, nor can it cover all aspects of that culture. Nor is it an account of contemporary Gaeldom. Rather, what is set out are events and people, stories and songs that have salience for Gaels in the former and current Gaelic-speaking areas.

Of course, many of the stories that survive are of battle, murder and sudden death, not because they were everyday occurrences, but because they were not, and therefore became the subject of story and song. It has been calculated that the total of deaths in all the affrays and skirmishes between the clans comes nowhere near the deaths caused in England by the Wars of the Roses.

I have written this book in the hope that it will give the reader a better understanding of Scotland's Gaelic culture and history: a taster for those visitors to the country who have an interest in, and a desire to learn a little more about, Scotland's Gaelic people and their place in the country's story. It is called *Travels in Another Country* because I once heard an experienced tour guide say:

> "I always tell my clients, we are entering the Highlands - another country!"

She was referring to the Gaelic-speaking areas in the north and west of Scotland and suggesting that they were somewhat primitive and set apart from the rest of the country.

The structure of the book in some respects mirrors that of the Luath Press series of guidebooks authored by Tom Atkinson that draw on Seton Gordon's *Highways and Byways* series of some decades earlier, but lacks the nature notes of either. It is loosely organised around local authorities or councils. In 1996, the Conservative government decided to abolish a system of large regional councils and smaller district councils, and merge their powers into thirty-two new unitary authorities. The new councils vary wildly in size. Some, for example Clackmannanshire, are the same as the old counties; some, such as Inverclyde, are the same as former districts that were replaced, and others, such as Highland, are the same as former regions. Not all council areas are covered and some have been grouped together. The reader will find what appears to be a disproportionate balance in the treatment of certain localities as against other areas. This is partly a reflection of the material to hand but also of the need to provide a corrective to the accepted tourism narrative of key sites. The book begins in the City of Glasgow and progresses in a roughly clockwise manner around the country.

This is not an academic book; references to sources are kept to a minimum, and instead, a select bibliography of the more useful reference books is provided. An appendix lists alphabetically the locations mentioned with grid references.

It is said 'Mas e breug bhuam e 's e breug thugam e' ('*If I lie, it's one I received*'). Any errors, omissions or solecisms are entirely of my own making. I apologise for this in advance. It is my hope that if you travel with this book you will learn about the Gaels in Scotland, their history and language, their songs and stories. May it enrich you.

Turas math dhuibh (*Bon Voyage*).

Geàrr-chunntas Eachdraidheil:
A Short Historical Overview

For the sake of convenience, it is useful to divide up the history of the Gaels in Scotland in the following manner:

- 4th to 6th centuries - the Age of Dál Riada, the first Gaelic kingdom in Scotland: the Scottii, originally shadowy Irish raiders, establish a foothold in Argyll and begin to build Scotland.
- 6th century - the Age of Columba: the power of the Word dominates, with cultivation of the high arts and book learning, missionary zeal and great monastic complexes.
- 9th century - the Age of the Vikings: devastation, disruption and destruction of the old order. Scotland is now in an international trade network but partially dismembered by Norse land grabs in the north and west.
- 9th and 10th centuries - the Age of the Gall-Ghàidheal: a period when the self-consciously, hybridised, Gaelicised Norse begin to carve out semi-autonomous polities in the West.
- 9th century onwards - the Age of the Unification of the Picts and Scots: as in the time of the Romans, the threat of external domination melds disparate territories into a strong coherent kingdom.
- 10th and 11th centuries and onwards - the Age of the Norse kingdoms of the islands, and Rí Innse Gall, the King of the Hebrides: shifting alliances and tensions between Norway and lands now Scottish.
- 14th century onwards - Linn an Àigh, the Age of Joy and the Lordship of the Isles: a maritime semi-independent territory provides a period of relative stability. A sophisticated, cultural, Gaelic renaissance, capriciously suppressed in 1493 by the Scottish Crown.

- 16th century - Linn nan Creach, The Age of Forays: the vacuum left by the Lordship of the Isles produces five attempts at its restoration and one hundred and fifty years of anarchy.
- 15th, 16th centuries and onwards - The Age of the Clans: with no central authority and rapacious 'lieutenants' exploiting opportunities for personal gain, kindreds rely on their swords rather than the law.
- Mid-17th century - The Age of the Civil War: the Stewart kings, desperate for forces in their struggle against Parliament, turn their attention to Gaelic fighting prowess, with little profit for the Gaels.
- 1560 to 1690 - The Age of the Reformed Churches: the whole-scale theft of church lands destroys the limited social care it provided. The lack of churches and qualified preachers, with or without Gaelic, weakens the Church's mission. More damaging still, a militant Presbyterianism, ascendant after 1690, brands many Gaelic Episcopalians as little better than apostates, exacerbating the cultural and racial bigotry that then characterised Lowland attitudes to the Gaels.
- 18th century - The Age of the Jacobite Risings: as with the sixty years of attempts at the restoration of the Lordship of the Isles, again the Gaels are sucked into two generations of futile struggle for the exiled Stuart dynasty. The last, in 1746, described authoritatively as an 'escapade', leads to semi-extinction of Gaels as a result of a severely rattled Government's near-genocidal response.
- 19th century - primarily The Age of the Clearances and of Emigration: by the middle of the century the bulk of Highland estates are in new ownership or in trust and the focus is on cash generation at all costs. People as tenants at will (the will of the landlord) are in the way of large-scale experiments in sheep ranching and, until 1886, have no defence in the law. The land is cleared of its population with many swept into congested coastal areas, described by an eminent historian as a 'rural slum'.

- 20th century - an age of sporadic but quickening recovery: an Act of the Scottish Parliament in 2005 grants Gaelic 'parity of esteem' with English, leading ultimately to legal recognition of the language. Scotland's census finds that 2.5% of people aged three and over have some skills in Gaelic in 2022. This is an increase of 43,100 people since 2011 when 1.7% had some skills in Gaelic.

Nota mun Ghàidhlig: *A Note on Gaelic*

Gàidhlig [ˈkaːlɪkʲ], or Scottish Gaelic, is a Goidelic language (in the Celtic branch of the Indo-European language family). It is commonly believed to have been brought to Scotland, in the 4th-5th centuries CE, by settlers from Ireland who founded the Gaelic kingdom of Dal Riata on Scotland's west coast in Argyll. After the conquest in 1018 by the Kingdom of Scotland of the Lothians, Gaelic reached its social, cultural, political, and geographic zenith. Most of modern Scotland was once Gaelic-speaking, as evidenced especially by Gaelic-language place names.

The division of Celtic languages into Q- and P-families depends on whether they retained the Indo-European qu-or substituted a p-. The substitution of p- for qu- probably happened in Europe during the first millennium BC and spread westwards, but not as far as Ireland. The p-/q- split is clearest in cognates retaining the same roots, e.g. Welsh *pen* ('head') and Irish *ceann* ('head'). The modern P-Celtic or Brythonic languages are Welsh, Cornish, and Breton. The language of Scotland at the time of the arrival of the Romans in c AD 70 was predominantly P-Celtic.

As a Goidelic language, Scottish Gaelic developed out of Old Irish. Colloquial speech in Scotland had been developing independently of that in Ireland since the 8th century and it became a distinct spoken language sometime in the 13th century. The 10th to 12th centuries marked the high watermark in a Gaelic world which embraced Ireland, Man and Scotland, as:

> men from one part of this Gaelic region involved themselves in the affairs of another part … and … practitioners of Gaelic high culture in Scotland looked to Ireland ... for leadership and learning.

A common literary language, Classical Common Gaelic, was shared by Gaels in Ireland and Scotland down to the end of the 17th century. The *Book of Common Order* by John Carswell, Bishop of the Isles, published in Edinburgh in 1567, the first book to be printed in Gaelic is in that language; Carswell's choice of as the language for his version of the *Book of Common Order* was quite deliberate. In an Epistle to the Reader, he addressed:

> … specially to the men of Scotland and Ireland, to such of them as desire to receive the true word of God in their hearts and minds...

While a pan-Gaelic culture remained in existence, Ireland was its centre. Gaelic Scotland benefited enormously from an ongoing infusion of Irish personnel throughout the later middle ages. But Gaelic Scotland was not a cultural dependency of Ireland, for she made innovative contributions to the common culture. We find no Irish parallel for the late medieval West Highland tradition of richly decorated monumental sculpture nor do we find an Irish parallel to *ceòl mór*, the classical music of the Highland bagpipe.

By the mid-14th century what eventually came to be called Scots emerged as the official language of government and law and at the end of the 15th century, Scots speakers were referring to Gaelic as Irish and their own language as Scottish. A steady shift away from Scottish Gaelic, partly driven by policy decisions by government or others and, some originated from social changes, continued into and through the modern era. In the 2011 census, 57,375 people, 1.1% of the Scottish population, identified as able to speak Gaelic. Nevertheless, there are revival efforts. In 2018, the census of pupils in Scotland showed 520 students in publicly funded schools had Gaelic as the main language at home, an increase of 5% from 497 in 2014. Although not an official language of the United Kingdom, it is classed as an indigenous language under the European Charter for Regional or Minority Languages. The Gaelic Language (Scotland) Act 2005 established a language-development body, Bòrd na Gàidhlig.

Caibideil 1: *Chapter 1*

Baile Ghlaschu: *Glasgow*

The journey commences in Baile Ghlaschu (Glasgow City). Known as Baile Mòr nan Gàidheal ('The Great City of the Gael'), it was and remains a significant Gaelic centre:

> Mairg thréigios inn, a Amhlaoíbh
> an ghuirt úaine ubhallmhaoíl.
>
> *Woe to him who neglects me,*
> *Amhlaoibh of the green orchard of apple trees.*

So begins a poem composed some 800 years ago by the Irish bard, Muireadhach Albanach Ó Dálaigh. He was addressing the son of the Earl of Lennox, demonstrating that the nobility of this area were Gaelic speakers. Amhlaoibh's residence could perhaps be rendered nowadays as Gart nan Ubhal and in English as Gartnaval.

As with most parts of Scotland, the northern part of Strathclyde has a complex cultural, political and linguistic history. The first known language here was British, closely related to Old Welsh, and Glaschu, the city's name, comes from that tongue. Glasgow is often translated as 'the dear green place' but unfortunately 'glas' and 'chu' mean 'green' and 'hollow'; 'dear' does not come into it, generous and hospitable though the inhabitants of the city are.

It might seem strange to start a journey through Gaelic Scotland in Greater Glasgow, home to a population of over 1,215,000, and the largest urban area in Scotland. However, Glasgow has a sizeable population of Gaelic speakers and the city has been important in the cultural and economic life of Gaelic Scotland. Indeed, in the 19th century when the Gaelic population was over 22,000, the title Baile Mòr nan Gàidheal was coined, testament to the vibrancy of its Gaelic population. In 2022, the census recorded 8,962 in a total population of 603,203 (1.5%); an increase of over 3,000.

Gaelic speakers named many parts of the area around Glasgow during a period of about 150 years from 1100 onwards, when the language was used by the aristocracy and church. The River Clyde made Glasgow a great trading centre and its name Cluaidh, sometimes rendered as Clutha, suggests that it was always seen as a beneficial force. The word Cluaidh is related to the Latin verb *cloare*, to cleanse, and is the root of the name of Rome's great sewer, the *Cloaca Maxima.* The name here refers to the spirit of the river, regarded as a great cleanser.

Oilthigh Ghlaschu: *The University of Glasgow*

Oilthigh Ghlaschu (The University of Glasgow) has a long association with Gaels. When The University was founded in 1451, it drew revenue from parish churches which were incorporated into the university. Kildalton, Kilchoman and Killarow in Islay, Dunoon in Cowal, and Rothesay in Bute are all in the Gàidhealtachd. Similarly, areas closer to Glasgow such as Arran, the Lennox, Argyll and the Isles, together with Galloway and Carrick to the south, were all Gaelic strongholds. The University was intended to draw in students from these Gaelic-speaking areas as well as from neighbouring Ireland, and Gaels could always be found within the University community.

John Mair, Principal of the University (1518-1523), did not speak Gaelic. He mentioned, however, in his *History of Greater Britain* (1521), that Gaelic was still the language of half the kingdom whose population was then more evenly distributed throughout the land than it has become since 1800. The Glasgow graduate Walter Kennedy, MA 1478, from Carrick in Ayrshire, an aristocratic poet, was criticised for his Gaelic background and habits of speech in a verbal 'flyting' or sparring by the poet William Dunbar. Kennedy replied that Gaelic should be the language of all true men in the kingdom. Kennedy's son, probably a Gaelic speaker, was made Rector of the University of Glasgow in 1525.

Many Gaelic-speaking graduates of Glasgow University have had eminent careers in the army, the civil service, the education system and the church. Others were poets, publishers and active promoters of the Gaelic language. One of the most distinguished was Professor Mànas MacIllEeathain (Magnus MacLean) (1857-1937), a Skyeman from Fàsach (Fasach, 'wilderness') and an eminent scientist and mathematician. He worked for a time at the university as assistant to Lord Kelvin and was the author of a number of scientific articles and books including *Modern Electrical Engineering* (6 Vols., London, 1918). MacLean was also a Gaelic scholar whose pioneering efforts led to the establishment of the Chair in Celtic at the University, though it is only since 1906 that Gaelic has been taught there as a degree subject.

But not all significant Gaelic characters at Glasgow University were employed by the Celtic Department. For example, the poet Donnchadh MacIain (Duncan Johnston) (1881-1947), a native of Islay, was a university employee. Leaving for the First World War with the 8th Argyll and Sutherland Highlanders, he penned the still popular love song 'Sìne Bhàn' ('Fair Jean') to his new wife:

Bruaillean cogaidh anns an tìr,
Faic an long a' togail sheòl,
Cluinn an druma 's fuaim na pìob',
Faic na suinn a' dol air bòrd.

Feumaidh mise triall gun dàil,
Chi mi 'm bàrr a croinne sròl.
M' eudail bhàn, Ò soraidh slàn,
Na caoin, a luaidh, na sil na deòir.

The call to war is heard throughout the land. See the ship raising sail, hear the drum and the music of the pipes, see the warriors boarding.

I must leave without delay. I see a flag at the top of its mast. My beloved fair one, farewell and do not shed tears.

Gassed in 1916, Johnston worked in the University's Department of Natural Philosophy until 1945. Many of his compositions reflect his interest in history and culture and his 'Birlinn Ghoraidh Chròbhain' ('Godred Crovan's Galley') is a great choir favourite:

Fichead sonn air cùl nan ràmh,
Fichead buille lùghmhor;
Siùbhlaidh i mar eun a' snàmh
Is siaban thonn ga sgiùrsadh.

Twenty heroes manning the oars, twenty strong strokes;
she travels like a swimming bird driven by sea spray.

Muinntir Ghlaschu: *People of Glasgow*

Iain MacPhàidein (John MacFadyen) was probably worthy of the title of Bàrd Ghlaschu (Glasgow's poet). He was born in Mull in 1850 and was a guard at the railway station in Hope Street. His humorous songs provide a vibrant picture of the lives of Glasgow Gaels. Cèilidhs and concerts, including the final concert of the Royal National Mod, still conclude with MacFadyen's 'Soraidh Leibh is Oidhche Mhath Leibh' ('Goodbye and Goodnight to You'):

Màthair uisge 'n tobair fhìor-uisg,
Cainnt ar sinnsir, brìgh na loinn;
'S faochadh tlàth o ànradh m' inntinn
Nuair bheir rann na glinn am chuimhn'.

Source of the well of pure water, the language of our ancestors,
essence of beauty; it's a welcome relief from my mental torture
when a verse reminds me of the glens.

The offices of the Clyde Port Authority are at 16 Robertson Street on the Broomielaw, by the River Clyde. Many Gàidheil seeking work as seamen made their way here. So many were employed on the Clyde ferry boats that it became known as 'The Skye Navy' and many Gaelic songs speak of the River Clyde. 'Fàgail Ghlaschu' ('Leaving Glasgow') is a popular homesick sailor's song:

An àm bhith fàgail Ghlaschu air madainn mhoich Dimàirt
Bha m' inntinn trom fo airtneal 's mi cho fad bho thìr mo ghràidh;
A' fàgail mo luchd-eòlais anns a' bhaile mhòr a' tàmh
Na deòir nan sruth om shùilean 's mi cur cùlaibh ri mo ghràidh.

Leaving Glasgow early on Tuesday morning my spirits were low, being so far from the place I love; leaving my friends who live in the city and leaving my beloved caused my tears to flow.

'Fàgail Ghlaschu' was composed by Ruaraidh Caimbeul (Roderick Campbell) from South Uist. He went to sea as a young man and endured a hard life of long hours, poor food and water shortages on many long voyages. Complaining of the lack of food on a MacLay ship he stated:

'S mur a till i do Ghrianaig
'S e siud a' bhliadhna bheir bàs dhomh
'S nach fhaigh mi aist'.

Unless she returns to Greenock this will be the year of my death as I cannot escape her.

George Square in the city centre has a number of statues of people who were important in the city's story. Perhaps best remembered by his fellow Gaels is Cailean Caimbeul (Colin Campbell), First Baron Clyde. He commanded the Highland Brigade at the Battle of Balaclava during the Crimean War. Facing a charge from Russian cavalry, he formed his men into a line only three rows deep and successfully beat off the attack, an action immortalised in the phrase 'The Thin Red Line'.

His fellow Gaels also honoured him, for example, in a poem 'Fàilte Thighearna Chluaidh' ('Welcome to Lord Clyde') composed by Iain MacDhùghaill à Àird Ghobhar (John MacDougal from Ardgour) on the General's return from the East Indies in 1860:

Aig Baiteal Alma b' fhàbharach
Dar rìoghachd thu bhith làthair ann
Nuair bhrosnaicheadh na Gàidheil leat
Chaidh misneachd chàich am mòid leis:
'S aig Balaclàbha, 'n taice ris,
Gun d' dhìon thu 'n acarsaid 's an luingeis
A bha snàmh air bhàrr na tuinne,
'S b' fhiach iad millean stòrais.

At the Battle of Alma it was in our country's favour that you were present. When you urged on the Gaels everyone else's courage increased. And at Balaclava, in support, you defended the harbour and the ships which were floating on the waves; they were worth a million.

Argyle Street in Glasgow was home to two publishing houses of importance to the history of Gaelic publications – Gilleasbaig Mac na Ceàrdaich (Archibald Sinclair) at No. 62 and MacLabhrainn (MacLaren's) at 360-362.

Partaig: *Partick*

To the west, in Partick South Church, Ceòlraidh Ghàidhlig Ghlaschu (the Glasgow Gaelic Musical Association) hold their weekly practices. This Gaelic choir, like others in the city, was founded in the 1890s and is popularly known as 'The GGs'. It has gained the premier Gaelic choral singing award, Sgiath Mhic Shimidh agus Mhorair Thulaich Bhàrdain (the Lovat and Tullibardine Shield) sixteen times.

Many Gaels lived in Partaig (Partick, 'little copse') including the Argyllshire poet, Donnchadh MacIlleRuaidh, (Duncan Reid), who composed a well-known rallying song for the Gaelic language, 'Suas leis a' Ghàidhlig' ('Forward, Gaelic'):

Tha mòr-shruth na Beurla a' bagradh gu cruaidh
Ar cànan 's ar dùthchas a shlugadh a suas;
Ach seasaibh gu dìleas ri cànain ur gaoil,
'S chan fhaigh i am bàs gu ruig deireadh an t-saoghail.

The torrent of English strongly threatens our language and our heredity. But stand up faithfully for the language we love and it will not be killed off till the world ends.

Born in 1849 in Clachan in Ceann Tìre (Kintyre), Duncan worked as a book-keeper for the wood merchants, George Halliday Ltd. He was particularly interested in encouraging learners of the language and wrote *A Course of Gaelic Grammar* (1895) and *An Elementary Course of Gaelic* (1908).

Togalaichean aig Crois Charing:
Significant Buildings at Charing Cross

The largest venue in the city for Gaels was once Tallaichean Naomh Anndrais (Saint Andrew's Halls) at Charing Cross. Built in 1877, the largest of the three halls, An Talla Mhòr ('the Great Hall'), could house 4,500. It was there that on one night in the 1950s the singer Aonghas MacLeòid à Scalpaigh (Angus MacLeod from Scalpay, Harris) was prevailed upon to give eight encores. A member of the audience, the Harris bard Murchadh Moireasdan (Murdo Morrison), recalled:

> Cha leigeadh iad e far an àird-ùrlair. Sheinn e ochd òrain, fear às dèidh fear. Bha a chridhe, 's a chànan, 's a chuimhne cho aontaichte anns a h-uile òran a sheinneadh e. Shaoileadh tu gun robh thu dìreach ann am brògan a' bhàird a rinn an t-òran!
>
> *They would not let him off the stage. He sang eight songs one after the other. His heart, his language and his memory were united in each song he sang. You would think you were in the very shoes of the bards who composed them!*

In this area of Glasgow is a building as important to Gaelic as any in Scotland, Sgoil Ghàidhlig Ghlaschu (the Glasgow Gaelic School) on Berkeley Street. This was the first school in Scotland to offer education through the medium of Gaelic for ages three to eighteen. The school opened its doors at this location in 2005 and the pupil roll now stands at over 800; demand for Gaelic-medium education in Glasgow continues to increase.

Churches of all denominations played an important role in the life of the Glasgow Gaels. The history of Eaglais Naomh Chaluim Cille (St. Columba's Church) on St Vincent Street goes back to the foundation of the Glasgow Highland Society in 1727. Its minister, an t-Urr. Tormod MacLeòid (Rev. Norman MacLeod) (1783-1862), was nicknamed Caraid nan Gàidheal ('friend of the Gael'), thanks to his philanthropy. He coined the church's motto:

> Taigh mo Chridhe, Taigh mo Ghràidh
>
> *House of My Heart, House of My Love.*

Later, Saint Columba's minister was Raibeart Blàrach (Robert Blair) (1837-1907), from Dùn Omhain (Dunoon). He edited the Gaelic poems of the Islay poet William Livingstone and was one of the translators of the Revised Version of the Bible into Gaelic. The congregation and minister of St Columba's Church were instrumental in founding Comann Gàidhealach Ghlaschu (the Glasgow Gaelic Society) in order to provide welfare to the Gaelic poor of the city. It was Blair who took the Penny Readings, informal social gatherings under the aegis of the church, and from these meetings emerged territorial associations such as Comann an Eilein Sgitheanaich (the Glasgow Skye Association) and Comann Leòdhais is na Hearadh (the Lewis and Harris Association). These societies remain active in the city today.

Baile a' Ghobhainn: *Govan*

Govan, south of the river, in Gaelic is Baile a' Ghobhainn ('town of the smith'), a misunderstanding of the meaning of the word 'goban' which seems to derive from the pre-Gaelic, Brythonic name for a hill. It has been suggested that this referred to the moot or dempster hill that once stood beside Govan Old Parish Church.

During the Middle Ages, Govan was the site of a ferry crossing to Partick, used by seasonal cattle drovers. The writer Daniel Defoe painted a picture of a Highland gentleman in the city's streets in 1706:

> *a man in the mountain habit (kilt) with a broad sword, targett (targe, shield), a pistol or perhaps two at his girdle, a dagger and staff, walking down the Gartnaval street as upright and haughty as he were a lord – and withall driving a cow.*

Although Defoe was poking fun at the man's pretensions, such a sight would not have been uncommon in Glasgow then.

By the later 19th century, Govan was an obvious destination for Gaelic settlers from the Highlands seeking employment in the heavy industries which fringed the banks of the river Clyde. In 1883, Còmhlan Phìobairean Phoilis Bhaile Ghobhainn (the Govan Police Pipe Band) was established, one of the first non-army pipe bands. With burgh re-organisation in 1912, it became Còmhlan Phìobairean Phoilis Ghlaschu (Glasgow Police Pipe Band). Under the leadership of Pipe Major Seonaidh Dòmhnallach, Seonaidh Roidein à Uibhist a Deas (John MacDonald from South Uist), it won the first prize at the World Pipe Band Championships seven times.

In 1975, following local government re-organisation, the City of Glasgow Police and five adjoining police forces amalgamated to form Strathclyde Police, giving rise to the formation of the Strathclyde Police Pipe Band. Led by Pipe Major Ian MacLellan, the band won six successive World Pipe Band Championships (1981-1986); an unprecedented achievement.

Govan is also the city's main media centre with both the BBC and STV established there. BBC Gàidhlig produces Gàidhlig programmes for BBC Alba, the first TV channel to be delivered under a BBC licence by a partnership. This is a joint venture between the BBC and MG ALBA, the operating name of Seirbheis nam Meadhanan Gàidhlig (the Gaelic Media Service), which was formed under the Communications Act, 2003. MG ALBA replaced Comataidh Craolaidh Gàidhlig (the Gaelic Broadcasting Committee), which itself had been renamed under the Broadcasting Act, 1996. Prior to that, the body was known as Comataidh Telebhisein Gàidhlig (the Gaelic Television Committee), established under the Broadcasting Act 1990.

Caibideil 2: *Chapter 2*

Siorrachd Dhùn Breatann an Iar: *West Dunbartonshire*

Great Western Road is the main road north and west out of Glasgow to Balloch in Siorrachd Dhùn Breatann an Iar (West Dunbartonshire). This county, not now considered Highland, had Gàidhlig-speaking pockets until the middle of the 20th century. It has often been said that this was a Highland county with a Lowland fringe, that being the towns of the northern shore of the Clyde and the city of Glasgow.

Before it reaches Balloch, the road west snakes along the north shore of the River Clyde. As the estuary widens into the Firth of Clyde, it is spanned by the arc of Drochaid Arasgain (the Erskine Bridge). Arasgain is an older Brythonic name that may have some sense of 'riverside'. Nestling beneath the bridge is Cill Phàdraig (Kilpatrick, 'Church of St. Patrick', Ireland's patron saint). St. Patrick is believed to have been a Briton who was kidnapped in the area and enslaved in Ireland. This rare dedication to him perhaps recalls that tradition. This is also where the Roman Antonine Wall, constructed after 143 AD, stopped. Beyond the wall lay 'Old Scotia'.

That term was used in the early medieval period to define the territory of those who lived north of the physical barrier of the Antonine Wall. To the medieval Scots, this was truly Scotland, as opposed to the mixed populations of North-Welsh-speaking Britons and the polyglot towns of Inglis and Flemish speech communities south of the Wall. The Wall may have had perhaps only two generations of continuous use, but it left a permanent physical and psychological imprint on the landscape and mind of early Scotland.

That this was a border zone for a long period is well illustrated by the next major landscape feature to be named by the Gaels, Dùn Breatann (Dumbarton, 'fort of the Britons'). The name derives from 'dùn', a fort in Gaelic, and their word for Britons. It was captured by the Vikings in 871, further weakening the last British kingdom in the north and allowing the Gaels to extend into their territory. Dumbarton's strategic location at the mouth of the River Leven controlled entry into Loch Lomond and hence access into the heart of Scotland. Small wonder it gave rise to the saying:

Trì gearastain na h-Albann – Dùn Breatann, Dùn Chailleann is Madaigein na Mòine.

Three fortresses of Scotland – Dumbarton, Dunkeld and Rannoch Moor.

The rock on which the fort stood is referred to for the first time as Al Cluathe as early as 658 AD and for several hundred years thereafter. In modern Gaelic this would be Creig Chluaidh ('rock of the Clyde'). The place also appears in the proverb:

Cho bodhar ri Creig Chluaidh

As deaf as Dumbarton Rock

a variant on the better-known version:

Cho bodhar ri cloich

As deaf as a stone.

As the road crosses the River Leven, Ben Lomond looms to the north. Early Celtic peoples believed that bodies of water, particularly rivers, were inhabited by an animating spirit such as the great cleansing goddess of the Clyde. Running water was thus the most important feature in the landscape and gave its name to the loch, and the high land around the loch also gained its name from the river.

This naming system was originally followed here: the loch was known as Leamhain (Leven, 'elm water') and the mountain and loch names were the same. The region is known in Gaelic as Leamhnachd (the Lennox), also from the river name. However, the hill is now called Beinn Laomainn (Ben Lomond, 'beacon mountain'), presumably a site for beacon fires in the past, with the mountain's name ultimately adopted for the loch.

Most people know about Loch Lomond from the Victorian song, 'The Bonny, Bonny Banks of Loch Lomond', recently given a new lease of life by the rock band, Runrig. The song is often described as an 18th-century Jacobite song that describes an apparently Gaelic notion of a high road to life and a low road to death. In reality the song is one of many late 19th-century compositions. The notion of 'high' and 'low' roads of life and death is not part of Gaelic culture.

Nithean Os-nàdarra: *The Supernatural*

Once, the three winter months from Samhain, 1st November, to Latha Faill Bhrìghde, 1st February, were presided over by the one-eyed Cailleach ('old woman' or 'hag') or Cailleach Bheur ('sharp-dealing hag associated with mountains') who impersonated and dwelt in the winter storms. She is also known as Beire, the Gyre-Carline, and Mag Moullach. The enemy of growth to the detriment of man and beast, she hurries about switching the grass and blasting vegetation with a magic wand. Her reign ends nominally in February, when she is at last overcome by the sun, but not without a struggle. She raises Spring storms and in the period known as A' Caillich she makes her final effort to arrest growth. Latha na Cailleach, the Auld Wife's Day (March 25th, which, up to 1600, was Scotland's New Year's Day), is the traditional date of her final overthrow.

But she was not the least of the supernatural beings in the Gaelic landscape. We now speak generically of 'fairies' but these phenomena can appear in many guises.

There was a' bhean-nighe (a woman washing at a lochside), often a premonition of death; a' ghruagach (a Loireag – interested in the arts of cloth making, for example the waulking of the tweed to shrink and tighten the weave); Peallaidh or Peallag, was an ùruisg ('urisk'), with very matted long hair and teeth, practising fishing and haunting lonely and out of the way places. A classic character was Peallaidh an Spùit (Peallaidh of the Spout) who along with his neighbour Brùnaidh an Easain (Brownie of the Little Waterfall) features in a verse naming the best-known urisks in Breadalbane. Peallaidh lived at Moness near the town of Obair Pheallaidh (Aberfeldy, 'the mouth of the Peallaidh'), to which he has given his name. Brownie of the Little Waterfall also lived in the same stream, just above Peallaidh. They came out at night to annoy the townsfolk.

Other apparitions were: Caoineag bheag a' bhròin ('the little wailer of sorrow'); Gainnisg was heard before a storm; the Glaistig inhabited the loch shore and was a danger to travellers; the Each-uisge ('the water horse'), asking of evil and a risk to young unwary women; Na frìdean were small fairy people who could form a host and transport people many miles from home; Cearbaire carried the spirits of those who fell in battle to heaven, and is drawn from of Christian traditions, and Cailleach nan Gàg was a fearsome apparition with whom parents threatened their children if they did not wash.

At the foot of the loch is the small town of Bealach (Balloch, 'pass'). The name refers to a pass through the hills, leading towards the east. For centuries, until the Second World War, it was through this pass that thousands of cattle were driven to markets in the South.

Beyond Balloch, the Arden roundabout is the point at which most visitors are informed that they are officially entering the Highlands. The reason is that this is where the geology of the land changes along a fault line stretching across Scotland from the island of Arran in the southwest to Stonehaven in the northeast: the Highland Boundary Fault. This physical boundary is now conflated with the Highland Line.

Caibideil 3: *Chapter 3*

Earra-Ghàidheal agus Bòd – Tìr-mòr: *Argyll and Bute – The Mainland*

The Arden roundabout also marks the boundary of the local authority area of Earra-Ghàidheal agus Bòd (Argyll and Bute). According to the 1881 population census, the year when people were asked for the first time which language they spoke, six out of ten of the population, in the area approximating to today's council boundaries, spoke Gaelic. Up until the Second World War, 6% of the people round the shores of Loch Lomond and the immediately surrounding areas had Gaelic and there are archival recordings of some of these speakers.

Earra-Ghàidheal (Argyll, 'coastland of the Gael') and the area of Mid Argyll constituted Dal Riada, named after the territory in Ireland where the Scots originated. At its greatest extent, Argyll stretched from Kintyre to Loch Broom. The land to the south of Ardnamurchan was known as Oirthir a Deas (the south coast), while the northern area was called Oirthir a Tuath (the north coast). The present local authority area of Argyll and Bute covers a land area of 690,946 hectares and, after Highland, is the second largest local authority by area in Scotland. It is also dramatically described as the Heartland of the Gael, the place from whence their Scottish colony grew. Its dominant clan was Na Caimbeulaich (the Campbells) but following their incorporation of other lesser families such as the Lamonts and the MacNaughtons, their huge kindred could be more appropriately described as the Argyllshire men.

Gleann Freòin: *Glen Fruin*

West from the Arden roundabout is Gleann Freòin (Glen Fruin), most likely named from its river and based on freòine meaning 'rage'. It is the site of a clan battle in 1603 between Clan MacGregor and the Colquhouns of Luss. This battle turned into a bloody rout for the latter but had dire consequences for the victorious Clan MacGregor. The reason for the battle is enshrined in the proverb:

B' fheàrr nach do rugadh a-riamh mult dubh an earbaill ghil.

It would have been better if the black wedder with the white tail had never been born.

The proverb is also linked to a steep mound truncated by the A82 road some three kilometres north of the Arden roundabout and almost opposite the gates to Rois Dubh (Ross Dhu, 'dark point'), the seat of Colquhoun. Two MacGregor men, it is said, slaughtered and ate the proverbial sheep. The Colquhoun chief had the men promptly hanged from his gibbet on Tom na Croiche (Gallows' Hill), the truncated mound near Ross Dhu. Alasdair of Glenstrae, the MacGregor chief, sought revenge and battle ensued with heavy losses for the Colquhouns. Alasdair MacGregor had little time to savour his victory and a lament composed sometime later recounts the events of the Battle of Glen Fruin:

Dheagh MhicGriogair nam bratach,
'G an robh gliocas is pailteas,
Tha thu 'n ciste chaoil ghlaiste fon fhòid.

Nuair a dhìrich sibh 'm bruthach
'S a ghlaodh sibh 'Bad Giuthais!',
Bha luchd nan ad dubha fo leòn.

Fine MacGregor of the banners, where there was wisdom and plenty, you are in a narrow, locked coffin beneath the sod.

When you breasted the hill and you shouted 'Bad Giuthais!', the gang of black hats were in dire straits.

'Bad Giuthais' ('pine copse') was the MacGregor battle cry and black hats was a derogatory term for Lowlanders.

James VI was outraged and had the whole Clan MacGregor 'put to the horn'. This method of declaring a person an outlaw was by giving three blasts on a horn and publicly proclaiming the fact. In effect, every single member of the clan was outlawed and could be hunted down as if they were wild prey. On 31st January 1611, James:

in his accustomed disposition to clemency and mercy,

graciously allowed that any MacGregor who should:

slay another of the same name of as good a rank as himself,

would be granted a free pardon. Depending upon the rank of the victim, MacGregor heads could reap rewards ranging from £130 to £1000. The prevailing crown attitude of the time that they and their kind were:

> very proud, suspicious, avaricious, full of deceit and evil invention against his neighbour in any way to circumvent him. Besides all this they are so cruel in taking of revenge that neither they have regard to person, age, time or cause; so are they generally all so far addicted to their own tyrannical opinions that, in all respects, they exceed in cruelty the most barbarous people that ever has been since on the beginning of the world

would have done little to help the MacGregor's defence that the Earl of Argyll had "been fishing in drumly (murky) waters" and had a hand in the affair.

In addition, a law proscribed the name MacGregor, which is why people now of the name Gregory, Greg or Reid, from the adjective ruadh ('red-haired'), explain that they are really MacGregors. It is claimed that the distinguished family of Gregory professors at Aberdeen University were originally MacGregor and indeed the distinguished Norwegian composer Edvard Greig was descended from an emigre Scotsman, Alexander Greg, originally MacGregor.

The story of the Battle of Glen Fruin is often used to highlight the barbarity of Highlanders being visited on the settled Lowland society of the Colquhouns – a persistent trope first peddled in the 15th century. But it is likely that the majority of the men on both sides in the battle were Gaelic-speaking and shared the same culture.

Though the song 'The Bonny Bonny Banks' is a 19th-century romantic construct, a poem by the Victorian poet William Wordsworth has a genuine

Gaelic connection. He was among the earliest tourists to Loch Lomond and in 1803 he went to Loch Katrine, to the east, to view locations mentioned in Sir Walter Scott's epic poem 'The Lady of the Lake'. Wordsworth had heard from a friend, who had made the journey earlier, of the impact upon him of the singing of a young woman while she worked in a field by the loch shore. It is likely that his friend's recollection was of the voice of a local Gaelic-speaking woman singing to lighten the drudgery of her work. Wordsworth wrote:

Will no one tell me what she sings?
Perhaps the plaintive numbers flow
For old, unhappy, far-off things,
And battles long ago:
Or is it some more humble lay,
Familiar matter of to-day?
Some natural sorrow, loss, or pain,
That has been, and may be again?

Whate'er the theme, the Maiden sang
As if her song could have no ending;
I saw her singing at her work,
And o'er the sickle bending;
I listened, motionless and still;
And, as I mounted up the hill,
The music in my heart I bore,
Long after it was heard no more.

Had Wordsworth's friend enquired locally, the song would undoubtedly have been identified. We have no idea what this haunting song of 1801 was, but Gaels often lightened activity by singing, a custom practised and recorded well into the 1950s. One such song is 'Feasgar Foghair air Achadh Bhuana' ('Autumn Evening in the Harvest Field'). By custom, the youth of a village would pair up to harvest the corn. A girl who had been crossed in love failed to persuade a lad to join her. Working alone, she outpaced the others who were working in pairs and composed the song as she progressed speedily with the harvest:

Feasgar foghair air achadh bhuana,
Saoil sibh fèin nach mi bha suarach!
H-uile tè 's a fear fhèin ri gualainn
Mo leannan donn-sa, gur fhada bhuam e.

Nàile! 'S e mo rùn-s' an cùirteir,
Sgrìobhas litir 's dhan aithn' a dùnadh;
Thèid a-staigh gu bòrd na cùirte,
'S thig a-mach gu cridheil, sunndach.

Nàile! 'S e mo ghaol an saighdear,
Aig am bi na h-airm a' boillsgeadh;
Sgian bheag nan casan daoimean;
'S fhada shiùbhlainn leat an oidhche.

'S trom mo cheum air sàil mo bhrògan,
Dol don chlachan air Di-Dòmhnaich;
Bho nach fhaic mi tighinn am chòmhdhail,
Am fleasgach donn sin a gheall mo phòsadh.

Ach ma thig thu gu bràth an rathad,
Feuch gun tadhail thu 'n taobh-s' na h-abhainn;
An gaol a bh' againn bidh e 'n glèidheadh,
Gus an càirich saor an snaigheadh.

On an autumn afternoon in the harvest field, how I was despised! Every girl with her man at her shoulder, my brown-haired lover far from me.

Truly! My beloved is the courtier who can write a letter and knows how to seal it, who goes to dine at court and emerges cheerful and lively.

Truly! My love is the soldier whose arms gleam; the small dagger with the diamond hilt; far would I travel with you in the night.

My step is heavy going to church on Sunday because I do not see coming towards me that brown-haired young man who promised to marry me.

But if you ever come this way make sure you visit this side of the river; the love we had will be preserved until a joiner mends the carving

Originally the road from Glasgow to Fort William lay on the east side of the loch. However, from 1724 onwards, the military commander General Wade chose to route his new military road from Inveraray to the garrison at Fort William on the western side of Loch Lomond. It was known as 'The Great Communication' or the King's Highway. Subsequent investment favoured the military route and much of the current route of the A82 was constructed by Thomas Telford in the 19th century. The old route on the east shore of the loch remained the droving road it had been for some three centuries, finally being abandoned with the passing of the droving trade after the Second World War. The old route is now The West Highland Way, a long-distance footpath, over 150 kilometres long, running from Glasgow to Fort William. In the past, people *not* driving cattle to market took to the water, it being more comfortable and easier to take a boat rather than journey overland.

Rob Ruadh: *Rob Roy*

From the early 17th century, groups of Clan MacGregor, who had been pushed eastwards from their ancestral homes around the eastern shores of Loch Awe, occupied the area at the head of Loch Lomond. The most renowned of these MacGregors was Rob Ruadh (Rob Roy, 'red-haired Robert') (1671-1734), who, in his own lifetime, became the subject of myth-making. A relative of the MacGregor chiefs and a minor landowner, he supplemented his income, as was normal, by acting as a drover or dealer in Highland cattle. He would take large numbers of beasts from the north and west and walk them south to the Lowland markets, particularly Crieff. The system depended upon cattle owners entrusting their stock to men of probity who would take them safely to market, manage their sale and then return with the proceeds. Rob

Roy appears to have made poor business judgements and then hit upon the ruse of declaring himself bankrupt. Unfortunately, the Earl of Breadalbane, one of his major creditors, took this as a personal insult and pursued Rob Roy remorselessly. His success in largely staying out of the clutches of the Earl was recorded as early as the 1720s in a book entitled *A Highland Rogue*. Since then, many stories have been associated with his name and in the 1817 novel, *Rob Roy*, by Sir Walter Scott, his tale was internationalised.

For non-Gaelic audiences, Rob Roy acted in some senses as a cipher for his people and for Gaelic culture. The recounting of his exploits strengthened the process of stereotyping Gaelic society. Thus in 1882 it was entirely normal for the Communist philosopher Engels to talk about the whole of Scottish Highland society being "a bunch of terrible cattle-thieves" which was "part of their heritage".

In the contact zone between the arable lowlands and the pastoral Highlands, the presence of so many herds of cattle being driven to market inevitably tempted some to engage in a spot of rustling. What was perhaps unusual about Rob Roy was that he operated comfortably in both zones and his cunning enabled him to evade retribution. He also operated a system of blackmail. Nowadays the term is generally used to describe extortion from a victim with threats of exposing some misdemeanour. However, its original meaning was more akin to protection money and its description in Gaelic as 'màl dubh' ('black rent') has given rise to the English term 'blackmail'. Rob Roy encouraged his near neighbours to pay him an annual rental not to rustle their cattle and sheep and, if someone else did, to secure their safe return. An author writing in 1808, explained the arrangements:

> Regular contracts were drawn up by the proprietors in which it was stipulated that if less than seven cattle were lifted … then no redress should be required, but if the number stolen exceeded seven [it] was designed lifting, the MacGregors became bound to recover. In … 1720 four score of sheep were stolen [from] Stirling of Craigbarnet, some 12 miles from Glasgow. The MacGregors on hearing intimation set out in pursuit of the thieves, who happened to be the Camerons of Lochaber, traced them to their recesses in Inverness shire, and after six weeks, restored the whole flock with the exception of four sheep.

Rob Roy died peacefully in his bed in 1734 and his grave site is in Both Chuidir (Balqhuidder, meaning unclear).

Loch Long agus Loch Slòigh: *Loch Long and Loch Sloy*

The road forks at An Tairbeart or Tairbeart Loch Laomainn (Tarbet of Loch Lomond), with the A83 road to the left leading to the sea loch of Loch Long ('ship loch'). Between this salt water and the fresh water of Loch Lomond there is a small neck of land, barely over a kilometre wide. The name Tairbeart is composed of two Gaelic words meaning 'to carry' and 'across', in other words, a boat portage. Mariners wishing to gain quick access to Loch Lomond dragged their ships that short distance overland. The near contemporary saga by Sturla Thordarsson of King Haakon's campaign against Alexander III in 1263 recounts that a section of the Norwegian fleet was dragged across this portage in order to harry the shores of Loch Lomond:

Drew boats over dry land
For many a length.
Those warriors undaunted
They wasted with war-gales
The islands thick-peopled
On Lomond's broad loch

Less than two kilometres northwards from Tarbet is Inbhir Dhubhghlais (Inveruglas, 'grey estuary'). Here is an electricity generating hall, the first of the modern hydro-electricity schemes constructed after the Second World War, powered by water from Loch Slòigh (Loch Sloy, 'loch of the multitude') in the hills above. The loch's name is also the battle cry of Clann Phàrlain (Clan MacFarlane). There is a ruined castle on a small wooded island just offshore that was formerly Clann Phàrlain's stronghold before it was destroyed by naval bombardment during the Cromwellian invasion of Scotland in 1651. Such bombardment was not exactly novel, but it must have been a nasty shock for the MacFarlanes who believed themselves safe on their island stronghold.

So renowned were the MacFarlanes' nocturnal cattle lifting activities that the full moon is still referred to in Gaelic as 'Lòchran MhicPhàrlain'

('MacFarlane's lantern'). As if to cement their reputation, their cruinneachadh, or rallying call, was 'Togail nam Bò' ('Lifting the Cattle'):

Thogail nam bò,
Thogail nam bò,
Thogail nam bò thèid sinn;
Thogail nam bò,
Ri uisge 's ri ceò
Ri monadh Ghlinn-crò thèid sinn.

Lifting the cattle, lifting the cattle, lifting cattle we will go; lifting cattle despite rain and mist to the moor of Glen Croe we will go.

Glen Croe lies to the west. 'Thogail nam bò' is now best known as a bagpipe tune.

Clach nan Tarbh: *Pulpit Rock*

Soon the road passes a rock face into which a niche has been cut. This is Clach nan Tarbh ('the stone of the bulls'), now known as Pulpit Rock. Its creation speaks of poverty and piety. In 1825, parishioners living in the northern part of the parish wearied of the distance they were required to walk to church services in Arrochar, some thirteen kilometres each way. The Reverend Proudfoot responded to his parishioners by promising that if they built him a pulpit he would come and preach to them. The parishioners cut the hole in the rock to form a space large enough to accommodate the minister, an elder and the precentor. A wooden pulpit was fixed to a platform bolted onto the rock. During the services, the congregation sat on the ground. Services were held during the summer months for about 75 years until a mission church was established in Ardlui. When the West Highland Railway was built, it passed to the west of the rock, avoiding this religious landmark.

But why was it once known as the 'stone of the bulls'? There is a traditional tale that a large red bull from England came north to challenge a black Scottish bull. In the verbal, and then physical, contest on Beinn Mhùrlaig (Ben Vorlich, 'mountain at the inlet'), the rock was dislodged and rolled down the hill to this spot. Ultimately, the black bull killed the red bull. The tale is closely related to an ancient Irish hero tale, 'Táin Bó Cuailgne' ('The Cattle Raid of Cooley'), and has echoes in the American ballad, 'The Little Brown Bull'.

Àrd Laoigh (Ardlui, 'height of the calf') lies at the boundary of the three ancient kingdoms and language groups of Brythonic Strathclyde, Dalriada of the Gaels and the kingdom of Alban of the Picts, as indicated by an ancient monument on the west side of the road almost opposite the Falls of Falloch road sign. The Clach nam Breatann (sic) ('stone of the Britons') is among a number of local names that indicate this ancient boundary. The hamlet of Ardlui dates only from the 1890s when the West Highland Railway Company created a station here, in part because they required a bunkering halt for their steam locomotives.

Naomh Faolan: *St. Fillan*

But the railway's major halt was beyond here, through Gleann Falach (Glen Falloch, 'hidden glen') to A' Chrìon Làraich (Crianlarich, possibly meaning 'aspen site'), where once two railway lines converged with two military roads. Westwards, the road and railway line pass through Na Srathaibh (the Straths, now Strath Fillan). In the 1881 census, almost all the residents in this area were Gaelic speakers and as late as 1961 upwards of a fifth of the community was still speaking Gaelic.

St. Fillan of Munster, an Irish missionary lived here from about 695 to 770. So saintly was this missionary monk that his popularity rivalled that of St. Columba, the premier saint of the Celtic Church. The remains of his monastic settlement and the church dedicated to his memory are some five kilometres west from the junction at Crianlarich, on the banks of the River Fillan. A deep pool there was once considered holy, and the waters were fabled for their restorative qualities. To quote one source:

> Lunatics were brought here, bathed in the water, bound and left overnight. If by morning the bonds had been released, they were considered cured.

The cairns of white pebbles placed there by supplicants remain.

Dail Rìgh (Dalrigh, 'valley of the king') seems to have a genuine association with King Robert the Bruce. Fleeing westwards to safety following defeat at the Battle of Methven in 1306, he was ambushed by his MacDougall enemies. Bruce supposedly evaded capture by slipping off his cloak and leaving it and its fastening in the clutches of his would-be captor. A 10th-century jewel, the Brooch of Lorne, remains in the possession of the MacDougalls and, while its direct association with Bruce may be unlikely, the skirmish probably did occur.

Taigh an Droma (Tyndrum, 'house on the ridge') was originally an 18th-century change house on Wade's King's Highway, where the road forked westwards to Oban. A change house was where, approximately every 20 kilometres, the horses pulling the stagecoach were changed. Breasting the hill above Tyndrum takes one into the ancient territory of Bràghad Albainn (Breadalbane, 'upper part of Alba [i.e. Scotland]'). To the right of the road is Beinn Dòbhrain (Ben Doran, meaning uncertain), its bare flanks rising steeply from the broad valley floor. The mountain is the subject of one of the finest nature poems ever composed in Scotland, 'Moladh Beinn Dòbhrain' ('In Praise of Ben Dorain'):

> An t-urram thar gach beinn
> Aig Beinn Dòbhrain;
> De na chunnaic mi fon ghrèin,
> 'S i bu bhòidhche leam:
> Munadh fada rèidh,
> Cuilidh 'm faighte fèidh,
> Soilleireachd an t-slèibh
> Bha mi sònrachadh;
> Doireachan nan geug,
> Coill' anns am bi feur,
> 'S foinneasach an sprèidh
> Bhios a chòmhnaidh ann;
> Greadhain bu gheal cèir,
> Faghaid air an dèidh,
> 'S laghach leam an sreud
> A bha sròineiseach.

Donnchadh Bàn nan Òran: *Fair-haired Duncan of the Songs*

Its composer Donnchadh Bàn nan Òran ('fair-haired Duncan of the songs') was born nearby in 1724. He became the Earl of Breadalbane's forester here and in Coire Cheathaich ('misty corrie'). His poem, constructed as a series of variations in the manner of a pìobaireachd (the classical music of the Highland bagpipe), runs to 554 lines. He describes and praises Ben Dorain, its vegetation and contours, streams, trees, bushes, birds and the varieties of deer that inhabit it. Looking today at the mountain's scraped flanks, it is difficult to envisage the landscape Duncan saw.

There have been several attempts at rendering the poem in English, by Hugh McDiarmid, by Gaelic poets Derick Thomson and Iain Crichton Smith and, most recently, by Alan Riach. The poet Aonghas MacNeacail stated that:

> Alan Riach brings Duncan Bàn fully into the 21st century: the sustained richness of language, rhythmic drive and flow of thought mirrors the original …

This is Riach's version of the beginning of the poem:

Praise over all to Ben Dorain –
She rises beneath the radiant beams of the sun –
In all the magnificent range of the mountains around,
So shapely, so sheer are her slopes, there are none
To compare; she is fair, in the light, like the flight
Of the deer, in the hunt, across moors, on the run,
Or under the green leafy branches of trees, in the groves
Of the woods, where the thick grass grows,
And the curious deer, watchful and tentative,
Hesitant, sensitive: I have had all these clear, in my sight.

Duncan Bàn's many compositions were transmitted orally as songs but their quality ensured their early transcription by the minister of Lismore, Donald MacNicol. In 1768 'Moladh Beinn Dòbhrain' was published in a collection of Duncan Bàn's poems.

Beyond Inveroran is Achaladair (Achallader, 'field of hard water'), the former home of the Fletcher clan. It is said that these Fletchers were a sept of Clan MacGregor, but their reputation as arrow makers earned them the nickname which they adopted once the name MacGregor was proscribed in 1603. Here stands a ruined 16th-century tower house, and guidebooks say that the Massacre of Glencoe was planned here. Plotting to murder some MacDonalds was undertaken in Edinburgh and London, but, in 1691, there was a meeting here between King William of Orange's envoy, John, Earl of Breadalbane, and clan chiefs. John Campbell, with promises of government gold, attempted to buy the loyalty of those chiefs who had refused to accept the legitimacy of the usurping government of the 'Glorious Revolution' of 1688. To these Gaels it was repugnant to depose a rightfully anointed king and their monarch remained James VII of Scotland and II of England. Nor did they trust Campbell, who was renowned for his wiliness. They refused the gold, which many of them badly needed, but conceded that they would sign the Oath of Allegiance once they had received royal permission from James's exiled court in France. For one small sept of Clan Donald, that of Glencoe, their principled stand was to prove fatal.

Mòinteach Raineach: *Rannoch Moor*

Northwards, the road dips into the dished expanse of around 130 square kilometres of the boggy moorland of Mòinteach Raineach (Rannoch Moor). This was the seat of the glacier that lay here until some 14,000 years ago. The name Raineach means 'bracken' (*Pteridium aquilinum)*, a widespread member of the fern family. However, the original name for this area was Madagan na Mòine, a name now preserved in the proverb:

> 'S ann eadar roinn Labhair agus Madagan na Mòine a tha feairt na h-Alba.
>
> *It is between the point of Lawers and the deepest part of the moss that lie the strengths of Scotland.*

The A82 skirts the western side of the moor. It now appears incapable of sustaining any habitation, yet the title of a beautiful 17th-century song,

'Bothan Àirigh am Bràigh Raineach', ('Sheiling in the Brae of Rannoch'), locates it here. This love song, by an unknown woman, speaks of her àirigh ('a shieling'), one of a collection of huts where young women spent the summer tending the cattle that grazed on the mountain pasture:

Nuair a thèid thu gu fèill
'S e mo ghèar-sa thig dhachaigh,
Thig mo chrios à Dùn Èideann
Is mo bhrèid à Dùn Chailleann.
'S cuim a bhitheamaid gun eudail
Fhad bhios sprèidh aig na Gallaibh?
Gheibh sinn crodh às a' Mhaorainn
Agus caoraich à Gallaibh.
'S ann a bhios sinn gan àrach
Air àirigh 'm Bràigh Raineach.

When you go to the market you'll bring me home the gear I want. My belt will come from Edinburgh and my marriage kerchief from Dunkeld. Why should we be without riches while the Lowlanders have cattle? We'll get cows from the Mearns and sheep from Galloway. We will rear them on a sheiling on Brae Rannoch.

Gleann Comhann: *Glencoe*

Practically no place in the Highlands resonates so strongly with history and mythology as Glencoe. To start with, the name's meaning has been altered to emphasise the bathos of the location: Gleann Comhann is simply 'valley of the narrow river' but now it is often called the 'Glen of Weeping', immortalising the events enacted here at dawn on the 13th of February 1692.

That morning, government soldiers, who had been billeted for a fortnight as guests, turned on their MacDonald hosts and murdered 38, including many of the leading members of the community as well as MacIain, the 12th Chief. Many more might have died had the operation not been botched, although some of those who escaped into the wintry hills undoubtedly died of exposure in the snow. But these bare facts are now surrounded with fantasy.

According to some tourist guides, it is received wisdom that the Massacre was an anti-Catholic act. Perhaps one of the most persistent items of 'fake news' in Scottish history is that the efforts by the Stewart dynasty to regain the throne were a 'Papist' plot. However, in relation to the Glencoe victims, their religion was not relevant, and, in any case, they were Protestants, if Episcopalian. For others, it was simply clan rivalry, the cloak of a government sanctioned operation being an ideal opportunity for Campbells to take revenge on their MacDonald rivals. This distortion has arisen because the commander of the government forces was Robert Campbell of Glenlyon, but most of his men subsequently named, though never prosecuted, had Lowland names. To reduce the Massacre of Glencoe to a narrative of MacDonalds versus Campbells obscures the fact that the conflict was between a Lowland government and the Gaels generally.

Nor was the demand for a subsequent enquiry a result of any real concern over the killing of a few Gaelic Highlanders. That was a trivial matter when one considers the Privy Council's order of 1685 to deal with the normally consistently loyal, but on this occasion rebel Argyllshire men, which ordered that all:

> are to be killed, or disabled ever from fighting again … Let the women and children be Transported to remote Isles.

This official act of exemplary 'justice' in order to encourage the signing of The Oath of Allegiance to King William by tardy chiefs would have passed largely unnoticed in Anglophone Society were it not for the manner in which it was executed. Turning on your hosts and murdering them in their beds, no matter who they were, was regarded as Murder under Trust and, even in the more 'civilised' South, was regarded as a gross violation of the ancient laws of hospitality. The murderers were never prosecuted.

The road descends into Glencoe proper, giving views across to Coire Gabhail (perhaps 'hollow of capture', but generally now called 'the hidden valley'). A rockfall at its mouth, that obscures the valley, has created a natural amphitheatre, in effect a stockade where animals could be corralled. It is likely that some animals so held were the result of raids and were hidden from their owners here.

Beside this valley mouth rear the buttresses of Bidean nam Bian ('pinnacle of the hides'), three steeply sided ridges that extend north into the Glen. These ridges are Geàrr Aonach ('short ridge'), Aonach Dubh ('black ridge') and, most easterly, Beinn Fhada ('long hill'), now known collectively as the Three Sisters. This recent bundling for mountaineering purposes has given rise to modern mythic explanations of the name. Visitors are sometimes told that these buttresses were named in memory of three siblings, survivors of the Massacre of Glencoe.

In the middle of the glen is Signal Rock, where Campbell of Glenlyon, the commander of the military detachment, purportedly set a signal fire; another of the Glencoe myths. Despite the careful preparations, the official death toll of 38 was surprisingly small. There are tales of miraculous escapes: one man is said to have leapt across the River Coe to avoid being shot; another tale tells of the removal of an child's pinkie by a compassionate soldier in order to show his colleagues his bloodied dirk as proof of a kill.

Am Bàrd Mucanach ('the Muck Bard'), who is believed to have been in Glencoe as a guest of MacIain on the night of the Massacre, was probably the author of the contemporary 'Murt Ghlinne Comhainn' ('The Glencoe Murder'), a marbhrann ('elegy'). One of its images is of cuirp gheala ('white bodies'), probably indicating that the victims' corpses were stripped, as was the practice, of recyclable clothing. The tone is restrained, asserting that had the MacDonalds been given warning few Redcoats would have lived to tell the tale.

Altogether more vividly blood-soaked is the song by the Rev. Donald MacCallum, a crofter's son from Craignish in Argyll. He was the author of a small volume of songs but is chiefly remembered as one of the three of four ministers of the Established Church who had the moral courage to stand up for the people in the crofter agitation. He has the rare distinction for a man of the cloth of being arrested on a charge of "inciting the lieges to violence". The fine was paid by well-wishers. His sense of injustice finds full expression in this verse of his elegy for the Glencoe victims, published in 1884 at the height of the 'Crofters' War':

Dhùisg an raoir an gearan geur mi,
Las mi 'n lòchran air dhomh èirigh
'S chunna' mi mo mhac na shlèitrich
Fhuil ga thrèigsinn 's e gun deò.

O nach mis' a thuit an ciad fhear
Chum 's nach fhaicear leam-sa m' eudail,
Anns an leabaidh leòinte, reubte
Leis na bèistean a bha gun tròcair.

Last night the anguished moan woke me,
I lit the lamp on rising
And saw my son cut down
Blood streaming from him, lifeless.
Oh why was I not first to fall
That I might not have seen my beloved
In bed, wounded and ripped apart
By the beasts who had no compassion?

The soldiers, having completed their bloody work, proceeded to pillage the glen. The Massacre took place after a period of winter called na mìosan marbh ('the dead months'), generally from December to April. Food supplies stored in times of plenty were beginning to run out. It is therefore remarkable that some 700 head of black cattle and an equal number of sheep and other domestic animals were driven afterwards into the garrison at Fort William. The cattle represented the bare minimum winter carrying stock; the bulk of the summer additions had been sold off as surplus to the needs of the community and driven to southern livestock markets. The older beasts, no longer capable of bearing calves or surviving the lengthy walk to market, would have been butchered to provide a small amount of smoked or salted meat to supplement the basic diet of oatmeal, milk and cheese, the daily fare of most Highlanders before the introduction of the potato in the 18th century. The single farm in Glencoe today would be hard-pressed to produce a tenth of those numbers of animals.

Uamh Oisein: *Ossian's Cave*

Westwards from the buttresses, the flanks of Bidean nam Bian are sheer cliff faces punctured by deep clefts. The most prominent of those is known as Uamh Oisein ('Ossian's Cave') and was traditionally the home of this Gaelic Homer. Quite apart from his virtues as a poet, this blind bard was reported to be gargantuanly fat, hence the vastness of his eyrie in the crags. The Gaels said of him:

> Bha e dall, bodhar, bacach, 's bha naoidh dealgan daraich na bhroinn; 's e 'g itheadh na càin a bh' aig Pàdruig air Èirinn.
>
> *He was blind, deaf, lame, and had nine oaken skewers in his belly; and was eating the tribute Patrick had over Ireland.*

Aengus of Ulster had committed himself and his successors to donate 500 cows, bars of iron, shirts, mantles, and sheep to the religious houses founded by St Patrick in Ulster, instead of three pennies per head for every person baptised.

Seumas Bàn MacMhuirich: *James 'Ossian' Macpherson*

As with Homer, no one poet was solely responsible for the range of ballads described as Ossianic and once enjoyed in Gaelic Scotland. The popularity of these medieval ballads was such that they remained current until the early 20th century and were the wellspring of the poetry of James 'Ossian' Macpherson, a body of work that has been described by one academic as perhaps the most significant Scottish literary production.

In 1760, James Macpherson (1736-1796) published his volume *Fragments of Ancient Poetry,* collected in the Highlands of Scotland, and translated from the Gaelic or Erse Language. What has become known as Ossianic verse (after its purported 3rd-century author, Ossian) had an influence in the 19th century second only to William Shakespeare. In his little book Macpherson had collected oral and written sources to construct his version of a national epic. Although scholars and poets had published 'native' sources and used them for their own creations, such works were not 'ennobled' by the epic form that Macpherson had given to the older ballad form. He had literally translated a specific culture to the 'higher sphere' of classical culture.

The philosopher of national literature, Johann Gottfried Herder (1744-1803), was enthralled by the poems of Ossian and saw these works as the key to a new vision of popular poetry in the North. His 1773 collection, *Von Deutscher Art und Kunst*, opens with an essay on ancient poetry that mentions Ossian, with the second being about Shakespeare. This slim volume, with a contribution from Johann Wolfgang von Goethe (1749-1832) among others, is often seen as the manifesto of *Sturm und Drang*, the literary and artistic movement.

Intellectuals all over Europe began to perceive their own traditions in a different light. They ceased mimicking classical models and used sources in their own countries or areas outside the classical sphere. These they supported, as with Ossianic productions, with long explanatory texts to support the construction of a unique national heritage.

South of the border the accusation was that the translation was a hoax and no such epic had ever existed. The controversy simmered on for years and led to a personal feud between Macpherson and Samuel Johnson (1709-1784), which remains an anecdote gleefully recounted in many an encyclopaedia article. This view has come to dominate the literary and scholarly discourse on the subject of Macpherson's works and has since overshadowed all debates on the phenomenon associated with Ossian and its influence on European literature.

The Finnish national epic, *The Kalevala,* by Elias Lönnrot (1802-1884) is today probably the most important work that sprung from Macpherson literary impulse. Lönnrot largely used the technique of collecting from disparate 'folk' sources to produce a coherent epic much as Macpherson's did. The Finns mark the 28th of February as Kalevala Day, marking the anniversary of the publication of their national epic. Meanwhile, Macpherson's Ossianic works are largely derided or simply ignored. As one critic has stated:

> That Macpherson's works were removed from the canon of the most important works of European, and, indeed, world literature, might thus be regarded as a matter of nationalist narrow-mindedness and dogmatic notions on translation and textual criticism.

Despite sterling efforts at revision, it is still possible for a recent academic paper to make the facile statement that:

> The proud Scotsman (Macpherson) bought himself a burial site in Westminster Abbey, but the proud Englishman (Johnson) earned his resting place there. On one side of the sanctuary lies the foremost practitioner of poetic falsehood in modern history, and on the other side, also in The Poets' Corner, lies England's supreme moralist and

critic, a good and great man who so memorably defended truth in life and literature.

Johnson, as we now know, was not above a little bit of 'embellishment' himself.

Loch Lìobhann: *Loch Leven*

For the first time since leaving Glasgow, the road now returns to sea level and the shores of Loch Lìobhann (Loch Leven, 'loch of the smooth water') a location that, last century, inspired the composition of a fine song in praise of home by Alasdair MacFhraing (Alasdair Rankin), 'Mo Ghleannan Taobh Loch Lìobhann' ('My Glen beside Loch Leven'):

Fàile cùbhraidh an fhraoich tighinn thar mullach nam beann
Agus chì thu 'n damh ruadh air an fhrìth ann;
'S ged shiùbhladh tu Alba chan fhaic thu aon ghleann
Tha cho bòidheach rim ghleann taobh Loch Lìobhann.

The fragrant scent of heather coming over the summits of the hills, and you'll see the red deer in the forest there; even if you travelled throughout Scotland you wouldn't see a single glen as beautiful as my glen by Loch Leven.

Eilean Munda (Munda's Isle) in Loch Leven is the chapel site where the MacIain MacDonald chiefs were traditionally buried. The island is named for a saintly hermit; it was common for men in this hermetic tradition to select isolated locations as far north as Iceland, in order to pursue their penitential path to salvation. In such locations, they were also protected from the attentions of wild animals and men less saintly than themselves. The subsequent choice of such locations as the final resting place for prominent members of the community had the additional advantage of their remains not being dug up by carrion eaters.

The shore road towards Fort William passes Baile a' Chaolais (Ballachulish, 'village at the narrows'). The disused slate quarries here once employed many Gaelic-speaking men and the people of South Ballachulish were nicknamed muinntir na sglèat ('the slate people'). At these quarrying operations, and also during the construction of the earliest hydro-electric schemes at the beginning of the 20th century, bilingual 'gangers' had to be employed to instruct the mainly monoglot Gaelic work squads.

American forces in the Second World War used First Nation people as radio operators, figuring out that their messages would be incomprehensible to the eavesdropping enemy. A slight twist to this demonstration of the value of minority languages is found in the tale of the wartime escape by three Ballachulish quarrymen, William Kemp, Sandy MacDonald and James 'Ginger' Wilson, who escaped from captivity in Germany by using only Gaelic as a means of communication. They succeeded in getting home.

The twenty kilometre River Leven drains a series of small lochs to the north-west of Rannoch and flows westward to Loch Leven, forming, during its course, the border between the shires of Inverness and Argyll.

An Iar Air Tairbeart: *West of Tarbert*

Returning south and west from the Tarbet junction with the road to Inveraray, is Arrochar, which lies in Latharna a Deas (South Lorne). In 1881, more than four out of five people here were habitually speaking Gaelic. Meeting the needs of such speakers in areas like the parish of Arrochar was always a challenge to Church authorities. In 1678, Dumbarton's Presbytery heard of the distances people had to travel in the Luss church area and the 'ruggedness of the way'. It was necessary that a church be built at Tarbet for:

> about the number of four hundred souls that are now living in ignorance.

But when the Rev. Archibald McLachlan resigned in 1701 after 41 years, his reasons were:

> infirmities of body and various secular discouragements,

namely the lack of a church, manse and glebe. His 400 church-less souls would all have been Gaelic speakers. A new church was provided in the

1820s to be almost immediately emptied with the departure of the bulk of the congregation to the new Free Church in the Disruption of 1843.

Gleann a' Chrò: *Glen Croe*

Wade's military road ran along the floor of Gleann a' Chrò (Glen Croe, 'Cattle-fold Glen'), using the old drove road that climbed in a series of switchbacks to reach the pass at what is now known as the Rest and Be Thankful. The name is taken from an inscription on a stone erected by Government soldiers who, in 1756, marked their construction achievement much in the fashion of Roman legionaries completing similar roads almost two millennia earlier. The road had no strategic purpose, but it just happened to run to Inveraray, the seat of the Duke of Argyll, who then had more than sufficient political influence to adjust the military's priorities to his own advantage.

Gamekeeper Gilleasbaig Mac an t-Saoir (Archibald MacIntyre) (1854 -1922) composed 'Òran Ghlinne Chrò' ('Glen Croe Song'), expressing sadness when, in 1914, he had to move his flock of sheep out of the glen to make room for deer and sportsmen:

Bidh fèidh nam fuar-bheann
A-nis air ghluasad
Is gràisg de dh'uabhraich
A' dol nan còmhdhail;
Bidh màidsear cuagach
A' caitheamh luaidh' orr'
'S gruing is gruaim air
Mur dèan e 'n leònadh.

The deer of the cold hills are now on the move with a rabble of toffs going out to meet them; a limping major firing lead at them, frowning and sullen if he fails to wound them.

Descending back to sea level, the road sweeps to the right of a hump-backed bridge on the military road. It is known as the Butter Bridge. The name comes from the river which, as its Gaelic name, Allt Beinn Ime ('stream of the butter hill'), suggests, flows down from rich butter-producing pastures in the hills to the east, once used as summer grazing by the communities that inhabited this now emptied glen. The young women lived in bothies known as àirighean ('shielings') and made butter and cheese from the plentiful milk. Young men might join them of an evening and naturally love songs were composed. One such was 'Thug mi 'n oidhche raoir san àirigh' ('I spent last night in the sheiling'):

> Thug mi 'n oidhche raoir 's mi bruadar
> Mar ri nìghneagan na buaile
> B' fhìnealt uasal mìn na gruagaich
> Seinn nan duanag air an àirigh.
>
> Thug mi 'n oidhche raoir san àirigh
> Thug mi 'n oidhche raoir san àirigh,
> Chaith mi 'n oidhche cridheil coibhneil,
> Mar ri maighdeanan na h-àirigh.
>
> *I spent last night in my dreams with the sheiling maidens, elegant, noble, delicate young women singing songs at the àirigh.*
>
> *I spent last night at the sheiling, I spent last night at the sheiling, I spent a kindly cheerful evening with the sheiling maidens.*

This little river drains into Loch Fyne by Ardkinglass and the road south from here to Dunoon enters the territory of Còmhghall (Cowal), one of the four sections of ancient Dál Riada. Còmhghall was the name of one of the seven sons of the legendary King Erc, who gave their names to many parts of Scotland.

In Dun Omhain (Dunoon, 'hill [fort] on the river'), stands a statue to Mary Campbell, who had a profound influence on Robert Burns. Mary was born in 1764 at Achadh Mòr (Auchamore, 'big field'), near Lochranza in Arran, although the family had links to Ceann Loch Chille Chiarain (Campbeltown, 'head of the loch of St. Kieran'). Burns called her 'Highland Mary' and planned to marry her. Sadly, before that could happen, she became ill and died in the very 'Highland' but Lowland port of Grianaig (Greenock, 'gravelly place').

To the south of the town of Dunoon is Caisteal Tollard (Castle Toward, 'height of the caves'), once the home of Clan Lamont and scene of a bloody Campbell reprisal. When the bloodletting at Inverlochy in 1642 had left the Clan Campbell kindred prostrate, the Lamonts attacked them, having seen their acquisitive neighbours encroach upon their own lands. In tradition, an early rehearsal of the Glencoe Massacre, the again-ascendant Argyllshire men sought hospitality at Castle Toward and then slaughtered the Lamonts while they slept. In reality, they offered leniency to the besieged families and then slaughtered the lot, sparing neither sex nor age.

From Lochgilphead, the B83 to the Mull of Kintyre runs south through Cnapadal (Knapdale, 'hill field') and Tairbeart Loch Fìne (Tarbert of Loch Fyne) to Ceann Tìre (Kintyre, 'land's end'). The peninsula, once treated administratively as one of the Inner Hebrides, was formerly held by the MacDonalds, but following the bitter struggle with the Argyllshire men, they had, by the beginning of the 17th century, lost control of the area. It was this relentless, scheming erosion of their estates that was the context and ultimate reason for Clan Donald's involvement with Montrose in the Wars of The Three Kingdoms. An Anglocentric view of these Wars suggests that much of it was conducted along gentlemanly lines. While this might, perhaps, have been true for England, this was not the case north of the Border and particularly across the Irish Sea.

Alasdair Mac Cholla Chiotaich: *Alasdair, Son of Left-handed Coll*

The conflict enabled Alasdair mac Cholla Chiotaich ('Alasdair, son of left-handed Coll' or Alexander MacDonald) the most renowned of all the warriors of Gaelic Scotland, to come to prominence. In 1644, he led a force of some 1500 mainly Ulstermen to Scotland to support the Royalists against the Covenanters. Alasdair linked up with the Royalist Seumas nan Cath ('James of the Battles', or James Graham, First Marquis of Montrose). Given Alasdair's status within Clan Donald, he was also able to raise men among his fellow clansmen and other anti-Campbell kindreds. In the subsequent campaign against the Covenanter armies of the Scottish state and particularly the Argyllshire men, Mac Colla and Montrose won a series of victories from Tobar Mhoire (Tippermuir, 'Mary's well') to Cill Saidhe (Kilsyth, 'Church of St. Sadhabh').

Alasdair divides opinion, then and now; his enemies claimed he was a cannibal. Though described as Montrose's Lieutenant, he was the military strategist of that campaign. His nickname was Fear Thollaidh nan Taighean ('destroyer of houses'), as he conducted a scorched earth policy against the Campbell kindred's lands, killing all Argyllshire men he could find. By one account some 900 were killed. Argyllshire tradition records an incident that resonates with the many instances of alleged church burnings, in which he burned down a building full of women and children, the place becoming known as Sabhal nan Cnàmh ('barn of bones'). As often with stories of the burning of churches, the tale is probably apocryphal.

A fairly contemporary song is addressed to Alasdair and is attributed to Diorbhail Nic a' Bhriuthainn (Dorothy Brown) who lived on the Isle of Luing in Argyll. She apparently composed it after seeing his ships pass through the sound of Luing on an expedition against the Campbells – her own people.

Alasdair, a laoigh mo chèille,
Cò chunnaic no dh'fhàg thu 'n Èirinn?
Dh'fhàg thu na mìltean 's na ceudan
'S cha d'fhàg thu aon d'leithid fèin ann,
Calpa cruinn an t-siubhail eutruim,
Cas chruinneachadh 'n t-sluaigh ri chèile ;
Cha dèanar cogadh as t-eugais,
'S cha dèanar sìth gun do rèite.

Alasdair, my darling, who did you see or leave in Ireland? You left thousands and hundreds but you didn't leave one like yourself, light-footed with rounded calves, the bringer together of people; war cannot be waged without you and peace can't be achieved without your agreement.

In a context where apparently innocent passengers on ships travelling from Ireland were apprehended by Covenantors and had their hands bound before being flung into the sea on suspicion that they were there in support of the Royalist cause, atrocity followed atrocity.

Ultimately, Alasdair mac Cholla beat a tactical retreat from the Covenanting forces of David Leslie, leaving a small body of 300 men to hold Dùn Àbhartaich

(Dunaverty Castle, 'Àbhartach's Fort') at the very south end of Kintyre. These men negotiated a conditional surrender but were subsequently slaughtered by being flung from the cliffs of the castle at the insistence of the Covenanting army chaplain, Rev. John Nevay. Local tradition has it that the rocks below the castle are still stained with the blood of these men. A grateful Parliament awarded David Leslie a title and lands near Leven in Fife, and the ruins of his ostentatious Newark Castle now dominate the coastline near St. Monans. Alasdair mac Cholla himself was shot in cold blood at Knocknanauss in Ireland, having honourably surrendered to his opponents.

Mac Cholla's activities did have an unintended consequence for the fate of Gaelic in war-torn Kintyre. Its hold in the area was further eroded by the planting of Scots-speaking tenants from the southwest Lowlands to take up empty farm tenancies. Small burghs such as Inveraray and Campbelltown were established, accelerating language shift. That process was a slow one, as is demonstrated by a probably early 18th-century love song from the immediate area of Campbelltown, 'Dòmhnall nan Dòmhnall' ('Donald of the Donalds') in which his love praises a young man's manners and that of his clan; not Campbells in this instance but MacNeills:

> Dè! nam biodh tu mar shionnach air an tulaich ud thall
> Agus mise mar eala air bharraibh nan tonn
> Nàile, rachainn ad choinneamh agus mheallainn thu leam,
> Lùb ùr a' chùil chlannaich, ort tha m' anam an geall.
>
> *God! if you were like a fox on yonder knoll and I like a swan on*
> *the crests of the waves. Truly I would go towards you and I'd*
> *beguile you to come with me, young man of the curled locks,*
> *my soul longs for you.*

Returning north to the A83 road, the next town is the former burgh of Inveraray, the seat of Clan Campbell. The Heritable Jurisdictions Act of 1746 abolished judicial rights held by Scottish heritors, the feudal landholders of a parish. These were a significant source of power, especially for clan chiefs, such as the Duke of Argyll, since they gave them legal control over their tenants. These rights included the privilege of inflicting capital punishment for theft, by which a woman could be drowned in a pit, or a man hanged on a gallows.

This Act also returned control of the appointment of Sheriff-Principals to the Crown as had been the case when this position had been established in the 13th century. Over the centuries the majority had become hereditary, the holders appointing legal professionals known as Sheriff-Deputes to do the work. This was now reversed.

Inbhir Aora: *Inveraray*

In 1747, out of a total of £152,000 paid out by the government in compensation for the Scottish nobility's loss of these heritable rights, the Duke of Argyll received £25,000. This money went to meet the not-inconsiderable costs of his new residence at Inveraray. But the expense did not end there. It was said that some £250,000 was expended in the second half of the 18th century on the annual upkeep of the Duke's castle and its designed landscape. The neo-Gothic castle now stands alone on the banks of Abhainn Aora (River Aray, the name probably meaning 'water course'). The site of the planned village of Inveraray is technically not the proper name of the place. The former castletoun around the original castle was named from the point where the River Aray met the water of Loch Fyne, the Inbhir Aora. The re-siting of the village during the setting out of the designed landscape broke the link. The Duke of Argyll aped the Duke of Atholl in clearing people for aesthetic purposes.

The new planned town was set out with homes for linen mill workers and traders, though many of the people eked out a livelihood fishing herring in the sea lochs. A humorous song, 'Luinneag an Iasgair ('The Fisherman's Song'), tells of one lad's experience at a wedding in Inveraray. His own wedding would be dependent on a successful herring season:

> Ach bheir mi mo ghealladh dhuibh, òigridh a' bhaile,
> Ged is ann ann an cagar nach canainn ri daoine.
> Ma shnàmhas an sgadan am bliadhn' mar is math leinn
> Bheir mise dhaibh banais am Bail' Ionar-aora!
>
> *But village youth, I promise you this, even if it's in a whisper*
> *because I can't tell people yet. If the herring swim this year*
> *as we would wish I'll give them a wedding in Inveraray!*

The 20th-century poet George Campbell Hay was also inspired by the fishermen of Loch Fyne and their environment: his poem 'Luinneag' ('Lullaby') tells of his strong attachment to the place:

B' e gairbhe na gaoithe
chum an raoir mi nam chaithris.

Gaoth à deas air Loch Fìne
teachd gu fìochar le tartar.

Na tuinn chaoirgheal mu Gharbhail
neart na fairge 's a faram.

Is ann an raoir a bha 'n nuallan
Na mo chluasan 's mi 'n Sasainn.

It was the hardness of the wind that kept me awake last night.

A wind from the south on Loch Fyne coming fiercely with uproar,

waves blazing with foam round Garvel, the might of the sea and its clangour.

Last night its roaring was in my ears and I was in England.

Inveraray Parish church was built at the same time as the village and designed to serve the two language communities. The church is divided across the middle, creating two equal spaces for the respective services. The last Gaelic service took place in 1930.

A further ten kilometres on from Inveraray is A' Cheann-mhòr (Kenmore, 'big-headed place'). This small, planned village, occupying a promontory on the northern shore of Loch Fyne, was begun on the instructions of the 5th Duke in 1771. It was here that Eòghann MacColla, Bàrd Loch Fìne (Ewan MacColl, the Loch Fyne Bard) was born in 1808. When his parents emigrated to Canada in 1831, MacColl stayed as he was anxious to see his collection of verse into print. When he was 30, he went to work in Liverpool for eleven years. Most of his love songs were to Sìne Chaimbeul, Jean Campbell, who sadly married somebody else:

A nighean donn as grinne cruth,
As binne guth 's as caoine,
Ge geal an cobhar air an t-sruth
'S ann bhiodh e dubh rid thaobh-sa.

O 's truagh bhith 'n seo air Galltachd
Nuair tha 'n samhradh is mo chiad-rùn
A' strì cò 's grinne dheàrrsas nis
Air àirighean Ghlinn Creurain.

Brown-haired lass elegant of shape, with the most beautiful, tender voice, though the foam on the burn is white it would be black beside you.

O, I am miserable in the Lowlands when summer and my first love are engaged in a contest to see who shines most beautifully at the Glen Creran sheilings.

MacColl ultimately joined his family and died in Toronto in 1898, aged 90. His fellow countrymen recognised his worth and, in 1930, erected a cairn to his memory on the shore of Loch Fyne at Kenmore. On it is inscribed:

Mairidh ainm 's a dhuan cho fad 's is buan ar ceòl.

His name and verse will survive so long as our music survives.

On the coast further north on a promontory on Loch Crinan stands the 16th century castle of Dùn Treòin (Duntrune, 'fort of the mighty person'). It was once a MacDonald stronghold but, by 1616, the Earl of Argyll used it to muster his forces for an invasion of Islay. In a traditional tale, Colla Ciotach ('left-handed Coll MacDonald'), intending to stop them, sent his piper to reconnoitre. The piper gained entry to the castle but was captured. While imprisoned, he saw Coll's galley approaching. Fearing that they might fall into a trap, he played a pibroch composed on the spot and known as 'The Piper's Warning to His Master'. Coll recognised the warning immediately and sailed away. Belatedly, the Campbells realised what the piper was doing and as punishment cut off his fingers:

A Cholla mo ghaol, seachainn an caol,
Seachainn an caol, seachainn an caol,
Cholla mo ghaol, seachainn an caol,
Seachainn an caol,
Tha mise làimh, tha mise làimh.

Coll my beloved, avoid the straits, avoid the straits,
avoid the straits,
Coll my beloved, avoid the straits, avoid the straits,
I am imprisoned, I am imprisoned.

Seón Carsuel: *John Carswell*

While Duntrune castle survived the depredations of the 17th century, Caisteal Chàrn Asaraidh (Carnasserie Castle, 'castle of the cairn of the path') did not. It was burned by the same Atholl forces that destroyed Inveraray in 1685. Built between 1562 and 1575, it stands above the main road, just north of Kilmartin. It was the home of An Carsalach Mòr, Seón Carsuel (John Carswell), the first Protestant Bishop of Argyll following the Reformation in 1560. As his patron was the 5th Earl of Argyll, the lintel of the main door bears the words:

Dia Le Ua nDuibhne,
God [be] with the Campbells.

It was here in the 1560s that Carswell translated into Gaelic a key book of the Scottish Reformation, *The Book of Common Order,* a directory for the conduct of worship in the Reformed churches. Called *Foirm na n-Urrnuidheadh (Form of the Worship),* it was important in assisting the spread of the reformed doctrine. Its language is in an exuberant, classical Gaelic. The vernacular dialects of Ireland and Scotland belong to a single language and, in the late 12th century, a formalised standard variant of that language was created by medieval Gaelic poets, based on the then vernacular usage, for compositions of bardic poetry. Carswell thus used the Irish Classical Common Gaelic orthography. It is suggested that if it were not for his decision to use it, Scottish Gaelic today, like the Manx language, might be using an orthography more akin to English than traditional Irish.

Ministers of the 17th century Synod of Argyll, following Carswell's example, translated catechisms into Gaelic and set to work on a translation of the Bible. The Old Testament was completed by 1673 but was never printed. When the Bible was eventually translated into Gaelic, between 1755 and 1801, Argyllshire men played their part in the task, their most notable contributor being the Rev. Dr John Smith (1747-1807), a native of Glenorchy and minister of Campbeltown.

An t-Òban Latharnach: *Oban*

An t-Òban Latharnach (Oban, 'the little bay of Lorne') was once known as Loch a' Mhuilinn (Lochavualin, 'Mill Loch') and it developed around a distillery and jetty created here in the 18th century. The town is noted for two cultural events in the Gaelic world. Probably the most coveted awards in piping are the gold medals awarded every year at the Argyllshire Gathering in Oban and at the Northern Meeting in Inverness. The first Gold Medallist at Oban in 1873 was Donald Stewart MacDonald, piper to the Mackintosh chief and a native of Drochaid Chàrr (Carrbridge, 'bridge at the marsh'). In 1876, the winner was Calum Pìobaire (Malcolm MacPherson), piper to Cluny MacPherson. To win both medals in the same year is a feat that has been achieved on only eleven occasions in over 140 years, most recently in 2014 by Douglas Murray. Most winners have been Gaelic-speaking Highlanders.

Another first for Oban was to host the 1898 inaugural Mòd Nàiseanta Rìoghail (the Royal National Mod). At that time, the vast majority of the town's 4,000 inhabitants were Gaelic speakers. Today, Oban has 7,823 people of whom 328 speak the language.

East from Oban at A' Chonghail (Connel, 'the whirlpool') the former railway bridge carries the A828 from Connel to Ballachulish through the territorial area of Meadarloch (Benderloch, 'between two lochs'): namely, Loch Eiteabh (Etive) and Loch Leamhainn (Leven). At the head of Loch Etive is Dail an Eas (Dalness, 'the valley of the waterfall') which is associated with the tale of Deirdre and the Sons of Uisne. In Scotland, this tale was recorded in part by James 'Ossian' Macpherson in 1760, but John Francis

Campbell (1821-1885) undertook a systematic examination of the versions in both medieval manuscripts and oral traditions. These he published privately as *Leabhar na Feinne (Book of the Fingalians)* in 1874 and most of the English tales now circulating are derived from this source.

Dearshula is Clann Uisne: *Deirdre and the Sons of Uisne*

Colum Cruitire (Colum the Harper) was told that his wife would have a girl in their old age but was warned that her beauty would lead to bloodshed in Ireland. Colum took steps to prevent the fulfilment of the prophecy and their child, named Deirdre, was hidden away. She grew up:

> lithe and fair as the stately sapling, and as straight and proportioned as the young moorland rush. She was shapely in her person, lovely in her beauty, while her skin and her gait was like those of the swan of the lake and the hind of the hill. She was the blood-drop of the finest form, of loveliest complexion and of gentlest mien ...

But Deirdre's hide-out was discovered and she was taken to Connor MacNessa, King of Ulster. Infatuated, he determined to marry her, but one day she saw Naois, Ardan and Ainle, the three sons of Uisne. The youths are described as:

> ... the colour of the raven on their hair, their skin like the swan of the waves and their cheeks like the blood of the speckled-red fawn, while their strength and their stateliness were those of the salmon of the rapid stream and the stag of the brindled hill; and Naois had all above the slope of the two shoulders over the other people of Erin.

Deirdre fell for Naois:

Delightful to Deirdre was the youth,
Whose face was the brightness of day;
Of the lustre of the ravens were his locks;
Redder than rasps were his cheeks.

Inevitably, Deirdre eloped with Naois to Glen Etive along with his two brothers where their home was known as Grianan Dearshula (Deirdre's Sunny Bower).

It was luxurious:

> Bha grianan Dearshula air a thuthadh a mach le
> reang-roinneach nari glac agus le madh chriadh nam poll,
> agus air a linseadh le giubhas nan beann agus le cloimh-iteach
> nan ian.
>
> *The sunny-bower of Deirdre was thatched without with the*
> *long-stalked fern of the dells and the red clay of the pools,*
> *and lined within with the pine of the mountains and the down*
> *of birds.*

Soon a trusted friend was sent from Connor MacNessa to invite them back. He promised that no harm would come to them and, against Deirdre's wishes, they returned. But the king was still so enthralled with her that he broke his promise and had the three brothers killed, hoping to have Deirdre for himself. But even in death, she would not be separated from Naois. At the grave of her lover and his brothers, Deirdre said:

> Teann a nall, a Naois, mo ghràidh;
> Druideadh Ardan ri Aillean.
> Na 'n robh ciall aig mairbh,
> Dhèanadh sibhse àite dhòmhsa.
>
> *Move thou hither, O Naois, my love;*
> *Close thou, Ardan, over to Aillean.*
> *If dead had understanding,*
> *You would make a place for me.*

Deirdre leapt down beside Naois and died. The tale of the doomed lovers is also commemorated celestially: 'Slighe Chlann Uisnich' ('path of the Children of Uisne') is The Milky Way.

An Apainn: *Appin*

The road northwards reaches An Apainn (Appin, 'the Abbot's land'), once held by the abbot of the monastery dedicated to St. Moluag, situated on the offshore island of Lios Mòr (Lismore, 'great garden'). Moluag's name is connected to light, as is seen in a couplet in his praise by Angus, the Culdee:

Moluoc glan geldai
Grian Lissmoir di Alba

Moluag clear and brilliant
The sun of Lismore in Alba.

The name 'Moluag' is made up of the honorific mo ('my', signifying 'saint') and the name Lughaidh. But there is a tradition that Moluag is simply mo lùdag ('my little finger'), because the saint, in a race to the island with St. Columba, claimed Lismore by cutting off his little finger and throwing it ashore. Moluag is said to have introduced Christianity to Lismore where he died in 592. Despite this early conversion, echoes of the belief in omens of pre-Christian times continued in rhymes such as the following:

Chuala mi chuthag 's gun bhiadh am bhroinn;
Chuala mi am fearan am bàrr a' chroinn;
Chuala mi 'n suaircean shuas anns a' choill;
'S chuala mi nuala cumhachag na h-oidhche.
Chunna mi 'n uan 's a chùla rium;
Chunna mi 'n t-seiliche air lic luim;
Chunna mi 'n searrach le thulachain rium;
Chunna mi 'n clachran air ghàrradh tuill,
An eunarag 's mi 'm shuidhe cruinn.
'S dh'aithnich mi nach rachadh a' bhliadhna leam.

I heard the cuckoo with no food in my stomach;
I heard the ringdove on the top of the branch;
I heard the sweet warbler up in the wood;
And I heard the screech of the night owl.

I saw the lamb with its back to me;
I saw the snail on the bare flagstone;
I saw the foal with his hindquarters to me;
I saw the wheatear on a dyke of holes,
I saw the snipe while sitting crouched,
and I knew the year would not favour me.

The story of the rescue of the Appin Standard at the Battle of Culloden indicates active support in Lismore for the Jacobite cause. The MacGilleMhìcheil (Carmichael) family were the hereditary standard-bearers of the Stewarts of Appin. At Culloden, eight Carmichaels were either killed or wounded in defence of the standard. When the last fell, Donald, a young member of the Livingstone bodyguard, snatched the banner from the standard and escaped from the battlefield. When challenged by two dragoons, he turned and killed one, putting the other to flight. He ultimately succeeded in getting to Lismore and restored the banner to the Stewarts.

Dòmhnall MacNeacail: *Donald McNicol*

Donald McNicol (1735-1802) was appointed minister to the Lismore parish in 1766 at the age of 31. He was a poet and scholar who started on his own duanaire ('anthology of poems') focused on Ossianic themes. His parish was extensive, encompassing an area of 1450 hectares. A minister, who attended conscientiously to the needs of the people distributed over such an area, would have had little spare time. The stipend was poor, thanks to the meanness of the heritors, or landlords. When he came to the parish, his stipend amounted to only £64 and remained so for 24 years. Much of his work was written on scraps of paper and, amongst his documents, are eleven obviously home-made notebooks. Although much of his collection of old poetry has been lost, some 3,000 lines have survived, and these include a number of versions of poems and ballads which appear in the *The Book of the Dean of Lismore*. Miraculously, a cache of his papers has been discovered very recently.

One can perhaps understand the extent of McNicol's irritation when he learnt of Samuel Johnson's dismissal of the authenticity of any of the Ossianic poems which had been published by 'Ossian' Macpherson. In response, he wrote a very detailed and learned defence of the heritage of these ancient ballads which characteristically Johnston dismissed out of hand. McNicol could be forgiven if, as has erroneously been claimed, he had penned a traditional piece of invective – an aoir ('lampoon, satire') about the great savant.

The 'Òran don Ollamh MacIain' ('Song to Dr Johnson') includes unflattering descriptions such as:

> ceann puinnsein ('head of poison'); [with a brain little bigger than that of a] maighdeige-tràghad ('shore-whelk'); bratag sgreataidh ('ugly wasteland caterpillar'); seilcheag ghrànda, bhog, litheach ('foul, soft, slimy snail') and cartan ('botfly')

and continues in this vein for almost a hundred lines. Seamus Mac an t-Saoir (James Macintyre) (1727-99), a learned, fellow antiquarian colleague of McNicol's published this song anonymously in 1776. Johnson would have been blissfully unaware of the long tradition this poetry represented although it would have occasioned much hilarity amongst its Gaelic readers.

McNicol himself was capable of more than satirical verse when the occasion demanded. He was in love with Lilias, daughter of Campbell of Auchlian in Glenorchy and when he learnt that she was to marry Brian, a son of the Earl of Breadalbane, he composed a song,

'Mo shùil ad dhèidh' ('My eye following you'), which remains popular to this day:

> Nam biodh siud agam, mo lùth 's mo leum,
> Mi 'm shuidh air a' bhealach 's mo chù air èill,
> Gun dèanainn-sa cogadh gu làidir, treun,
> Mun leiginn mo leannan le fear tha fon ghrèin.
>
> *If I had my strength and the ability to leap, sitting at the pass with my dog on a leash, I would wage war robustly and bravely before I would let my sweetheart go with any man in the world.*

Hearing that Lilias was at Lochnell Castle, Donald went to ask her if she really was going to marry. When Lilias confirmed that she was, Donald set out on the road back to Lismore. After he had left, Brian suggested to Lilias that they have some fun at the expense of Lochnell's fool, the butt of everybody's humour. But the fool gave as good as he got. At last Lilias's fiancé, having run out of ideas, offered the fool a shilling if he would kiss Lilias.

He replied, "Were it her wish I would do it for nothing."

Her response was, "You are more of a gentleman than he," and she continued, "You will have your shilling, but it is I who will kiss you for showing me what an unmannerly fool I all but married."

Having kissed the fool, Lilias ordered a servant to find Donald and to tell him she wanted to speak to him urgently. So, Donald turned back and met Lillias who said, "If you have not changed your mind, I have changed mine."

"Does this mean that you are willing to marry me?" enquired Donald with surprise.

"Yes, now, if you wish," replied Lilias firmly.

They married in 1777 and enjoyed many years together.

Cailean Caimbeul is Seumas a' Ghlinne: *Colin Campbell and James of the Glen*

On the mainland opposite Lismore is Leitir Mòr (Lettermore, 'big sloping land'), the site of the 1752 killing of Cailean Caimbeul, Gleann Ùire (Colin Campbell of Glenure or 'the Red Fox'). According to tradition, a man with the second sight, Dòmhnall Mòr Òg Camshron (Big Young Donald Cameron) from the Braes of Lochaber, had foreseen the murder. Confident of everything happening as he foresaw, he came all the way to Onich, where he waited until he heard the report of the shot fired by Campbell's assassin on the other side of the narrows.

Seumas a' Ghlinne ('James of the Glen' or James Stewart of Acharn) was wrongly accused of complicity by inciting his kinsman Alan Breac to kill the Red Fox. The adjective breac in Alan's name means 'speckled' as of a rainbow trout, or a person's freckled or pockmarked face. Glenure, as judicial factor on the estate, was proceeding to eject some tenants at the time. Allegedly, when James Stewart was told what had happened, he said prophetically:

> Cò sam bith an ciontach, is mise an crionlach.
>
> *Whoever may be the guilty one, I am the victim.*

Two days later he was arrested and, while in prison at Fort William, he was denied all facilities for preparing his defence. It is obvious that James's trial was to be, in the words of one writer, "an impudent mockery".

The presiding judge was the Duke of Argyll, Lord Justice-General, and the jury were all Argyllshire men. Sometime later, a Campbell was taunted with the disgraceful justice meted out to James. He replied proudly that anyone could get a guilty man hanged but only mac Cailein Mòr (Campbell of Argyll) could get an innocent man hanged.

Cnap a' Chaolais ('knoll of the narrows'), sited to the left of the road as it crosses the bridge at Ballachulish, is one of many hanging spots used to dispense punishment to the victims of heritable jurisprudence, a lord's territorial right of 'pit and gallows'. The Duke's 1747 surrender of these rights did not prevent him from dispensing 'justice'.

Protesting his innocence on the scaffold, James recited the 35th Psalm of David. The psalm became known in the Highlands as Salm Sheumais a' Ghlinne ('James of the Glen's Psalm'):

Tagair, a Dhia, ri luchd mo strì: cuir cath ri luchd mo chath'.
Glac fhèin do thargaid is do sgiath, èirich, dèan còmhnadh
  math.

Ach chruinnich iad, is bha iad ait, air bhith dhomh ann an
  teinn,
Gun fios dhomh chruinnich cuideachd thàir, gun tàmh mi
  reubadh rinn.

Contend Lord, with those that contend with me and fight
with those that fight against me. Take up shield and buckler;
arise and come to my aid.

But when I was in distress, unbeknown to me attackers
gathered in glee against me. They slandered me without
ceasing.

In a manner similar to earlier Roman notions of exemplary justice, the authorities had a 30 foot gibbet erected on Cnap a' Chaolais. Usually, the gibbet was dismantled once the victim had been pronounced dead. Here, however, the authorities prevented anyone sympathetic to Stewart's plight from cutting down the gibbet by slotting its base into an iron sheath. The hanging took place on 8th November 1752, and, for a period of eighteen months, a constant guard prevented friends from taking the body down. When it began to disintegrate, the bones of the skeleton were joined together with wire and replaced on the gibbet. A monument to Seumas a' Ghlinne stands on Cnap a' Chaolais today.

The story of the 1756 shooting of the Red Fox is central to Robert Louis Stevenson's *Kidnapped*, a historical fiction adventure written for youth in 1886. Although some say disparagingly that it is simply Sir Walter Scott's *Waverly* rewritten for boys, one academic has suggested that Stevenson was a serious historian. It is claimed that in writing about Alan Breac Stewart, the man who was widely believed to have fired the fatal shot at the Red Fox (although recent research now points the finger at others), Stevenson drew on still current tales concerning the exploits of John Roy Stewart, the commander of the Appin Regiment at the Battle of Culloden. Serious historian or not, Stevenson's characterisation of Alan Breac closely follows tropes of representation employed by Sir Walter Scott some seventy years earlier. Alan Breac Stewart is recognisably the Gaelic Highlander, irredeemably Jacobite and a lost cause dreamer, in contrast to Lowlander David Balfour, a practical stolid, sensible citizen of a modern world.

The road east from Oban to Tyndrum passes Taigh Inbhir Obha (Inverawe House) once the home of Donnchadh MacDhonnchaidh of Inbhir Obha (Duncan Campbell), tacksman and officer in the 42nd Regiment, Black Watch. In 1758, when the regiment spear-headed General Abercrombie's disastrous assault on Fort Carillon on Lake George, Upper New York State, there were 3,867 Scottish soldiers, mainly Gaelic-speaking Highlanders, and 207 Scottish officers in America, representing close to a third of the total British force. They often found themselves in the thick of the fighting and bore the brunt of British losses. Such were their losses that, by 1762, the Black Watch could field only 480 soldiers, about half its original complement.

Donnchadh MacDhonnchaidh is Ticonderoga: *Duncan Campbell and Ticonderoga*

Major Duncan Campbell of Inverawe died at Fort Carillon in 1758 from wounds sustained while leading his men. These events form the background to a famous ghost story that pivots on two fundamental traditions of Gaelic society, hospitality and fosterage.

Each concept has its own proverbs. The saying:

> Aoigheachd Thormoid mhòir – fuirich, fuirich, tha a' chearc sa chliabh agus a' bhean sa chladach
>
> *Big Norman's hospitality – the hen's in the creel and the wife's at the shore*

implies a wholesome diet of eggs and shellfish and illustrates well the notion of true Highland hospitality which gladly shares its all, however little that may be, with a stranger.

Sayings relating to fosterage include:

> Co-dhaltas gu ceud, is càirdeas gu fichead.
>
> *Fostership to a hundred, kindred to twenty.*

The bond of fostering was stronger than that of blood, a sentiment reinforced in the proverb:

> Thèid trian daltachd ri goistidheachd
>
> *A third of fostership goes to sponsorship,*

meaning the bond to a foster father was three times as strong as that to a godfather.

In the extremely difficult choice made by Duncan Campbell the almost sacrosanct rule of hospitality trumps the deep bonds formed through fosterage.

As the story is now told, Duncan Campbell was at his home in Inverawe when a stranger arrived to explain that he had killed a man and was seeking sanctuary. Honouring the unwritten law of hospitality, Duncan duly hid the man in a cave on Cruachan, the mountain above Inverawe. Soon the stranger's pursuers arrived and Duncan was dismayed to learn that the victim was his own foster-brother. Yet he did not reveal the whereabouts of the murderer.

That night, the ghost of his foster brother appeared imploring him to give up the murderer, but Duncan had to refuse. A second night the ghost appeared again demanding his murderer be given up, but Duncan remained steadfast. For a third and final night, the ghost appeared, saying to him:

> "Chan urrainn dhuit a liubhairt thairis, oir leig thu leis a chasan a thoirt leis. Tachraidh sinn aig Ticonderoga."
>
> *"You could not hand him over, but let him escape. We will meet at Ticonderoga."*

The name Ticonderoga meant nothing to Duncan. The evening prior to the attack on Fort Carillon, Duncan received another visit from his foster brother's ghost, who reminded him of his promise that they would meet again. Mortally wounded in the futile assault, Duncan was buried near the site of the battle. Fort Carillon was known as Ticonderoga in the native American language of the area.

Beann Cruachan is Loch Obha: *Ben Cruachan and Loch Awe*

Ben Cruachan, to the east, the site of a Hydro-electric pump-storage scheme, rises to a height of 900 metres above Loch Awe. The name is usually translated as 'little heap' although some claim 'shoulder'. The word for 'thigh' is a homonym of Cruachan and spurious tales about the shoulder of the mountain being part of the early Dalriadic crowning rituals at Dunadd have confused thigh and shoulder. More pertinent, perhaps, is that the fabled seven-tiered palace of Queen Maebh, described in the ancient Gaelic tale 'Táin Bó Cúailnge' ('the Cattle Raid of Cooley'), was also known as Cruachan.

Seen from the sea, the mountain has a similar stepped aspect. It is celebrated in Peter MacIntyre's song:

Cruachan Beann 's e cho mòr,
Tha e sònraicht' ri fhaicinn;
Chan eil a leithid san Roinn Eòrp',
'S geal a chòta 'n àm sneachda.

Cruachan Mountain so very high, to see it is special; its like isn't to be found anywhere in Europe, its coat so white at the time of snow.

Loch Awe, lying below the mountain, is mentioned in the Lorne saying:

Eireachdas mnathan Loch Obha, am brèid odhar a thionndadh.

The elegance of the Loch Awe women, turning the dun clout inside out.

The loch takes the river name Abha (Awe, 'water') and is the heartland of the Campbells. Their battle cry highlights the central role of the Loch in the clan's psyche:

Is fad an eubh o Loch Obha, is cobhair o Chlann O'Duibhne.

Far is the cry from Loch Awe, and help from the race of O' Duibhne.

The Campbells claim descent from Diarmad O'Duibhne, one of the members of the Fianna of the Ossianic ballads. The saying is supposed to have originated at the time of a defeat of the Argyllshire men by the Gordons at Allt Chuailleachain in Glenlivet in 1594. This battle is said to be the last time that the Highland harp was used on the battlefield before it was replaced by the Great Highland Bagpipe.

Sgeulachd Fhraoich: *The Legend of Fraoch*

The legend of the death of a warrior named Fraoch is popularly associated with Fraoch Eilean, one of the Loch Awe islands. A woman called Mai had a daughter whom the hero Fraoch loved. Mai was jealous because Fraoch did not love her instead and she determined to destroy him. When Mai's daughter fell ill, she told Fraoch of an island with a single rowan tree on it, whose fruit would cure her daughter. The only problem was that at the foot of this tree lay a fierce monster.

Fraoch swam out and, as the monster was asleep, he safely returned with a bunch of the berries. Not satisfied, Mai ordered him to tear the tree from the root. But now the monster was awake and Fraoch had to fight for his life. The daughter threw him a gold knife, but in vain. Although Fraoch killed the monster, he died of his wounds. His eulogy says:

The hero lived, of matchless strength,
The bravest heart in battle's day.
Lovely those lips with welcomes rich,
Which woman liked so well to kiss;
Lovely the chief whom men obeyed,
Lovely those cheeks like roses red,
Than raven's hue more dark his hair,
Redder than hero's blood his cheeks;
Softer than froth of streams his skin,
Whiter it was than whitest snow;
His hair in curling locks fell down,
His eye more blue than bluest ice;
Than rowans red more red his lips.

Gleann Sreith (Glenstrae, 'glen of the row') on the eastern shores of Loch Awe was once held by the MacGregors, then indispensable to the Argyllshire men as their fighting arm. Matters between the clans began to sour after the MacGregor chief was somehow slain by an arrow on an island in Loch Rannoch. His son, Griogair Ruadh ('red-haired Gregor'), became a ward of mac Cailean Mòr (The Son of Big Colin, patronymic of the chief of the Campbells of Argyll). In 1562, when Griogair came of age and assumed leadership of his clan, Cailean Liath ('grey-haired Colin Campbell') of Glen Orchy, demanded conditions that would have compromised Griogair's authority as chief. Griogair struck first: he and his men set fire to an inn, killing eight Argyllshire men who were returning from a fair in Perth and triggering a period of intense conflict between the men of Argyll and the MacGregors. The MacGregors never regained Glenstrae and Griogair was executed personally by Cailean Liath in 1570. In 1603, their name was proscribed and the whole Clan 'put to the horn'.

Beyond Glenstrae is the Strath of Orchy, known as Gleann Urchaidh nam Badan ('Glen Orchy of the copses'), with the parish name of Dìseart Chonnain ('hermitage of Connan'), a name also appearing in Clachan an Dìseirt ('village of the hermitage'), the Gaelic name for Dalmally. One of several songs about the persecution of the MacGregors is located here:

Mi 'm shuidhe an seo am ònar
Air còmhnard an rathaid,
Feuch am faic mi fear-fuadain
Tighinn o Chruachan a' cheathaich.

Bheir dhomh sgeul air Clann Ghriogair
No fios cò 'n taobh a chaidh iad.

Cha d'fhuair mi ur sgeulaibh,
Ach a bhith an-dè anns na srathaibh.

Thall 's a-bhos mu Loch Fìne
Mas fìor mo luchd-bratha.

Ann an Clachan an Dìseirt
Ag òl fìon air na maithibh.

Bha Griogair mòr ruadh ann,
Làmh chruaidh air chùl claidheimh,

'S bha Griogair mòr meadhrach,
Ceann-feadhna 'n luchd-taighe.

I am sitting here alone on the level of the road looking out for a fugitive coming from Cruachan of the mist, who'll give me tidings of Clan Gregor or tell me where they're headed.
I have no news of them except they were yesterday in the straths, round and about Loch Fyne if my spies are telling the truth, and in Clachan of Dysart drinking wine with the nobles.
Big red-haired Gregor was there, a deadly hand wielding a sword and big joyful Gregor, head of our house.

Caibideil 4: *Chapter 4*

Earra-Ghàidheal agus Bòd – Na h-Eileanan: *Argyll and Bute – The Islands*

The Inner Hebrides comprise 35 inhabited and 44 uninhabited islands with an area greater than 30 hectares. Skye, Mull, and Islay are the three largest and also have the highest populations. Today the Inner Hebrides are administered by two separate local government jurisdictions: to the south, Argyll and Bute; to the north, Highland. Argyll and Bute has 23 inhabited islands, including Bute, Islay, Jura, Mull, Iona, Coll and Tiree; more than any other local authority in Scotland.

Colbhasa agus Orasa: *Colonsay and Oronsay*

In the southern Inner Hebrides are the islands of Colbhasa (Colonsay) and Orasa (Oronsay). Colonsay likely derives from ON, Kolbein's Island. The spelling of the name of Oronsay, North Uist as 'Orvinsaig' in a charter given by John, Lord of the Isles in 1469, when the lands were granted to his brother Hugh, supports the view that Orasa also derives from ON (*Orjiris-ey,* 'ebb-tide island'). It is a common name, with twenty to be found between the western shores and the islands. This Oransay is about 850 hectares in extent, and hilly in the north. Colonsay is about twelve kilometres long and averages five wide.

After his departure from Ireland in 563, St. Columba is said to have landed at Port na h-Iùbhraich ('port of the barge'), Oransay. Before leaving Ireland, he had vowed never to settle within sight of his native hills, and, discovering that he could still see them from Oransay, he moved on to Iona. We are on slightly firmer ground with the earliest mention of Colonsay, in the Latin form, *Colosus,* in Adamnan's *Life of St. Columba*, written about 693.

The Norse held Colonsay for some 400 years and many place-names such as the name of the main settlement at Scalasaig (ON, 'Skali's bay') demonstrate that. There are about a dozen places with the remains of chapels that were in use before the Reformation. The dedications were to Columba, Oran, Catan,

Ciaran, Coinneach, Maol Rubha, Moire (the Virgin Mary), Brìdghe (Bridget), and Catriona.

Colonsay was held until the 17th century by the Dubh Sìth (MacDuffies or MacPhees, meaning 'son of the black fairy'). The name-forms MacPhee, MacFee, and Duffy derive from the MacDuffies. The surname Shaw in Islay and Jura is also thought to derive from 'sìth'. MacPhee once held the prestigious role of clerk to the Council or Parliament of the Lords of the Isles.

Colla Ciotach: *Left-handed Coll*

After Sir James MacDonald's failed resistance to Campbell aggrandisement in 1615, one of his outlawed supporters, Colla Ciotach ('left-handed Coll'), Colla mac Ghilleasbaig MacDonald, escaped retribution by handing over nineteen of his allies, including Malcolm MacDuffie of Colonsay, to the Earl of Argyll. Malcolm was pardoned in 1618 and went back home. Coll also went back to his home island of Colonsay. The two men fought for supremacy in Colonsay where Malcolm clearly had the support of the local population. There are at least seven places on the islands known as Leab' Fhalaich Mhic a' Phì ('MacFie's hiding bed'). Malcolm was finally tracked down to a place at the southwestern end of Eilean nan Ròn ('island of seals'), where they found him crouching on a ledge of rock at the edge of the sea. The fugitive pleaded with Tòmas (Thomas), one of Coll's men:

> "Fàbhar, a Thòmais"
>
> *"Mercy, Thomas"*

who answered:

> "Fàbhar no fàbhar, is beag fàbhar a gheibhteadh o d' fheusaig ruaidh mun àm seo 'n-dè."
>
> *"None of your mercy; it's little mercy we would have got from your red whiskers this time yesterday."*

It is recorded that his killers extracted the lead balls from Malcolm's corpse for re-use.

It is said that Coll married twice, one tale recording that one wife had once been married to MacDonald of Keppoch. She was very much younger than himself. When she rejected his amorous advances with the words:

"'S e sin miolaran an t-seana choin ris a' chuilein"

"That's the fawning whine of an old dog to a puppy"

he in turn rejected her.

One of Coll's sons, Alasdair, subsequently the Marquis of Montrose's commander, was born in the Sabhal Bàn ('white barn') of the Abbey at Cill Orain (Kiloran, St. Oran's Church), the family home. On the night he was born, it was said that swords jumped out of their scabbards and muskets fired of their own accord – omens of his future career.

The 9th Earl of Argyll, after the execution of his father for treason in 1661, became owner of Colonsay. The Marquis sent one Donald Ballach as factor to the island, but his demands were so severe that it was claimed that he taxed the very shellfish on the shore. On the death of her husband, he would claim the widow's horse or cow, a common custom called 'calpa'. Around 1644, Coll Ciotach's son, Angus, visited the island. He met a widow taking her only cow as tribute to Donald Ballach. On learning this, Angus sent her home and then went to the factor's house. When Angus arrived Donald Ballach offered him snuff to which Angus replied:

"Have you a feather?" (to take the snuff)

"I do not," answered Donald Ballach. "If I had (i.e. the power of flying), I would not have been here this night."

Donald was dragged across the strand to the standing stone at Lèana na h-Eaglais ('marshy plain of the church') and shot with seven musket balls. The Marquis was warned that if he sent another man like Donald Ballach to Colonsay, he would be treated in the same manner.

The islands remained under Campbell control until 1701 when the lands were sold to Malcolm MacNeill from Knapdale, and these MacNeills held

Colonsay and Oronsay for the next two hundred years. Visiting Colonsay in 1836, Lord Teignmouth thought that the population, which was to reach its maximum of 904 in 1841, was "insufficient for the labour required" as a result of emigrations to America. It had been, he added:

> found necessary to supply the deficiency of hands by labourers from Islay and Jura.

Yet only ten years after this was written, the mass emigrations of the mid-19th century were in full swing.

Iain MacGillebreadh is Dòmhnall MacFhionghain: *John MacGilvray and Donald Mackinnon*

One man who did not leave was Iain MacGillebreadh, John MacGilvray, from Baile Raomainn. When, in 1860, Iain Òg Ìle (John Francis Campbell) recorded his version of the hero tale, 'Gaisgeach na Sgèithe Deirge' ('Warrior of the Red Shield') John MacGilvray was over 70 years of age. What is remarkable is that the story as written down in Campbell's *Popular Tales of the West Highlands* consists of thirteen solid pages of type – a feat of memory repeated many times in the four volumes.

In the same tradition of Campbell's informed scholarship was Dòmhnall MacFhionghain (Donald MacKinnon) (1839-1914) of Cille Chatain (Kilchattan, 'Saint Cathan's Church') in Colonsay, the first Professor of Celtic in Edinburgh University – an honour which many in 1882 felt should have gone to John Francis Campbell. However, Campbell had trenchant views on academic politics and never considered himself a candidate for the position.

MacKinnon is best known for his edition and translation of the Glenmasan manuscript, a late 15th-century Gaelic vellum manuscript compilation of versions of tales of the Ulster Cycle, such as the Táin Bó Flidhais and Oided mac nUisnig. He also left an account of life in Colonsay back to the period of the Potato Famine of 1846. He wrote that all the people in Lower Kilchattan in his youth, apart from his own family, emigrated to Canada around 1852. Bread loaves were unheard of, with milk and its products – butter, cheese, curds and cream – an important part of the local diet. The roots of brisgean ('silverweed') were gathered and eaten raw and also boiled like potatoes. The local value of this food was such that it was termed seachdamh aran ('seventh bread') and there was also a saying:

> Mil fo thalamh, brisgean earraich.
>
> *Honey from underground, the silverweed of Spring.*

A children's game then was to pluck the flowers of Gille-guirmein ('blue scabious'). Holding the flowers in the left hand with the right closed in a threatening attitude over it, they intoned:

> Gille, Gille-guirmein
> Mu 'n tèid thu mun cuairt
> Buailidh mi mo dhòrn ort!
>
> *Gille, Gille-guirmein*
> *If you don't go around*
> *I will hit you with my fist!*

The stalk was surreptitiously twisted beforehand and held in such a way as to allow it to unwind.

Some of the residents of Colonsay were identified as follows:

> Sgritheal, Sgrathal, Scalasaig,
> Carrachan nam machraichean,
> Daolagan Chill Òdhrain,
> Is daoine mòra Chill Chatain.
>
> *Sgritheal, Sgrathal, Scalasaig,*
> *Carrachan of the machair land,*
> *Beetles of Kiloran*
> *And the noble men of Kilchattan.*

General 'Jock' MacNeill is probably the best known of this MacNeill dynasty. At his death in 1904, the estate was bought by Donald Smith, Lord

Strathcona and Mount Royal. Smith, who was born in 1818 in Forres, left at the age of eighteen to work for the Hudson's Bay Company in Canada, and in twenty years rose from clerk to Chief Executive. He was a founding director of the Canadian Pacific Railway, High Commissioner for Canada in London, a member of the Canadian Parliament, Chancellor of MacGill University and reputedly the richest man in Canada. He received honorary degrees from fifteen universities in the anglophone world. The present laird is Donald Euan Palmer Howard, the 4th Baron Strathcona and Mount Royal.

Ìle agus Diùra: *Islay and Jura*

South of Colonsay is Ìle (Islay, perhaps 'flank shaped island'), the fifth largest Scottish island and the eighth largest island of the British Isles, with a total area of almost 620 square kilometres. It is the southernmost island of the Inner Hebrides and it lies around 40 kilometres (22 nautical miles) north of the Northern Irish coast.

Ceithir busa* fichead an Ìle (*from ON, *bólstaðr*, a farm)
Ceithir tìre fichead am Muile
Ceithir bailte fichead an Ceann Tìre.

Twenty four farms in Islay
Twenty four lands in Mull
Twenty four townships in Kintyre.

In its neighbour Diùra (Jura, ON, 'deer island', although its byname was An t-Eilean Bàn, 'blessed island'), Gaelic was spoken by nine-tenths of the population. The islands were overwhelmingly Gaelic-speaking until after the Second World War. A local was known as a Diùrach, but usually nicknamed 'each' ('horse').

There are no fewer than 52 churches, chapels, burial grounds and other ecclesiastical sites in Islay including Cill A Rubha (Kilarrow) of Maol Rubha and Kildalton (probably 'church of the foster child'), most likely a reference to St. John, the Beloved Disciple.

Somhairle: *Somerled*

These islands were never entirely Norse. Their hybrid nature is shown by the fact that the father of Clan Donald's founder, Somhairle, was Gille Bhrìde ('servant of St. Bride'). Gille Bhrìde had a Norse wife, and their son was named Sumarlidi (ON, 'summer traveller'), a common name among Vikings. That name became Somhairle and, now in English, Somerled. In a sea battle off Ardnamurchan, Somerled defeated Olaf, ruler of the Isle of Man, and in a subsequent settlement gained control over the southern Hebrides, including Islay. He married Ragnild, Olaf's daughter, to seal the bargain. From this union are descended the MacDonalds and the MacDougalls.

By 1153, his relations with the King of Scots had deteriorated and Somerled invaded the mainland with 160 galleys but was assassinated at Renfrew. After his death, his son Ragnvaldr (Ranald, 'ruler's counsellor') held Kintyre and Islay. Ranald was Ranald MacSomerled, and his son Donald MacRanald, but after Angus, Donald's son, all direct descendants took the name MacDonald.

Tighearnas nan Eilean: *The Lordship of the Isles*

Another of Somerled's descendants, Angus Òg, took 1800 men to aid Bruce at Bannockburn. For his loyalty, he was awarded the lands of Bruce's defeated enemies, principally that of the MacDougalls. This was the genesis of the Lordship of the Isles, a semi-independent realm that styled itself as a kingdom and eventually covered almost all the western seaboard of Scotland; from Antrim it stretched as far as Dingwall on the Moray Firth. The hegemony and power of the lordship was based on control of the sea. Military service usually consisted of the provision of galleys and crews, rather than mounted knights. Elite mercenary warriors, known as the gallóglaigh ('gallowglasses') emerged from this Norse-Gaelic society. Viking longships influenced the design of these birlinnean or longan-fada ('long ships'). That it was a maritime power is amply demonstrated by the 17th-century lullaby, possibly addressed to Dòmhnull Gorm, Chief of Clann Ùisdein (MacDonald of Sleat):

Long mo rìgh-sa
long nan eilean
gu bheil stiùir òir oirre
trì chrainn sheilich
gu bheil tobar fìon innt'
shìos na deireadh
agus tobar fìor-uisg'.

My king's ship, the ship of the Isles, it has a golden rudder and three willow masts and it has a well of wine down in the stern and a well of fresh water.

Administration within the Lordship was conducted by the Council of the Isles, a body which advised the incumbent Lord of the Isles. The Lordship issued its own charters; it was almost a state within a state and it was an overtly Gaelic institution. It brought relative stability to the western seaboard and over the century and a half of its existence created the context for a golden age of Gaelic culture – Linn an Àigh ('Age of Joy'). Among the learned orders, poets held pride of place as the intellectual leaders of medieval Gaelic society.

Ultimately, strife with the Crown led to the downfall of the Lordship. John of Dùn Naomhaig (Dunnivaig, 'Naomhag's or Naomhan's fort') and the Glens, along with his son Iain Catanach ('shaggy John'), were arrested, sent to Edinburgh and executed in 1494. The title of the Lordship of the Isles was annexed to the Crown and is now held by the Prince of Wales.

It is perhaps not an exaggeration to say that a Scottish monarch had one of the hardest jobs amongst the European monarchies: in a decentralised system, they had to depend on an aristocracy whom the eminent Victorian historian and essayist, Thomas Carlyle, characterised as:

> a selfish, ferocious, famishing, and unprincipled set of hyenas, from whom at no time, and in no way, has a country delivered any benefit whatsoever.

Monarchical rule was further weakened since, despite the Stewart dynasty's longevity, for half the time the heirs were minors and the realm was subjected to the rapacity of unscrupulous regents. Small wonder that one of the commonest quoted proverbs was:

> 'S feàrr caraid sa chùirt na mìle crùn airgid.
>
> *Better a friend at court than a thousand crowns of silver.*

These repeated royal minorities added to Scotland's internal strife and, from the time of the annexation, there was a bewildering spate of charters and leases, cancellations and re-grants of land. James IV and James V attempted to control affairs in the North and West and did not hesitate to play off clan against clan. Of the half dozen major risings in the islands between 1492 and 1545, the fact that the most serious was the last one simply emphasises the failure, even of James IV, to 'daunt' the isles. That their reputation was a mixed one is evident from the saying:

> Stiùbhartaich nan rìgh 's nan ceàrd.
>
> *The Stewarts of the kings and tinkers.*

Some historians consider that it might have been better to have allowed the Lordship to continue in a reduced and controlled form, using its authority to run the Western Isles on behalf of the Crown. With that authority undermined, and with the state unable, or unwilling, to deploy resources necessary to ensure firm rule in the West, it was every clan for itself and the long period of anarchy and feuding, Linn nan Creach ('The Age of Forays'), was the inevitable, though preventable, result.

Colin Campbell, the 3rd Earl of Argyll, as Lieutenant of the Isles profited from this anarchy, handing over the administration of what were in effect Crown lands in Islay to his own brother, Sir John Campbell of Calder. The title, Earl of Argyll, unlike the plethora of honorific titles from the 15th century and later, was a territorial designation akin to those of the old provincial earldoms. It probably reflected the Ri Airir Goidel ('King of the borderland of the Gaels'), one of Somerled's original titles, used until the early 14th century by his descendants. It has been suggested that when the Campbells became Earls of Argyll they were claiming a place in the Gaelic world roughly equivalent to that of Somerled's descendants, the MacDonald Lords of the Isles; a situation never accepted by the MacDonalds.

In 1543, the Earl was given a ten-year lease of Islay. But Dòmhnall Dubh MacDhòmhnaill ('black Donald MacDonald'), for the last forty years imprisoned in Edinburgh, escaped and was acclaimed as the rightful Lord of the Isles. He gathered a fleet, it is said, of 180 galleys and 4000 fighting men and sailed to Knockfergus in Ireland. But promised English gold came late and, when it did arrive in Mull, MacLean of Duart was accused of keeping too much of it for himself. The rebellion dissolved in mutual recriminations. Later an agent of the English Queen, Elizabeth, I said that the best solution to the Irish situation would be to foster "blood and feuds" between the Irish rebels and the island clans and added:

> "my lord of Argyll may do it best of any."

The Argyll in question was the devious, unfathomable Gilleasbuig Gruamach ('Archibald the grim'). King James VI shared Gilleasbuig's views on the fomenting of feuds to gain Crown objectives. It is a sad, but sobering, reality, said one historian, that when feuds in the Highlands are investigated, Crown intervention is usually found. But the clans often needed little encouragement.

Blàr Tràigh Ghruinneart: *The Battle of Gruinart Sands*

On 5th August 1598, the long-running territorial disputes between the MacDonalds of Islay and the MacLeans of Duart, in this case title to lands in Na Roinn Ìleach (the Rinns of Islay), came to a head. The MacLeans sought to take advantage of MacDonald weakness and fought them at Tràigh Ghruinneart (Gruinart Sands) to the south of Cill Naoimh (Kilnave, 'holy church'). James MacDonald of Dunivaig was victorious. Lachlann Mòr MacIllEathain, Triath Dhubhaird (Sir Lachlan MacLean of Duart) was killed along with over a third of the 800-strong MacLean force and the battle conclusively ended the dispute. As the song 'Ceann Tràigh Ghruinneart' ('At the Head of Gruinart Sands') relates:

’S ann aig Ceann Tràigh Ghruinneart
A dh’fhàg mi ’n curaidh
’S ann aig Ceann Tràigh Ghruinneart a dh’fhàg mi;
Fear a thàirneadh lann
’S a bhualadh buillean
Aig Ceann Tràigh Ghruinneart a dh’fhàg mi.

Clò-dubh, clò-donn
Clò mo chreich
Clò-dubh, clò-donn, clòthlan,
Gura daor a reic mi an clòthlan-dubh
Gura daor a reic mi an clòthlan.

It was at the head of Gruinart Sands
I left the hero
It was at the head of Gruinart Sands
I left him;
A man who draws a sword
And strikes blows
At the head of Gruinart Sands I left him.

Black cloth, brown cloth, cloth of my ruination,
Black cloth, brown cloth, batch of cloth,
Dearly did I sell that batch of black cloth,
Dearly did I sell that batch.

The reference to cloth in the second verse suggests that rent may have been paid in cloth by the MacLeans to the MacDonalds.

According to tradition, as the two sides were preparing for battle, a hairy, dark-skinned, hunch-backed dwarf came to Lachlan MacLean and offered his services. The man’s father was a Shaw from Jura and his mother was a fairy woman and he was thus called Dubh Sìth (‘black fairy’). He had to twist his ugly head to look up at Lachlan, who stood over seven feet tall. Lachlan, confident of victory, told Dubh Sìth that he could not bear the sight of him and refused his help. Instead, the dwarf offered his services to Sir James MacDonald and was accepted. Dubh Sìth climbed up into a rowan tree beside a well and waited.

The battle was fought on a hot day and during a lull in the fight Lachlan went to Tobar Nèill Neònaich ('the well of strange Neil'). As he knelt to drink, Dubh Sìth shot a crossbow bolt into the back of his neck. With Sir Lachlan's death, the MacLeans lost heart and were routed. They sought sanctuary at the church at Kilnave, but the MacDonalds set fire to the thatched roof. All the MacLeans inside were killed, except for one man, a MacMhuirich (Currie), who leapt through the roof, ran into Loch Gruinart and saved himself by submerging his body in the water and breathing through a reed.

Another reason given for Sir Lachlan's defeat was that he had failed to heed the advice of a wise woman, An Doideag Mhuileach ('the Mull Witch'), who had told him three specific things he should not do. He should not go anywhere near Nòstaig in Islay, take a drink from the well or raise his standard on Cnoc nan Ainglean ('knoll of the angels'). Lachlan ignored the Doideag's warning and his fate was sealed.

Uachdarain Shawfield: *The Shawfield Lairds*

Sir James's efforts to defend his people's just titles came to nought and it should come as no surprise to learn that, in 1614, a charter to Islay was granted to Sir John Campbell of Cawdor, or Calder, and, by 1629, the Calders had it all. The family's affairs in Islay were managed by a series of locally appointed administrators or 'tutors'. In 1716, it was decided to dispose of peripheral parts of the Cawdor estate and, by 1726, Daniel Campbell of Shawfield had acquired Islay. Shawfield House, his townhouse in Glasgow, had been looted by a mob in reprisal for Campbell's support for the hated 1725 Malt Tax. The £9000 he received in compensation from the Burgh of Glasgow aided his purchase of Islay.

There were four 'Shawfield' lairds in 122 years. They were powerful individuals, especially the first, known as the Great Daniel to distinguish him from his son of the same name. He was born in Kintyre around 1670, the second son of Walter Campbell of Skipness and, as such, went into trade, becoming a ship owner and merchant. He bought the small Lanarkshire estate of Shawfield near Glasgow.

The Shawfields were to change the face of Islay, and much of the island's landscape today is a result of their policies. 'Improvement' commenced in Islay, based on three principles: the enclosure of land, the consolidation of holdings into single farms and the separation of agriculture and industry. Daniel's own attitudes towards the local inhabitants of Islay have been described as at worst exploitative, at best patronising. Whether those 'improvements' were ultimately to the benefit of the people is a matter of opinion. Dr Storie of the University of London had no doubts; in her view, the changes were responsible for transforming, she said: an illiterate, superstitious population living on the edge of famine into a prosperous part of a thriving Victorian Scotland.

The tacksman class was first to be affected. When plans for a restructuring of the island with profit in mind were announced in 1740, rather than compete for leases, some of the tacksmen decided to establish the Argyll Colony around modern Fayetteville, North Carolina. At first, Highlanders were hesitant about leaving and their doubts were fomented by the anti-emigration propaganda of landlords wishing to keep hold of then-essential wage labour. In time, however, Highland immigrant communities flourished and beckoned their relations to join them.

Safely in Campbell hands, Islay remained unaffected by the Jacobite Risings and, after 1746, Shawfield received development funds from the Commissioners of the Annexed Estates. His proposals envisaged a new village that is now Bogha Mòr (Bowmore, 'big bay'), with a parish church, schoolhouse and a prison, thus catering for all the needs of the population. By 1768, Bowmore was one of the earliest planned villages in the Highlands.

The writer Thomas Pennant wrote of Islay at this time as a subsistence economy, permanently on the verge of famine and starvation. He describes an impoverished society on the fringes of Europe, riddled by bad health and superstition. As a doctor, George Campbell (1766-1858) had to confront those conditions. He was from a family who were tenants of Cionnabus (Kinnabus, possibly 'lady's farm) in the Obha (Oa, 'headland'), and today is best remembered for the love song, 'Fuirich, a Rìbhinn' ('Tarry, Beloved Lass'):

Cha dìrich mi bruthach 's cha shiùbhail mi còmhnard
Tuilleadh ri m' bheò 's mo smeòrach na tàmh
Ach èisdidh mi 'ghàir thig o bhàrr nan tonn mòra
'S dh'fhuiling mi bròn gu leòr air do sgàth.

Ò, fuirich a rìbhinn phrìseil, phrìseil
Fuirich a rìbhinn 's dìlse na càch;
A' mhaighdeann as luraiche, fuirich an Ìle,
Òg-bhean as dìlse chì mi gu bràth.

Fhuair mise litir 's mi fàgail na tìr seo,
O fhear a bha dìleas dhomh an dàimh;
Cha b' urrainn dhomh freagairt 's mo chridh' ann an Ìle
Glaist' aig an rìbhinn 's ise 'n Ceanntràigh.

I'll never climb a brae, nor will I travel a smooth plain,
Forever and anon my mavis is at rest,
But I'll lend my ear to the music from the crests of great waves,
And I've suffered enough sadness on your account.

Oh, tarry, precious, precious lass,
Tarry lass, more faithful than all others;
Loveliest of maidens, tarry in Islay,
The most faithful young woman I'll ever see.

On receipt of a letter as I left this land
From a man who was a close relation,
An answer I cannot offer as my heart remains in Islay
Held captive by the lassie who is in Kintra.

After the outbreak of war with France in 1793, emigration slowed down but, following peace in 1801, it rose to high levels. Landowners and government were concerned about the potential loss of labour and army recruits and rushed through a Passenger Vessels Act in 1803 to increase ten-fold the cost of transatlantic voyages. Emigrant numbers again fell. These waves of emigration consisted mainly of small tenants with some means and were a reaction to the many changes in rentals and tenure which were destroying the old way of life. These Highlanders had the resources to enable them to choose to go to the new world to improve their situation as masters of their own destiny. Such emigration was still one of rising expectations.

And yet the population of Islay rose. In 1811, it was estimated at about 11,500, a doubling in only 60 years. It was reported that:

> so greatly is the island improved … [that] … were all the farms to be let in 1810, the estate of Islay would … probably fetch £16,000 … [rental] … per annum.

This had increased from only £2,700 per annum in 1779.

Uilleam MacDhunlèibhe: *William Livingston*

Uilleam MacDhunlèibhe (William Livingston) was born near Bowmore in 1808 but he spent most of his life working as a tailor in Glasgow. He had an interest in history and learnt Greek, Latin and French. A nationalist and champion of Gaelic, he published a *Vindication of the Celtic Character* in 1850. Today he is best remembered for his poetry, particularly 'Fios chun a' Bhàird' ('Take This Message to the Poet'). Supposedly Livingston composed this poem after the departure, as a result of estate policies, of many of the cuthagan ('cuckoos', as the locals were nicknamed) from The Oa to Canada in 1862-63. That act might have been in the background but the immediate origin of the song, also known as 'Oran Bean Dhonnchaidh' ('Song to Duncan's Wife'), was that William had expressed a wish for some homespun cloth from Islay. The Rev. Robert Blair of St Columba's in Glasgow arranged for his mother to send the poet some of her own cloth with the note 'Fios chun a' Bhàird o Bean Dhonnachaidh'. In response Livingston sent her this poem:

Chan fhaigh an dèirceach fasgadh
No 'm fear-astair fois o sgìos,
No soisgeulach luchd-èisteachd;
Bhuadhaich eucoir, Goill is cìs;

Tha an nathair bhreac 'na lùban
Air na h-ùrlair far an d'fhàs
Na fir mhòr' a chunnaic mise;
Thoir am fios seo chun a' Bhàird.

Lomadh ceàrn na h-Oa,
An Lanndaidh bhòidheach 's Roinn MhicAoidh;
Tha 'n Learga ghlacach, ghrianach
'S fuidheall cianail air a taobh;
Tha an Gleann na fhiadhair uaine
Aig luchd-fuath gun tuath, gun bhàrr;
Mar a fhuair 's a chunnaic mise,
Thoir am fios seo chun a' Bhàird.

The beggar will not get shelter
nor will the traveller get rest from his weariness,
nor will a gospel preacher get an audience;
injustice, Foreigners and taxes have won;
the speckled adder is lying in coils
on the floors where once there grew
the big men that I saw there;
take this message to the Poet.

The district of the Oa has been stripped bare,
the beautiful Lanndaidh and MacKay's Rinns;
sunny Largie with its many hollows
has a pathetic remnant on its slope;
the Glen has become a green wilderness,
owned by hateful men without tenants or crops;
just as I found and as I saw
take this message to the Poet.

Running like a thread through many early 19th-century accounts was the growing realisation that, however successful improvements in agriculture and other traditional activities were, the growing pressure of population demanded other solutions. Walter Frederick Campbell, only eighteen, succeeded his grandfather, and, between 1816 and 1848, initiated many of the changes in agriculture and settlement that contributed to the present appearance of Islay: farms interspersed with small villages.

In 1824, there were 69 tenants of holdings but nearly 700 small joint tenants in nearly 100 townships and, although the proportion of those joint tenants did fall to a third by 1831, the Campbell policies were still some way from fulfilment. Meanwhile, the population continued to increase, reaching a maximum of 15,000 in 1831. Now the estate's challenge was not prosperity but overpopulation.

Under the Shawfields, there were never widespread clearances and emigration as in other parts. The hope was that employment schemes to attract tenants displaced from jointly held farms and some departures would be enough to control the population growth. In 1845, potato blight arrived and, in the following year, it was said that there were 5000 people in Islay facing immediate starvation. Despite strenuous Shawfield efforts, by 1848 the estate was sequestered and for five years it was administered by Edinburgh accountants. Many Highland estates were in trust by mid-century, administered by agents of trustees for the landlords' creditors. Their responsibility was to treat the property as an asset, run it efficiently, increase rental income and, where possible, increase its value for quick disposal. Financial imperatives were placed ahead of other considerations and the trustees cleared people. During this time there were several clearances, for instance, in Dùn Nosebridge (ON, 'turf fort') and in other townships in the Glen area. By the 1860s, net migration from Islay may have amounted to about one quarter of the population.

In 1853, a buyer was found. He was James Morrison, a London merchant banker and former Member of Parliament for the Inverness burghs, who reputedly created his wealth in 1837 by stockpiling black crepe in readiness for the mourning of King William IV. Much of the estate has remained in the hands of the Morrison family. Clearance continued, with 400 people emigrating from Islay in 1863 alone. John Granville Morrison, MP for Salisbury from 1942 to 1964, was created Lord Margadale in 1965, his title taken from a beloved sporting area (possibly ON, 'Merkland dale'). The current representative is Alastair Morrison and The Islay Estate Company Ltd owns 51,563 acres.

Iain Òg Ìle: *John Francis Campbell*

The Campbell connection with Islay did not end immediately. Just outside Ceann an Loch (Bridgend) stands an obelisk erected by the Glasgow Islay Association to a son of Walter, Iain Òg Ìle (John Francis Campbell of Islay) (1822-85) who has been described as the "father of Celtic folklore studies." He was Gaelic-speaking, well-educated and respected by his contemporaries. In addition to Gaelic, he was proficient in eight European languages. In the early decades of the 19th century, fieldwork collections contained folk songs and Ossianic verse but had little prose narrative. Iain Òg's work was to set the direction of future folklore studies in Scotland. He travelled extensively with his scribes, scrupulously recording tales, Ossianic ballads, songs, charms and anecdotes. John Francis described his work thus:

> The following collection is intended to be a contribution to this new science of "Storyology". It is a museum of curious rubbish about to perish, given as it was gathered in the rough, for it seemed to me as barbarous to "polish" a genuine popular tale, as it would be to adorn the bones of a Megathrerium with tinsel, or gild a rare old copper coin. On this, however, opinions vary, but I hold my own, that stories orally collected can only be valuable if given unaltered; besides, where is the model story to be found?

His great published work is the bilingual *Popular Tales of the West Highlands* (4 vols., 1860-62). In 1872 he also self-published the seminal *Leabhar na Feinne* (*The Book of the Fingalians*), a collection of Ossianic ballads culled from manuscripts held by libraries. Commenting critically on the prose poem *Dar-thula* that James Macpherson had published as one of the companion pieces to his epic poem *Fingal* (1762), he noted that it was related to the traditional tales, but the geography had been changed. He said drily that:

> Upon this geography learned men had found theories as to 'Selma', 'Bergonium' and vitrified forts of the stone period, which the ignorant who speak Gaelic ignore.

He had no interest in this 'learned' Anglophone invention.

Despite the work of people such as John Francis Campbell, there was at times a tone of moral superiority adopted by Victorian tourists. One such was W. A. Smith whose account of Islay was published in 1868. Smith said of the people that:

> ... ground down by a landed aristocracy who treat them like dogs they had gradually increased in poverty and misery ... possessed of a strange mixture of superstition and religion ...[and tied]... to a life of labour, immorality and devotion, pass they wearily to the grave.

Niall MacAilpein agus Donnchadh MacIain: *Neil MacAlpine and Duncan Johnston*

Among the Gaelic scholars Islay has produced is Neil MacAlpine (1786-1867) from Cill Chomain (Kilchoman, 'Comain's church'). He produced *The Argyleshire Pronouncing Gaelic Dictionary* (1832) and *A Pronouncing Gaelic Dictionary* (1847), the first Gaelic-English examples of their kind. They were cheap, originally appearing in large numbers in sixpenny parts. MacAlpine was the schoolmaster at Kilmeny School and also held posts as administrator of the Poor Law and Parish Registrar. His appeal to the authorities for famine relief in 1846, resulted in his landlord, Walter Frederick Campbell, sacking him from his teaching post. He died, near destitute, on Poor Relief.

A bard whose work is still sung at gatherings is Duncan Johnston (1898-1947) of Lag a' Mhuilinn (Lagavulin, 'mill hollow'), best remembered for a volume of poems published in 1938, *Crònan nan Tonn (Croon of the Waves*). He was then the janitor in the Department of Natural Philosophy at Glasgow University.

In summing up the history of Islay, the writer Norman Newton asks, "So what went wrong?" He answers his own question thus:

> cultural and economic imperialism. A vulnerable culture, its military resources broken by central government, situated in a fertile island which promised a good economic return, its communal

> society under threat from leaseholders and estates surveyors, its language beaten out of its schoolchildren and the scourge of over population as the Laird's policy started to take effect – these were the ingredients which transformed the headquarters of the Lords of the Isles to the fragile island we see today.

Since those words were written some 50 years ago, Islay has prospered, although Gaelic as a community language remains in a fragile state.

Gigha, Tiriodh agus Col: *Gigha, Tiree and Coll*

East of Islay and just off Kintyre's west coast is Gigha (ON, 'God's island'). When the Vikings arrived here, they must have encountered a monastic community on the island. Those monks must have echoed the saying:

> Is fuar gaoth nan coimheach.
>
> *Cold is the wind that brings strangers.*

That is thought to refer to the Vikings, who came from the north.

The Council of the Lordship of the Isles had four grades within the territorial kindreds that included the four thanes of MacKinnon, MacQuarrie, MacNeill of Gigha and MacNeil of Barra. We know of one Niall, chief of the MacNeills, whose early death evoked a moving elegy from his 'loved yokefellow', Aithbreac inghean Coirceadail (Aithbreac of Gigha). Aithbreac was not a professional poet, but even as a lay person she could allude quite naturally to a specific place in the far south-west of Ireland.

Poets were passing back and forth between Scotland and Ireland and the Gigha harper-poet, Giolla-Críost Brúilingeach, who visited the court of Tomaltach MacDiarmaid on the Rock of Loch Cè in the mid-15th century, makes no bones about what has brought him from Gigha to Connacht:

> I have come, good the reason, from Scotland to visit thee, as is meet, drawn by thy fame ... I have come to crave a boon from thee, from Scotland ... A harp in special grant me at my request, thou king.

Pedigree deerhounds were an integral part of any hunting endeavour and as such highly prized. Perhaps in the hopes of such a reward, in his poem 'Lámh Aoinfhir Fhóirfeas i nÉirinn' ('One Man's Arm Can Stop in Ireland'), Giolla-Críost extols the virtues of Tomaltach's hounds:

Míolchoin gharga ar iallaibh órdha
ag Tomaltach 's ceann ar cách;
sguir gu moch san aonach uallach
mán loch bhraonach bhuadhach bhláth.

Fierce deerhounds on gilded leashes are owned by Tomaltach, lord of all; horses in the morning in proud assembly round the mild, dewy, healing loch.

This Giolla-Críost belonged to the branch of the Mac a' Bhreatnaich, now rendered in English as Galbraith, a family of hereditary harpists based in Gigha, who sought the patronage of the Lord of the Isles. By the 16th century, the lordship had ceased to exist and, by the early 17th century, hereditary harpists were largely gone. Lowland settlers had begun to move into the peninsula.

James William Scarlett, son of Sir William Anglin Scarlett had purchased Gigha for £49,000 in 1865. His son, Lieutenant-Colonel William James Scarlett, built the mansion house of Achamore there and Gigha remained in the family's hands until 1919. In 1944, Gigha was sold to Sir James Horlick, who created the great gardens of Achamore, now owned, as is most of the rest of the island, on behalf of the community by the Isle of Gigha Heritage Trust.

Eilean Thiriodh: *Tiree*

North of Islay and southwest of Coll is the low-lying island Tiriodh (Tiree), with an area of 7,834 hectares and a population of around 700. In Tiree in the late 19th century, over half the islanders were monoglot Gaelic speakers, with the other half being bilingual in Gaelic and English. By 2011, the figure for Gaelic had decreased to 40%, still the highest percentage of speakers in the Inner Hebrides.

Tiree is fertile and its name Tìr Iodh ('land of corn') perhaps dates from the 6th century onwards when Tiree provided the monastic community in Iona with grain. Its fertility, however, little benefited its inhabitants, as the old saying bears out:

> Bheireadh Tir-iodh an dà bhàrr mur bhi eagal an dà mhàl.
>
> *Tiree would bear two crops, were it not for the fear of two rents.*

Early monasteries existed in Tiree and such settlements would undoubtedly have suffered from early Viking incursions. With the demise of Norwegian control in the area, following the Treaty of Perth in 1266, the island was part of the Lordship of the Isles. In 1517, the MacDonalds ceded control of Tiree to the MacLeans under their chief, Lachlan Catanach ('shaggy Lachlan'), who held on to the island until 1674. Then, with the expulsion of the MacLeans from their estates in Mull, Tiree came under the control of the Campbells and remains part of the Argyll Estates to this day.

In common with the practice in other islands such as Pabbay in the Sound of Harris, whisky distilling was carried out on a considerable scale. Even following the introduction of effective customs controls in the early 19th-century, illicit distilling continued. It has been said that it was encouraged by landlords as it made their rental incomes more secure. The price of barley was thus kept high in the west; according to report, twice as high as the cost in the Lothians. John, 5th Duke of Argyll, noted in 1802 that distillers were to be evicted from farms on Tiree and given £2 to remove, in the full understanding they would emigrate to America.

In 1779, Tiree had a population of approximately 2,500 but, by 1846, that number had risen to around 5000. The rise in population owed much to the activities of the kelping landlords and their willingness to subdivide their lands to the utmost in order to generate the increased supply of labour they needed. One of the symptoms of this increase in population was the implacable erosion of peasant status and the virtual disappearance of the peasant holding, capable both of maintaining a family and of providing enough cash to pay the rent.

These huge profits from kelp instead of being invested productively were spent as soon as, or indeed, before they were received. The windfall income that fell into their laps led lairds such as the MacDonalds to ape the lifestyle and extravaganza of English aristocrats. A contemporary journalist said:

> The effect was the same as that when a hawker of the [North American] backwoods spreads out his toys and trinkets. The vanity of the [island] chieftains was intoxicated and the solid advantages which the new tide in their affairs had opened up to them were bartered for the nearest baubles.

Lord MacDonald, with substantial kelping interests in Skye as well as in North Uist, was said at the peak of this kelping boom in the early 19th century to enjoy gross returns of £14,000, the equivalent of today's £1.2 million, The Duke of Argyll and MacNeil of Barra probably reaped almost as much, thanks to their fortunate ownership of seaweed-rich shores. But the kelping tenantry found themselves in a position doubly precarious. They were faced with rent screwed up to catch the individual's surplus, and a population now so much more numerous in relation to agricultural potential that individual possessions must inevitably be smaller. This was a dire situation aptly articulated by the Tiree saying:

> Lìonmhorachd làmh, ach san mhèis.
>
> *A multiplicity of hands, except in the dish.*

The saying implied that many hands are best for getting through work, except when round the dinner table; the more taking from the dish, the less each portion would be.

As social conditions in the Highlands and Islands deteriorated through the 19th century, emigration was stimulated. For some, but by no means all, emigration was a consequence of clearance. Some emigrants made their choices even without compulsion and many had high hopes for bettering their lot in the New World. The first Gaelic-speaking settlers came to an American continent largely uninhabited by European agriculturalists and the land they acquired was usually covered with dense forest of a sort that they would never have seen in Scotland.

For many of the emigrant poets, the wilderness was a shock and a disappointment. Poetry was used in much the same fashion as it had traditionally been used to define and reinforce the values of their society, particularly at times of crisis. The virgin, untamed forest is the central image of possibly the most famous of all of the poems of the emigrant generations 'Òran do dh'Aimearaga' ('Song to America') also known as 'A' Choille Ghruamach' ('The Gloomy Forest'):

Gu bheil mi 'm ònrachd sa choille ghruamaich
Mo smaointean luaineach cha tog mi fonn,
Fhuair mi 'n t-àite seo 'n aghaidh nàdair,
Gun thrèig gach tàlant a bha nam cheann,
Cha dèan mi òran a chur air dòigh ann,
Nuair nì mi tòiseachadh bidh mi trom.
Chaill mi Ghàidhlig seach mar a b' àbhaist dhomh
Nuair a bha mi san dùthaich thall.

Chan fhaigh mi innse dhuibh anns an dàn seo,
Cha dèan mo nàdar a chur air dòigh
Gach fios a b' àill leam thoirt do na càirdean,
San tìr a dh'fhàg mi rinn m' àrach òg,
Gach aon a leughas e, tuigibh reusan,
'S na tugaibh èisteachd do luchd a' bhòst,
Na fàidhean brèige a bhios gur teumadh,
Gun aca spèis dhuibh ach dèidh ur n-òir.

How lonely I feel in the gloomy forest,
My thoughts are restless, I can't raise a tune,
I have found this place so against nature,
That every talent in my head has deserted me,
I can't organise myself to compose a song,
Once I start I become depressed
I've lost my Gaelic compared to how it used to be
When I was back in the country over there.

I can't tell you in this poem,
My nature can't let me to express it
The news I would like to give to my friends,
In the land I left behind where I was raised as a child.
But all who read this, take heed of sense
And don't heed the propagandists
The lying prophets who will seduce you,
With no motive other than to get your money.

The poem was composed by John MacLean (1787-1848) a native of Caolas in Tiree, shortly after his arrival in Nova Scotia in 1821. He was a shoemaker who became honorary poet to the Laird of Coll, hence his usual name, Bàrd Tighearna Cholla ('poet to the Laird of Coll'). At the heart of the song to America is the disjunction between the dream and the reality of the New World. MacLean wanted his poem to be a warning to those who might have been considering emigration. He assumed the traditional role of the poet in Gaelic society: the spokesman for the community, helping to enforce its values and guide its decisions.

But compulsion did play a part in the waves of emigration. About 1846, Colonel John Campbell became Tiree factor for the Argyll Estates with a remit to reduce the population. Known as Am Bàillidh Mòr ('the big baillie'), Campbell's ruthlessness reduced the population to about 2,000 within twenty years and, as one writer said:

> awoke the deep hatred of the peasantry for himself and for his master.

Rèis Mhòr na Teatha: *The Great Tea Race, 1863*

Some chose the high seas rather than the gloomy woods, particularly a young man from Hianais (Heanish, ON, 'outlying headland'), who became a ship's captain. Dòmhnall 'ic Nèill 'ic Dhòmhnaill Ruaidh (Donald MacKinnon, 'son of Neil, son of red-haired Donald') skippered the *Taeping*, a tea clipper built in 1863 in Greenock, which took part in The Great Tea Race of 1866 and narrowly beat the *Ariel.*

A premium was paid for the first consignment of tea to reach London each season. The *Ariel* and the *Taeping* left Foochow together and on 6th September, after 99 days, they raced within sight of each other into the Thames. The *Taeping* drew less water and was able to tie up in the London docks twenty minutes ahead of the *Ariel.* The *Taeping* divided her winnings of ten shillings per ton with the owners of the *Ariel* and Captain MacKinnon divided the captain's £100 with Captain Keay of the *Ariel.* The distance of the shipping route is 24,767 km from London to Fuzhou via the Cape of Good Hope but the clippers took a longer route to obtain the best winds. Captain MacKinnon died of complications with rheumatic fever on his next voyage on *Taeping* and the ship itself was wrecked in the China Sea in 1871. *Ariel's* fine yacht-like lines always made her at risk of being swamped and she disappeared in 1872 en route to Australia.

Before these tragic events, a celebratory song, 'Deoch-slàinte nan Gillean' ('Health-drink of the Lads'), was composed by Iain MacFhionghain (Ian MacKinnon) from Mull, who was a carpenter on the *Taeping:*

Gun gabh sinn an t-òran a rinneadh do Dhòmhnall
Bhon tha e cho foghlaimt' air seòladh nan long:
Bhon fhuair e an t-urram eadar China is Lunnainn
Gur feàrr leam na m' uile gun bhuidhinn e 'n geall.

Bha 'n Ariel bhòidheach gar feuchainn aig seòladh –
Gur h-i a bu chòir a bhith còmhl' rinn san àm;
'S le mheud 's fhuair thu dh'fhòghlam an toiseach do thòisich,
Gun bheat thu iad còmhla 'n àm crosadh na line.

'S i ghearradh an fhairge mar shiosar air caimrig
Is Chinaman mailidheach na dhealbh air a sròin;
'S i thàirngeadh an t-sùrdag air bhàrr nan tonn dubhghorm,
Mar fhiadh anns a' bhùireadh air chùl nam beann mòr.

Nuair thogadh tu h-aodach am bàrr a cruinn chaola
'S i shnàmhadh gu h-aotrom mar fhaoileag nan tonn;
Gaoth tuath 's i na frasan mar luaidhe ga sadadh,
Is fuaim aig a darach 'n àm sgapadh nan tonn.

Gur mis' th' air mo lèireadh sa mhadainn 's mi 'g èirigh,
An drùchd air mo lèine 's mi èisleanach fann;
An Sìona na dunach gam lot leis a' chuileig;
Gum b' fheàrr a bhith Muile fo dhubhar nam beann.

We'll sing the song that was composed for Donald
since he has such knowledge of sailing the ships;
and since he gained the honour between China and London
his winning of the wager I prefer to all things.

The Beautiful Ariel was vying with us at sailing –
she certainly ought to have been beside us that time;
but, thanks to those skills gained at your very beginning,
you beat both ships together when crossing the Line.

She'd cut through the ocean like scissors through cambric,
with a heavy-browed Chinaman portrayed on her prow;
she'd make a fine skipping on the crest of dark billows
like a deer in the rutting behing the high bens.

When you'd hoist up her canvas to the peaks of her thin masts,
She would sail along lightly like the gull of the waves;
The north wind with showers like lead shot would pound her,
And her oak would resound as she clove through the seas.

I am filled with great sorrow as I rise in the morning
with the dew on my shirt, feeling feeble and ill,
in miserable China, being nipped by mosquitoes –
I'd rather be in Mull beneath the shade of the hills.

Folklorist John Gregorson Campbell (1836-1891) was the Free Church minister appointed to the Tiree and Coll parishes by the Duke of Argyll in 1861. He was fluent in several languages including Gaelic, and a collector of traditional stories. Just before his death, work began on collating the first of four books of tales; three were published a few years after his death. His collection is significant in that he transcribed the tales precisely as dictated by their narrators.

Iain MacIlleathainn, Bàrd Bhaile Mhàrtainn:
John MacLean, the Bard of Balmartine

Amidst cultural richness, poverty persisted, compelling many to leave. 'Òran Mhanitòba' ('Manitoba Song') was composed by Iain MacIlleathainn, Bàrd Bhaile Mhàrtainn ((John MacLean, the Bard of Balmartine). MacLean was born in 1827 in Balmartine ('Martin's village'), the largest township on Tiree and remained there all his life. He composed the song when a group of MacLeans emigrated from Baile a' Phuill (Balephuil, 'village of the pool') to Manitoba in 1878:

Gur muladach mise 's mi 'n seo gun duin' idir
A thogas, no thuigeas, no sheinneas leam dàn;
Le dùrachd mo chridhe, soiridh slàn leis na gillean
A sheòl thar na linne gu Manitobà.

Bu ghrianach ar madainn nuair bha sinn nar balaich,
Gun chùram, gun ghearain, gun teannachadh màil;
Le ceòl is làn aigheir, cha laigheadh an smalan
Air a' chomann a bh' againn am Baile nam Bàrd.

'S chan fhaic mi san àm seo ach caoraich air bheanntan:
Chan eil as a' ghleann ach fear Gallda no dhà:
'S am beagan a dh'fhan dhiubh air rudhachan mara
Gan iomain gu cladach 's gam feannadh le màl.

Luchd fhèilidh is osan is bhonaidean cocte
Bha riamh air am moladh air thoiseach sna blàir,
Tha iad gan cur thairis gu dùthaich mhì-fhallain
'S gun nì air an aire ach am fearann chur fàs.

How sad am I without a single companion
who can raise, understand, or sing a song with me;
with all the goodwill of my heart, I bid a fond farewell
to the lads
who sailed over the ocean to Manitoba.

How sunny was our morning when we were young lads,
without anxiety or complaint, or the screwing of rent;
with music and the fullest fun, no gloom would descend
on the companionship we had in the Town of the Poets.

I can see nothing at present except sheep on the hillsides;
only a couple of Lowlanders can be found in the glen;
and the few who have remained on the ocean's headlands
are being driven down to the shoreline and flayed by rent.

The wearers of kilts and hose and cocked bonnets
who were always extolled in the battle's front line;
they are being sent overseas to a place that's unhealthy,
and the perpetrators are concerned only with laying waste
to the land.

Much of MacLean's output was concerned with local matters, speaking out on behalf of the people as in the song above. He was active in the Land League. In 1886, disturbances over the lease of land at Grianal (Greenhill, 'green field') prompted the estate to send a force of policemen to Tiree to serve summonses on the leaders of the Land League. The force headed for the village of Balephuil, known locally as Baile nam Bàrd ('village of the bards'), being noted for its many poets; 34 according to one estimate. There the policemen were routed and left the island. The Duke then sent Marines who marched in with fixed bayonets. The crofters were under strict orders not to resist and six were arrested, sent to Inveraray jail and released on surety of £20.00 each, paid by Lachlan MacQuarrie, a merchant from Balmartine. The six were tried in the High Court in Edinburgh and five were sentenced to six months in prison. MacLean was among them and his song 'Òran nam Prìosanach' ('Song of the Prisoners') makes it clear whose side he is on:

Is tha luchd-àiteachaidh an eilein ìosail
Fo ghrunnan millteach, gun àite còmhnaidh,
'S e 'n-diugh 'na fhàsach aig luchd am mìoruin
A chuir sa phrìosan ar gillean òga.

An Inbhir-aora, toll dubh a' chruadail
Gun dhùnadh suas iad a Luan's a Dhòmhnach;
Ach bha de dh' uaisle an com MhicGuaire
Nach biodh iad uair ann nam fuasgladh òr iad.

Theich na tràillean bho chùis na h-aimhreit
Mar nì an t-aingidh gun aon an tòir air;
Gun deach an tilleadh; cha robh ach breugan
An cùirt Dhùn Èideann; bu lèir siud dhòmhsa.

The inhabitants of the low-lying island
in subjection to a destructive minority, have no place
to live;
today it has been laid waste by those who despise us,
who have put in prison our young lads.

In Inveraray, that black hole of hardship,
they were incarcerated Monday and Sabbath;
but there was sufficient nobleness in MacQuarrie's breast
to ensure that they would not be there one hour if gold could release them.

The wretches fled from the scene of the confrontation
as the wicked flees when no man pursues him;
they were driven back; there was nothing but lies
in the Edinburgh court; that was clear to me.

Another notable Balmartine resident was Pipe Major John MacDonald of the 79th Highlanders who fought in the Crimean War. When storming the Heights of Alma at the head of the regiment, a volley struck down his companion piper while a bullet went through the bag of John's own pipes. He picked up his dead companion's pipes but in the heat of the moment, he played a dance tune instead of a march. Today he is known as the composer of the march *The 79th's Farewell to Gibraltar.*

Cola: *Coll*

Cola (meaning obscure), is located west of Mull and is known by the epithet Cola Chreagach Chiar ('dark, rocky Coll'). It is about 21 kilometres long by five wide and has a permanent population of around 220. Àirigh nan Gobhar (Arinagour, 'goat shieling'), located on the east coast, is the island's main settlement. A native of Coll is known as a Colach. There is a rhyme that refers, tongue in cheek, to the character of the Colaich and other islanders:

> Chan fhaic am Muileach nach sanntaich; na shanntaicheas am Muileach, goididh an Colach 's na ghoideas an Colach, cuiridh an Tiristeach am falach.
>
> *What the Mull man sees, he wants; what the Mull man wants, the Coll man steals; what the Coll man steals, the Tiree man hides.*

Breacachadh (Breachacha, 'speckled field') has two adjacent castles. Old Breachacha Castle is the 15th-century stronghold of the MacLeans of Coll, the island having been granted to John MacLean in 1431. This castle was superseded by a new dwelling in 1750 and it was restored to liveable condition in the 1960s. The newer Breachacha Castle was constructed in the mid-18th century and Samuel Johnson and James Boswell stayed there on their tour of the Hebrides.

An Gille Riabhach: *The Brindled Lad*

On the farm of Grìseabol (ON, Grisapool, 'pig farm') there are two places associated with the name An Gille Riabhach ('the brindled lad'), the first being Leum a' Ghille Riabhaich ('leap of the brindled lad'). It is said that in a skirmish between MacLeans and MacNeils, the unarmed Gille was confronted by an axe-wielding MacNeil tailor. The tailor tried to strike the Gille Riabhach but the Gille, who was standing with his back to a stream, sprang backwards, crossing it and landing on the elevated bank opposite. The tailor, enraged, threw the axe after him, whereupon the Gille, picking it up, leapt back immediately and dispatched the tailor. The stream is about twelve feet wide with the opposite bank about six feet above the one from which he sprang. The other spot which bears the same name is on level ground and is marked by stones about fourteen feet apart, marking the distance the Gille Riabhach is said to have jumped from a standing start.

In the late 18th century, Coll's some 1,000 inhabitants were suffering the same destitution and overpopulation already described in Tiree. By the mid-19th century, half the population had chosen to leave, many of them moving to Australia, Canada, or South Africa. In 1848, Alexander, the heir of the MacLeans of Coll, emigrated to Natal in South Africa. In 1856 his father, Hugh MacLean, decided to sell Coll. In the 2011 census, the island's population was recorded as just under 200, representing nearly an increase of one fifth over the previous decade.

An t-Eilean Muileach is Eilean Ì: *Mull and Iona*

East of Coll lies An t-Eilean Muileach (the Island of Mull), the second largest island of the Inner Hebrides with an area of almost 990km^2. Its name is pre-Gaelic in origin and has no connection to headland names such as Mull of Kintyre. Following 19th-century clearances and the Potato Famine, Mull's population has fallen from 10,000 to about 3,000 today.

The song 'Muile nam Fuar-bheann Mòr' ('Mull of the Cold High Mountains') by merchant seaman Iain Dòmhnallach (John MacDonald) (1883-1940) was apparently composed as he was sailing to New Zealand as a young man. It could be described as the island's anthem:

> O, b' àlainn leam riamh bhith coimhead 's a' ghrian
> A' ciaradh san iar mar òr,
> 'S Caol Muile mo ghaoil fo dhubhar nan craobh,
> 'S na luingis a' sgaoileadh sheòl;
> 'S do mhonaidhean àrd le ceò air am bàrr,
> 'S na fèidh len cuid àil nan còir;
> B' e dùrachd mo chrìdh' bhith tilleadh a-rìs
> Do Mhuile nam fuarbheann mòr.

O how I always loved seeing the sun fading to gold in the west, and my beloved Sound of Mull shaded by trees, with ships spreading sails; and your high uplands with mist-shrouded peaks and the deer tending to their young there; my heart's desire is to return again to Mull of the cold high mountains.

The 1881 census, the first to contain a language question, revealed that the vast majority of Muilich (Mull people) habitually spoke Gaelic. As in other parts of the Highlands and Islands, this would be changed by the educational system. Before 1872, Gaelic was extensively used in schools in the area, but the arrival of mandatory national education led to its total exclusion from classroom and playground, a severe blow to the status of Gaelic in the minds of many speakers. This had a considerable effect on language transmission to the next generations. Educational policy in Argyll was as dismissive of the local language as was the policy in Inverness-shire and Ross and Cromarty. Gaelic was officially introduced as a subject to the curriculum only after the First World War when it was reluctantly taught to native speakers as a second language, with English as the medium of instruction.

Creag an Iubhair is An Dubh Àrd: *Craignure and Duart*

Creag an Iubhair (Craignure, 'yew-tree crag'), a ferry port, is the main entry point to the island. The short sailing from Oban passes the headland of An Dubh Àrd (Duart, 'the dark height'); its castle of the same name is home to the island's primary kindred, the MacLeans. An early chief of the MacLeans married the daughter of the first Lord of the Isles and received Duart Castle as dowry. The clan surname MacLean is the anglicisation of Mac Gille Eathain ('son of the servant of [St.] John') and their names were often Eachann (Hector) or Lachann (Lachlan). Hence the jibe against them:

Mar mhadadh ag òl eanraich, tha ainmean Chlann Ghilleathain: Eachann, Lachann, Eachann, Lachann.

MacLean names sound like a hound slurping soup: Eachann, Lachann, Eachann, Lachann.

Dating from the 13th century, Duart consists of a strong curtain wall as well as a substantial tower that was added around 1390. In 1678, in the culmination of a long vendetta against the clan, Archibald Campbell, 9th Earl of Argyll, was instructed by the Privy Council to seize Mull and suppress the MacLeans. Campbell took charge of Duart Castle and ejected the MacLean elite from Mull. Government troops and their families garrisoned Duart Castle. A short distance from the castle is the tiny 'English' graveyard. The garrison petitioned to have the plot consecrated rather than be buried among the 'heathen' Episcopalians in the nearby Kilpatrick graveyard.

Ultimately slighted, the remains of the castle were abandoned in 1751. In 1911, the ruins were bought and restored by Sir Fitzroy Donald MacLean, 26th Chief of Clan MacLean. Later in the 20th century, the Soviet spy Donald Maclean's decision to betray his country was formed here. The double agent was a British diplomat who sent high-level, top-secret information to Moscow as a member of the Cambridge spy ring. In the book *A Spy Named Orphan*, the origin of his convictions is said to have come from a MacLean clan summit, held at Duart Castle in 1912. His grandfather had been a shoemaker in Tiree.

Tartan nan Leathanach: *The MacLean Tartan*

A MacLean tartan is specifically referred to in connection with lands in Islay. In a crown charter of 1588, granted to:

> Hector Makclene, son and heir-apparent to Lachlan Makclene of Doqart the feu-duty of these land is specified as:
>
> *Pro Norrabollsadh 60 ulnas panni, albi, nigri et grosei coloris.*
>
> *For Norraboll sixty yells of cloth, white and black and green.*

These are the only colours in the oldest authenticated MacLean tartan, the Hunting Sett of Duart. A poem in praise of Sir Hector MacLean, chief of Duart, contains the following verse:

Bu mhiann leam am breacan tlàth,
Breacan uain' 'us dubh 'us geal
Datha sàr Mhic-Ghilleain am flath
Siud an laoch a fhuair mo ghaol.

Dear to me the tartan plaid,
The plaid of green and black and white
The colours of the brave MacLean
The hero who has my love.

It was perhaps inevitable that the MacLeans were included in the slur:

Leathanach gun bhòst, Domhnallach gun tapadh, Caimbeulach gun mhòr-chùis: trì rudan ainneamh.

A humble MacLean, a listless MacDonald, a non-pompous Campbell: three rare things.

Loch Buidhe: *Loch Buie*

It is possible to do a circuit of Mull, first taking the A849 road to Fionnphort and Iona. A side road south leads to Loch Buidhe (Loch Buie, meaning 'yellow loch' but here signifying 'noble'). By the shore is Caisteal Màigh (Moy Castle, 'castle of the plain'). The surviving fabric of the castle is from the early 15th century with additions before abandonment in 1752. It was home to a sept, a powerful family within a clan, of the MacLeans who often spell their name in English as 'MacLaine'. This branch of the MacLeans was known by the patronymic Sliochd Mhurchaidh Ruaidh ('descendants of red Murdo'). History does not relate why they earned the following epithet:

Locha Buidhe, ceann-uidhe nam mèirleach.

MacLean of Lochbuie, destination of thieves.

Archibald MacLaine of Lochbuie was advised in 1779 to set his estate on long leases and get a military commission. The pay of an army captain then was £182, over twice the amount of his highest rented farm and equal to nearly a fifth of his entire 1783 rental. When Murdoch MacLaine of Lochbuie gained a commission as Lieutenant Colonel of the Dumbartonshire Fencibles in February 1794, he made an offer to his tenantry which constitutes the best surviving example detailing the actual mechanics of estate recruiting. He said that he would not give his men any of the government's five guineas bounty. Instead, he offered to reduce rent by 30 shillings on any possession held by the recruit's family for a duration of five years. Thus, he pointed out, the bounty to the recruit's family would total £7.10.0 which was £2.5.0 more than the government subsidy. Lochbuie got 50 men and pocketed the 250 guineas. The sum probably went to pay his own debts.

An Ros Mhuileach (the Ross of Mull), the largest peninsula of Mull, at 28 kilometres long, makes up the southwestern part of the island. It is bounded to the north by Loch Scrìodain (Loch Scridain, 'scree loch') and to the south by An Linne Latharnach (the Firth of Lorne). Here the tack of Peighinn a' Chrois (Pennycross, 'pennyland of the cross') was held by a MacLean who lent his name to a pipe tune, known variously as 'Captain MacLean of Pennycross', 'MacLean of Pennycross's March', and 'MacLean of Pennycross's Welcome to the 93rd', composed by William Ross (1823-1891) of Knockbain, Ross-shire.

Just two miles east of Bun Easain (Bunessan, 'foot of the waterfall') is the small crofting township of Àird Tunna (Ardtun, possibly 'enclosure headland'). Of the wider area, the 8th Duke of Argyll wrote in evidence to the Napier Commission into the plight of the crofting population:

> In 1846 and the following years the aspect of the population and the numerous wretched hovels erected by squatting cottars along the roadsides, was most painful. It resembled nothing so much as the descriptions given of the poorest part of the West of Ireland.

Despite the 7th Duke's earlier financial difficulties and resultant land disposals, the Argyll estate held on to holdings in the area and the 8th Duke was part of a landholding hierarchy in the Ross of Mull whose policies had led to the conditions described. Nor was it necessary to make the journey to the West of Ireland; such scenes were replicated up and down the west coast of Highland Scotland.

'Leanabh an Àigh': 'Child of Joy'

Close by Àird Tunna is a monument to Mary MacDonald (1789-1872), a poet whose best-known work was set to a tune later named after Bunessan.

On her marriage to Neil Macdonald, the couple had to move to Siaba (not meaning, as has been stated in a recent TV documentary 'six cows' but denoting 'drifting sand'), a moderately prosperous crofting community. They were there for a brief time before all the people were cleared away so that the land could be converted into a single sheep farm. The couple returned to the Bunessan area and here Mary, a devout Baptist, composed poems and hymns. One hymn, entitled 'Leanabh an Àigh' ('Child of Joy'), was set to a traditional air. This was heard by Lachlan MacBean when he was collecting tunes for his 1888 book, *Songs and Hymns of the Scottish Highlands,* and he translated the title of Mary's hymn into English as 'Child in the Manger', naming the tune to which it was sung 'Bunessan'. This tune has since achieved an ever wider audience. The editors of the 1925 book *Songs of Praise* asked the English writer Eleanor Farjeon to write another hymn to the tune. The result was 'Morning has Broken'. The original hymn begins:

Leanabh an àigh, an leanabh aig Màiri,
Rugadh san stàball, Rìgh nan Dùl;
Thàinig don fhàsach, dh'fhuiling nar n-àite
'Son iad an àireamh bhios dha dlùth.

Ged a bhios leanabain aig rìghrean na talmhainn
An greadhnachas garbh is anabarr mùirn;
'S geàrr gus am falbh iad, 's fàsaidh iad anfhann,
An àilleachd 's an dealbh a' searg san ùir.

Cha b' ionann 's an t Uan thàinig gar fuasgladh
Iriosal, stuama, ghluais o thùs;
E naomha gun truailleachd, Cruithfhear an t-sluaigh;
Dh'èirich e suas le buaidh on ùir.

The child of joy, the child who was Mary's, born in the stable, Lord of the Universe; came to the wilderness to suffer in place of us, happy are those who are close to him.

Although earthly kings have children in high pomp and with much joy, they are soon gone and they grow weak, their beauty and their shape withering in the grave.

Nothing is equal to the Lamb who came to free us, humble and modest when he first moved, saintly, with no impurity, this creator of humanity, he rose up with victory from the grave.

The singer Cat Stevens's 1971 recording of 'Morning has Broken' led to the song becoming known internationally.

Eilean Ì: *Iona*

The road west from Bunessan reaches the sea at Fionnphort (Fionnphort, 'white landing place'). From there, a car ferry crosses to Eilean Ì (Iona). The earliest forms of the name enabled place-name scholar William J. Watson to show that the name originally meant something like 'yew-place'. But more recent names are Ì, Ì Chaluim Chille, Eilean Idhe ('island of Iona'), and Ì nam Ban Bòidheach ('Iona of the beautiful women'). The modern English name comes from the Latin variant, *Ioua*, a spelling changed to Iona about 1270 when a transcription error, caused by the similarity of the letters n and u, arose. W. J. Watson would have been exasperated by recent social media speculation that the name may have a Norse connection, *Hiōe* being supposedly 'island of the den of the brown bear'.

Iona was the site of an important monastery. According to tradition, the monastery was founded in 563 by the monk Columba, originally called Criomhthann ua Cuinn. His name, meaning 'wolf', was changed, appropriately, to Colm Cille ('dove of the church'). He had been exiled from his native Ireland as a result of his involvement in the Battle of Cul Dreimhne and he and twelve companions went into exile on Iona, founding a monastery there. The monastery thrived and played a crucial role in the conversion to Christianity of the Picts in the 6th century, and of the Anglo-Saxon kingdom of Northumbria in 635. Many satellite institutions were founded, and Iona became a renowned centre of learning; its scriptorium produced important manuscripts, including, probably, the original texts of the *Iona Chronicle*, thought to be the source for the early Irish annals. *The Book of Kells* may have been produced in Iona at the end of the 8th century. Around this time, the island's high crosses were sculpted, perhaps the first such crosses to include the ring around the intersection that became characteristic of the Celtic cross.

Iona's prominence was diminished as a result of Viking raids that began in 794. After its treasures had been plundered several times and its monastic community massacred, Columba's relics were removed and divided between Scotland and Ireland in 849 when the monastery was abandoned. In 1549, an inventory recorded that 48 Scottish, eight Norwegian and four Irish kings rested in Rèilig Odhrain ('Oran's graveyard'). This is also the final resting place of John Smith, the former Labour Party leader, who loved Iona and was buried there in 1994.

Iona Abbey is the best-preserved ecclesiastical building surviving from the Middle Ages in the Hebrides. The 8th Duke of Argyll presented the island's religious buildings and sites to the Iona Cathedral Trust in 1899. In 1938, George MacLeod founded the Iona Community, an ecumenical Christian community of people from differing Christian traditions and walks of life. The Community restored the abbey to its current state. At the time of the 2011 census, the island's population had grown to 177 usual residents. The place still brings forth the strong emotion evoked by Columba himself:

Ì mo chridhe, Ì mo ghràidh
An àite guth manaich bi geum bhà
Ma thig an saoghal seo gu crìoch
Bithidh Ì mar a bha.

Iona of my heart, Iona of my love
In place of the voice of monks, there will be the lowing of cattle
Should the world come to an end
Iona shall always be as it was.

Stafa: *Staffa*

Back in Mull, the island circuit can be continued by taking the road from Àrd Ceann Locha (Kinloch, 'height of the head of the loch') to An Sàilean (Salen, 'the small inlet') on the east coast of the island. About ten kilometres off Mull to the west is the roughly 30-hectare island of Stafa (Staffa, ON, 'stave island'). Staffa came to prominence after a visit in 1772 by the botanist, Sir Joseph Banks, who extolled the beauty of the basalt columns in general and the island's main sea cavern in particular. Other personalities followed, including Queen Victoria and Felix Mendelssohn. The latter's overture, *From the Hebrides*, composed in 1830, brought further fame to the now-deserted island. The work is usually called *Fingal's Cave*, evoking the Ossianic hero Fionn mac Cumhaill. James 'Ossian' Macpherson had re-purposed a Scots version of his name, Fingal, that had been used by the poet Barbour in the 14th century, meaning 'white stranger' and, according to Banks, a local guide told him that the cave was so named. In Banks's own words:

> We asked the name of it, said our guide, the name is Finhen; what is Finhen? said we. Finhen MacCoul – whom the translator of Ossian's works has called Fingal.

Banks was not well served by his guide and the issue was fully examined by Faujas de Saint Fond in 1784. He explains that "the boiling motion of the water" would account for:

> the ancient and real name of this cave in the Erse [Gaelic] language being, the melodious cave.

In the face of such Anglophone imaginings, it was possible for a Frenchman:

> through enquiries of several persons well skilled in Gaelic

to explain the true meaning of An Uamh Bhinn and set it out in detail. However, despite these efforts, the name Fingal's Cave persists and its original meaning, according to the *Scotland in Trust* magazine (Spring, 2011), is "still uncertain".

Grùilinn: *Gruline*

At Grùilinn (Gruline, 'stony land') is the mausoleum to Lachlann MacGuaire (Lachlan Macquarie) CB, (1762-1824). The Gaelic-speaking Macquarie was the last autocratic Governor of New South Wales from 1810 to 1821 and is considered to have played a major role in the shaping of Australian society in the early 19th century. His tenure is not without controversy. In 1816, Macquarie gave orders that led to the Appin Massacre, when at least fourteen aboriginal Gundungurra and Dharawal people were killed by British soldiers.

Gruline was a gathering place, a *þing* ('Thing') of the early Norse period. Historian Alex Woolf believes that each island or group of small islands would have had its own assembly site. Along with Gruline, only Tinwhil or Hinnisdale in Trotternish, Skye, Tiongal in Lewis and Finlaggan in Islay can be identified in the Hebrides. As well as having judicial, administrative and political roles, a 'Thing' was a social gathering at which individuals from the area's families could trade, take part in sporting competitions, negotiate alliances, make arrangements regarding marriages and inheritance and, of course, drink. It was here also that Clan MacLean mustered for war.

An Sàilean is a small village on the east coast of the island on the Sound of Mull, roughly halfway between Craignure and Tobermory. The full name is Sàilean Dubh Chaluim Chille ('Black Salen of St. Columba'). Until the early 1800s, the site of the village was no more than a junction of tracks. Lachlann MacGuaire, the Laird of Gruline and Ulva, decided that there was a commercial advantage in establishing a village and harbour on the nearest point to his estates on the Sound of Mull and so Salen came into being.

Tobar Mhoire: *Tobermory*

From Salen it is a few kilometres to the port of Tobar Mhoire (Tobermory, 'Mary's well') formerly known as Tobar Maol Rubha ('St Maol Rubha's well'). The name refers to a well located nearby which was dedicated before the Reformation to the Virgin Mary. Tobermory is located on the east coast of Misinis (Mishnish, ON, 'goat headland'), the most northerly part of the island, near the entrance to the Sound of Mull. It was built by the British Fisheries Society, a body formed largely by Scottish landowners to exploit the rich marine resources off the west coast. The Society established the model of utilitarian planned settlements that subsequently spread across the Scottish landscape. Tobermory began in 1788 as such a settlement to support the fishing industry, its layout based on the designs of Thomas Telford. It has a current population of about 1,000.

Legend has it that the wreck of a Spanish galleon, laden with gold, lies somewhere at the bottom of Tobermory Bay. By some accounts, a ship of the Spanish Armada, the *Florencia*, maybe, *Florida* or perhaps even, *San Francisco*, taking the route around Scotland to Spain in 1589, anchored in Tobermory to take on provisions. After a dispute over payment, the ship caught fire and the gunpowder magazine exploded, sinking the vessel. In her hold, reputedly, was £300,000 in gold bullion. Other sources claim the vessel was the *San Juan de Sicilia* or *San Juan de Baptista,* carrying only troops. According to that account, the island's chief, Lachlan Mòr MacLean, struck a deal with the Spanish commander to re-provision and refit the ship in return for military intervention on his side against the MacDonalds. The traditional Gaelic story of the destruction of the galleon is that it was blown up by the jealous wife of a MacLean tacksman who was interested in a Spanish lady aboard, the bomb being smuggled into the ship by her page.

There have been several treasure searches, including that of the scandal-ridden 11th Duke of Argyll's futile 1960s effort, but treasure has yet to be raised from the bay.

Caibideil 5: *Chapter 5*

A' Ghàidhealtachd – Tìr-mòr: *Highland Council Area – The Mainland*

To the north of the local authority area of Argyll and Bute, across the bridge at Ballachulish, is the local authority area of A' Ghàidhealtachd (Highland) and the district of Loch Abar (Lochaber, 'confluence loch'), so named because all the main rivers flow into it. The road follows the shores of Loch Linne. This latter name is a 'ghost' name in the sense that the 'linne' refers simply to a channel. On the opposite shore from here is Corran ('sickle'), referring not, as is supposed, to the sand spit but to the narrow promontory. From Corran there is a ferry across to Àird Ghobhar (Ardgour, 'height of the goats') on the western side of the loch. Below Corran Ferry, the stretch of water is known as An Linne Sheileach ('the brackish channel'), while above is An Linne Dhubh ('the dark channel'). The loch shore road to Fort William is more recent – before 1785 the old military way to Fort William was inland through the Laraig Mòr ('big defile'). The villages that once existed along that route have vanished; their inhabitants cleared away at the beginning of the 19th century.

The immediate locality of Fort William is Inbhir Lòchaidh (Inverlochy, 'confluence of the River Lochy' [with Loch Linnhe]). The modern name commemorates the 1690 establishment of a garrison named in honour of King William III. It re-used the site of a 1655 Cromwellian citadel, one of a series of strongholds that were largely demolished by a nation that detested them. Although seen as symbols of oppression and heavy taxation, the ten years of the Commonwealth were an unprecedented period of law and order in Lochaber, as elsewhere in Scotland. The government-appointed English judges dispensed impartial justice, a new phenomenon in Scotland. A contemporary Scottish law lord, Lord President Gilmour, exasperated by praise for these paragons of virtue, testily remarked:

> "Deil thank them! they had neither kith nor kin."

Fort William has only ever been known in Gaelic as Gearasdan Dubh Inbhir Lòchaidh ('black fortress of Inverlochy'), the epithet referring to grimness. At various times the town has been called Maryburgh, Gordonsburgh and Achintore in English. In the 19th century the town council, in a romantic move, applied the name of the now partially demolished fort to the town as a whole. The town has a population of 5,603,231 of whom speak Gaelic.

North of the Fort and across the narrow River Nevis is the town's burial ground. At its entrance is the original stone gateway into the fort, salvaged in the 1890s, when the West Highland Railway bought the site for marshalling yards. Above the arch is a memorial to Alan Cameron of Erracht, who is quoted in the Introduction. He raised the 79th regiment that later became the Cameron Highlanders. At the outbreak of the war in America in 1775, Thomas Gage, Commander-in-Chief in North America, asked for Highland levies of 5000 men, a demonstration of perceptions of the military value of the Gael. In 1790, the 4th Duke of Gordon and the 4th Earl of Breadalbane and other grandees all believed they could raise men. But Alan of Erracht was perhaps the most optimistic; from 1787 to 1791 repeatedly offering to raise men in the Highlands. In the 18th and 19th centuries, fighting men were the area's major export after cattle and sheep. The land was emptied of young men.

When the 79th Regiment was formed by Cameron, none of the volunteers had English and he had to use Gaelic terms in order to make them understand his instructions when drilling them. Hay was tied to the left foot and straw to the right, and when he wanted them to march, he cried:

> "Feur, stràbh, feur, stràbh!"
>
> *"Hay, straw, hay, straw!"*

In this way they came to understand the command, "Left, right, left, right." When he wanted them to turn right he shouted:

> "Taobh a' phutain!"
>
> *"The button side!"*

When he wanted them to turn left he called:

> "Taobh tuill!"
>
> *"Button-hole side!"*

The route from Fort William to Mallaig is now popularly known as 'The Road to the Isles'. The name first appeared in a book entitled *Songs of the Hebrides* published in 1917, with words by the Rev. Kenneth Macleod to a popular tune composed by Pipe Major John McLellan DCM, called 'The Bens of Jura'.

Immediately outside Fort William, the name A' Chorpaich (Corpach, 'body place') appears on road signs. It was here that the water-borne catafalques bearing the remains of the high-born, such as MacBeth, reached salt water. They remained here for one last night before the catafalque was transferred to sea-going ships to bear the body south to join the many Scottish and Norwegian kings laid to rest in Rèilig Òdhrain, the royal burial plot in Iona.

The Camerons, the clan that came to predominate in Lochaber, once resided close by on Eilean nan Craobh ('tree island'), one of several islands in Loch Iall (Loch Eil, probably 'thong loch' referring to its long thin shape). While the Camerons' rallying cry is:

> Chlanna nan con, thigibh a seo agus gheibh sibh feòil
>
> *Sons of the dogs, come ye here, and you will get flesh*

their cath-ghairm ('war-cry') is:

> Dà thaobh Loch Iall 's dà thaobh Lòchaidh, Loch Iall, Loch Iall!
>
> *Both sides of Loch Eil and both sides of Lochy, Lochiel, Lochiel!*

Further west, Achadh Do Liubha (Achdalieu, 'Do Liubha's field'), named in memory of a saint, is the site of a scene in the long life of Sir Ewan Cameron of Locheil (c.1637-1719). Locked in mortal combat here, he is supposed to have bitten out the throat of a sergeant from the Cromwellian garrison in Fort William.

Beyond Achdalieu, Coire Beag (Corrybeg, 'little corrie') was the home of Màiri NicEalair (Mary MacKellar) (1836-1890), poet, translator and campaigner for Gaelic language and culture. The daughter of a baker in Fort William, she married Iain MacKellar, captain and joint owner of a coasting vessel which carried cargo from the western seaboard of Scotland to the Baltic seaports. Mary used to accompany him on voyages and survived shipwreck on at least one occasion. After a judicial separation from her husband, she settled in Edinburgh and her poems and songs, in Gaelic and English, were published in 1880. Her translation of Queen Victoria's second series of *Leaves from our Journal in the Highlands* has been described as, "a masterpiece of forcible and idiomatic Gaelic". Her song 'Am Maraiche 's a Leannan' ('The Sailor and his Sweetheart') is in the form of a conversation between a sailor and his girlfriend:

O, leam bu mhiann a bhith san luing,
'S an stiùir a bhith nam làimh
An uair bhios muir gu nualanach,
Na glinn 's na stuaghan àrd,
A' brùchdadh barra-gheal fo a sròin,
'S le crònan seach a sàil;
I 'g èirigh eutrom air gach tonn,
Is fonn oirre ri gàir'.

O how I would like to be in the ship with the helm in my hand when the sea is howling in its glens and high waves are rushing white-topped under her bow and crooning over her stern as she rises lightly on each wave, deriving pleasure from the sea sounds.

Her little *Tourist's Hand-book of Gaelic Phrases for The Highlands*, published around 1890, reflects the very different nature of the visitor then:

Cò leis an oighreachd so?

Whose estate is this?

Mharbh mi sia paidhrichean de choilich ruadha.

I have killed six brace of red grouse cocks.

Sin sùlaire, tilg air.

There's a gannet, fire on it.

Such phrases would have little currency today.

The 'Road to the Isles' now crosses a burn, An Dubh Lighe ('the dark flood'), and enters the lands once held by the MacDonalds of Clanranald in Arisaig and Morar. This is Gleann Fhionnain (Glenfinnan, possibly 'Finan's glen'). By the loch shore is Dail Naomh ('holy dale') where there was once a burial ground. Here is Alexander MacDonald of Glenaladale's monument to the first recruits of Prince Charles Edward Stuart, some 1100 men who gathered here on 19th August 1745. The Prince raised the standard of his father (called 'the Old Pretender' from the French word *prédentant* meaning 'claimant') on the hillside near the railway line and viaduct. The statue was added to the original shooting lodge in 1834.

"A Madness" was Cameron of Locheil's contemporary description of Charles's attempt, while an authority on the Jacobite cause now describes it as "an escapade". Yet little has been written on the motivations of the Highlanders who gathered in Charles' support. Professor Hume Brown, the first Professor of Scottish History at Edinburgh University thought that:

> The dominating idea in the mind of the average Highlander was that he was engaged on a Highland raid on a large scale.

In response, John Lorne Campbell wrote in his seminal book *The Highland Songs of the '45* (1933):

> ... this statement, like others of the same kind, owes its conscious or unconscious genesis to what would now be described as the influence of anti-Gaelic propaganda. In its unenlightened aspect it was represented by the dread of English mothers that the Prince's followers would devour their children alive. Uttered as it is with the weight of Professor Hume Brown's scholarship behind it, it becomes a verdict based upon insufficient evidence, which it is the duty of an impartial criticism to reject and overthrow.

Campbell felt that Gaelic poems and songs of the time did not display barbaric greed. Instead, for him the predominant sentiments were a passionate attachment to the rightful Royal House coupled with hatred for the usurping Williamite and Hanoverian dynasties and a sense of humiliation at having been bested by a people whose lack of physical and military prowess had long been a subject of Highland scorn.

Despite Campbell's efforts, in 1974, Gordon Donaldson, the Historiographer Royal, simply parroted Hume Brown in saying that the Highland clans saw their campaigns as opportunities for a revival, on a grand scale, of the traditional collection of booty in the Lowlands. Ironically, this was from the same historian who stated mournfully in 1981 that:

> It takes a long time for the findings of scholars to filter through to the popular mind ... a good error never seems to die. It is a great pity that so many authors ... continue instead to feed the public on outdated, discredited notions.

The Prince had arrived from Dail an Lèigh (Dalilea, 'meadow of the doctor') in the company of one of the poets featured in Campbell's anthology. This was Alasdair mac Mhaighstir Alasdair (Alexander MacDonald). Born in the 1690s and living until about 1770, he is regarded as the most original of Gaeldom's 18th-century poets. He worked as a teacher with the Society in Scotland for Propagating Christian Knowledge (SSPCK) and his collection of poems, *Ais-Eiridh na Sean-Chanoin Albannaich* (*Renaissance of the Old Language of Scotland*), was published in 1751. He was "out" in the 1745 Rising and much of his political poetry celebrates his ardent Jacobitism. His often inventive and explosive verse is rooted in Gaelic poetic tradition but shows the influence of his classical reading and his knowledge of Scots and English verse. His poem 'Òran Don Phrionnsa' ('Song to the Prince') has benefited from a fresh and powerful translation by the poet Taylor Strickland. His soaring lyrics perfectly capture the motivation of the Highlanders as expressed by Campbell:

O, hì-rì-rì, tha e tighinn,
O, hì-rì-rì, 'n Rìgh tha uainn,
Gheibheamaid ar n-airm 's ar n-èideadh,
'S breacan-an-fhèilidh an cuaich.

'S èibhinn liom fhin, tha e tighinn,
Mac an Rìgh dhlighich tha uainn,
Slios mòr rioghail d'an tig armachd,
Claidheamh us targaid nan dual.

’S ann a’ tighinn thar an t-sàile
Tha ’m fear àrd as àille snuadh,
Marcaich’ sunndach nan steud-each
Rachadh gu h-eutrom ’san ruaig.

Samhail an Fhaoillich a choltas,
Fuaradh froise ’s fadadh-cruaidh;
Lann thana na làimh gu cosgairt
Sgoltadh chorp mar chorc’ air cluain.

Torman do phìoba ’s do bhrataich
Chuireadh spiorad bras’ san t-sluagh,
Dh’ eireadh ar n-àrdan ’s ar n-aigne,
’S chuirte air a’ phrasgan ruaig.

Tairneanach a’ *bhomb* ’s a’ chanain
Sgoilteadh e ’n talamh le ’chruas,
Fhreagradh dha gach beinn ’s gach bealach,
’S bhòdhradh a mhac-tall’ ar cluas!

Gur mairg d’ an èideadh san là sin
Còta grànd’ de ’n mhàdar ruadh,
Ad bhileach dhubh us cocàrd innt’
Sgoiltear i mar chàl mu ’n cluais!

Here he comes now out of exile.
Our arms are wrapped in cloak and welcome.

His arrival thrills. This son of our rightful king
has looks to kill. A striking side view
with slick sword and plaited shield. My knight
in shining armor from overseas
is a tall, graceful rider whose caracole stuns any
light horse insurgence.
Rarest appearance, his skyful glare of March:
a rainbow’s splinter, the rain-grey rush.

One swing of that sword
would scythe our enemy, like an oat field.

Beneath the pipe's baleful blast,
all under one banner, renewed spirit
unfurls, suffuses us: dispossessed

then enriched by the passion to run
the rabble out, and as the cannons call
each switchback and beinn respond

thunderously. Their coda rings our ears
and the earth cracks open... Poor lad
on that day, still in his fancy dress

or uniform. Coat as red as a fox.
What is that broken over his head?
A cocked hat, like charred cabbage.

Ailean Dearg: *Red Alan*

On a tidal island to the north is Caisteal Tioram ('dry castle'), one of many castles that suffered as a result of the upheavals of the Jacobite Risings, but this time at the hands of its owner, Ailean Dearg ('red Alan MacDonald'), chief of Clanranald. When Ailean Dearg joined the Jacobite Rising of 1715 he torched his castle, purportedly to prevent it again falling into Government hands; the Royal Navy controlled the sea, and coastal areas were potentially vulnerable to attack. He was also known as Ailean a' Chridhe Mhòir ('Alan of the big heart') on account of his small stature but generous spirit. He was later mortally wounded at the Battle of Sheriffmuir on 13th November and, seeing him fall, the Clanranald clansmen faltered, but MacDonald of Keppoch shouted to them:

> "Dìoghaltas an-diugh, tuireadh a-màireach!"
>
> "*Revenge today, mourning tomorrow!*"

and pressed forward to rout the government's left wing. Prophetically, according to tradition, the state-of-the-art house Ailean Dearg had built for his fashion-conscious wife in South Uist, Caisteal Ormacleit (Ormaclete Castle), caught fire on the night before his death. The clan took his death hard, as is clear from the saying;

> Cò ris a thèid mi g' am ghearan, 's gun Mac Mhic Ailein am Mùideart?
>
> *To whom can I make my complaint, and no Clanranald in Moidart?*

In 'Deoch-slàinte Ailein Mhùideartaich' ('A Toast to Alan of Moidart'), composed by Iain mac Dhùghaill 'ic Lachlainn (John, 'son of Dougal, son of Lachlan'), Ailean is described as a warrior, a hunter and a skilled seaman whom many women love and admire. The last statement is a common theme in bardic praise but, on this occasion, it may have a ring of truth to it. When, in 1692, he tardily presented himself to Colonel John Hill, the Fort William garrison commander, in order to take the Oath of Allegiance to William III, Hill described Alan as the most handsome man he had ever seen. When James Boswell heard this praise song during his journey to the islands along with Dr Johnson in 1773, he was so taken with it that he had it translated into English:

Siud an t-slàinte chùramach,
Òlamaid gu sunndach i,
Deoch-slàint' an Ailein Mhùideirtich
Mo dhùrachd dhut gun èirich.

'S iomadh maighdeann bharrasach
Ga math dan tig an earrasaid,
Eadar Bail' a' Mhanaich, agus
Caolas Bharraigh 'n dèidh ort.

Tha pàirt an Eilean Bheagram dhiubh
'S cuid san Fhraing 's san Eadailt dhiubh
'S chan eil latha teagaisg nach
Bi 'n Cille Pheadair treud diubh.

That's the mindful toast
Let's drink it cheerfully,
A toast to Alan of Moidart
My good wishes for your rising.

Many a superior maiden
Who well becomes her robes
Between Balivanich and the
Sound of Barra longs for you

Some are in Eilean Bheagram [South Uist]
Some in France and in Italy
And there's never a religious service in Kilphedar
Without a flock of them in attendance.

Dòmhnall an 13mh Mac 'ic Ailein: *Donald, 13th Chief of Clanranald*

Ailean's father Donald, chief from 1670, was a colourful character and the subject of many tales. Undoubtedly, the strangest concerns a companion in the guise of a huge black toad. It haunted Donald wherever he went and made itself at home at Caisteal Tioram. On one occasion it was said that Donald locked it in the dungeon and then launched his galley for a short excursion to Arisaig. But he had barely set sail when the creature was seen swimming in pursuit, happily breasting the waves, and, on reaching the vessel, showing every sign of enjoying the expedition more than any on board. To complicate matters, the toad began to show signs of resentment at the attempts which Donald made to avoid him. After years of misery, the chief succeeded in getting rid of this uncanny beast, but its disappearance is shrouded in mystery According to popular belief it was devoured by a lion, the said lion being presented to Donald as a gift from the Marquis of Argyll. Both gift and act are improbable.

Eilean Bàn: *White Island*

Further east on Loch Morar is Eilean Bàn ('white island') the site of a Roman Catholic seminary or, as Simon Fraser of Lovat put it, his dìseart ('deserted place' or 'hermit's retreat') or sanctuary, where as a fugitive he sheltered after the '45. His men had taken the precaution of securing all the boats on the loch, but a party of Redcoats launched a naval tender and made for Lovat's hideout. The soldiers burned the seminary, and, too old and infirm to run, Lovat surrendered. A recent exhibition at the Museum of Scotland, 'Stern and Wild' – a line from Lord Byron's poem *Lochnagair* – stated that he died in prison. This shields us from the truth. Tried by his peers in 1747 at Westminster, he was found guilty as an 'abandoned traitor'. His sentence read:

> You, Simon, Lord Lovat, return to the prison of the Tower; from thence you must be drawn to the place of execution; when you come there, you must be hanged by the neck, but not till you be dead, for you must be cut down alive; then your bowels must be taken out and burnt before your face, then your head must be severed from your body, and your body divided into four quarters, and these must be at the King's disposal.

However, he received clemency from the King; they just beheaded him at Tower Hill, the last peer of the realm so to die.

Beinn Nibheis: *Ben Nevis*

As the road northwards leaves Fort William for Spean Bridge, there are unrestricted views eastwards to the highest mountain in the United Kingdom. Beinn Nibheis (Ben Nevis), at 1345 metres, rises above the town and a whisky distillery stands between the road and the mountain. This operation once proudly proclaimed its product as the 'Dew of the Mountain' but it seems that their marketing people had only a hazy understanding of the meaning of the name Ben Nevis.

A number of fanciful explanations of the word 'Nevis' exist, but the most consistent one is that it is related to the Latin word for a cloud, *nebus*. All very satisfactory and all the better for having a nice classical connection. Unfortunately, it is wrong.

In the Gaelic landscape naming system, the river names the loch and then the loch lends its name to the surrounding land and mountains. The river name in this instance probably simply meant ‘wet’ but it was commonly believed to derive from uabhas (terror), and the area does have a forbidding reputation. For the distillery to call its spirit ‘the dew of the mountain’ is an own goal to a Gaelic speaker.

Oddly for such an awesome hill, Ben Nevis is dismissed in the saying:

> Beinn Nibheis mhòr a’ glaodhaich na laighe-siùbhla ’s cha tànaig aiste ach an luchag-fheòir.
>
> *Great Ben Nevis howling with its birth-pain and all that came out of it was a field mouse.*

Dòmhnall Dubh: *Black Donald*

The older of the two Inverlochy castles is situated on the east bank of the river Lochy to the north of the town. This 13th-century castle was a potent statement of baronial power realised by the then-ruling magnates, the Comyns, and the location guards access to the Great Glen to the north. It was here, in 1431, that an ancestor of Cameron of Erracht, Dòmhnall Dubh (‘black Donald’), joined the forces of the Crown under the Earls of Mar and Caithness only for that royal army to be routed by Donald, Lord of the Isles. ‘Pìobaireachd Dhòmhnaill Dhuibh’ (‘Pibroch of Black Donald’), one of the oldest Gaelic songs, refers to that Black Donald. When Clan Donald was victorious they took musical revenge on what they saw as Cameron treachery:

> Pìobaireachd Dhòmhnaill Dhuibh,
> Pìobaireachd Dhòmhnaill;
> Pìob agus bratach
> Air faich Inbhir Lòchaidh.

The piping of Black Donald,
the piping of Donald;
Pipes and banner
on the field of Inverlochy.

Blàr Inbhir Lòchaidh: *The Battle of Inverlochy*

Two hundred years later another battle took place beneath these walls on Goirtean Odhar ('dun-coloured field'). During the Wars of the Three Kingdoms, a series of intertwined conflicts were fought between 1639 and 1653 in the then-separate countries of England, Scotland and Ireland, Here below the castle wall, the Marquis of Montrose's royalist force of some 1500 men defeated a force almost twice its size.

Montrose and his commander Alasdair mac Colla Chiotach (Alexander, 'son of left-handed Coll') were near what is now known as Fort Augustus. They were aware that a pursuing force of 3000 Argyllshire men was only some 40 kilometres behind them at Inverlochy. Instead of marching directly back down the glen, Alasdair persuaded Montrose to surprise the Earl of Argyll with a flanking march. They crossed some of the toughest, snow-bound terrain in the Highlands to mount the attack. Just before dawn on Sunday 2nd February 1645, Argyll, dismayed at the sight of the Royalist army and suffering from a dislocated shoulder, left the command of his army to Donnchadh Caimbeul Achadh Breac (Sir Duncan Campbell of Auchinbreck) and retired to his birlinn, a vessel that the MacDonalds disparagingly nicknamed 'An Dubh Luideanach' ('black whore') on Loch Linnhe. As he left, yet more supporters of Montrose joined the fray; the chorus of a song said to have been composed at this time as a body of MacGregors, MacNabs, and Stewarts marched through Argyll's lands to join Montrose at the battle of Inverlochy goes thus:

Gabhaidh sinn an rathad mòr,
Olc no math le càch e!

We will take the high road,
Let them take it ill or well!

In the song 'Là Inbhir Lòchaidh' ('The Day of Inverlochy'), the poet Iain Lom ('bald John'), of the MacDonalds of Keppoch, gives an eye-witness account of the battle. As the poet says:

Chaidh an latha le Clann Dòmhnaill

The day was with Clan Donald.

Argyll watched helplessly as the royalist forces overwhelmed the Argyllshire men, with more than 1500 of them killed, many drowning in the river Lochy while trying to escape:

Sgeul a b' àite nuair a thigeadh,
Air Caimbeulaich nam beul sligneach,
H-uile dream dhiubh mur a thigeadh,
Le bualadh lann 'n ceann gam briseadh.

'N latha a shaoil iad a dhol leotha
'S ann bha laoich gan ruith air reothadh:
'S iomadh slaodanach mòr odhar,
A bh' air aodann Ach' an Todhair.

More pleasing still was the news of the crusty-mouthed Campbells: as each group of them appeared, sword blows smashed their heads.

The day they thought would be theirs they were chased by heroes through the frost; many great yellow idlers lie stretched out on Ach' an Todhair.

Alasdair MacColla, having already accounted for some 30 opponents, offered the captive Auchinbreck the choice of beheading or hanging, occasioning the still commonly used reply:

Dà dhiù gun aon roghainn.

Two evils and no choice.

Alasdair miscalculated his broadsword's swing and trepanned the unfortunate Duncan.

An Canàl Cailleannach: *The Caledonian Canal*

Northwards on the road from Fort William to Inbhir Garadh (Invergarry, 'confluence of the River Garry'), the major feature in the landscape is the Caledonian Canal which has been known in the past as both Amar-Uisge a' Ghlinne Mhòir ('waterway of the Great Glen') and Sligh'-uisge na h-Alba ('waterway of Scotland'). Following the brutal suppression of the Gaels after the 1745 Rising and the death in 1788, without a legitimate heir, of Charles Edward Stuart, the prospect of a further armed rising in the North receded. No longer a military threat, Gaels were seen as subjects for improvement, so the Highlands could now make an economic contribution to the nation. The Canal, created partly as a safe inland route for 32-gun frigates to the north of Scotland, was the realisation of a dream for Thomas Telford, "The Colossus of Roads" and Father of Civil Engineering, who championed its construction. It was one of the first government-funded employment schemes requiring the muscle power of many Highlanders to build a series of canals and locks linking four lochs and two rivers. The southern river, the Lochy, reaches the sea at Inverlochy.

Na Seumasaich: *Jacobitism*

Jacobitism was a largely 17th- and 18th-century movement that supported the restoration of the House of Stuart to the British throne. The name is derived from *Jacobus,* the Latin version of James. When James II and VII was forced into exile in 1688, Parliament argued that he abandoned the throne and offered it to his Protestant daughter Mary and her husband William III. Jacobitism was a complex mix of ideas, but supporters argued monarchs were appointed by God or divine right, and could not be removed, making the post-1688 regime illegitimate.

Jacobitism had armed support in the Western Scottish Highlands, and Aberdeenshire (20,000 Scots fought for the Jacobites in 1715, compared to

11,000 who joined the government army) and in areas of Northern England, Wales, and South West England. The movement had an international dimension; several European powers sponsored the Jacobites as an extension of larger conflicts. There were Jacobite risings in 1689, 1715, 1719 and 1745, along with abortive French-backed invasion attempts in 1708 and 1744.

The Rising of 1745 has provided much romantic writing about the devasting Highland Charges; the bloody defeat at Culloden; Prince Charles's evasion of capture with a price tag on his head; the heroism of his supporters such as Flora MacDonald; and his escape to France. These events were immortalised in many well-known Jacobite songs in Gaelic, such as 'Mo run geal òg,' and in English, such as 'The Skye Boat Song', 'Will ye no come back again?' and 'The Hundred Pipers'. While the Gaelic songs are contemporary with the events they describe, those in English are not. They were written by Robert Burns, James Hogg, Lady Nairne, and other named songwriters during the 19th century.

While the 1745 Rising had succeeded in taking control in Scotland and forced the recall of troops from Europe, the defeat at Culloden and withdrawal of French support in 1748 ended Jacobitism as a serious political movement. Whig historiography viewed Jacobitism as marginal to the progression towards present-day Parliamentary democracy. Nowadays, historians suggest that Jacobitism should be seen as an ongoing political idea and a strain of social and political conservatism running throughout British history.

Following the usual pattern, the river has given its name to the loch, but the English name Loch Lochy confuses many commentators. They read it tautologically as 'Loch Loch' and suggest that this loch was the last to be named in Scotland and the Gaels had run out of imagination. But Lochy has nothing to do with 'loch'. The river has the name of a spirit called Luga and it seems probable that this is the river of the 'black goddess' identified by early classical geographers.

Joseph Hobbs set up the Great Glen Cattle Ranch in the river valley. Travelling north from Fort William, on the left-hand side of the road close to the ranch's Shelter Number Two, there are three mounds of stones. They mark the point at which a cortège of mourners from Fort William, bearing a coffin for burial, would lay down their burden and men from Spean Bridge would take over, or vice versa. The largest of the three stone cairns was erected to the memory of Dr William Kennedy of Lianachan (1810-51) whose coffin once rested here. 1400 men attended his burial at Kilmallie, outside Fort William. The other two cairns were erected later in memory of his brothers.

Am Fògarrach Mu Dheireadh: *The Last Outlaw*

Eòghann Bàn a' Choire Bhuidhe ('fair Ewan MacPhee of the yellow corrie') was probably the last outlaw in the Highlands. He established himself and his family on an island in Loch Chuaich (Loch Quoich) where he recognised neither law nor landowner. Attempts were made to apprehend him, but he defended his stronghold with the use of firearms. John Cameron of Coire Choille (Corriechoille) was largely responsible for his arrest. Eòghann was said to have helped himself to some of John's sheep and eventually he was arrested and sent to prison. His now poverty-stricken family moved to Fort William and when they became ill, Dr Kennedy nursed them. He caught typhus from them and died in 1851.

The sign to the left shortly afterwards points to Highbridge, where once a high-arched bridge, completed in 1736, crossed the Spean River on the military road linking the forts of William and Augustus. It was here in the 1950s that Calum I. Maclean, the folklore collector, recorded many songs and stories in Gaelic from John MacDonald of Highbridge, John the Bard.

Fear Tìr an Dris: *The Tacksman of the Land of Bramble Bushes*

One of John's tales was about Donald MacDonald, Fear Tìr an Dris, and the first shots of the 1745 Jacobite Rising. On learning that Prince Charles had raised his standard at Glenfinnan and had been joined by his chief, Donald gathered a few of his tenants and barred the Highbridge to a force of Royal Scots coming from Fort Augustus. By subterfuge, he gave the impression of there being a far larger force and the Government detachment surrendered. Donald then followed his Prince all the way to Derby and back. He was with the Jacobite army when it turned to savage the pursuing government forces at Falkirk in February 1746. During that Jacobite victory, Donald ran up to a party of Argyllshire militia, mistakenly assuming that these plaided Highlanders were part of the Prince's army. Captured, he was subsequently hanged in

Carlisle, under English jurisdiction. On the scaffold, Donald reaffirmed that he was neither a rebel nor a Catholic. To him, the Stewart heirs of James the VII of Scotland, II of England, were still rightful monarchs and he was one who professed the Reformed form of worship, as most Highlanders did, but accepted the rule of bishops. In other words, he was Episcopalian. In his novel *Waverley*, Sir Walter Scott's portrayal of the bravery of the defiant Highlanders at the Carlisle gallows is said to draw heavily on the story of Donald of Tìr an Dris.

The newer bridge over the river Garry is further north and to the east. Spean Bridge's Gaelic name is Drochaid Aonachain ('bridge at the marketplace'), referring to the fact that major road junctions often served as important meeting points where business was transacted.

The road from Spean Bridge heading east to Dalwhinnie passes through the area of northeast Lochaber that is now largely known for the Creag Meagaidh National Nature Reserve in the Monadhliath Mountains. The reserve extends from the shoreline of Loch Laggan to the high summits of the hills that form the whaleback ridge surrounding the great crater of Coire Ardair. The summit of Creag Meagaidh ('rock of the boggy place') is the highest at 1130m. The upland area was designated as a Site of Special Scientific Interest in 1964 and extended in 1983 to cover just under 4,000 hectares. The earliest historical records for Creag Meagaidh are from the 17th century when the area was farmed by tenants who grew crops on the lower slopes and grazed cattle on the higher ground during the summer.

Blàr a' Mhaoil Ruaidh: *The Battle of Mulroy*

Immediately east of Spean Bridge and just before Roybridge, is Maol Ruadh (Mulroy, 'red lump'). On 4th August 1688, 500 MacIntoshes along with a similar number of MacKenzies, drawn from the government militia garrison in Inverness, were defeated at Mulroy by around 200 MacDonalds of Keppoch and 500 Camerons and MacMartins. At issue was a stretch of land here at A' Cheapach (Keppoch, 'the tillage land') claimed by Lachlan, the MacIntosh clan chief. The law upheld his claim but the MacDonalds of Keppoch held it by virtue of long occupancy, occasioning a feud of nigh on 300 years duration. Leading the Keppoch clan was Coll MacDonald, who had been studying at

St Andrews University when he succeeded his father as chieftain six years earlier.

When the MacIntoshes crossed the River Roy, they found their opponents holding the higher ground on the slopes of Mulroy. Coll executed a classic Highland Charge down the slope and routed the MacIntoshes. Among the prisoners captured was Lachlan, the MacIntosh chief, who was forced into a written agreement regarding the tenancy of Keppoch. While the Battle of Mulroy has been described as Scotland's last inter-clan battle, some have argued that the involvement of government militia means that the last purely clan battle was at Altimarlach near Wick, fought in 1680 between Argyllshire men and Sinclairs.

A modern account of the engagement recounts that MacIntosh's standard-bearer is said to have leapt across the River Roy at a spot where his enemies did not dare attempt to follow. However, Gaelic oral tradition recorded in the 1950s has an account in which the agility of the fugitives is of less consequence than the ownership of the pursuing dogs. The notes on this tale, recorded in 1951 by Calum I. MacLean from Allan MacDonald in nearby Roy Bridge, tell us that:

> Three or four men ran away – MacIntosh asked whose men they were. Keppoch replied that the dogs were his, whoever the men belonged to. The men were killed. There is a leap, Leum an Tòisich, where two MacIntoshes jumped … MacIntosh was loyal to the King … He asked the King for Keppoch, and the land was given to him. MacDonald said, "We got it with swords, but you got it with a pretty mouth."

Iain Camshron à Coire Choille: *John Cameron of Corrychoille*

Shortly a side road to the right leads to Coire Choille (Corrychoille, 'wood corrie'), the home of John Cameron or 'Corrie', the most famous drover of all. Dealing in livestock was a mainstay of the Highland economy particularly during the 19th century, with cattle being brought to markets in Lowland Scotland to be sold to dealers for onward transmission to the cities of the South. It was a big, risky business. At two of the three Falkirk trysts, or markets, in September and October 1827, a total of 130,000 cattle and 200,000 sheep changed hands. Corrie declared that he had stood at all three Falkirk trysts for 50 years.

Tales about Corrie's prowess as a dealer, as a man of integrity and of independent spirit spread all over the Highlands. He was a folk hero of the Gaels; one of their own who had prospered and could outwit any Lowlander. He was once asked whether he was a greater man than even the Duke of Wellington.

> "Hoot, toot!" replied Corrie, "that's too much, too much by far, by far."
>
> "Not a bit," continued the other, "do you think the Iron Duke could do as well as you?"

Corriechoillie eventually answered, "The Duke, no doubt, he was a clever man; very, very clever; but I'm not so sure, after all, if he could manage twenty thousand sheep, besides black cattle, that could not understand one word he said, Gaelic or English, and bring every hoof of them to Falkirk Tryst! I doubt it, I doubt it."

Corriechoillie reputedly died in the saddle in 1856 and was buried in the graveyard at Cille Choirill, near Roy Bridge.

Ailean nan Creach: *Alan of the Forays*

High above the road to the east stands Cille Choirill (St. Kerril's Church). Tradition has it that the church came to be built by Ailean, considered the 12th chief of the Camerons, who is known to have been appointed in 1472 as Keeper of Caisteal an t-Stròim (Stromeferry, 'castle of the current'), then a MacDonald stronghold in Lochcarron. His nickname, Ailean nan Creach ('Alan of the forays'), was a result of his many raids and skirmishes; he is said to have:

> made 32 expeditions into his enemy's country for the thirty-two years he lived, and three more, for the three-fourths of a year that he was in his mother's womb.

In his ultimate raid, around 1480, upon MacIntosh lands, Alan perished. However, it was said that towards the end of his life, Ailean felt remorse for his many black deeds, and sought penance. He consulted one of a trio of celebrated witches, Gormshuil Mhòr na Mòighe ('big blue-eye from Moy'). Gormshuil and her companions are recorded in the saying:

> Luideag is Doideag, is Corrag nighean Iain Bhàin;
> Cas a' Mhogain riabhaich à Gleann Comhann;
> is Gormshuil Mhòr bhàrr na Màighe.
>
> *Raggie and Frizzle, and Fair John's daughter Finger;*
> *Brindled Hogganfoot from Glencoe,*
> *and Big Blue-eye from Moy.*

Her advice was that he should seek divination by means of the Taghairm, a rite that has a range of interpretations including 'calling', 'invoking', 'petitioning' and 'conjuring'. It was said to be the most effective means of raising the Devil and getting unlawful wishes gratified. It was described as "giving supper to the devil" and consisted of roasting cats alive, one after another, for some days, without tasting food. If duly sustained, it summoned a legion of demons in the guise of black cats with their master at their head. Alan followed the witch's instructions and proceeded to roast the cats. The screeching of the tortured felines soon attracted other cats and one tradition has it that as the house began to fill with demons, Alan's companion cried out but got the resolute reply:

> Ge b' e chì no chluinneas tu, cùm an cat mun cuairt.
>
> *Whatever you see or hear, keep the cat turning.*

Finally, a gigantic one-eyed black cat called Cam Dubh, said to be the king of the tribe, appeared and warned him that unless he released the tortured animal, he would be torn to pieces. Alan agreed to release his victim on condition that the king would tell him the best means of atoning for his past misdeeds.

> "You must," said the King, "build seven churches, one for each of your seven great forays."

In addition to Cill Choireil, in fulfilment of his contract with the King of the Cats, Alan is said to have built churches at Kilmallie, Kildonan, Kilchoan in Knoydart, Arisaig, Morvern and Kilkillen at Loch Laggan. However, he was defiant to the last, and not one of his churches had a roof.

The land to the east was once MacPherson country. In the Jacobite rising of 1745, the then chief was Ewen MacPherson of Cluny. Known as Cluny MacPherson, he was a leading supporter of Prince Charles. After Culloden, his fine, new house was torched, his father dying of a broken heart amidst its ashes and Cluny went into hiding, spending the next nine years protected by his kinsman. A government report stated that:

> he haunts the houses of his kindred and his wife's in the day time, and he has proper places of retirement in the night time, to which he repairs by turns, according to the danger he ...[fears]... he's in, from the different motions of the troops.

The most famous of his many hiding places was a small cave on Ben Alder, known as 'The Cage'. Eventually, he escaped to France, lived in some poverty in Dunkirk and died there on 30 January 1764. He was the uncle of the poet James 'Ossian' Macpherson.

The Cluny estates were then managed on behalf of the Crown by the Commissioners for Forfeited Estates. The Commission began the process of evicting the tenants and consolidating the holdings into a single sheep farm, and, by 1790, there were around 20,000 sheep in the parish of Laggan alone.

Seumas is Anna Grannd: *James and Anne Grant*

The church at Lagan Choinnich (Laggan, 'St. Kenneth's hollow') was built five years before 1779 when the military chaplain James Grant became minister. The parish then extended for about 60 kilometres from northeast to southwest and was 30 kilometres in breadth at its widest, although the bulk of the population lived in a corridor of 32 kilometres long and five wide. The population in 1790 was 1,512. Then there were only two heritors or major landowners, the Duke of Gordon and Colonel Duncan MacPherson, 'Cluny' MacPherson's son. Grant noted that there were no shoemakers in the district, the people making their own shoes, but there were three or four brogue makers, three house carpenters, seven tailors, one blacksmith, one mason with two apprentices and five or six weavers.

James Grant married Anne MacVicar in May 1779. She learnt Gaelic and was able to speak with the people and also to translate a few of their songs. On his death in 1801, she was left to bring up eight children, reluctantly moving to near Stirling in June 1803. To make ends meet, she published her reminiscences in 1806, under the title of *Letters from the Mountains.* The book was a success. In later life, she wrote:

> When I first went to the Highlands, and, from not knowing the language, could not taste the charms of their poetry, the sentiments of their music, or the delights of manners more courteous, and conversation more intelligent, than are anywhere else to be met with among rustics. When first I wandered untaught and forlorn amid the desolation of brown heaths and dusky mountains, I was at times charmed with particular scenes, but the general effect was as much lost on me as on these tourists: I was like the ignorant maid who tried her master's violin all over, and could never find where the tune lay.

'Mrs Grant of Lagan's Strathspey', a violin tune in her honour, is contained in Gow's *Repository of the Dance Music of Scotland,* Part 4.

Calum 'Pìobaire' Mac a' Phearsain: *Calum 'Piper' MacPherson*

Calum 'Pìobaire' Mac a' Phearsain, one of the legendary figures in the piping tradition, was born in Raasay in 1824. His father, Angus, had been trained by the MacCrimmons in Skye and he passed these traditions to his son who succeeded his father as piper at Cluny Castle.

His patron was Eòghan Mac a' Phearsain (Ewan MacPherson), the 20th chief from 1817, and always known as Seann Chluainidh ('Old Cluny'). Calum's home at Cataig (Catlodge, 'wild cat place') became a school for teaching pìobaireachd and he taught his own five sons and many of the young men of Badenoch. He used both staff notation and canntaireachd ('chanting') to teach.

In the canntairached method of instruction, the teacher sings or hums the tune to the pupil, generally using specific syllables which signify the sounds to be produced by the bagpipe. Calum Pìobaire seems to have been a particularly exacting tutor, insisting on pupils practising up to twelve hours a day, but his efforts produced some of the finest pipers of their day. He himself won many prizes, including Bonn Òir Cruinneachadh Earra-Ghàidheal (Argyllshire Gathering Gold Medal) in 1876 and, ten years later, he carried off the first prize in a major three-day piping competition in Edinburgh, though he was then over 60 years old. By Catlodge stands the 1960 memorial to Calum Pìobaire erected by Comann Ghlaschu Bhàideanach (Glasgow Badenoch Association).

Below the road westwards from Spean Bridge is the church of Cill mo Naomhaig (Kilmonivaig, 'St. Naomhag's Church'). Now regarded as an important location in recalling the events described in Diana Gabaldon's *Outlander* series, Kilmonivaig's dedication recalls the saint Naomhag ('little sainted one'), an Abbot of Lismore who established a church near here.

Eòghan MacLachlainn: *Ewen MacLachlan*

The current church was built in 1812 when Dr Thomas Ross was parish minister. Ross is credited with recognising the signs of brilliance in the young Eòghan MacLachlainn (Ewen MacLachlan) (1775-1822) and encouraging him in his studies. MacLachlan, though born into an impoverished family above Kinlochleven, was educated at Aberdeen University. He was Assistant Librarian to Kings College, Aberdeen from 1800-1818 and headmaster of Aberdeen Grammar School from 1810-1822. He translated the first eight books of Homer's *Iliad* into Gaelic and also composed and published his own *Gaelic Attempts in Verse* (1807) and contributed greatly to the 1828 Gaelic-English Dictionary. One of his best-loved compositions is 'Ealaidh Ghaoil' ('Love Song'):

Gur gile mo leannan nan eal' air an t-snàmh,
Na cobhar na tuinne 's e tilleadh gu tràigh,
Na 'm blàth-bhainne buaile 's a' chuach leis fo bhàrr,
No sneachd nan gleann dosrach ga fhroiseadh mun bhlàr.

Fairer is my beloved than the swimming swan, the foam on waves returning to shore, warm creamy meadow milk in a bowl, or snow falling in the leafy glens.

However, if MacLachlan were to be remembered for only one work then it should be his translation into conventional orthographic Gaelic of the 16th-century manuscript of the *Book of the Dean of Lismore*. Its Fortingall writers had written their late medieval Gaelic using the standard Scots orthographic conventions of the day. The task was fiendishly difficult and, had it not been for MacLachlan's ability and knowledge, the text might yet defy scholars.

On the breast of the hill, to the west of the road stands the Commando Memorial, a sculpture of three soldiers by Scott Sutherland. It commemorates the men who trained in the landscape west of the monument in order to be tough enough to undertake operations behind enemy lines during the Second World War. In the adjacent Garden of Remembrance, families have scattered ashes and left tributes to loved ones who lost their lives serving in Commando units in more recent conflicts.

The road to the west here is signposted to Achadh na Cairidh (Achnacarry, 'field of the fish-trap') where New Achnacarry Castle stands, the Commando headquarters in World War II and still the seat of the chief of the Camerons. It is said that the original name of the place was Achadh nan Crò ('field of the cattle-folds'), kept well-stocked with stolen cattle which the MacMillans and the MacPhees rounded up for the Cameron family. The following rhyme about the local MacMillans seems to suggest their thieving habits:

Tha Maolanaich ann an Airceig,
Bu mhath aig slaodadh na creich' iad.
Fhad's a mhaireas nì aig Cataich,
Cha bhi ac' ach leum air.

In Arkaig are MacMillans,
expert at cattle raiding.
While Sutherland has any cattle
they will raid them.

And again:

> MacGhilleMhaoil à Loch Abar nan craobh,
> Ghoideadh e caor' air aghaidh bhearraidhean.
>
> *MacMillan from Lochaber of the trees,*
> *would steal a sheep on the brow of precipices.*

The fighting prowess of Gaelic Highlanders was appropriated by the state. From the War of the Spanish Succession (1757-63) until the Battle of Waterloo in 1815, some 50,000 Gaelic-speaking Highlanders served in British marching regiments. This was a disproportionate number of the available young men in a community which never exceeded more than 350,000. Often regarded as "the enemy within," they were undoubtedly cannon fodder. Battlefield casualties during this period fell most heavily on Highlanders, to an estimated 15% of their number. The proportion of English casualties was only a third of that.

The symbol of the kilted Highland soldier came to represent the military might of the British Empire in the 19th century. Highlanders were described as "a warlike, intrepid, hardy mountain race" and some commentators suggest that the association of hardiness with mountaineers perhaps subconsciously prompted the War Office to send the commandos to train in the mountains around Achnacarry.

Similarly, the author Alisdair Alpin MacGregor, writing in 1949, felt that:

> the record of the Western Isles for courage in war-time is well known

but resulting from:

> … as with most native races, an insensibility to those loftier feelings … found in the more civilised members of human society – an insensibility bred of primitive belief and environment renders them courageous and callous in face of danger.

MacGregor's views were echoed in 1961 by Campbell Nairne in his book *The Trossachs* where he reveals to us that:

> [b]eneath an appearance of impassivity the Highland Celt is in fact much more emotional than the Anglo-Saxon; more easily elated and more easily cast down. Traditionally, he attacks obstacles with tremendous dash, but if they do not yield at the first onset he can rarely be persuaded to make a second attempt. The Anglo-Saxon, and the Englishman in particular, never seems to know when he is beaten; that is one of the secrets of his strength. But the Gael does know, and if he fights on it is with the courage of despair.

Thus, that bravery was regarded as abnormal, having to be harnessed and appropriately channelled. But once they had taken the 'King's Shilling', as the recruiting bounty was referred to, the strong cohesion of a language community and the kinship of clansmen led to high levels of *esprit de corps* and acts of undoubted bravery. Ultimately, these notions created a logic in the later 19th century that caused the Department of War to order all Scots, regardless of language and cultural affiliation, to don the kilt, a garb, according to one commentator:

> hitherto regarded by many as an outward symbol of the dirty, feared and despised Gaelic Highlander.

Blàr na Lèana: *The Battle of the Shirts*

Twenty kilometres north of the Commando Memorial, on the eastern shore of Loch Lochy, is the site of a clan fight now known as the Battle of the Shirts. In 1544, the Earl of Huntly, as the Crown's authority, attempted to deal with Iain Mùideartach (John of Moidart), *de facto* chief of the Clanranald sept of MacDonalds. The legal heir, Raghnall Gallda ('foreign Ronald') was the son of a Fraser mother; in feud with the Frasers, John of Moidart had raided their lands in Abertarf and Stratherrick. Hugh, the Fraser chief and Ronald's uncle was thus a leading member of the force that Huntly assembled to punish the MacDonalds. Huntly led his forces westward into Clanranald territory but achieved little and so withdrew to his Gordon homeland. The Frasers headed north and were ambushed at Blàr na Lèana on the narrow isthmus between the head of Loch Lochy and the southern shores of Loch Oich.

The heavily outnumbered Frasers had no means of escape. The Fraser chief, his heir and almost all his men fell under a hail of arrows, cut to pieces by double-handed broadswords. An almost universally accepted assertion tells us that:

> Clan tradition of the clans involved and all histories written since the period have stated that the name was derived from the fact that the day was so hot that both sides threw off their chainmail hauberks and Plaids, fighting in their shirts.

Other sources have even claimed that the men took an intermission to cool off with a dip in the waters of the loch. That would have been some hike from the site identified on the 1876 Ordnance Survey map that was then about half a mile away and would have been a far greater distance in the 16th century since the Caledonian Canal raised the level of Loch Lochy by nearly four metres to reduce the depth of the cutting between Loch Oich and Loch Lochy. As a near contemporary English description shows, the clans' champions, and particularly the well-armed Frasers, would mostly yet be wearing chain-mail tunic – a habergeon with lighter clansmen in a heavily padded surcoat, an aketon. No matter how hot the warrior was, the laborious effort of divesting himself of the mail and the aketon amid hand-to-hand combat would have been suicidal. A century later the primary virtue of the then commonly worn fèileadh mòr 'belted plaid', was that it could be cast off with ease, as amply demonstrated by such a tactic at the battle of Kilsyth on 15th August 1645. *The Chronicles of the Frasers,* written around this time and accentuating the carnage, thus claimed that towards the end:

> most fought in their shirts, running at each other like mastives.

As so often with the treatment of Gaelic, much is either lost in translation or bowdlerised. As one would expect, the low-lying ground between the two lochs was marshy and it was that feature that gave the place its name, Blàr na Lèana ('field of the swampy meadow'). However, it is now popularly known as Blàr na Lèine ('field of the shirt'). Lèine ('a shirt') sounds a little like lèana ('a field'). The shirts and the impromptu bathing are inventions.

Among the fallen was the legitimate Clanranald heir, Ronald, and the extinction of the direct line led to very public ructions over the claims to that chieftainship nearly 300 years later.

Tobar nan Ceann: *The Well of the Seven Heads*

Immediately beyond the swing bridge over the Caledonian Canal, on the shores of Loch Oich, is Tobar nan Ceann ('well of the heads'). Crowning the well is an obelisk capped by an effigy of seven heads and a protruding dirk or dagger. As the inscription in Gaelic, Latin, French and English explains, the monument was commissioned in 1815 by Alasdair MacDonell, or as he styled himself 'Ranaldson', 15th chief of the Glengarry sept of Clan Donald.

It commemorates the washing of seven heads in this well in 1663. Alasdair Mòr, chief of the Keppoch sept, and his brother Raonall Òg, on their return from their education in Rome, quarrelled with their uncle, Alasdair Buidhe ('yellow' here signifying 'noble'). Evidently, their uncle wanted the chiefship, and, under the pretext of personal injury, decided to get rid of the brothers. The assassination was carried out by two of his sons, Ailean Dearg ('red Alan') and Dòmhnull Gorm ('blue-black Donald'), aided by Alasdair of Inverlair and his six sons. Alasdair Buidhe duly succeeded the murdered chief.

Iain Lom, John MacDonald, the Keppoch Bard, exhorted his fellow MacDonalds to avenge the death of their young chief but to no avail. He then took his entreaties to Sir James MacDonald of Sleat. This resulted in a commission issued by the Privy Council listing persons to be put to the sword. Sir James's half-brother in North Uist, Gilleasbaig Ruadh MacDhòmhnaill ('red Archibald MacDonald'), nicknamed An Ciaran Mabach ('the sallow stutterer'), was instructed to bring several chosen men to the mainland. In September 1665, the Uist men along with Iain Lom took their revenge and killed Alasdair of Inverlair and his six sons. On their way to Invergarry to present the heads to MacDonell of Glengarry, they are said to have washed them in a well by Loch Oich that has since been called The Well of the Seven Heads. These events did take place but, since the motif of washing heads in wells exists elsewhere in such tales, the addition of the well for hygienic purposes is perhaps a little embellishment. Nor is it certain that the number of skulls was seven, itself a potent number. Iain Lom's song 'Murt na Ceapaich'

('The Keppoch Murder') which helped persuade the MacDonalds to bring Alasdair and his sons to justice, describes the murder scene:

B' iad mo ghràdh na cuirp chùbhraidh
Anns 'm bu dlùth cur nan sgian
'S iad 'nan sineadh air ùrlar
'N seòmar ùir gan cur sios,
Fo chosaibh Shìol Dùghaill
Luchd spùilleadh nan cliabh;
Dh'fhàg àlach nam biodag
Mar sgàile ruidil ur bian.

The fragrant bodies beloved by me, close packed with stab wounds, were stretched out on the ground, laid low in an earthen chamber beneath the feet of the Seed of Dougal, plunderers of breasts; the blows of daggers left their skin with the appearance of a sieve.

Alasdair Buidhe, unpunished, held on to the chieftainship.

Creag an Fhithich: *Raven's Rock*

Iain Lom had only to travel a couple of kilometres north with his evidence as the seat of the Chiefs of the MacDonells of Glengarry was on Creag an Fhithich ('raven's rock'), overlooking Loch Oich. Its situation was a strategic one at a time when movement was mostly by water. The ruins of this castle, most likely dated to between 1610-1640, and its vicissitudes, though dramatic, were not dissimilar to many other Highland castles. Major enhancements were barely completed when in 1645 it was damaged by Covenanters. In 1654, it was burnt and partially dismantled by General Monk, Commander of the Commonwealth Army in Scotland. Subsequently restored, the Invergarry lands were declared forfeit in 1690 following the first Jacobite Rising and the castle was occupied by Government troops. During the 1715 Rising, Glengarry regained possession, only to see the castle re-occupied by Government forces and then burned down. It was restored again at the end of the 1720s, this time by Thomas Rawlinson, the Quaker manager of the Iron Works. On the failure of that venture around 1736, Glengarry regained the castle as his home, only to have it finally destroyed after the 1745 Rising. In 1838, the Glengarry portion of the estate was sold to the Marquis of Huntly, ending MacDonell possession.

The last Glengarry chief to reside partly in the area was Alexander 'Ranaldson' MacDonell of Glengarry. His fame is largely due to Henry Raeburn's full-length portrait of 1812 that now hangs in the Scottish National Gallery in Edinburgh. Raeburn portrays him in the style that Alasdair wished, clothed in full Highland dress with all the accoutrements of a chief and a haughty demeanour. A flamboyant figure, he maintained a large 'tail' – a retinue of servants to attend to his every whim. His lavish lifestyle was well in excess of the rents and sales of land, some sold at an exorbitant price to the Caledonian Canal Company, making builder Thomas Telford's life a misery. Accounts of the last resident chief paint a picture of a high-handed, obstructive and pilfering bully. His fellow Gaelic speakers seem to have agreed since his epithets were either fiadhaich ('wild') or garbh ('rough'), suggesting a person who was a bit of a bruiser. Sir Walter Scott, who knew him, was sometimes irritated by his arrogance but described him as a picaresque soul. It is thought that Glengarry was the model for Scott's portrayal of Fergus, the proud, mercurial chief of Clan MacIvor in his novel *Waverley*. He certainly lived up to the characterisation of his clan in the saying:

> Spagadagliog Chlann Dòmhnaill is leòm Leathanaich.
>
> *MacDonald swagger and MacLean pretence.*

The debts MacDonell bequeathed his heirs forced them to sell up and leave Glengarry. There is some irony in the fact that this had been the treatment he meted out to his own tenantry. He had a habit of forcing sons to enlist in the army and, once they were fighting and dying elsewhere, evicting their parents.

His ancestors seem to have been more in the mould of the traditional Highland chief. Sìleas na Ceapaich in her lament for Alasdair Dubh, 11th Chief of Glengarry, compares him to a great oak tree:

Bu tu 'n t-iubhar thar gach coillidh,
Bu tu 'n darach daingeann làidir,
Bu tu 'n cuileann,'s bu tu 'n droigheann,
Bu tu 'n t-abhall molach blàthmhor;
Cha robh do dhàimh ris a' chritheann
Cha robh do dhligheadh ris an fheàrna;
Cha robh do bheag annad den leamhan;
Bu tu leannan nam ban àlainn.

You were the yew above every forest, you were the strong steadfast oak, you were the holly and the black thorn, you were the apple tree, rough-barked and many-flowered. You had no kinship with the aspen, owed no bonds to the alder; there was none of the lime tree in you; you were the darling of beautiful women.

Affection for woodlands is an ancient Gaelic tradition shown by the ethnonym 'Goídil', now 'Gàidheal', that they use for themselves: a borrowing from their early Brythonic neighbours meaning something like 'forest-people' or 'wildmen'.

In 1860, Edward 'Bear' Ellice (1781-1863) added the Glengarry portion of the estate to his Glenquoich holding and there he entertained up to a thousand guests a year. Ellice, inter alia, was a co-owner of eight sugar estates in Grenada, British Guiana, Tobago and Antigua. In the 1830s, the British government emancipated the slaves, and Ellice received compensation to the tune of about £35,000 for the liberation of over 300 slaves.

Am Fèileadh Beag: *The Little Kilt*

Immediately below the caissons of the newer bridge over the river Garry are the remains of a furnace belonging to Rawlinson's Iron Works. Along with the York Building Company, established in Bonawe in Argyll, also in the early 1720s, their entrepreneurial business model was to exploit the abundant timber resources of the area, producing charcoal from coppiced timber as fuel to smelt iron ore shipped to the furnaces. Although the Bonawe operation lasted for many decades, Invergarry survived a mere seven years. But because the operation of the Invergarry iron furnace was the supposed reason for the invention of the little kilt, a story of black propaganda is attached to this place.

In the period leading up to the devolution referendum in Scotland in 1979, Hugh Trevor-Roper, Regius Professor of Modern History at Oxford University, launched a media campaign to undermine support for the government's proposals. As part of that, he wrote a conference paper claiming, amongst other things, that the little kilt had been invented by the manager of the Invergarry furnace. The paper, subsequently published in 1983 in *The Invention of Tradition*, is widely regarded as conclusively demonstrating that Highland cultural attributes such as the kilt were largely the invention of Sir Walter Scott and others for the King's visit to Edinburgh in 1822. According to one academic, this theory of invented tradition has achieved almost iconic status and Trevor-Roper's paper is cited as a noted exemplar. Unfortunately, to quote another academic, the paper is "blotted with inaccuracy". It was a deliberate piece of black propaganda, designed to suggest that Scottish culture was bogus. His plan worked. The Devolution Bill was defeated, the Labour government fell and its author was ennobled by a triumphant Margaret Thatcher.

The fiction still has wide currency. In November 2019, the national body responsible for both built and intangible heritage promoted a song and light show at Edinburgh Castle – 'The Castle of Light'. Its script stated:

> The visit [of King George IV to Edinburgh in 1822] was stage-managed by Walter Scott with much of what we think of today as Highland Dress and Scottish ceremonial tradition invented for the occasion.

Despite the agency being advised about the canard, it continues to be promoted.

The 80-kilometre road west to Kyle starts from Invergarry and heads towards the coast, past five different lochs. The first three are freshwater – Loch Garry, Loch Loyne and Loch Cluanie – while the latter two are sea lochs – Loch Duich and Loch Alsh. Loch Garry is fed by waters from Loch Quoich upstream on the River Garry. Both lochs have been dammed for the production of hydroelectricity, the scheme being completed in 1962. As we saw, Glen Garry used to be the home of the Clan MacDonell of Glengarry, but the population has been reduced to a handful of sporting estates. The main activities now are fly-fishing, shooting and forestry, with little tourism apart from hill-walking.

The turning signposted An Tom Donn (Tomdoun, 'brown mound') leads to Gleann Chuaich (Glen Quoich, 'glen of the quaich/hollow') and thence to the sea at Ceann Loch Shùirn (Kinlochhourn, 'head of the loch of the berry gap'). It is possibly a former resident, a MacIntosh from Luinne in Knoydart, who is remembered in the 18th-century love song, 'Iain Ghlinne Cuaich' ('Ian of Glen Quoich'). This song of unrequited love may have been composed by a woman from the area of Fortingall in Perthshire, whose family had come to Lochaber about 1689. She laments the fact that he has forsaken her and says that she has never loved another man:

> Ach Iain, a ghaoil, cuime leig thu mi faoin air chùl,
> Gun chuimhn' air a' ghaol a bh' againn araon air tùs.
> Cha tug mise mo spèis do dh' fhear eil' tha fon ghrèin
>   ach thu,
> 'S cha tabhair nad dhèidh gus an càirear mi fhèin san ùir.

> *But John, my dear, why did you leave me lonely, forgetting the love that we shared at first? I didn't give my affection to another man in the world, and I won't again till I'm put in the ground.*

The lands to the north and west were extensively cleared of people. At the west end of the vastly expanded loch, created by the damming of the glen, is Cluainidh (Cluanie, 'meadow place'), and its inn which was built in 1787. It was a change-house on the military road to Bernera Barracks in Glenelg and it became a staging post for cattle drovers passing through from Glen Shiel. Across the loch is Cluanie Lodge, a Victorian hunting lodge that services hunters on the Glenquoich Estate. This deer forest is one of the oldest in Scotland and was part of the former lands of the MacKenzies of Kintail. With the death of Francis Humbertson MacKenzie in 1815, most of the Seaforth estates, including Kintail, were sold. Later in the 19th century, the people of Kintail were subjected to an estate regime enabled by an inherited Russian fortune, a wholly different breed of proprietor from the relatively benevolent MacKenzies.

Walter W. Winans, heir to the fortune made by his American father in Czarist Russian railways, held hunting and shooting rights over some 1,000 hectares in Srath Farair (Strathfarrar, 'strath of the River Farar', possibly meaning 'flowing'), Gleann Canaich (Glen Cannich, meaning uncertain) and Gleann Afraig (Glen Affric, meaning uncertain). His domain stretched from Ceann a' Chnuic in Gleann Moireasdan (Glen Moriston, meaning uncertain) to Cill Fhaolain (Killilan, 'Church of St. Fillan') in the north, and from Loch Dubhthaich (Loch Duich, 'St. Duthac's Loch') in the west to within ten miles of A' Mhanachainn (Beauly, 'the Monastery') in the east. All these areas had been cleared of people, creating a deer forest with harsh injunctions against the keeping of stock by the few who remained.

Depopulation had a profound impact on these localities. Writing in 1878, a Mr. Chisholm said:

> In Glen Cannich even within my own recollection, there were a number of people comfortably located. Of the descendants of Glen Cannich men, there lived in my own time one Bishop and fifteen priests; three colonels, one major, three captains, three lieutenants and seven ensigns. Such was the class of men who had their early education in the glen or in Strathglass, and now there are eight shepherds, seven gamekeepers and one farmer in Glen Cannich.

Today there are even fewer people living in this glen.

Another of the series of change-houses on the old military road at Shiel Bridge, further west from Cluanie, closed in 1907 so that, according to one source:

> the deer might not be disturbed by anyone taking shelter for the night.

Such was Winans's concern for his precious deer that, in 1884, he prosecuted a local crofter, Murdoch Macrae, for grazing his pet lamb on estate land. The failure of Winans's prosecution established the right to roam, a key element in opening some of the British landscape to the public.

Further to the west again, by a bridge over the river Shiel, is the site of the Battle of Glen Shiel, fought here for three hours on the 10th of June 1719. This was the penultimate effort of the Stuarts to regain their throne, this time with the aid of the Spaniards. It ended in failure and also caused the destruction of Caisteal Eilean Donnain ('the castle of Donan's isle').

This is the route to Skye that Samuel Johnson and James Boswell took in 1773. Having left Inverness on the 30th of August, by the afternoon of the 1st of September they were at Achadh nan Seileach (Achnashellach, 'field of the willows'). No one knows how many people lived in Achadh nan Seileach in 1773 but "considerable numbers" was Johnson's description of the crowd that surrounded them. Boswell wrote later:

> At Auchnasheal we sat down … and they brought us out two wooden dishes of milk which we tasted. One of them was frothed like a syllabub.

Achnashellach was cleared of its people. Here, at the ruins of his forebear's home, the Canadian author Hugh Maclennan, writing of "such sweeps of emptiness" in *The Scotsman's Return* (1961), said:

> above the sixtieth parallel in Canada, you feel that nobody but God has ever been there before you, but in a deserted Highland glen, you feel that everyone who ever mattered is dead and gone.

The hills about here, now collectively lumped together by the climbing fraternity as 'The Five Sisters of Kintail' (all have their own individual names) are the setting of 'Chan e dìreadh na bruthaich' ('It's not the Climbing of the Brae'), a Kintail fugitive song:

> Chan e dìreadh na bruthaich a dh'fhàg mo shiubhal gun treòir,
> No teas ri là grèine nuair a dh'èireadh i oirnn.
> Laigh an sneachd seo air m' fheusaig is cha lèir dhomh mo bhròg.
>
> 'S gann is lèir dhomh nì 's fhaisge ceann a' bhata nam dhòrn.
> 'S e mo thaigh mòr na creagan, 's e mo dhaingeann gach fròg:
> 'S e mo thubhailte m' osan, 's e mo chopan mo bhròg.

Ged a cheannaichinn am buideal chan fhaigh mi cuideachd nì òl.
'S ged a cheannaichinn seipean chan fhaigh mi creideas a' stòip.
'S ged a dh'fhàdainn an teine chì fear foille dheth ceò.

It's not climbing the brae that has weakened my step or a sunny day's heat when the sun's at its height: this snow has lain on my beard and I can't see my shoe.

I can barely see nearby things – the staff head in my fist; my great house is the rocks, my stronghold each cranny, my towel is my stocking, my cup is my shoe.

If I should buy a bottle, I'd find no one to share it, and if I bought a chopin, I'd not get credit for a stoup. If I should light a fire, I'd be betrayed by its smoke.

The song describes life as a fugitive. Its composer, Farquhar MacRae, was outlawed around 1615 for murdering Donald MacRae, MacKenzie of Kintail's factor. Apparently Donald went to Farquhar's house to demand the rent. But as Farquhar's wife had no money he took a cow and a copper kettle in lieu of money. Farquhar pursued him and killed him. He paid blood money to Donald's family but when a friend of the dead man upbraided him for the murder, Farquhar replied:

Ma mhurt mis' e, nach do dh' ith sibh fhèin e; gun d' fhuair 's gun do chosg iad an èirig!

If I murdered him, it was you who ate him; they got and spent the reparation money.

He took to the Kintail hills for seven years. According to custom, after this seven-year period, he could return home with no fear of punishment. He was reputed to be one of MacKenzie's best fighting men and this may have encouraged the chief, after some initial reluctance, to forgive him.

Caisteal Eilean Donnain: *Eilean Donan Castle*

On the shore of Loch Dubhthaich (Loch Duich, 'St. Duthach's Loch') is Eilean Donan Castle, originally, perhaps in the 13th century, a far larger castle entirely encompassing the small rocky island. The island may have housed a religious community dedicated to the memory of St. Donan. In 1331, when Randolph, the then Guardian of Scotland, paid a visit to the castle, its warden hung the heads of 50 victims from the castle walls as an act of zealous, retributive justice.

The locality is linked to Nigh' n Ìomhair, a deprecatory by-name for the adder. A lady called nighean Ìomhair ('Ivor's daughter'), wife of John MacKenzie, Constable of Eilean Donnain, was suspected of having poisoned, in about 1550, John Glassich of Gairloch to snuff out his claim to the Kintail estates. This act may possibly have given rise to the application of the name to the snake.

The Constable's keep, by then very much smaller, was destroyed in May 1719 by Royal Navy forces who took the castle and detonated kegs of Spanish gunpowder that had been placed there for safekeeping. The shattered ruin lay in that state until the 1930s. By 1932, Lieutenant Colonel John MacRae-Gilstrap, a British army officer, spent the equivalent in today's terms of £30 million of his wife's brewing fortune on its restoration. The castle was in part realised by Farquhar MacRae of Auchtertyre who claimed to have had:

> a dream in which he saw, in the most vivid detail, exactly the way the castle originally looked.

But one author expressed her unhappiness with the restoration in strong terms, saying:

> I was horrified and repelled by the ruined picture which obtruded itself on the outraged surroundings, the remains of the castle being in the throes of a rebuilding which must permanently disfigure the landscape.

Few now feel that, and the castle is perhaps the most photographed in Scotland.

Despite the fact that Eilean Donan Castle houses what purports to be his battered sword, there has been an almost complete erasure of local Gaelic bard Iain MacMhurchaidh (John MacRae) who enjoys the unenviable reputation of being one of America's first prisoners of war. MacRae had joined the Loyalist forces against the American revolutionaries and was captured by them. His poem 'Tha mi sgìth 'n fhògar seo' ('I am tired of this banishment'), composed in captivity, is of such quality that it returned to his homeland after the author's death in captivity:

Thoir mo shoraidh le caoimhneas,
Gu Tòrr Luinnsich nan smeòraichean.

Far an tric bha mi ma bhuideal
Mar ri cuideachda shòlasaich.

Chan b' e 'n dram a bha mi 'g iargain,
Ach na b' fhiach an cuid stòireannan.

Sìos is suas tro Ghleann Seile,
'S tric a leag mi damh cròiceach ann.

Gheibhte bric air an linne,
Fir gan sireadh is leòis aca.

Tha mi nis air mo dhìteadh
Ann am prìosan droch bheò-shlàinteach.

Bear my greetings with kindness to Torr Luinnsich of the thrushes where I often shared a bottle with a joyful company. It wasn't the dram I longed for but the worth of their stories. Up and down Glen Shiel, I often felled the antlered stag there. Salmon could be caught in the pool, men seeking them with lights. I am now condemned in an unhealthy prison.

A number of the villages and their inhabitants in the wider parish of Sgìre Chomhghain ('Comhghan's Parish') appear in the ditty:

Steàrnairean a' Chaoil, faoileagan Abhairnis,
Taighean dubha Rèaraig, pàlaisean Bhaile Mac Ara.
Diùranais an eòrna, clòbhair Ach nan Darach,
Druim Buidhe nan deargannan, Earbarsaig nan con clomhach.

Terns from Kyle, gulls from Avernish,
Black houses in Reraig, palaces in Balmacara,
Durinish of the barley, Drumbuie of the fleas,
Erbusaig of the scabby dogs.

The A87 road leaves the mainland at Caol Loch Aillse (Kyle of Lochalsh, 'strait of the foaming loch') and is carried over to Skye by the 1995 bridge. It is connected to Inverness by the Kyle of Lochalsh railway line, built in 1897 to enable the transport of thousands of barrels of salt herring. Industry of such scale did not survive much beyond the First World War.

Taobh Loch Nis: *Loch Ness-side*

The road from Invergarry east to Loch Ness continues alongside the second loch in the series of four lochs that make up the Caledonian Canal. Loch Obhaich (Oich, formerly named Abha, 'fresh water') is on the line of the original construction of the Great Communication: the network of military roads linking fortified points and the resurrected Roman-era model of General Wade following the 1715 Jacobite Rising. Paradoxically, the speed of movement allowed by these new roads worked well for the Jacobites. It was here that Prince Charles's small army turned south for its lightning march to Edinburgh in August 1745, evading the hesitant efforts of Sir John Cope, the government military commander of Scotland, to intercept it. The buoyant mood of the army as it sped along Wade's newly created road is perhaps best displayed by a contemporary song:

Nam bithinn fhèin am shia bliadhn' deug,
Nam bithinn fhèin mar b' àill leam;
Nam bithinn fhèin am shia bliadhn' deug,
Gum falbhainn fhèin le Teàrlach.

Luchd nam breacan, luchd nam breacan,
Luchd nam breacan sgàrlaid;
Luchd nam breacan ballach, uaine,
Dol mu thuath le Teàrlach.

If I were sixteen years old, if I were as I wish to be; if I were sixteen years old, I would go with Charlie.

People of the plaids, people of the plaids, people of the scarlet plaids; people of the green striped plaids going north with Charlie.

Fort Augustus at the foot of Loch Ness was named in honour of a son of its builder, King George II. The fort was originally known as Cille Chuimein (St. Cuimein's Church), since it was located near the site of a church dedicated to Cumin, the second abbot of the monastery of Iona. Part of the ramparts of the fort remain incorporated into what was, until fairly recently, Fort Augustus Abbey School.

The present-day route to Inverness follows the northern shore of Loch Ness. Immediately on leaving Fort Augustus and just offshore is a crannog, a man-made island, on which an Iron Age homestead was constructed. The name derives from crann ('tree trunk or length of timber'). This particular crannog now rejoices in the name Cherry Island although it is unlikely that its 17th-century resident, Ailean na Lèine Deirg ('Alan of the red shirt'), would have given that as his address. To him, it was Innis na Ceàrdaich ('island of the smiddy'). Alan seems to have been a freebooter rather than a blacksmith, but by the time he came to occupy the crannog local tradition regarded it as an ancient site used by a magical smith. How 'cherry' came into the picture is not related.

Dòmhnall Donn Bhoth Fhionndain: *Brown-haired Donald of Bohuntine*

The area immediately to the north on Loch Ness side seems to have been a regular haunt for men such as Alan and Dòmhnall Donn Bhoth Fhionndain ('brown-haired Donald of Bohuntine'). His place of origin means 'Fintan's

Hut' and is one of five remembered in a saying:

> Tha còig bothain an Loch Abar, tha còig gasgan ann am Bàideanach is còig còigean ann an Srath Èireann.
>
> *There are five huts in Lochaber, five gasgs (strip of land) in Badenoch and five còigs (fifth-divisions) in Strathearn.*

Donald was a renowned cattle reiver and poet, yet little concrete is known of him other than he was of the family of the tacksmen of Bohuntine, who were referred to as Sliochd an Taighe ('the family of the household') and as Sliochd na Ban-fhigich ('the family of the weaver-woman'). The poem 'Nighean Tighearna Ghrannd' ('The Laird of Grant's Daughter') composed by his girlfriend paints a picture of a good-looking, well-dressed man:

> Tha do phearsa cuimir dealbhach,
> 'S math thig èideadh dhut is armachd;
> Bu tu 'n curaidh treun, neo-chearbach
> 'S meanmnach anns an tuasaid.
>
> 'S math thig fèile dhut san fhasan
> Bonaid gorm is còta breacain,
> Osan geàrr is trì chur ghartan
> 'S glas lann air do chruachann.
>
> Chan eil òganach cho ainmeil
> Riut sa cheàrna seo de dh'Albainn:
> 'S mairg a dhùisgeadh suas gu feirg thu
> 'N àm nan arm a bhualadh.
>
> *Your form is shapely and handsome, well do dress and armour become you; you are the brave, efficient hero, courageous in the fight.*
>
> *You suit a fashionable kilt, a blue bonnet and a plaid coat, short hose and thrice plaited garters, a grey sword on your hip.*

There is no youth as famous as you in this part of Scotland; pity anyone who incurs your wrath at the time of the clash of arms.

Around 1690, Donald fell in love with Mary Grant but her father, the Grant chief, disapproved. Donald was taking a risk as it was said of the Grants:

Cha bhigean air Granndach gus am faigh e an lite

A Grant is in a foul mood until he gets his porridge

Despite her father's opposition, Mary decided to elope with Donald who hid in a nearby cave until she could join him. Unfortunately, he was lured to a house where he was encouraged to drink to excess, and once asleep, he was disarmed and captured. He describes the incident in the following verses:

Mìle mallachd don òl,
'S mairg a dhèanadh dhe pòit;
'S e mo mhealladh gu mòr a fhuair mi.

Mìle marbhphaisg don dram,
Chuir an daorach nam cheann,
'N uair a ghlac iad san Àirde Tuath mi.

Mas d'fhuair mi bhith mach,
'S a bhith 'm armaibh gu ceart,
Bha rag mhèirlich nan cearc mun cuairt domh.

Bha trì fichead is triùir
Ga mo ruith feadh nan lùb,
Gus na bhuin iad mo lùs le luaths 'uam.

A thousand curses on drink, anyone in thrall to it is to be pitied; I have been greatly deceived.

A thousand curses on the dram, that caused intoxication in my head, when they captured me in the North.

Before I could get out and properly arm myself, the arrant hen thieves surrounded me.

There were sixty-three chasing me around the bends, till they exhausted me with their speed.

Calling the Grants 'hen thieves' is a choice insult. After lying in prison for some time, Donald was executed. Tradition has it that his sister Kate was present at his execution and, as his head was being severed from his body by the axe, his tongue uttered the words:

"A Cheit, tog an ceann!"

"Kate, lift the head!"

Uilebheist Loch Nis: *The Loch Ness Monster*

On the shores of Loch Ness is Druim na Drochaid (Drumnadrochit, 'ridge at the bridge'), the centre for the story of the Loch Ness Monster, perhaps the world's most famous water spirit. A guidebook states that:

> the first sighting of the Loch Ness monster was by St. Columba in 565 AD. The first modern sighting was in 1932 and scientific studies have not proved the existence of Nessie one way or the other!

Having such a saintly eyewitness might be considered by some as convincing evidence for the creature's existence. However, we need to consider the context. Its source is Adomnán, Columba's hagiographer, writing shortly after the saint's death and making a point about the power of the sign of the Christian cross to dispel malign spirits. He tells us that Columba had deliberately lured the monster to the surface by having a young monk swim in the water. The man-eating monster duly showed up for this toothsome morsel but was banished by the saint's use of the sign of the cross. This demonstration of the all-powerful might of the new religion's symbol happened in the river Ness and not in the loch. In the river, the spirit was a great goddess, Nessa. Was Adomnán having a sly joke and portraying Nessa as a horrible man-eating monster? Suffice it to say that she has now been set aside in the narrative by something akin to a plesiosaurus.

Undoubtedly people have seen unexplained features in the loch and, as late as 1932 and beyond, Gaelic-speaking locals would have been comfortable with the notion of a water spirit, regardless of its form. In a footnote, W. J. Watson in his book on Celtic place names recounts that when once asking a local resident, Pharlan MacPharlan, whether he had seen the water bull that inhabited Loch Katrine, he was told in all seriousness by Pharlan that:

"No, he had not seen the bull itself but he had seen its calf."

The dominant hill to the southwest of Drumnadrochit is Meall Fuar Mhonaidh (Mealfourvonie, 'lump of the cold moor'). Beside it is Lòn na Fola ('bloody meadow'), the site of a skirmish between MacDonalds and MacKenzies around 1600. In reprisal for the MacKenzies' seizure of Strome Castle in Wester Ross, the MacDonalds had raided the MacKenzie lands of Cill Chrìosd (Kilchrist, 'Christ church') in the Black Isle and burned the congregation inside the church while their piper marched around the outside, playing loudly to drown the sound of screaming. However, they and their leader, Ailean Dubh ('Black Alan' MacDonald of Lundie) were ambushed by the vengeful MacKenzies at Lòn na Fola. Alan, the only survivor according to one source:

> escaped naked, without clothes or arms by a leap he gave desperately over the most ill-favoured lynn (pool) which he nor any other man did never before or afterwards.

The place where Alan made his leap is known as Leum Ailean MhicRaonaill ('Alan MacRanald's leap'). Legal action taken by a Reverend John MacKenzie in 1622 does prove that the raid did take place, but the prodigious leap and the additional story of church burning belong to a tradition of many similar tales associated with historic events. A pipe tune bearing the name is still played.

To the west of the point where the river Ness issues from the loch is the estate of Dochfour. In 1833, slave owners were paid approximately £20 million in compensation for some 40,000 enslaved people freed in the colonies of the Caribbean, Mauritius and the Cape of Good Hope, i.e. £500 per head. This represented around 40% of the British Treasury's annual spending budget and has been calculated as equivalent to around £16.5bn in today's terms. Approximately half went to absentee landlords in the UK, with the largest total compensation sum being made to Prime Minister William Gladstone's father, who received £106,769 for losing his 2,508 slaves used across nine plantations. When the Baillies of Dochfour, by then Bristol merchants, with James Evan the city's pro-slavery MP, 'lost' their 2,500 slaves, the government paid them £110,000. That compensation would be worth over £13 million today. It allowed the family, like others, to buy land in the Highlands. Many later cleared their lands of people to make room for sheep. In 1839, Evan Baillie had architect William Robertson remodel Dochfour House as an ornate Italian villa.

Inbhir Nis: *Inverness*

Inbhir Nis (Inverness, 'estuary of the river of the Goddess Nessa') was the site of a strategic, royal castle guarding northern access into the Great Glen. There were struggles for control of this location for many centuries.

Inverness, the regional 'capital', has a population of almost 47,000 of whom 1,456 are Gaelic speakers. The city is home to both the Gaelic Society of Inverness and to Bòrd na Gàidhlig, the former a venerable society dedicated to the study and promotion of the language, while the latter is a government agency tasked with maintaining and developing the language. Bòrd na Gaidhlig was established with all-party consensus in the Scottish Parliament in 2005. The city is also home to Highlands and Islands Enterprise, the successor body to the Highlands and Islands Development Board, established by an Act of Parliament in 1965 for the social and economic well-being of the Highlands. The then Secretary of State for Scotland, Willie Ross, admitted that:

> the Highlander was on the nation's conscience.

Caibideil 6: *Chapter 6*

Na h-Eileanan Siar – Tuath: *The Western Isles – North*

To the west of the Highland Council's mainland area is an island archipelago of more than 50 substantial islands, in extent 2,178.98km^2, with the conjoined areas of Lewis and Harris being the largest island in Scotland. The distance from the Butt of Lewis to Barra Head is roughly 210 kilometres. According to the 2022 census, its fifteen inhabited islands had a total population of 26,200. The majority had some Gaelic skills (57.2%). This was far higher than the next highest council areas, Highland (8.1%) and Argyll and Bute (6.2%). In all other council areas less than 3% of people aged three and over had some Gaelic skills.

The name of the parliamentary constituency is now Na h-Eileanan an Iar (the Isles of the West), but these islands are also often called the Hebrides. The name 'Hebrides' originated in an Irish kindred named the Uì Ibdaig, descendants of one Oengus Ibdach (Angus the Hebridean). 'Ibdaig' is the presumed Gaelic form of what the Romans called *Hebudes,* which became, via scribal error, the Hebrides. The island chain is also called Innse Gall ('isles of the foreigners'), referring to the Norse who settled in the islands from the 9th century. Other names have been Na h-Eileanan Tarsainn (Crossways Islands) and Na h-Eileanan Siar (the Western Isles), the form preferred by the local authority, Comhairle nan Eilean Siar.

However, the southern portion from Harris to Barra, part of Inverness-shire before local authority reorganisation in 1975, was grouped in Poorhouse legislation as The Long Island Combination. Another name was coined in 1962 when a BBC television mini-series was set on the island of Benbecula. The theme tune, 'The Dark Island', remains a favourite with Scottish musicians and was originally called 'Dr MacKay's Farewell to Creagorry' according to some sources, although it was a Dr Grey who bade farewell to Creagorry.

Many of the earlier names in the Hebridean islands have been replaced by names of Scandinavian origin, with the northern part of the largest island known as Leòdhas (Lewis), thought to mean 'house' in Norse, a name that was once applied to the whole island. From the place-name evidence, it is very clear that the new settlers completely dominated the existing population, most likely Pictish-speaking. The Norse seem to have imported slave women from Ireland while dispatching Hebridean slaves to populate Iceland.

From that Norse settlement until the Treaty of Perth which ceded the Western Isles to the Scottish crown in 1266, a close relationship existed between these two island groups. They share place-names in common: for example, Berneray or *Bjarnarey* ('Bjorn's island') an uninhabited island in the Vestmann Islands of Iceland. The islands are named perhaps for the Hebridean slaves who were brought there, although Vestmenn or Westmen also applied to the Irish. *The Landnámabók*, a Medieval Icelandic written work that describes the settlement (*landnám*) of Iceland in the 9th and 10th centuries, states that there were *papar* (Gaelic monks) there before the Norse arrived and a number of place names named after these *papa*r exist. There are also Icelandic personal names of Gaelic origin, including *Njál* (Niall), *Brján* (Brian), *Kjartan* (Muircheartach) and *Kormakr* (Cormac), while the village *Patreksfjörður* was named after St. Patrick.

In the Hebrides, many Norse colonists intermarried and adopted Gaelic, while their conversion to Christianity contributed to Gaelicisation. Gaelicised Scandinavians dominated the region of the Irish Sea until the 12th century. They founded the long-lasting kingdoms of Man, Dublin and Galloway, as well as taking control of the Norse colony at York. Within a matter of generations, the colonists had been hybridised to become a race known as the Gall-Ghàidheil ('foreign Gaels'), a term used for Gaels of Norse identity. Over time, these Norse-Gaels became ever more Gaelicised, disappearing as a distinct group but leaving a lasting influence. Several kindreds have Norse-Gaelic roots, such as Clan Donald, with one progenitor called Dòmhnall MacRaghnaill (son of Ragnall, perhaps ON, *Rögnvaldr*, meaning 'ruler'); Clan MacDougall from Dubh Gall or 'dark foreigner'; and MacLeod, possibly from *ljótr* meaning 'ugly', or more likely from an older word *leuhta,* suggestive of 'shining' or 'brightness'.

Eilean Leòdhais: *Isle of Lewis*

Lewis and Harris are the two parts of a single island of over 2,000 kilometres^2, making it the largest island in Scotland. It sits at the head of the Western Isles chain. Lewismen were sometimes nicknamed bioraich ('dogfish'), but the island has the more poetic epithet of Eilean Fraoich ('heather island'), immortalised in a song of praise by Uilleam MacCoinnich (William MacKenzie):

Eilean fraoich, Eilean fraoich,
Eilean fraoich nam beann àrd',
Far an d' fhuair mi m' àrach òg,
Eilean Leòdhais mo ghràidh.

Isle of Heather, Isle of Heather, Isle of Heather of the high hills, where I was brought up, my beloved Isle of Lewis.

The most northerly point of the island is Rubha Robhanais (the Butt of Lewis or 'the point of the hole headland') in the district of Nis (Ness, from the ON, 'headland'). Ness stretches from Eoropie in the north to Dell in the south, and northeast to Skigersta, and consists of about sixteen villages including Lionel, Habost, Swainbost, and North and South Dell, all names with Norse roots. It was, before Brexit, the most north-westerly community in the European Union. Ness is part of the Galson Estate which is owned and managed on behalf of the community by Urras Oighreachd Ghabhsainn (the Galson Estate Trust).

Am Britheamh: *The Breve*

The small fortified crag of Dùn Èistean in Ness was once the ancestral home of the Lewis branch of Clan Morrison and is remembered in connection with the deeds of Alan Mòr, Am Britheamh (the Morrison Judge of Lewis). Tradition recounts that Niall Odhar ('dun-coloured Neil MacLeod') attacked the Morrisons who took shelter in Dùn Èistean. The MacLeods arrived at night and one of Neil's men shot a Morrison with an arrow named Baobh an Dòrlaich ('the fury of the quiver'), the last arrow of the eighteen that should be used. In response, Alan Mòr sprang across the ravine that separates Dùn Èistean from Ness and demanded that they surrender the culprit. When the MacLeods denied all knowledge Alan reproached them for cowardice and said:

> If you have come to fight, you ought, according to the laws of war from the creation of the world, to have waited till there was light enough to see each other.

This was a Scandinavian notion that it was wrong to slay after dark. To them, the mere killing of a man was of less importance than the manner in which it was committed. In the Icelandic saga *Brennu-Njál (The Story of Burnt Niall)*, atonement for assassination was only twelve ounces of silver. However, if the killing was done at night, it was murder and a capital offence.

Alan demanded Neil's doctor see the wounded man and Neil consented. Alan took the doctor under his arm and leapt back across the ravine with him. The Morrisons managed to flee from Dùn Èistean to the mainland, Neil in pursuit. Alan Mòr, who was very strong, set his two brothers to row in competition with himself, and composed and sang 'An t-Iorram Niseach' ('The Ness Boat Song'):

> 'S truagh nach robh mi fhìn 's Niall Odhar
> An lagan beag os cionn Dhùn Odhail
> Biodag am làimh 's esan fodham;
> Dhearbhainn fhèin gun deigheadh i domhainn
> 'S gum biodh fuil a chlèibh mu ghobhal,
> 'S gun dèantadh feòil 's gun dèantadh sitheann
> 'S gum biodh biadh fo ghob an fhithich.

> *What a pity Niall Odhar and I weren't in a small hollow above Dùn Odhail, a dagger in my hand and he beneath me. I would confirm that it would go deep, that the blood of his body would be around his crutch, and meat and game meat would be prepared for the raven's beak.*

Despite the fine song, Neil overtook the brothers at Dùn Odhail where all three were killed and buried.

Sula Sgeir

More than 60 kilometres north of Ness is Sula Sgeir ('gannet skerry' from the ON *'súla sker'*), a small island, uninhabited, apart from a hermit's cell. There is a similarly named Suleskjer in Utsira, Norway. Sula Sgeir is best known for its population of gannets. The flesh of the young gannet, or guga, is relished only in Ness today, but in the 16th century, it was served even at royal feasts as a 'whet' or appetiser. In the autumn of each year, a group of Ness men spent about a fortnight on Sula Sgeir, harvesting under licence a maximum of 2,000 young birds. Demand for their catch means that the birds are rationed to ensure a fair distribution of the catch. Bird resources were once exploited on all the Hebridean islands but this is now the only Scottish example, although the practice remains common in the Faroe and Icelandic islands. The annual harvest by Ness men has been interrupted by Covid restrictions and bird flu in recent times.

There are further Scandinavian resonances at Teampall Mholuaidh (St. Moluag's Church), an Episcopal church in Eòropaidh (Europie, meaning 'Jōrunn's farm'). Unusually, this Norse name *'Jōrunn'* is female, here probably meaning 'lover of horses', but the dedication is to a Celtic saint, Lughaidh. The T-shape plan of the church has similarities with the 12th century Gardar Cathedral in Greenland and it would have been built under Norse patronage on an earlier Christian site. A research project to identify the chapel sites of Lewis and surrounding islands recorded 37 such sites. Teampall Mholuaidh was associated with shallow-tide sacrifices to the sea god Shony, not ceasing until the 1670s, a late survival of pre-Christian rituals. Their persistence was conceivably a result of the widespread failure of the Reformed Church to provide adequate pastoral care to local Gaelic-speaking congregations for almost a century and a half following the Reformation of 1560.

An Taobh Siar agus Barabhas: *Westside and Barvas*

The area of An Taobh Siar agus Barabhas (Westside and Barvas) occupies the western part of the island and incorporates a large number of crofting townships between Siabost (Shawbost, ON, 'sea farm') and Borgh (Borve, ON, 'fort'). Crofting still plays an important role in the lives of many of the people and, despite ongoing depopulation, roughly 3,000 islanders live in this rural environment. It is clear from the census that Gàidhlig was spoken almost exclusively in all communities in this part of the island between 1881 and 1901 and, in a large proportion of crofting townships, was the only language of the majority of residents. In 1891, for example, almost no one spoke English in places like Còig Peighinnean Bhuirgh (Fivepenny Borve). From 1900, the number of Gaelic monolingual persons fell significantly, a result of the influence of the compulsory school system which used English exclusively in the classroom, though Gaelic remained the language of the home.

In the village of Baile an Truiseil (Ballantrushal, 'village of the Trushal stone') is Clach an Truiseil, a standing stone nearly six metres high. Its name comes from the ON *thrus*, 'a goblin'. This megalithic stone is commemorated in the pipe tune 'Major David Manson at Clachantrushal', composed by a local man, Pipe Major Donald Maclean (1908-1964). Known as Big Donald MacLean, he joined the Seaforth Highlanders in 1926 and, within ten years, became Pipe Major of the 2nd Battalion Seaforths and the youngest Pipe Major in the British army. Captured at St Valery in 1940, he spent the next five years as a prisoner of war. While imprisoned, he wrote the tune that probably commemorates a visit by retired Canadian Army Major David Manson to Donald's home in Ballantrushal.

The township of Barabhas (Barvas, ON, 'fort by the mouth of the river') developed around a road junction where the road from Ness to the north meets the road south to Carloway and onwards to Uig. The main road across the Barvas Moor continues to Steòrnabhagh (Stornoway). The parish remains the strongest Gaelic-speaking community in Scotland with the 2022 census recording 1608 speakers; over half the population.

The epithet:

> Iasgach muinntir Bharabhais
>
> *The fishing of the Barvas folk*

refers to the alleged habit of the people of Barvas of waiting to see how other areas got on with the fishing before setting out themselves.

Steòrnabhagh: *Stornoway*

Steòrnabhagh (Stornoway, ON, 'rudder bay') is the principal town of Lewis, with a population in 2022 of 4,468, 834 of whom speak Gaelic. The town is often referred to as Steòrnabhagh Mòr a' Chaisteil ('Big Stornoway of the Castle'), that castle being the seat of Siol Thorcaill, the Lewis branch of the MacLeods. It was demolished in the 17th century. One castle resident, the clan chief, Torcul, is recorded in a late 15th-century song, 'Moladh air Torcul MacLeòid Leòdhais' ('In Praise of Torquil MacLeod of Lewis'):

Fhuaras mac mar an t-athair,
math ar flathaibh ar n-eòlas,
do fhriothàil a aoibh 's a aigneadh
's mè 'gà chaidreabh i Leòdhus.

Adèara mè dhà h-aithle,
D' èis a aithne is a eòlas,
nach dtànaig fear a aoise
as fearr nà an rì-se Leòdhuis

Madh leis ò Charraig Bhoirbhe
sèad as soirbhe fhuair file,
do bhronnadh mac mheic Thorcuil,
dò roichinn tìr a fhine.

I have found a son like the sire, good in our knowledge of princes; he served me with his cheer and his spirit while I was in his company in Lewis.

I shall assert thereafter, after acquaintance and knowledge, that there is no man of his age who is better than this king of Lewis.

Had he from the rock of Bergen a jewel the most precious that poet ever won, the son of Torcul's son would bestow it were I to reach the land of his kin.

Stornoway has long been associated with salt herring. The MacLeods of Lewis were engaged in the lucrative 16th-century trade in salt and dried fish caught in their fishing grounds which had long been exploited by other northern Europeans. This trade drew the covetous attention of the Scottish kings, James VI in particular. The difficulties of securing the yearly payment of Hebridean rents occupied the authorities' agenda in the late 1590s. This fight against tax evasion was the predominant motive behind the invasion of Lewis in October 1599 by around 600 hired soldiers and 'colonists'. The King rashly anticipated the 'colonists' would deliver over £4000 sterling annually.

James's exploitation plans did not include the islanders. Such was his regard for the inhabitants of Lewis that he recommended:

> slauchter, mutilation, fyre-raising, or utheris inconvenieties

if necessary, to clear them out of the way. Initially, he planned to murder all of the native inhabitants in order to facilitate settlement but was persuaded that this was impractical. Indeed, James was thwarted a second time when he attempted, in 1607, to induce the Marquis of Huntly to 'extirpate' all the inhabitants of the Uists, a pogrom that was not eventually acted upon, although evidently not on humanitarian grounds.

In a manner that had much in common with the slightly later Plantation of Ulster, James had awarded rights to a group of eleven noblemen, largely from Fife, to colonise the Isle of Lewis. Their plan was to exploit the island's natural resources, pay the king large sums of money and in the process commence the 'civilising' or de-Gaelicisation of the islands. This attempt at expropriation has led one academic to suggest that Highland Scotland became:

> … an imaginary zone in which the spatial process of colonial penetration and development were practised on a small scale before being brought to bear on much of Africa and Asia.

The elegant name by which this band is known, The Gentleman Adventurers of Fife, suggests something more akin to a Sunday school outing rather than the armed invasion that in reality it was. In 1599, 'The Gentlemen' quickly built in the area of Stornoway now called South Beach and so the town owes its existence to the establishment of this embryonic colony.

Unsurprisingly, the MacLeods determined to confront the new settlers. After failed negotiations, the settlement was attacked and their ship, their lifeline, was captured. The MacLeod assaults ultimately killed 80 of the settlers and finally forced The Adventurers to abandon their colony. The struggle, however, weakened the MacLeods and the way was open for the MacKenzies to take over; James VI granted the MacKenzies a number of commissions against the MacLeods; in essence, leave by the Crown to attack Lewis and seize MacLeod land. The MacKenzies established their base at the head of Loch Seaforth, a name with which they have since been associated. The process was consolidated by the wily Ruairidh (Roderick) MacKenzie of Còigeach. He had been entrusted, in 1611, with the clan territories on behalf of his nephew Colin. Ruairidh was better known as the Tutor of Kintail.

The last MacLeod leader was Neil mac Ruairidh mhic Chaluim, or Niall Odhar. His small band of whom, unusually, over twenty are known by name, held out on the island of Bearasaigh (Berisay, ON 'stone island') in Loch Roag. Ejected from his base, Neil ultimately surrendered to the authorities in the hopes of clemency. He was taken to Edinburgh and, on 30th March 1613, charged with fire-raising, murder, theft and piracy. He received no clemency from the King and was swiftly hanged at the Mercat Cross on 1st April. The Gentleman Adventurers never faced charges.

Following this land grab, practically all the country from Strathnaver in the north to Ardnamurchan in the south was either MacKenzie property or under their vassalage. Both the Tutor of Kintail and Colin, the heir, were criticised for imposing high rentals on their Kintail and west coast tenants. Indeed, a Gaelic proverb in common currency was:

> Trì mallachdan an tuathanaich, an Taoitear Sàileach,
> reothadh Cèitein agus ceò Iuchair.
>
> *The three curses of the farmer, the Tutor of Kintail, frost in*
> *spring and mist in the dog-days.*

The MacKenzies in their turn suffered occupation. Perhaps the oldest surviving man-made structure in Stornoway is behind Amity House, the Port Authority Office. This is the foundation of the citadel built in 1654; a large, square building with thick ramparts to absorb cannon fire. It was part of the Cromwellian Protectorate's occupation of Scotland that was consolidated by General Monck who remained military governor of Scotland until 1660. Great citadels were built at Ayr, Perth and Leith, and twenty smaller fortresses were built at strategic locations across Scotland, including Stornoway.

Scotland's loss of its national identity and its hostility towards the Commonwealth occupation required the maintenance of an army that, even when much reduced by the end of 1657, still stood at 11,000, and in consequence required the levying of high taxes. It was this army of occupation which enabled General Monck to effect a putsch which saw the return of the exiled Charles II in the Restoration of the Monarchy of 1660, and Monck's professional army, from which the modern British army grew, included regiments such as the Royal Scots and the Coldstream Guards. All the citadels were demolished.

Dithis de Chlann 'ic Coinnich à Steòrnabhagh: *Two Stornoway MacKenzies*

With the Restoration came more settled times, and MacKenzie ownership of Lewis lasted for over 200 years until a new buccaneer, James Matheson, appeared on the scene. But the Seaforth period produced two eminent MacKenzies whose names are as well-known elsewhere as they are in their native Stornoway; the first in India and the second in Canada.

Colin MacKenzie, a merchant's son, was born in Stornoway around 1754. He was an army officer before becoming the first Surveyor General of India. He surveyed southern India, making use of local interpreters and scholars to study religion, oral histories, inscriptions and other evidence. His collections, consisting of thousands of manuscripts, inscriptions, translations, coins and paintings, are an important source for the study of Indian history and are now in the India Office Library. He was awarded a Companion of the Order of the Bath in 1815. He died in Calcutta in 1821.

In 1990, a Winnipeg-based employee buy-out of the northern grocery and merchandise posts of the Hudson's Bay Company revived the name the North West Company. That revived name has links to Stornoway in the person of Sir Alexander Mackenzie who was born in 1764 in Luskentyre House where Martin's Memorial Church now stands. Alexander Mackenzie is one of the great names in the history of North American exploration.

As was the case with so many Gaelic-speaking Highlanders, Mackenzie had emigrated to the New World. He joined the fur-trading business which was later absorbed into the North West Company and was the chief rival of the Hudson's Bay Company. Mackenzie wanted to identify a river which might go north or east to the Pacific, providing new opportunities in the fur trade. He reached the Pacific coast of what is now British Columbia in July 1793 and became the first white man to cross the continent of North America from coast to coast. Earlier, in 1789, he identified an important river route to the Arctic, now called the Mackenzie River, at a place called Whale Island in the Beaufort Sea. He is also commemorated in the Mackenzie District of the North-West Territories, Mackenzie Valley, Mount Mackenzie and the Mackenzie Pass.

In 1812, he returned to Britain and, like another fur-trading colleague Edward 'Bear' Ellice in Invergarry, he used his fur-trade wealth to buy a Highland estate, in his case, that of Abhach (Avoch, 'water place') in the Black Isle. He was reputed to have been a benevolent laird.

MacMhathain is Bodach an t-Siabainn: *Matheson and Leverhulme*

In 1844, Lewis had a new owner with cash to spend but who was perhaps less benevolent to the islanders. James Matheson, originally from Lairg, Sutherland, paid £190,000 for the island; a huge sum that had been acquired through the illegal opium trade in China.

Matheson built Lews Castle near Stornoway, clearing more than 500 families off the land by arranging their emigration to Canada. In 1845, he began a programme of improvements on the island, including drainage schemes and road construction and, by 1850, he had spent £329,000 on Lewis. By 1855, he had 'assisted' nearly 2,000 people to emigrate.

The next 'merchant prince' to arrive in Lewis made his money in soap. William Lever, Lord Leverhulme, the first non-Gaelic owner, paid £143,000 in 1918. Together with his brother, James, William had established Lever Brothers, one of the first companies to manufacture soap from vegetable oils. It is now part of the Anglo-Dutch transnational business, Unilever.

Leverhulme was known in Lewis as Bodach an t-Siabainn ('the Soap Man'). Soap wealth was poured into Lewis. In a little over three years, Leverhulme spent some £2 million on industrialisation schemes, largely based on fishing, which he believed would transform economic and social conditions in the islands. However, returning ex-servicemen wanted land rather than the factory jobs Leverhulme offered them. By 1920, Lever Brothers had serious financial difficulties and, needing to make significant savings, Leverhulme decided to concentrate his efforts in Harris, where the fishing village of An t-Òb (Obbe, ON, 'bay') was renamed Leverburgh.

In 1923, Leverhulme invited the people of Lewis to take the land, but only those in the Stornoway area accepted his gift. He sold off as much of the island as he could, but many of the buyers were only interested in creating shooting and fishing estates. When Leverhulme died in 1925, the Board of Lever Brothers ceased all development in Harris and Leverhulme's schemes for the Western Isles perished, having achieved little.

But there was and is a successful export from the islands, Harris Tweed, which partly owes its international reputation to the efforts of one estate owner, Catherine Herbert, Lady Dunmore. Harris Tweed is made from pure virgin wool dyed and spun, handwoven and finished in the Western Isles. This was once an entirely manual process, the wool being dyed with natural dyes derived from local plants and lichens, then processed and spun, before being handwoven.

This small cottage industry, serving local needs, began to change when, in 1843, Catherine Herbert took responsibility for the Dunmore estate in Harris. She noticed the high quality of the tweed cloth produced locally by two sisters from the village of Strond and commissioned them to weave lengths of tweed with the Murray tartan. She then promoted tweed as a fashionable cloth for sporting wear and it soon became the fabric of choice for the aristocracy, including members of Queen Victoria's court. The Harris Tweed industry grew, reaching a peak production figure of 7.6 million yards in 1966, much of it woven in islanders' own homes. The definition, quality standards and protection of the Harris Tweed name and the Orb stamp are enshrined in the Harris Tweed Act of 1993.

Trì Dòmhnallan Ainmeil: *Three Famous Donalds*

Lord Leverhulme's 1923 gift of Lews Castle and 69,000 acres of land to the people of Stornoway included over 1300 crofts. In 1912, on one of these crofts, number 5 Tong, Màiri Chaluim Alasdair (Mary Anne MacLeod) was born, one of ten children whose father was a crofter and fisherman. English, learned at school, was her second language. Mary Anne emigrated to America in 1930, one of tens of thousands of young Scots who left for the United States or Canada during this period.

As one account has put it, she:

> started life in America as a dirt-poor servant escaping the even worse poverty of her native land.

All that changed when she met Fred Trump at a party. She became Bean Thrump (Mrs Trump) and, in 1946, she gave birth to Donald John Trump, the 45th and 47th President of the United States. His name most probably came from Màiri Anna's maternal grandfather, Donald Smith. President Trump's patronymic in Gaelic would be Dòmhnall Iain mac Màiri Chaluim Alasdair.

Another Donald, this time a MacLeod, is widely regarded as one of the greatest pipers of the 20th century, both in terms of his competitive prowess and as a composer of memorable pipe tunes. Born in Stornoway in 1916, he enlisted in the Seaforth Highlanders in 1937 and became Pipe Major within four years. During the Second World War, he saw action in France with the 51st Highland Division and was captured at St. Valery. He managed to escape and was picked up by the Resistance. He was the only Gaelic speaker among other Scots escapees, and the story goes that he responded in Gaelic when challenged and was presumed to be Eastern European. He made it back home, eventually returning to France to pipe the 7th Seaforth Highlanders across the Rhine.

During the post-war years, Donald MacLeod excelled on the competition circuit. Between the late 1940s and early 1960s, he won the Gold Medals for pìobaireachd at Inverness and Oban and eight clasps from the Northern Meeting, as well as eight Silver Stars, the top March, Strathspey and Reel award. Donald had considerable powers of composition, sometimes at very short notice. Once, at the Northern Meeting, he had only written two of the four parts of his subsequently famous jig 'The Seagull', but entered the light music competition nevertheless, improvising the last two parts on the platform. Similarly, on another occasion, while waiting for the competition judges to come to a decision, he picked up the programme sheet and started writing on it. By the time the results were announced, he had composed another enduring jig, 'The Judges' Dilemma'.

He left a legacy of many fine pipe tunes, compositions such as 'The Man from Skye', 'Butterfingers', 'The Duck', 'MacLean of Lewis' and 'Crossing the Minch'. An exceptional tutor to young pipers, his six books of pipe tunes and a collection of ceòl mòr, pibroch, supplemented with recordings by himself of 230 tunes, remain an invaluable teaching aid.

A fellow Stornowegian was Donald B MacLeod (1932-1984), popularly known as 'Donnie B', a TV presenter, best known for appearing on the BBC1 afternoon show, Pebble Mill at One. MacLeod was also known for his role as presenter of several ground-breaking travel documentaries including 'MacLeod's America', 'MacLeod's Russia', and 'MacLeod's Japan'. The 'B' in his name was simply 'B': Donny was one of several Donald MacLeods in his class, and teachers identified them as Donald 'A', 'B', 'C' etc.

Both these men would have known the rhyme used to characterise the town's areas:

> Fithich dhubha Ìonacleit, slìogairean shìos a' bhaile, daoine uasal Ceann a' Bhàigh, spàgairean Ghiùrsiadair.
>
> *Black ravens from Newton, sneaks from down the town, noble folk from Bayhead, clumsy folk from Guershader.*

Cogadh agus Eilthireachd: *War and Emigration*

The Isle of Lewis made a disproportionately large sacrifice in the two World Wars. The losses suffered in World War I were 1,300, accounting for about 8% of the total population or one man out of every six, whilst the UK as a whole suffered just over 2%. The Lewis War Memorial in Stornoway records all these casualties, though they are also commemorated in many localities. The memorial takes the form of a Scottish Baronial Tower over 26 metres high. Internally, a separate chamber was allotted to each of the four parishes of Lewis, each bearing the inscriptions of every one of the fallen. Among them was Iain Rothach (John Munro) (1889-1918) who has been described as:

> the first strong voice of the new Gaelic verse of the 20th century.

An exceptional scholar, Munro enlisted in the 4th Seaforth Highlanders, won the Military Cross on 13th April 1918 and was killed in action three days later. Although, tragically, little of his verse survives, his war poem 'Ar Tìr 's na Gaisgich a thuit sna Blàir' ('Our Land and the Heroes who fell in Battle') is an exception:

Fhuair sinn sìnt' iad le 'm bàs-leòintean
an dust eu-dreach', na bha chòrr dhiubh,
nan laighe sìneadh mar mheòir-shìnt'–
smèideadh, stiùireadh,
sparradh ùr-oidhirpean oirnne,
strì air n-adhart, strì còmhla,
an taobh a thuit iad dol còmhl' rinn,
null thar Còmhnard na Strì.

Bi am chuideachd geàrr-ùin',
dùin do rosg-sgàilean air d' shùil
'n seòmar ionmhais do smaoin
's caoin-sholas òg-mhaidne, ciùin-mhaidne, òg-mhèis
ga lìonadh, a' briseadh tre uinneag a' chùil –
'n àite taighe, tadhal d' anma,
fasgadh cuspairean a' mhùirn,
an sin – tog, taisg dealbh orra
nan laighe mar thuit san raon,
fairich, cluinn,
...
An smèideadh, an cainnt rinn,
'n rùn-gnìomh air an tug iad an deò
suas, nan càradh
air an àr-làr,
air a ghlèidheadh dhuinn beò
mar gun snaidheadh fear seòlt'
cuimhneachain cloiche gun phrìs.

We found them lying with their fatal wounds
in formless dust, what was left of them,
lying stretched out like pointing fingers –
beckoning, guiding,
spurring us on to fresh efforts,
pressing forward, pressing together,
the very way where they fell when with us
they crossed the battlefield.

Stay with me for a moment
close the lids on your eyes
in the treasure-house of your thoughts
with the soft light of young-morning, calm-morning,
June-morning
filling, breaking through the back window –
instead of house, penetrating your soul,
enveloping the objects of love,
then – make, store a picture of them
lying as they fell in the field,
feel, hear
...
their beckoning, their speech to us,
the reflex in which they
expired, fixed
on the battle-floor,
preserved for us alive
as if some sculptor had hewn
marble memorials.

An *Iolaire*: HMY *Iolaire*

The loss of HMY *Iolaire* ('eagle') in the early hours of New Year's Day 1919 was the island's worst single loss of life in the First World War. 174 Lewis and 7 Harris servicemen drowned at the Beasts of Holm in sight of the Stornoway harbour lights. Despite the yacht's proximity to the shore, the exposed location and stormy night made the sea dangerous, even for the few experienced swimmers aboard. Thanks to the bravery of John F. MacLeod from Port of Ness, the bulk of the survivors got ashore using a line he secured to the rocks. As dawn rose, one sailor was rescued from the mast. The tragedy is the subject of a poem by an Arnol man, the Rev. John MacLeod, 'Banntrach Cogaidh' ('War Widow'). His mother was widowed that morning when he was only one year old:

Sgaoil i 'aodach air gàrradh,
briogais bhàn is lèine gheal,
crios gorm leathann,
còrd geal caol.
Bha mi air clach ri taobh,
bonaid cruinn air mo cheann,
bonaid m' athar.
Deise ghorm na stiallan
mar reub iad bho chorp i
nuair fhuair iad e
fuar bàthte air an tràigh,
air a pasgadh le làmhan gràidh
is cridhe brist',
mar deise rìgh dol gu banais.

She spread his clothes and belongings on the wall, white trousers and shirt, a broad belt, a narrow white cord. I was sitting on a stone by her side, a round cap on my head, my father's cap. A blue uniform in shreds as they had ripped it from his cold body when they found him drowned on the beach, now folded by loving hands and a broken heart: like a king's wedding uniform.

The island saw sustained emigrations during the inter-war years. For every 100 people in Lewis, eight were killed in the war and a further ten emigrated. Most memorable was the departure of the SS *Metagama* on 21st April 1923, taking away 300 young Hebrideans, all but twenty being young men with an average age of 22, in search of a new and better life. Within the year, 800 other young people left Lewis and other islands. Commenting on the exodus of young men and women from the Western Isles, a contemporary magazine stated:

> They ... are sure to be an acquisition to the land of their adoption. What is Canada's gain is unfortunately our loss.

Most of those seeking a new life continued to keep in touch and a few returned for good, such as Am Bàrd Mhealboist (The Melbost Bard), Murdo MacFarlane. Some of his songs recount his experiences on the Canadian prairie but undoubtedly his best-known song is a rallying cry for the Gaelic language, 'Cànan nan Gàidheal':

O, chànain ta leth ri mo chridh',
M' aran, m' annlan is m' anail 's mo smior,
'S tu cho aost ri fraoch dosrach nam frìth,
Shloinneadh òg leat beinn, leitir is sgurr,
Albainn gad easbhaidh 's gad dhìth
'S clàrsach-aon-teud is cuislean gun fhuil.

Suas togamaid Gàidhealtachd nuadh
Le eanchainn, braon-gruaidh agus dòirn,
Gàidhealtachd às 'n dèanar uaill,
Àit' àrd uasal aig cànan is ceòl,
'S biadh-beatha aig spiorad 's aig brù
Ri fhaotainn gun dhìth air do bhòrd.

O language which is so close to my heart,
My bread, my sustenance, my breath and my strength,
As old as the bushy heather on the moors,
Used to christen every hill, slope and peak;
Without you, a Gael would be
A one-stringed harp and a bloodless artery.

Let us build up a new Gàidhealtachd
With our intelligence, our sweat and our fists;
A Gàidhealtachd of which we can be proud,
In which language and music are held in high esteem,
May a lifetime of fulfilment for the spirit and body
Be forever found at your table.

In earlier days, emigration was an irrevocable separation from loved ones. One of the many songs of loss and separation is 'Cumha do dh'Aonghas 'ic Ailein' ('A Lament for Angus Son of Alan'), composed by his brother Donald Smith. Angus, a widower aged 63, left for Canada around 1840, taking two of his sons with him.

Gur e mis' tha fo mhulad ann an cumha mo bhràthar,
a dh'fhalbh às an tìr seo o dhaoine 's o chàirdean,
's a chaidh a mheasg na coill' fhiadhaich tha giùlain
  biastan an fhàsaich,
far nach fhaighear soisgeul ri iarraidh 's nach èirich grian
  air an t-Sàbaid.

Chan e do bhòidhchead no d' àilleachd tha mi 'n-dràsta ri
  'g acain
ach nach fhaic mi gu bràth thu latha Sàbaid no seachdain,
sinn cho fada bho chèile 's tha 'n cruinne-cè 's e cho
  farsaing,
sinn gun sgrìobhadh gun leughadh och, gu sgeula thoirt
  eadrainn.

How sad am I lamenting my brother who left this land and kin and people to go among the wild forests that sustain the beasts of the wilderness, where there's no access to the gospel and the sun doesn't rise on the Sabbath.

It's not your beauty or your handsomeness that causes me to sigh but that I won't see you ever again on a weekday or a Sunday. We are as far apart as the width of the world, we are unable to read or write so we cannot exchange news.

Sixteen kilometres south of Stornoway, Acha Mòr (Achmore, 'big field') is one of only two inland settlements on Lewis; a person not up to their job is said to be a:

> Maraiche an Acha Mhòir.
>
> *An Achmore sailor.*

Strì an Fhearainn – Na Lochan, Ùig, Beàrnaraigh: *The Land Struggle – Lochs, Uig and Bernera*

Just beyond Baile Ailein (Balallan, from 'Alan's town'), a long village at the head of Loch Èireasort (Loch Erisort, ON, 'Harris firth') is the Pàirc Memorial, one of several memorials commemorating the land struggle in Lewis. The name A' Phàirc ('the Park') refers to a deer forest. In 1872, a Select House of Commons Committee examined whether the substitution of deer in place of sheep was against the interests of the community. Its slanted report did nothing to halt the loss of potential agricultural land to sporting interests. By 1884, 110 deer forests, 2,000,000 acres in extent, had been created in the Highlands and, by the 20th century, 34% of crofting counties' land was under deer forests. In 1957, the last time the figures were published, there were 2.8 million acres of land devoted to deer forests.

Settlements in South Park had been cleared by James Matheson in the 19th century and, in 1887, Lady Matheson's agents decided that the former 42,000 acre sheep farm should now be converted into a sporting deer park. In the Pàirc Deer Raid, some 160 crofters marched into this new deer forest and set up camp. In response, the Secretary of State dispatched troops to deal with the 'outrage'. Six of the leaders were committed for trial in Edinburgh, well covered by the press. The men were charged with mobbing and rioting but were represented by their own legal team. The jury took only half an hour before returning a verdict of Not Guilty on all charges against each of the six men. The cairn erected in 1994 to commemorate the events and the local people involved was designed by the artist Will MacLean.

Perhaps the area's best-known resident was Calum Kennedy, born Malcolm Martin Kennedy in Marabhaig (Marvaig, ON, 'sea bay') in Lochs in 1928. The most successful Gaelic singer of his generation, his first major success was to win the World Ballad Championship in Moscow in 1957. He went on to win the Gold Medal at the National Mod, become a television favourite and produce many commercially successful records.

One of the nine wards used to elect members to the Western Isles Islands Council is Sgìr' Ùig agus Càrlabhagh (Uig and Carloway); the parish of Uig is one of the island's four civil parishes. The name Ùig is generally accepted to be derived from the ON *vík* or 'bay'. The area was a fruitful recruiting ground for soldiers for the 78th Seaforth Highlanders, largely recruited in four waves in 1778, 1793, 1794 and 1804. The district recorded 1,923 residents in 1841, prior to evictions that occurred over the next decade. The most notable evictions resulted in the passage of hundreds of people on the emigrant ships *Marquis of Stafford* and *Barlow* in 1851. At the turn of the 20th century, there were 1,631 residents in the district and the population dipped below 1,000 for the first time after World War II. Uig's current ageing population is now at the lowest recorded level of around 400.

Beàrnaraigh Mhòr (Great Bernera or 'Bjørn's Island') is an island of 21km^2. At Circeabost (Kirkibost or 'church farm') in the southeast of the island, is located the first planned crofting township in the Outer Hebrides, created in 1805 by the allotting of crofts to individuals by the MacKenzie estate. The tenants of this planned village were all evicted in 1823. It was the location in 1874 of another 'riot' when crofters refused to remove their stock to make way for the expanding sporting estates. They were threatened with military coercion. This did not occur and, in the legal case that followed, the eviction notices were rejected; one of the first recorded victories for small tenants at will. The village was resettled in 1878 and the original 1805 croft boundaries are still in use.

Breacleit (Breaclete, ON, 'cliff with the broad ridge') is the central village in Great Bernera. It was once a settlement of twelve crofts surrounding the natural harbour of Loch Beag ('small loch'). In 1851, the Chamberlain to Sir James Matheson proposed that all the tenants of the village should be evicted and sent to North America. Although not fully implemented, it left the village with a population of just three families, later supplemented through evictions elsewhere, notably the clearance of villages in the south of the island.

Breaclete was the birthplace of the Scottish printer and publisher Calum MacDonald (1912-1999). He founded the literary journal *Lines Review* in 1952. As a principled publisher, MacDonald used proceeds from his general printing business to specialise in the publication of poetry and was instrumental in advancing the work of many major Scottish poets, including Hugh MacDiarmid, Sydney Goodsir Smith and Norman MacCaig.

Another famous son of Bernera was an t-Oll. Dòmhnall MacAmhlaigh (Professor Donald MacAulay), an innovative Gaelic poet and academic, who died in 2017. He is best known for the 1968 collection of his poems *Seòbhrach às a' Chlaich* (*Primrose from a Stone*) and for the highly influential *Nua-Bhàrdachd Ghàidhlig: Modern Scottish Gaelic Poems* (1976), which he edited. An example of his work is 'An t-Sean Bhean' ('The Old Woman'):

Choisich thu crotach
le do bhata
sìos ris a' ghàrradh;
stad thu 's thog
thu cudthrom do chrom-chinn
chuir thu do bhois
eadar do shùilean 's a' ghrian.

As an dubhar sin
dh'amhairc thu air an àiteach,
air an t-sreath a bha an crann a' cur thairis,
air crìochan na lota,
's air an t-sliabh
('s thug thu sùil mas robh bhò ann an geimhil).

Is thionndaidh thu an uair sin
do chasan
gun gaoth a' dol eadar iad 's an talamh,
is thill thu rag iad
a-steach
(le do bhata
's do làmh anns a' bhalla)
don aitreabh
far an robh am maide-buinn air fàs na
arrasbacan.

Is shuidh thu an sin air do chathair.

You walked, feeble,
with your stick
down by the wall;
you stopped and raised
the weight of your bent head,
you put your hand
between your eyes and the sun.

From that shade
you stared out at the spring,
at the furrow the plough turned;
at the boundaries of the croft
and the mountain
(and you looked to see the cow was not trapped).

And you turned, then.
your feet –
no space between them and the ground –
and walked them stiffly
in
(with your stick
and a hand on the wall)
to the house
where the threshold had grown
into an obstacle.

And you sat there in your seat.

To the south is the community of Eadar Dà Fhadhail (Ardroil, 'between two fords'), an elongated township of re-settled crofts from settlements cleared in the 1830s to create sheep farms. This particular clearance evicted the tenants of the five townships of Capadal (Capadale), Peighinn Dhòmhnaill (Penny Donald), Baile Ghobhainn (Balgowan), Baile Ghreusaich (Balgreasach) and Earastadh (Erista). The inhabitants were forcibly sent to other parts of Lewis, notably Swainbost in Ness, but also to Canada.

Dòmhnall Iain Aonghais (Donald MacIver) (1857-1935), also known as Dòmhnall Ruadh a' Bhodaich Bhàin ('red-haired Donald of the fair-haired old man'), was a son of a Gaelic schoolmaster and missionary. He composed the well-known song 'An Ataireachd Bhuan' ('The Endless Surge of the Sea') when he was visiting Uig, accompanied by his uncle Dòmhnall Bàn Crosd, who had left Carnish in 1851 for Canada. While they were walking around Carnish, long cleared of all its inhabitants, the uncle remarked:

> "Chan eil nì an seo mar a bha e, ach ataireachd na mara."
>
> *"There is nothing here as it was, only the surge of the sea."*

The song won first prize at the 1908 Mod:

An ataireachd bhuan,
Cluinn fuaim na h-ataireachd àrd,
Tha torann a' chuain
Mar chualas leam-s' e nam phàist,
Gun mhùthadh gun truas
A' sluaisreadh gainneimh na tràghad
An ataireachd bhuan,
Cluinn fuaim na h-ataireachd àrd.

Ag amharc mun cuairt,
Cha dual dhomh gun a bhith 'm pràmh:
Chan fhaic mi an tuath
Dom b' shuaicheant' carthannas tlàth –
Nam fògarraich thruagh,
Chaidh 'm fuadach thairis air sàl,
'S cha chluinn iad gu buan
Mòr-fhuaim na h-ataireachd àird.

The endless surge of the sea, hear the sound of the high swell;
the thunder of the ocean is as I heard when I was a child,
unchanging, without pity, swooshing on the sand of the shore.
The endless surge of the sea, hear the sound of the high swell.

Looking around I can't help but be dejected. I don't see the people known for their compassion and kindness – as miserable exiles, they were cleared across the sea, and will never again hear the great sound of the high swell.

Fir-tàileisg Leòdhais: *The Lewis Chess Pieces*

In 1831, the Lewis Chess Pieces were found in a sand dune at or near Peighinn Dhòmhnaill, by Calum nan Sprot (Malcolm MacLeod), and they are among the most important parts of Scotland's heritage. They constitute four, almost complete, medieval chess sets. The traditional story of the chessmen used to be told in a ceilidh house when Rev. A. J. MacKenzie was a youth and his account is one of several variants of the tale:

> When the MacKenzies took over Lewis, their clansmen from Kintail took the land. Amongst them was Calum Mòr, who got Baile na Cille and rough pasture in the Àrd Mhòr beyond the mountains. His cattle used the summer grazing under the charge of the Gille Ruadh, the Red Gillie. One day the Red Gillie spotted a ship at anchor and waited to see what would happen. At moonrise, he saw a youth rowing a small dinghy ashore.
>
> The Gille Ruadh saw he was holding a weighty bundle and spoke to the youth, who told him he was tired of living with a rough crew and had decided to escape. As he had no money, he had taken the playthings that the sailors amused themselves with, hoping to be able to sell them. The Gille Ruadh, overcome by greed, killed the lad.
>
> The Gille Ruadh set out for home, hiding the treasure nearby, and then told Calum Mòr about the ship at Àrd Mhòr, suggesting that he should plunder her. Calum Mòr was horrified and banished the Gille Ruadh from Balnacille, and he was prevented from retrieving his treasure. The Gille Ruadh tried his fortune around Stornoway, where he was arrested for crimes and hanged on Gallows Hill.
>
> That is a tradition of the treasure that was discovered in 1831 by Calum nan Sprot who, while herding his cattle, saw one of the beasts

rubbing itself against a sand bank, and saw her pull out some whitish objects with her horn. Calum examined them and took them to be idols which he did not understand. But a gentleman from Stornoway, Mr Ryrie, heard of the discovery and dug out all of the pieces since Calum would not meddle with them. Calum received an award of £30.00. Mr Ryrie made a handsome profit.

The British Museum is of the view that the chessmen were probably made in Norway's medieval capital, Trondheim, in the 12th century. They were therefore already some 600 years old when the Gille Ruadh supposedly buried the crew's playthings. This is a good example of a traditional tale being associated with a specific hero, Calum Mòr, and rare treasure. Some commentators feel that the pieces were only ever transient; that the chessmen were hidden (or lost) after some mishap occurred during their carriage from Norway to wealthy Norse towns such as Dublin on the east coast of Ireland. The large number of pieces and their lack of wear may suggest that they were the stock of a trader.

This theory ignores the fact that chess was a high-status game among the Gallo-Norse elite of the Hebrides also. Fir-tàileisg ('chessmen') are mentioned in song, and gaming pieces turn up in archaeological contexts. One possible alternative suggestion is that they may represent gifts to the not-too-distant religious settlement of Tigh nan Cailleachan Dubha ('the house of the black women') at Mealastadh (Mealista, 'bent-grass place'), by tradition the site of a nunnery. The sets may have been deposited there for safekeeping as seems to have been the case with the earlier Pictish treasure of St. Ninian's Isle in Shetland. That is only one theory, but there is no reason to believe that the pieces were of too high status for the Hebrideans.

Dualchas Ùigeach: *Uig Traditions*

Dòmhnall Càm (Donald MacAulay) (c.1560-c.1640) was Chief of the MacAulays and a great hero who lived in various fortified locations around Uig: on the stack that bears his name at Mangarstaigh (Mangersta, ON, 'monk place'), at Loch Bharabhat by Crabhlastagh, (Crowlista, meaning uncertain) and at the 'castle' at Valtos.

Dòmhnall Càm went one summer to the Flannan Isles and the Morrisons of Ness, hearing the MacAulays were away from home, raided Uig. When Dòmhnall returned he learnt that the Morrisons and their spoil were resting in the fortress of Dùn Chàrlabhaigh (Dun Carloway), said to have been built in the 4th century by the giant, Darg mac Nu-Aran. The MacAulays approached: one, An Gobha Mòr ('the big smith'), was set to guard the door and prevent anyone escaping, while Dòmhnall Càm, using two dirks which he stuck at different levels into the walls of the Dùn, managed to climb to the open top of the structure. Dòmhnall Càm's men gathered bundles of heather which were handed up, set alight and thrown down into the Dùn. This was repeated until all the inmates were smothered or burnt. It is said that Dòmhnall Càm and his men destroyed much of the fabric of Dùn Chàrlabhaigh.

A grandson of Dòmhnall Càm was Sgàire MacAmhlaoibh (Zachary Macaulay). Born in Inveraray in 1768, he became a leading slavery abolitionist and was a founder of London University and a Governor of British Sierra Leone. He was the father of Thomas Babington Macaulay, the Whig historian and politician.

Another Uig tradition relates to Fionnlagh Ciar ('swarthy Finlay MacRitchie') of Mealista. About 1460, the MacLeods of Pabaigh (Pabbay, 'priest island') had murdered every son of Dugald MacAulay except thirteen-year-old John Roy MacAulay, who was fostered with Fionnlagh Ciar at Mealista. The MacLeods now sought to get hold of the MacAulay heir and promised solemnly not to harm the youth. So, with these guarantees, John Roy came into Norman Macleod's care. Nonetheless, Fionnlagh Ciar remained anxious about his foster son's safety.

The MacLeods then proposed that John Roy accompany them on a winter deer hunt eleven kilometres south to the border with Harris. Caught in the hills by heavy snowfall, the party took shelter for the night in a sheiling called Tobhta Choinnich ('Kenneth's bothy'). There the MacLeods stripped John Roy naked and tied him to a large boulder intending him to die from exposure long before morning.

At Mealista, Fionnlagh Ciar had retired for the night but a supernatural being appeared to him in a dream alerting him to John Roy's plight. Startled awake, Finlay told his wife, only to be informed that he was too anxious about the youth. She advised him to go back to sleep. Again he had the same dream but was again told to forget it. Yet again the same being appeared to him and repeated the two previous warnings, adding that if he did not go immediately to John Roy, the boy would not be alive in the morning. Fionnlagh Ciar roused his wife and told her to milk the cow into a pot and heat the milk on the fire. He set off and arrived just as John Roy was nearing death from exposure, but his foster father revived the lad with a drink of warm milk. He put him on his back and they arrived back at Mealista before daylight.

John Roy escaped the clutches of the Pabbay MacLeods and reached the safety of his relatives in Mull. Once a fully grown man, he returned to wreak vengeance on the villains and reclaim his estate.

Na Hearadh: *Harris*

Returning to the east side of the island, the A859 crosses the boundary between Lewis and Na Hearadh (Harris) at Abhainn a' Mhuil (Mulhagery, possibly 'river of the shingle beach'). Up to the time of local government reorganisation in 1975, Lewis was administered from Dingwall, the seat of Ross-shire Council; Harris, as part of Inverness-shire Council, was administered from Inverness. The division was fixed on old parish and clan sept territorial boundaries.

The etymology of Harris is uncertain but perhaps derives from the ON *hærri*, meaning 'higher', a reference to the area's high hills. That the Gaelic name, Na Hearadh, was also an earlier term for the Rinns of Islay, an area of elevated land in an otherwise low-lying island, makes this meaning more plausible.

Harris managed to stay out of the clutches of the MacKenzies, but ultimately the MacLeod hold on Harris ended, when in 1834, George Murray, 5th Earl of Dunmore, bought the estate following the bankruptcy of Alexander MacLeod of Berneray. Within five years the people of South Harris were cleared from their homes by a posse of Glasgow policemen, aided by soldiers acting at the behest of the Earl who offered a £1 per person incentive for those electing to leave. Not long after his return in 1865 from serving with the Confederate forces in the American Civil War, Charles Adolphus, the 7th Earl, built the Scottish baronial-style Caisteal Abhainn Suidhe (Amhuinnsuidhe Castle).

In 1868, the North Harris estate was sold to the banker Sir Edward Scott, after whom the school in Tarbert is named. His son, Sir Samuel, retained the tenancy of the North Harris Estate after it was purchased by Lord Leverhulme for £20,000 in 1919. Since then, the castle and estate have changed hands several times but remained in private ownership until 2003. In that year, the estate passed into community ownership, but not the castle or the fishing rights.

At the southern extremity of Harris is An t-Òb, a community that in 1919 became the hub of Leverhulme's fishing operations. Traces of the project are still to be seen in the village. In 1920, it was renamed Leverburgh and work started on a new pier and shore infrastructure for processing the catch from 50 trawlers, at an estimated cost to Leverhulme of £500,000. By 1924, Leverburgh was ready, and twelve Great Yarmouth drifters landed such a quantity of herring that extra female employees were taken from the mainland to handle the catch. Some of these women were likely known to the fishermen since the work of these Clann-nighean an Sgadain ('herring girls') took them as far as Yarmouth. The Herring Girls were fundamental to the fishing industry on which ports such as Stornoway, Lerwick, Lowestoft and Yarmouth were built. They followed the annual migration of the herring shoals clockwise around the north of Scotland, gutting, salting and packing herring into barrels for sale and export, notably to the Baltic, Germany and Russia.

Roghadal: *Rodel*

Roghadal (Rodel, ON, 'rood valley') on the south-eastern coast of Harris was historically the island's capital and main port. Adjacent is Tùr Chliamhainn (St. Clement's Tower) erected in the 1520s and the finest pre-Reformation church in the Western Isles. It has a well-preserved group of canopied wall tombs; a rare survival of such late medieval funerary monuments. The church was built by Alasdair Crotach ('humpbacked Alasdair'), so called as a result of wounds received in battle. He was the 8th Chief of the MacLeods of Harris and Dunvegan and he broke with tradition in choosing to spend his final years in Harris and be buried there. Abandoned after the Reformation, the church was restored in 1873 at the behest of the Dowager Countess of Dunmore.

By tradition, the 17th-century poet Màiri nighean Alasdair Ruaidh (Mary, 'the daughter of red-haired Alasdair') is said to be buried in Rodel. She was a member of the Dunvegan 'court', but possible displeasure at the tone of some of her work led to her banishment to Scarba in the Small Isles or Mull. According to tradition, she regained favour and returned to Sir Norman MacLeod's house in Berneray. It was during her exile that she composed 'Luinneag MhicLeòid' ('MacLeod's Ditty'):

'S mi am shuidhe air an tulaich
Fo mhulad 's fo iomcheist,
'S mi coimhead air Ìle,
Is ann dem ìongnadh san àm seo;
Bha mi uair nach do shaoil mi
Gus 'n do chaochail air m' aimsir
Gun tiginn an taobh seo
Dh'amharc Dhiùraidh à Sgarbaidh.

Gun tiginn an taobh seo
Dh'amharc Dhiùraidh à Sgarbaidh;
Beir mo shoraidh don dùthaich
Tha fo dhubhar nan garbhbheann,
Gu Sir Tormod ùr allail
Fhuair ceannas air armailt,
Is gun cante anns gach fearann
Gum b' airidh fear t' ainme air.

As I sit on the knoll, forlorn and unquiet, gazing on Islay, what causes me to marvel now is that there was a time I never thought, till my fortunes changed, that I would come here to view Jura from Scarba.

That I would come here to view Jura from Scarba: bear my greetings to the land which lies in the shadow of the rugged peaks, to the strong and renowned Sir Norman who has won headship over an armed host, for it was said in every part that one of your name was worthy of that.

A renowned religious poet, Iain Moireasdan, Iain Gobha na Hearadh (John Morrison, 'John the smith of Harris') (1790-1852), was born in Rodel. Among his compositions is a long poem 'An Nuadh Bhreith, no Gleachd an t-Seann Duine agus an Duin' Òig' ('The New Birth, or the Struggle between the Old and the Young'). He also composed 'A' Mhisg' ('Drunkenness'), reflecting his support for the Temperance Movement:

> Mhill a' mhisg ort do bhiùthas 's do chliù chuir mu làr;
> Dh'fhàg i creacht' agus spùillt' thu gun iunntas gun tàin,
> Mheall i riamh thu le sùgradh, gun d' lùb thu da càil,
> Is dh'fhàg i don ghràisg nad spòrs thu.
>
> Is i mhill ort do reusan 's troimh'-chèil' chuir nad cheann,
> Mar bhrùid air bheag cèille 's le dèistinneachd cainnt;
> Bidh riasladh air Beurla 's "De'il take ye" 's "God damn"
> Bidh tric air gach ceann de d' chòmhradh.
>
> *Drunkenness has ruined your reputation, and brought your prestige to ground level; it has left you plundered and destroyed, without wealth or cattle. She always deceived you with merriment, you bent to her will and she left you as sport for the rabble.*
>
> *She ruined your reason, confusion in your head, like a beast with little sense using disgusting language; struggling with English, and "De'il take ye" and "God damn" often bookend your conversation.*

Before leaving Harris, mention should be made of the composer of what is regarded as the Harris anthem, 'Chì mi 'n Tìr' ('I see the land'). This song was composed by Seonaidh Dhòmhnaill 'ic Cumhais (John MacCuish). In 1919-1920, in his early twenties, he was on the ships *Shuna* and *Glenamoy* when he composed his song of praise for Harris:

> 'S ged 's creagach cruaidh e, cha toir mi fuath dha,
> Far bhàrr a' chuain, àite as bòidhche sheallas.
>
> 'S ged 's creagach grànnd e, an tìr ri h-àireamh,
> Chan eil nas àille far bhàrr na mara.

Chì mi 'n tìr san robh mi nam bhalach,
Tìr nan suinn, Leac a' Lì nam shealladh;
Chì mi 'n tìr san robh mi nam bhalach.

Although it is craggy and hard, I won't hate it;
from an ocean view it is the most beautiful of places.

Although it is craggy and ugly, of all places counted,
there's none lovelier from a sea view.

I see the land where I was a lad; land of heroes,
Leac a' Lì in view. I see the land where I was a lad.

Beàrnaraigh agus Pabaigh: *Berneray and Pabbay*

A ferry service links Leverburgh with Beàrnaraigh (Berneray, ON, 'Bjorn's island'), and it in turn is connected to North Uist by a causeway. Traditionally this island was known in Gaelic as Beàrnaraigh na Hearadh (Berneray of Harris) to distinguish it from Beàrnaraigh Cheann Bharraigh (Berneray of Barra Head), now simply Barra Head. More recently Gaelic speakers have also used Beàrnaraigh Uibhist (Berneray of Uist) to refer to the northern Berneray and also to distinguish it from Beàrnaraigh Leòdhais (Berneray of Lewis).

Iain Eàirdsidh MacAsgaill (John Archie MacAskill) was born in Beàrnaraigh in 1898. He was a well-known and talented piper in the Camerons during World War I and during his time as a policeman in Glasgow. In 1924, he took advantage of a government scheme to emigrate to Australia where he died in 1933. Relatives brought his remains back to Berneray in 2010. His poems were published in the book *An Ribheid Chiùil* (*The Musical Reed)* (1961) including 'Moladh Deireannach' ('Final Praise'):

'S gur sgianach cathain 's lach an t-sùnnd
'S giadh air cùrsa fògradh
Gu bial nan uamhaichean sa Chùl
'S leaba liùnn an dòbhr-chu.

’S ro phailt buntàta as deirge maoin
Ri claisean craobhach eòrna,
’S bruaich tholmach mhurain meanbh air sgaoil
A ghormais taobh a choitcheann.

’S tha ’n fhairge bhon ear ’s an fhairge bhon iar
Gu gàireach, fiadhaich, cròiceach,
Tighinn briseach tormanach is dian
Gu carra, bial a’ chòpaidh.

’S gum b’ èibhinn leam bhith ann air chuairt
Sa gheamhradh ghruamach reòite,
’S mo lorgan saor bhon talamh chruaidh
Air brollach fuar nan tòrr-sneachd.

The barnacle geese are timid and the ducks contented, the geese bound on an exile course to the opening of the Cùl caves and to the otters’ watery lairs.

The sea from east and the sea from west comes noisily in wild, rumbling, seething, headlong confusion against the rocks, foaming and frothing.

I’d be happy walking there in the sombre, freezing winter, my footprints freed from the hard earth on the chill slope of the snowdrifts.

Tormod MacLeòid Ùnais, Fear-taca Bheàrnaraigh: *Norman MacLeod of Unish, Tacksman of Berneray*

In 1739, Norman MacLeod of Unish led a party that seized almost 100 people, mainly young, from the Isle of Skye and the Bays of Harris intending to transport them to America as indentured labour, a form of bondage used against petty criminals. His captives had never been indicted of any crime. In October his ship, the *William*, was damaged by storms and put into Donaghadee in Ireland where the prisoners were landed and locked up.

They managed to escape into parts of the neighbouring countryside. Despite Norman's efforts to round them up, Gaelic-speaking locals drew their presence to the attention of the magistrates of Donaghadee who issued warrants for the arrest of Norman and the ship's captain. Both, however, escaped. The Magistrates conducted an enquiry and the captives, many of whom barely exceeded ten years of age, all corroborated the fact that they had been violently seized. They were found temporary lodgings near Donaghadee and from there most of them settled on the lands of the Earl of Antrim. Few ever returned home. Their ship became known as 'Soitheach Nan Daoine' ('Ship of the People'), and it is by this name that the incident is remembered. Norman was not a lone actor in this affair. His father, Donald MacLeod, and Alexander MacDonald of Sleat, in collaboration with his brother-in-law, Norman MacLeod of Dunvegan, planned to profit by deporting their own people and their families to work alongside slaves in the plantations of America. All mounted a stout defence of their innocence and attempted to shift the blame on to young Norman.

It has been suggested the threat of prosecution over the affair kept both MacDonald of Sleat and MacLeod of Dunvegan from supporting the final Jacobite Rising in 1745. Young Norman remained in hiding in Ireland, but, in 1745, he returned to Skye, joined the Government forces and received the captaincy of the MacLeod Independent Companies. On his father's death in 1783, Norman succeeded him as Tacksman of Berneray. Norman died in May 1803 in his 88th year and was succeeded by his nephew, Alexander. The following year, on his bankruptcy, Alexander sold the estate to George Murray, 5th Earl of Dunmore.

Angus MacAskill (1825-1863) from Berneray was a natural giant. The 1981 Guinness Book of World Records says that he, at 2.36 metres, was the tallest non-pathological giant in recorded history. His father, Norman MacAskill, was 1.75 metres tall and Angus was an ordinary-sized baby. The family ultimately settled in the fishing community of Englishtown, Cape Breton Island, around 1831.

Of the islands in the Sound of Harris, Berneray is the largest and is now the only one populated.

There was once an important ecclesiastical community centred on the neighbouring island of Pabaigh (Pabbay, ON, 'priest'). The island once supported a three-figure population, exporting corn, barley and illicit whisky, and the latter activity was the excuse given by the estate when the island was cleared for sheep in 1846. Most of the chief of MacLeod's stewards of St. Kilda were Pabbay men and the island was traditionally the home of Clan Morrison.

Hiort: *St. Kilda*

These Pabaigh stewards had a 64 kilometre sea journey before they reached the isolated westerly archipelago of which Hiort (Hirta or St. Kilda) is its only once-inhabited island. Neither the meanings of the English nor Gaelic names are clear, but the English form is thought to refer to a well, while the Gaelic name may contain an old word for death. The name applies to the whole group of islands and sea stacks as in the saying:

À Hiort gu Peairt.

From St Kilda to Perth.

A number of other sayings refer to St. Kilda, for example:

B' fheàrr leam gun robh e ann an t-Hiort!

I wish he were in St Kilda!

This was said of someone one wished to be rid of.

Pòsadh Hiortach

A St Kilda wedding

is a marriage between close relations.

While a threat to a badly behaved child was:

Cuiridh mi a Hiort thu air muin mairt!

I'll send you to St Kilda on a cow's back!

With Hiort are three other islands Dùn (Dun), Sòaigh (Soay, ON, 'sheep island'), and Boighreigh (Boreray, ON 'fort island'), whose combined sea cliffs are the highest in the United Kingdom. Several islands of the name Boreray exist though it is perhaps unlikely that St. Kilda's Boreray was the island in question when the advice was given:

Na toir bò a Paibeil 's na toir bean à Boighreigh.

Do not take a cow from Paible nor a wife from Boreray.

St. Kildans kept sheep and a few cattle and grew a limited amount of crops, such as barley and, later, potatoes, on the better-drained land. But survival here depended on the exploitation of the seabirds breeding on the islands, especially gannet and fulmar. These they harvested as eggs and as young birds that they ate both fresh and cured. There are a large number of cleitean ('stone bothies') used for storing dried birds, fish, hay and turf on St. Kilda. A 1764 census described daily consumption for each of the 90 inhabitants as:

36 wild fouls (fowls) eggs and 18 fouls.

These fowling activities involved considerable skills in climbing, especially on the precipitous sea stacks. One fatality was Ìomhar (Imar or Ivor) whose widow laments his death in a narrow geodha ('gully') on Sòaigh. Published first in a 1777 anthology by the Rev. Eòghainn MacDhiarmaid (Eoin MacDermid), the song is sometimes known as the 'Cumha Hiortach' ('The St. Kilda Lament'). His mother, sister and brother, along with his widow, observed what happened, but there was nothing that they could do but weep:

'S ann thall ann a Sòaigh
Dh'fhàg mi 'n t-òg mach robh leumnach
Làmh a dhèanadh na h-acfhainn
'S a thoirt dhachaidh na sprèidhe.

'S ged a chaidh thu sa chreig ud
Cha b' e 'n t-eagal a leugh thu
'S ann a rinn do chas sraonadh
'S cha do dh'fheud thu riamh èirigh.

Bha d' fhuil air a' chloich ud
Bha do lot ann 'n dèidh leumaidh
Bha thu muigh air bhàrr stuaidhe
'S muir gad fhuasgladh o chèile.

It was over in Soay I left the young man who was not easily startled; the one who would make equipment and bring home the cattle.

And although you went to that rock it wasn't fear that caused it; it was the fact that your foot took a false step and you couldn't rise above it.

Your blood was on that stone, your wound made you ill; you were out on the crests of waves, the sea tearing you apart.

Cholera and smallpox struck this isolated and low disease-resistant community hard. In 1727, the loss of life was so high that there were too few to man the boats, and new families were brought in from Harris. By 1758, the population had risen to 88 and almost 100 by the end of the century. The slow growth was due to high infant mortality, not helped by the islanders' use of fulmar oil on the child's umbilical cord. The resulting tetanus infection led to lockjaw and death. In 1851, 36 islanders emigrated to Australia, in part as a result of the laird's closure of the church and manse for several years during the 1843 Disruption. The people had deserted the Established Church en masse.

St. Kilda never fully recovered from the loss, and, eventually, in August 1930, the remaining 36 inhabitants were evacuated to the Scottish mainland at their own request. The island was bequeathed to the National Trust for Scotland in 1957 and, in recognition of its natural uniqueness, was designated as Scotland's first World Heritage Site in 1987. It subsequently received a second inscription for its built heritage. The Ministry of Defence established a base on Hiort in the late 1950s for tracking missiles fired from South Uist.

Such is the wealth of tradition from Hiort that, in 2004, the singer and cultural historian Anne Lorne Gillies produced a CD, *An Long Hirteach* (*The St. Kilda Mail-boat*), a collection of over twenty songs. Amongst them is a love song which seems to be addressed to Iain Òg Ìle ('Young John of Islay'),

John Francis Campbell, the 19th-century editor of the four-volume *Popular Tales of the West Highlands:*

'S gura mise tha gu h-uallach
O là thàinig an duin' uasal
'S mo chuid ribinnean mun cuairt dhomh
'S cumaidh iad mo ghruag air dòigh.
Mo ghaol òigfhear a' chùil duinn
Dhan tug mi mo loinn 's mi òg.

Thog iad ormsa mar sgeula
Gun robh mo chriosan ag èirigh
Giùlainidh mise siud eutrom
O nach dèan e eucoir oirnn.
Mo ghaol òigfhear a' chùil duinn
Dhan tug mi mo loinn 's mi òg.

Sguiridh mi shùgradh ri gillean
Ged bu mhath leam a bhith mire
On tha 'n Caimbeulach gam shireadh
Cha tèid mi tuilleadh nan còir.
Mo ghaol òigfhear a' chùil duinn
Dhan tug mi mo loinn 's mi òg.

How cheerful I am since the day the nobleman arrived;
with my ribbons surrounding me, keeping my hair in place.
My love is the brown-haired youth to whom I gave my young
love.

They have said of me that my belts are rising, I will bear that
lightly so it won't be counted as our crime. My love is the
brown-haired youth to whom I gave my young love.

I will stop dallying with young men even though I enjoyed it.
Seeing Campbell is after me I won't go near them again.
My love is the brown-haired youth to whom I gave my
young love.

If the object of the young woman's desire was indeed correct, her wishes could never have been fulfilled given the enormous social divide that existed between them.

Caibideil 7: *Chapter 7*

Na h-Eileanan Siar – Deas: *The Western Isles – South*

Uibhist a Tuath: *North Uist*

A causeway links Berneray to Port nan Long (Newtonferry, 'harbour of the ships') in Uibhist a Tuath (North Uist, possibly 'corn land'), where once a ferry ran.

Dùn an Sticir: *Fort of the Skulker*

Less than a kilometre to the southwest of Newtonferry and ten north of Loch nam Madadh (Lochmaddy, 'loch of the dog mussels') is Dùn an Sticir ('Fort of the Skulker'), located on a small island in the loch of the same name. The original structure began life as a broch, one of a type of high-status Iron Age dwellings now grouped under the term Complex Atlantic Roundhouses. Dùn an Sticir was probably built in the period between 200 BC and 200 AD, as most such brochs were.

Ùisdean mac Ghill' Easbuig Chlèirich (Hugh 'the son of Archibald the clerk', or Hugh MacDonald) of Sleat, as the Factor for the MacDonald estates in North Uist, lived here in the 1580s. It is said that in 1586 he hatched a plan to murder his cousin, Donald Gorm, 8th Chief of the MacDonalds of Sleat. He bungled the arrangements by mixing up two letters: one, an invitation to his cousin to attend a banquet and the second, instructions to his assassin to dispatch Donald. After his plan was discovered, he fled to Dùn an Sticir. He was smoked out of there and eventually captured when he again tried to escape a siege of his other stronghold, Caisteal Ùisdein, Hugh's Castle, in Skye. As punishment, he was starved to death in the dungeon of Duntulm Castle in Skye.

A report dated 1616 stated:

> Lochmaldie on the coast of Uist is a rendezvous for pirates.

It was an important fishing harbour before the decline of commercial herring fishing. Nowadays, the same good harbour makes Lochmaddy the ferry port for the island, connecting North Uist to Skye and to Harris.

Dà Bhàrd à Uibhist a Tuath: *Two North Uist Poets*

Iain MacFhearchair (John MacCodrum) (1693-1779), a poet and wit, lived in Hòghagearraidh (Hogarry, ON, 'field at the rocky mound'). Later in his life, he served as bard to MacDonald of Sleat. An anecdote has it that when James 'Ossian' Macpherson was collecting stories from the Fenian Cycle, he asked the poet:

> "A bheil dad agaibh air an Fhèinne?"
>
> *"Do you have anything of the Fianna?"*

In reply, punning on the alternative sense of owing a debt, MacCodrum quipped:

> "Chan eil agus ge do bhiodh cha ruiginn a leas iarraidh a-nis."
>
> *"No, and if I did it would be pointless to ask for it now."*

More significantly, however, was the testimony of his patron, Sir James MacDonald, who in October 1763, wrote a letter to Doctor Hugh Blair that stated:

> The few bards that are left … repeat only detached portions of these poems. I have often heard and understood them, particularly from one man called John MacCodrum … I have heard him repeat, for hours together, poems which seem to me to be the same with Macpherson's translation.

Although he composed many poems, MacCodrum was illiterate, and as no one took down his poems from his own recitation, many of these have been lost. In one of his most popular songs 'Smeòrach Chlann Dòmhnaill' ('Mavis of Clan Donald'), he praises his native island:

Ma mholas gach eun a thìr fèin
Cuim thar èis nach moladh mise?
Tìr nan curaidh, tìr nan cliar
An tìr bhiadhchar, fhialaidh mhiosail?

'N tìr nach caol ri cois na mara
An tìr ghaolach, chaomhach, channach
An tìr laoghach, uanach, mheannach
Tìr an arain, bhainneach, mhealach.

An Cladh Chomhghain mise rugadh
'N Àird an Rùnair fhuair mi togail
Fradharc a' chuain uaibhrich chuislich
Nan stuagh guanach cluaineach cluiceach.

Measg Chlann Dòmhnaill fhuair mi m' altrum –
Buidheann nan seòl 's nan sròl daithte
Nan long luath air chuantaibh farsaing
Aiteam nach ciùin rùsgadh ghlaslann.

If every bird praises its own land, why then should not I? Land of heroes, land of poets, the abundant hospitable, estimable land.

The land not narrow near the sea, the delectable, mild comely land, the land of calves and lambs and kids, the land of bread and milk and honey.

In Comhghan's Churchyard I was born, in Àird an Runair I was reared, in sight of the proud throbbing sea, of the sportive, fickle, playful waves.

Among Clan Donald I was nursed – the folk of sails and coloured banners, of swift ships on wide seas, a people not mild when baring grey blades.

To the north of the road junction at Clachan na Lùib (Clachan or 'village of the loops') is the township of Corùna named for the Peninsular War battle of Corunna. Dòmhnall Ruadh Chorùna ('red-haired Donald of Corunna'), Donald MacDonald (1887-1967), was a stonemason here and a veteran of World War I. He was one of Scotland's greatest war poets, called by one authority "The Voice of the Trenches" and best known for the song 'An Eala Bhàn' ('The White Swan') which he composed during the Battle of the Somme. It is both a war song and a love song addressed to Magaidh Dhòmhnaill Raghnaill Saighdeir (Maggie, 'the daughter of Donald son of Ranald the Soldier') from Lochmaddy, the woman whom he hoped to marry:

A Mhagaidh, na bi tùrsach a rùin ged gheibhinn bàs –
Cò am fear am measg an t-sluaigh a mhaireas buan gu bràth?
Chan eil sinn uile ach air chuairt, mar dhìthein buaile fàs
Bheir siantanan na bliadhna sìos 's nach tog a' ghrian an àird.

Tha mise 'n seo 's mo shùil an iar on chrom a' ghrian san t-sàl
Mo dhùrachd leig mi às a dèidh ged thrèig i mi cho tràth,
Gun fhios am faic mi màireach i nuair dhìreas i gu h-àrd
Is iomairt lann gu bhith ri chèil' nuair 's lèir dhuinn beul an là.

Oidhche mhath leat fhèin a rùin nad leabaidh chùbhraidh bhlàth;
Cadal sàmhach air a' chùl 's do dhùsgadh sunndach slàn
Tha mise seo san truinnsidh fhuar 's nam chluasan fuaim a' bhàis
Gun dùil ri faighinn às le buaidh – tha 'n cuan cho buan ri shnàmh.

Maggie, my love, do not grieve even if I die – where is the man among us who is immortal? We are all of us on a brief journey just like the field flower that grows and succumbs to the changing season, the sun no longer able to revive it.

I am here gazing westwards since the sun sank in the sea. I took my sincere farewell of her, feeling she left me too soon and not knowing if I shall see her again tomorrow as she rises skywards, for battle will be joined when we see the glimmer of day.

Goodnight, my love, in your warm fragrant bed, a quiet sleep to you and a joyous, wholesome awakening. I am here in a cold trench, the sounds of death constantly in my ears, with little hope of emerging victorious – and the sea is too wide to swim.

He never did marry Magaidh but he was happily married to Anna Ruaraidh 'Ic Nèill (Anne MacDonald). He had begun composing Gaelic poetry at the age of thirteen but, as a result of the education system, he could neither read nor write Gaelic. He recalled his school days in the poem 'Òran nan Sgoilearan' ('Schoolchildren's Song'), saying that all the students were "hungry, deprived, barefoot, bare-headed" and "encouraged" to learn English. Fortunately, most of Dòmhnall Ruadh's poems and songs were transcribed before his death, with 57 poems and songs being first published by Gairm Publications in 1969.

Càirinis: *Carinish*

Càirinis (Carinish, ON, 'Kari's headland') is in the south of North Uist, about three kilometres from the causeway to Benbecula. The township contains Teampall na Trìonaid ('Trinity Temple'). An entry in the MacDonald history, *The Red Book of Clanranald* reads:

> Beathog inghen Shomhuirle do bhi na mnaoi riagalta & na cailligh duibh...do thoguibh Teampall Chairinis an Uibhist.
>
> *Beathag, daughter of Somerled, was a religious woman and a Black Nun. It is she that erected Teampall Chairinis in Uist.*

The ruined structure is a Medieval Augustinian nunnery. In 1601, The Battle of Carinish took place at Fèithe na Fala ('ditch of blood') near the nunnery. This fight was part of two years of feuding between Clan MacLeod of Dunvegan and Clan MacDonald of Sleat which ended with a MacDonald victory and an enforced peace. The MacLeods had sent Dòmhnall Glas ('grey Donald' of Drynoch, Skye) with 40 men to raid the island. On learning this, the Uist families sought sanctuary in Teampall na Trìonaid. Dòmhnall Glas easily took possession of the Teampall and decided to rest briefly there before they returned with their loot to Harris.

News of the raid reached another Donald, Dòmhnall mac Iain 'ic Sheumais (Donald, 'son of John, son of James'). This young man was a member of Clann Ùisdein, the MacDonalds of Sleat. Aged about eighteen, he was invited by his foster mother, Nic Còiseam, to farm her lands on the island of Eriskay. It was said that few could shoot an arrow with such dexterity or use his sword, An Lainnire Riabhach ('the speckled blade'), so skilfully. It was also said of him:

> A neart mar dharag na coille, a chumadh cho direach ri giuthas na beinne, 's a chorp cho sùbailte ri cuilc nan lòn.
>
> *His strength so like the oak of the forest, his form as straight as the mountain pine and his body as supple as the pond reed.*

Donald and his twelve-strong bodyguard immediately made their way north. At the ford over to Beinn na Faoghla (Benbecula), he met a Dòmhnall mac Iain who said:

> "Tha latha buana foghair agam ort!"
>
> *"You owe me an autumn's harvest day!"*

The other Donald retorted:

> "Ma tha, chan fhada bhitheas!"
>
> *"If so, it shall not be for long!"*

and he joined them. A little later the small band encountered a man carrying a load of peat. Donald asked him what he was being paid for his efforts. That conversation went thus:

"Coig sgillinn."

"Five shillings."

Donald replied:

"Coisich còmhla ruinne,'s gheibh thu duais gu math nas feàrr, is urram nach bi faoin na luirg."

"Walk with us and you will get a much greater reward and high regard along with it."

The man joined them and when the fifteen arrived at Carinish, at dawn, Clann na Làir ('children of the mare') as the MacLeods were nicknamed, were preparing to leave. Donald divided his men into three companies. Five, he stationed behind a hill some distance from the church, five others, closer, and he and his companions moved to within arrow range of the Teampall. He ordered them to take steady aim and to make sure that each brought down one man. They were then to retreat to where the second company was stationed, again fire at their pursuers and finally run to the hill occupied by the remainder, where they would all make a determined stand.

Once the MacLeods spotted the puny company attacking them, they rushed upon them and were picked off just as Donald intended. The planning worked so well that when the MacLeods reached the hill the two groups were almost equal in number. Confident that victory was theirs, the MacDonalds charged forward. However, an arrow struck Donald in the thigh and he retired hurt, but the MacLeods were soon in full retreat and only two of them escaped alive.

It is said that his foster-mother followed Donald and arrived just as the fray was ending. She extracted the arrow and, as she did so, had the young women who had gathered around her sing the chorus of the song 'A Mhic Iain 'ic Sheumais' ('Son of John, son of James') she was composing, in order to divert Donald's attention from the pain:

A Mhic Iain 'ic Sheumais
Tha do sgeul air m' aire
Latha Blàr a' Chèithe
Bha feum air mo leanabh.

Là Blàr na Fèithe
Bha do lèine ballach
Bha fuil do chuim chùbhraidh
A' drùdhadh tron anart
Bha mi fhèin ga sùghadh
Gus na thùch air m' anail.

Son of Iain, son of James you are on my mind. The day of Blàr a' Chèithe my beloved was needed. The day of Blàr na Fèithe your shirt was speckled, the blood of your fragrant body soaking through the linen. I was sucking it till I choked.

Beinn na Faoghla: *Benbecula*

A 1960s causeway links North Uist to Benbecula. The name seems to derive from Peighinn nam Fadhla ('pennyland of the fords'). 'Peighinn' is very similar phonetically to the unstressed form of beinn ('mountain') which is now used.

Baile a' Mhanaich (Balivanich, 'town of the monk') is the principal community in the island. The name possibly relates to an ancient monastery, Teampull Chaluim Chille, a church dedicated to Columba, lying to the south. An airfield to the north, built during World War II, became the control centre for the Hebrides rocket range, established in 1957 at the height of the Cold War. There was once a substantial military community here.

Baile nan Cailleach (Nunton, 'nun town') contains Teampall Mhuire (Mary's Church) and the graveyard that was the burial place of the later Clanranald chiefs. Immediately adjacent is Nunton House, an early 18th-century laird's house, the former seat of the MacDonalds of Clanranald. The new house utilised the stones of the old religious establishment of Mary's Church. Prior to that, the MacDonalds resided at Borve Castle, a medieval keep or hall-house, probably dating to the late 14th century. Its construction is traditionally attributed to Amie, first wife of John, Lord of the Isles, although one version is that the builder was a chief who had been spooked out of his older haunt of Dùn Buidhe ('noble fort') by a premonition of death delivered by Luideag an Uillt ('the ragged lady of the stream'). The construction of the new house dates from the Nunton family succession to the title of Clanranald on the death of the chief, Ailean Mùideartach, at the battle of Sheriffmuir in September 1715.

In the early 19th century, the chief, Ranald George, got into financial difficulties and sold his lands to Colonel John Gordon of Cluny, a ruthless, evicting landlord. Later landowners saw the future of the estate in hunting, shooting and fishing terms, much as the penultimate owners – a sporting syndicate – did. In November 2006, the syndicate sold the assets of the 302km^2 estate, including Benbecula, South Uist and Eriskay, for £4.5 million to a community-owned organisation, Stòras Uibhist, set up to manage it in perpetuity.

Uibhist a Deas: *South Uist*

Across the modern causeway is Uibhist a Deas (South Uist), the second-largest island in the Western Isles. Beyond the causeway over Loch Bee, to the east of the A865 road, on the slopes of Ruabhal (Rueval), is a statue of Baintighearna nan Eilean (Our Lady of the Isles), designed by Hew Lorimer and dedicated in 1958. It was commissioned by Canon John Morrison, the local parish priest, who became known as 'Father Rocket' as a result of his resistance to a proposed missile testing range. The original proposals would have covered much of Uist and also involved the construction of facilities for building missiles. Ultimately, the Ministry of Defence built a scaled-down base to test missiles and an RAF missile range with a tracking station on St. Kilda. Opposition also resulted in the novel *Rockets Galore!* by Sir Compton Mackenzie, subsequently made into a film, and 'Òran nan Rocaidean ('Rocket Song') by Dòmhnall Ruadh Phàislig:

> Uibhist agus Barraigh
> Cha bhi leanabh na fear liath ann
> Leòdhasaich is Hearaich
> Dol nan sradagan dhan iarmailt;
> Sgitheanaich is Muilich
> Air am buileachadh dhan t-sìorr'achd
> 'S na h-Eileanan an Iar
> Air an lìonadh le plàigh

There won't be a child or a grey-haired elder in Uist or Barra; Lewismen and Harrismen disappearing skywards in showers of sparks; Skyemen and Mullmen consigned to eternity and the Western Isles filled with a plague.

The Deep-Sea Range for the evaluation of new missiles remains a feature of island life.

Togh Mòr (Howmore, ON, *'haugr',* 'big burial mound') lies to the south. Here are the remains of a once substantial religious settlement, its Teampall Mòr ('large church') also known as St Mary's, possibly dating back to the 13th century. This fragmentary group of two medieval churches and two chapels is one of the most important religious sites in the Western Isles. By the end of the 17th century, the buildings were probably ruinous, but Caibeal Chlann 'ic Ailein (Clanranald's Chapel) continued as the burial place of the Clanranald chiefs. The most celebrated historical artefact at Howmore lay in the graveyard. The so-called Clanranald Stone, a late 16th-century stone panel carved with the Clanranald arms, weighs 166 kilograms, yet in 1990 it disappeared from Howmore and was found in London five years later. It is now housed in Kildonan Museum in South Uist.

The landscape to the east of Howmore is dominated by the Lewisian Gneiss hills of Gèideabhal (ON, 'goat mountain'), now known as A' Bheinn Mhòr and Hecla. Hecla has a volcanic shape and shares the same name as the Icelandic volcano Hekla. Evidently it was a significant sea marker for voyaging Vikings.

Flòraidh NicDhòmhnaill agus Niall MacEachainn: *Flora MacDonald and Neil MacEachen*

In the area of Geàrraidh Bhailteas (Garryvaltos, 'fertile land of the river mouth') is Àirigh Mhuilinn (Milton, 'sheiling of the mill'), the tack where Flòraidh nighean Raghnaill 'ic Aonghais Òig (Flora, 'daughter of Ronald son of young Angus') was born and spent her childhood. Her name in English is Flora MacDonald but here she is referred to as Flòraidh Àirigh Mhuilinn (Flora of Milton) and never as Fionnghal as is sometimes supposed. A memorial dedicated to this Jacobite heroine stands at the remains of the township. Flora, a young woman of the tacksman class, was used as 'cover' for Bonnie Prince Charles's escape from the clutches of the tightening Government dragnet in South Uist. It was not the first time that royal princes had disguised themselves as young women. Charles's own grandfather, James VII, escaped thus from Westminster Palace while Louis XVIII fled from revolutionary Paris in the same way.

Less well understood is the role of the daoine uasal ('the local gentry'), who, while acting as officers in the locally recruited government militia, were instrumental in both the Uists and Skye in securing the Prince's liberty. Moreover, the role of a South Uist man, Niall MacEachainn (Neil MacEachen) of Howbeg, who was almost certainly in the French Secret Service, was crucial in ensuring the safety of the Prince. Local Uist tradition acknowledges the part played by this 'MacDonald for the Prince', as a book about him is titled. The traditional tales of the period have as much to say about Niall as they do about Flòraidh.

Neil, a relation of Flora MacDonald, studied for the priesthood at the Scots College at Douai in France. He was fluent in Gaelic, Greek, Latin, English and French before he returned to South Uist at the time of the 1745 Rising. He was Charles Edward Stuart's personal guide while the Prince was a fugitive. He returned to France, where he was given a commission in Ogilvy's Regiment under the name Neil MacDonald, possibly because the French had difficulty pronouncing MacEachen.

When Neil died in 1788, his son Jacques MacDonald had already begun a promising military career in the French army, and, by dint of ability, became one of Napoleon's Field Marshals. Jacques visited South Uist in 1825 and, as he recorded in his journal, travelled on what he describes as a road that "diminishes into a track" across an "immense wasteland" and "a country which seems desolate". When he reached his father's birthplace, he was met by a group of his relatives. More islanders began to arrive until around 600 people gathered to greet their distinguished guest.

Dà Bhàrd à Uibhist a Deas: *Two Poets of South Uist*

At Snaoiseabhal (Snishival, meaning uncertain) is a monument to two eminent local bards, Dòmhnall Iain Dòmhnallach and Dòmhnall Ruadh Mac an t-Saoir.

Dòmhnall Iain Dhonnchaidh (Donald John, 'son of Duncan') (1918-1986) belonged to Peighinn nan Aoireann (Peninerine from 'penny land of the Mass'). He was a poet, songwriter and author. His book, *Fo Sgàil a' Swastika (Under the Swastika's Shadow)*, gives a vivid account of the grim privation of World War II prison camps but resonates with the spirited sense of comradeship among the captives. A fine collection of his poems and hymns, entitled *Chì Mi* ('I See') was collected and edited by local man, Bill Innes. Donald's poetic influences were wide and varied, yet his work is deeply rooted in the local tradition which held the belief that such talent was a bestowal beyond education. As his contemporary Donald Allan MacDonald said:

> Chan eil de dh' fhoghlam air an t-saoghal a dhèanadh duine na bhàrd.
>
> *There's not sufficient education in the world to make a man a poet.*

The plaque on the monument has lines from his poem 'Feasgar Beatha' ('Evening of Life'):

> Dia a chruthaich do bhràthair, 'S co-dhiù 's ann dubh no 's ann bàn.
>
> *God fashioned your brother, whether dark or fair he be.*

The second bard commemorated on the Snishival monument is Donald's uncle, Dòmhnall Ruadh mac Aonghais Ruaidh ('red Donald, son of red Angus') or Dòmhnall Mac an t-Saoir, Bàrd Phàislig (Donald Macintyre, the Paisley Bard). He was born in Snishival in 1889. Leaving school at the age of fourteen, he was apprenticed as a stonemason but joined the Camerons at the start of World War I. As Cameron of Locheil's personal piper, he exhibited great bravery during the battle of Loos. Following the war, his search for work took him ultimately to Paisley, hence the name the Paisley Bard. He first made his name as a poet when he represented the Snishival crofters in the 'Case of the Dogs', their resistance to efforts by the estate owner, Lady Cathcart, to stop crofters from keeping dogs without permission. Their success prompted Dòmhnall to compose two songs about the events: 'Cùirt nan Con' ('Court of the Dogs') and 'Triall gu Cùirt nan Con' ('Going to the Court of the Dogs'). In his large corpus of songs is the amusing 'Bùth Dhòmhnaill 'ic Leòid' ('Donald Macleod's Pub'), commemorating a well-known establishment run by Skye man, Donald MacLeod:

Chì thu dìsnean is tàileasg gan càradh air bùird,
Bidh gach nì mar is còir eadar Dòmhnall 's a bhùth,
Gheibh thu pàipear ri leughadh le speuclair dhad shùil,
'S chì thu staidhre dol sìos, àit' bhios riatanach dhuinn
Ann am bùth Dhòmhnaill 'ic Leòid.

Ann am bùth Dhòmhnaill 'ic Leòid bidh gach seòrs'
  innte cruinn,
Thig o thaobh Abhainn Chluaidh 's cuid tha nuas às
  na glinn.
Bidh a' chàbraid cho cruaidh ann an cluasan do chinn,
'S ged bhiodh bàrd ris gach gualainn dhiot 's fuaim ac'
  air seinn
Ann am bùth Dhòmhnaill 'ic Leòid.

"Cuir a-nuas leth tè chruaidh," thuirt fear shuas mun
  cheann àrd,
"Gloine fìon," thuirt fear shìos air bheil fìor choltas ceàird.
"Happy Day, come away," labhair tè reamhar, bhàn
A bha bhlàth air a sròin, gun do thòisich i tràth
Dhol a bhùth Dhòmhnaill 'ic Leòid.

You'll see dice and draughts laid on a table; everything will be as it ought between Donald and his pub; you'll get a newspaper to read and specs for your eyes and you'll see a stair going down – to a place we all have need of – in Donald MacLeod's pub.

In Donald MacLeod's pub, all types congregate, some come from Clydeside and some down from the glens. The racket will be so loud in your ears as if you had a bard on each side of you singing loudly, in Donald MacLeod's pub.

> *"Send across a half of the hard stuff" said a man at the top of the bar. "A glass of wine," said a fellow down the other end who had the look of a right tinker about him. "Happy Day, come away," said a fat, fair woman, the colour of whose nose showed that she started young frequenting Donald MacLeod's pub.*

Welcoming *Sporan Dhòmhaill* (*Donald's Sporran*), an anthology of his songs in 1968, just four years after the poet's death, the scholar Coinneach Dòmhnallach (Kenneth MacDonald) said of Dòmhnall Ruadh's poetry:

> It seems to me that we will not see the like of his poetic quality in Gaelic again. His was the richness of language, an inheritance of his South Uist upbringing that he broadened by study of the works of poets who had gone before him. And yet while it was not from dictionaries that he derived his cainnt gheur-fhaclach nam bàrd, expressive language of the poets, those interested in vocabulary will long study his work.

Donnchadh Clachair: *Duncan the Mason*

Donnchadh Clachair ('Duncan the Mason' or Duncan MacDonald) had perhaps the largest and most varied repertoire of stories and songs recorded by any single Scottish Gael. Duncan was almost certainly directly descended from the MacRury seanchaidhean (hereditary historians and storytellers to the MacDonalds of Sleat). He was recorded for the Irish Folklore Commission by Calum I. MacLean. One of Duncan's tales took three nights of recording to capture in its entirety, and the transcripts are now housed in the archive of the School of Scottish Studies in Edinburgh.

The premier place in the Gaelic storyteller's repertoire is occupied by long hero tales derived from the secular literature of the medieval period. A comparison of an introductory episode of one tale of Donnchadh's with an incomplete 17th-century manuscript written in Kintyre in 1690 shows such similarities that it is quite possible that the story was learned by heart from a manuscript before 1700 and passed down to Duncan, substantially unchanged for almost three centuries.

Among the favourites tales are historical legends of clan feuds, robbers and archers, some of them migratory tales of European tradition. One of Duncan's tales concerns an instantly recognisable example of archery skill. It features Gille Pàdraig Dubh, Black Gilpatrick, a 17th-century MacIntyre whose descendants are still in South Uist.

Gille Pàdraig: *Gilpatrick*

Gille Pàdraig went to Clanranald's rent house with sacks of grain to pay the rent. When Clanranald's measurer complained that the measure was short, Gille Pàdraig slit the man's throat and made up the measure with blood. On learning this, Clanranald was in a dilemma: the murder could not go unpunished, but he was reluctant to fall out with Gille Pàdraig because, as a noted archer, he was too useful to him. Clanranald devised a plan and sent for Gille Pàdraig to come to him at Ormacleit, bringing with him his son, Iain Dubh. He said that he had laid a wager with a guest that his archer could, from a distance, break an egg on his son's head with an arrow without harming him.

Gille Pàdraig duly set out with his son for Ormacleit. There they were welcomed and then prepared for the challenge. Gille Pàdraig made his son stand in front of him with Clanranald and his lady and the guest observing. He took an arrow from his quiver and stuck it through the garter on his right leg and then took another arrow and stuck it through the garter on his left leg. The egg was then placed on the top of his son's head. Then Gille Pàdraig took the third arrow from his quiver, took good aim and shot the egg sky-high.

"Very good," said Clanranald, "I am pleased that you performed the feat in the presence of the stranger. But will you tell me now, what was your reason for sticking an arrow through each garter?"

"Yes," said Gille Pàdraig, "if I had done my son any harm, one would have landed in you and the other in the lady."

"Away, away!" said Clanranald. "It's no good trying to do anything with you."

However, no further action was taken against Gille Pàdraig.

This is obviously a variant of the William Tell legend but is too well established in South Uist to be derived from published translations of the Swiss story. A variant also exists in Barra.

Ceit, Bean Eàirdsidh Raghnaill: *Kate, Archie MacDonald's wife*

In 1953, Eàirdsidh Raghnaill (Archie MacDonald) of Gearraidh Sheilidh (Garryhallie, 'fertile land of willows') a crofting township some ten kilometres to the south of Snishival, made the following observation: "My wife has a song". From this modest statement, fieldworkers went on to record over 200 songs from Ceit, Bean Eàirdsidh Raghnaill (Kate, Mrs Archie MacDonald) (1897-1977). Among her wide repertoire was the song 'Mo nighean chruinn donn' ('My neat brown-haired girl') about a hapless man going night-visiting, describing the many obstacles he faced. He had to escape in a hurry, leaving his trousers behind. His advice to young men in a similar situation was to wear the kilt:

'S nuair ràna mi 'n doras bha 'n glas air mo shròin,
Bha tuilleadh 's a' chòir a dhlùithean air.

Bha triùir san rathad, an clobha 's a' bhrà,
'S am bùileasg gu h-àrd 's e gliongadaich.

'S an cuilean beag giobach bha 'n iomall na luatha,
Thug e trì uairean ionnsaigh orm.

Nuair ràna mi 'n leaba gun d' fhuair mi i làn,
Bha tuilleadh 's mo ghràdh nan sìneadh innt'.

Bha tè dhiubh ruadh 's tè cho dubh ris a' ghual,
Tè eil' agus cuailean grìs-fhionn oirr'.

'S gun d' dh'èirich am bodach 's a bhata na làimh,
"Nach glac sinn am gàrlach mì-mhodhail."

'S a-mach air an uinneig a ghabh mi gu h-àrd,
'S a' bhriogais gun d' dh'fhàg mi 'n dìochuimhn' i.

Bu chruaidhe mo thurtar a' tuiteam air làr,
Na each air an t-sràid is cruidhean air.

Mo mhallachd air gill' thig nam dheaghaidh gu bràth,
A bheireadh a' bhriogais a shuirghe leis.

’S e ’n t-èileadh beag preusant a b’ fhasanta leam,
Gus suidh’ ann an cùirt nan nìghneagan.

When I arrived at the door the lock was level with my nose and there were too many deterrents on it.
There were three things in the way – the tongs, the quern and the pothook jingling up above.
And the furry little puppy by the fire attacked me three times.
When I made it to the bed I found it full. There was more than my darling stretched out in it.
One was red-haired, one as black as coal and another with brindled locks.
The old man got up with his stick in his hand saying “Let’s catch the ill-mannered rogue!”
I fled out the top window forgetting to take my trousers.
I hit the ground with a thump louder than a shod horse makes on a street.
My curse forever on any lad who comes after me and wears trousers to go courting.
The kilt is my choice of attire for sitting in the company of young ladies.

Ceòlas

Since its establishment in 1996, Ceòlas has grown from a week-long music and dance school to become a leading Gaelic culture, heritage and arts organisation. From its base at Cnoc Soilleir (‘shining knoll’) in Dalabrog (Daliburgh, ON, ‘fort valley’), Ceòlas provides a programme of traditional arts classes and events. Cnoc Soilleir is itself a joint venture by Ceòlas and Lews Castle College/University of the Highlands and Islands.

Èirisgeigh: *Eriskay*

The main road south is carried by a 2001 causeway to the island of Èirisgeigh (Eriskay, ON, 'Eric's island'). It has a population of around 150. In 1550, a visitor noted that Eriskay was a small community taking advantage of excellent fishing grounds nearby, which is pretty much how it stayed for 300 more years. Everything changed in 1838 when Eriskay, along with South Uist, Benbecula and Barra, was purchased by Colonel Gordon of Cluny. He cleared most of the islands of people to create sheep ranches. Eriskay's land was too poor to support many sheep so Colonel Gordon permitted some of the people displaced from elsewhere to resettle there. As a result, Eriskay's then population of 80 rapidly expanded to over 400 people.

The island is known for the song 'An Eriskay Love Lilt', one of many Gaelic songs transcribed by the singer and composer Marjory Kennedy-Fraser after a visit to the island in 1905. Better known among Gaelic speakers is Father Alan MacDonald's 'Eilean na h-Òige' ('Island of Youth'):

Sùlair' amaiseach a's t-earrach
Staigh an caraibh tìr e:
Tighinn an caise, sgeithidh paisgte,
Fear nach caisgt' a chìocras.
Thall 's bhos iad, chan eil fois ac'
Sloistreadh crost' gun sgìos ac',
Cromadh, tomadh fo na tonnan –
Lìonadh bhronnan shìos iad!

Corr chas-fhada, stob 'm bun cladaich,
'N riochd bhith ragaicht' reòthta.'
'N ann fo ghcasaibh tha i seasamh?
'M bi i feast san t-seòl ud?
Cailleach ghlic i, cha do chleachd i
Cluich an cuideachd ghòraich –
Rogha suthainn bhith gun duine
'N cuid rith' grunnach' lònain.

In spring the unerring gannet comes in close to land: flying impetuously, wings folded back, his hunger cannot be satisfied. Here and there, without rest, sloshing, cross, never tired, dropping, dipping under the waves – filling their bellies down below!

The long-legged heron, a stick by the shoreline, as if she was stiffened and frozen. Does she stand there bewitched? Will she be like that forever? She's a wise old woman, not in the habit of playing in foolish company – she'll always choose to be alone whenever she wades through a pool.

On 2nd August 1745, the privateer *Du Teillay* landed Prince Charles Edward Stuart with his 'seven men of Moidart' near a spot that is now called Coilleag a' Phrionnsa ('Prince's Shell Strand'). On arrival, Charles met the local tacksman, Fear Bhaghasdail (Alexander MacDonald of Boisdale), who urged him to go home. Charles is reported to have said, "I am come home sir!" before sailing for the Scottish mainland. Today, the strand is home to a flower called the White Striped Pink Sea Bindweed, the seeds of which are said by tradition to have fallen from Charles's pocket. However, this creeping perennial plant, although rarer in northern Scotland, is common in coastal parts of Britain and Ireland.

Eriskay has a more recent claim to fame because of the story of the SS *Politician*, a general cargo ship of the Harrison line, en route to Jamaica and New Orleans. When the ship was wrecked off the island in 1941 there were 264,000 bottles of whisky aboard. It is said that some 24,000 bottles disappeared before the authorities arrived and in the aftermath, several islanders were sent to prison briefly. Compton Mackenzie's 1947 novel *Whisky Galore* loosely based on these events, was subsequently made into Ealing Studios' most successful film. A more local production by South Uist poet Roderick Campbell was the song 'Òran a' Pholitician' ('Song of the Politician'):

Thàinig bàt' air tìr san àite seo
A dh'fhàg mise fo mhìngean
Fhuair mi aiste dram no dhà
'S e sin a dh'fhàg cho tinn mi;

’S mar a tha mi an-diugh cho truagh
Cha ghluais mi ach le dìcheall
’S e na dh’òl mi dhan Spey Royal
Chuir am bròn air m’ inntinn.

Chuala mi gun robh i ann
’S gu robh an t-àm dhol innte
Gu robh stuth innte gu leòr
Bha brògan agus sìod’ ann
’S an t-uisge-beatha mar bha an còrr
Gach brand is seòrs’ bha sgrìobhte
’S ged bha ’n ola dhubh gu h-àrd
Bha chuid a b’ fheàrr gu h-ìosal.

A ship has grounded in this place and that’s left me discontented. I got a dram or two out of her and that’s what’s left me so ill. Today I’m feeling so poorly I can only move with a great effort; it was the amount of Spey Royal I drank that has left me depressed.

Like everyone else I heard that she was there and it was time to go aboard, that there was plenty cargo below, shoes and silks and like everything else plenty whisky of every known brand and, although there was black oil above, the best was below deck.

Barraigh is Bhatarsaigh: *Barra and Vatersay*

Barraigh (Barra) is the second most southerly inhabited island of the Hebrides after the adjacent island of Bhatarsaigh (Vatersay) to which it is connected by a short causeway. Once thought to be more isolated, its location led to the coining of the saying:

Ged ’s fad a-muigh Barraigh, ruigear e.

Although Barra is far out, it can be reached.

The island is reputedly named for St. Finbarr of Cork. In 2011, over 60% of the population of 1,174 were Gaelic speakers.

In 1493, the Lord of the Isles granted the Lairdship of Barra to Giolla Adhamhnáin Mac Néill (Chief of Clan MacNeil). Basing themselves at Caisteal Chìosamuil (Kishmul Castle), they were renowned mariners and it was said of the chief:

> Chan ann a h-uile latha a thèid MacNèill air each.
>
> *It's not every day that MacNeil mounts his horse.*

Inevitably, he practised a little piracy. The Barra men were not alone in this, however, and a commonly applied quip about nefarious practices was:

> Tha taobh dubh 's taobh geal air, mar a bha air bàta Mhic lain Gheàrr.
>
> *He has a white side and a black side, like the boat of Short John's son.*

The 'he' in question was Archibald MacDonell who was a noted reiver and followed a known practice of pirates in having his boat and sails of different colours on each side. Such men fell foul of the authorities by attacking English ships during the reign of Queen Elizabeth I. On being summoned by King James VI to Edinburgh to account for himself, the then MacNeil chief, Ruaraidh an Tartair (Rory the Turbulent), is said to have claimed in his defence that he thought the king would be pleased as Elizabeth had beheaded his mother, Mary, Queen of Scots. An amused James released him. Sadly, this supposed act would have been uncharacteristically lenient; James, had he got his hands on Ruaraidh, would have strung him up along with the rest of the, to his mind, 'pesiferous' Gaels.

The islanders evicted from Barra by Gordon of Cluny's clearances in 1838 were dispersed to the Scottish mainland, Australia, New Zealand, the United States and Canada. Barra was restored to MacNeil ownership in 1937 when the island was bought by Robert Lister MacNeil, an American architect who was evidently the 45th chief of the clan. In 2000, his heir, Ian Roderick, let

Kishmul Castle to Historic Scotland, on a 1000-year lease for an annual rental of £1 and a bottle of whisky. In 2003, he transferred ownership of the Barra Estate to the Scottish Government; the inhabitants have the right to take possession of the estate if they so wish.

The main port is Bàgh a' Chaisteil (Castlebay) where Kismul Castle sits on a small islet in the bay. The date of the castle's construction is likely to be after the 1427 grant of the island of Barra to the MacNeils. A tale is told of MacNeil's herald surmounting the ramparts to announce:

> Thoireadh gach sluagh cluas is èisteadh gach cinneach rim ghuth. Tha MacNèill Mòr Bharraigh air èirigh o bhòrd is faodaidh prionnsaichean an domhainn a-nis suidhe sìos gum biadh.
>
> *Let all the people and all nations listen to my voice. The Great MacNeil of Barra has risen from his table and the princes of the world may now sit down to eat.*

The talented singer and tradition bearer, Flòraidh an Tàilleir (Flora MacNeil) (1928-2015), was originally brought to wider public attention by the American musicologist Alan Lomax during the early 1950s. One of her well-known songs has been mistakenly thought to be Irish. Dòmhnall Ruadh ('Red Donald') and Catriona ni' n Aonghais (Catriona, 'daughter of Angus') from Ceann Tangabhal (Kentangaval) were betrothed, but before the marriage, Donald went to An Iùbhraidh (Newry) in Ireland on a grain ship in order to purchase whisky for the wedding. But there Donald met a rich woman who fell madly in love with him, and he, forgetting his vows to his Barra sweetheart, married her. It was from the jilted Catriona's ensuing sorrow that the song 'An Gille Dubh-Dhonn' ('The Auburn-Haired Lad') arose:

> 'S e na dh' fhalbh air bàt an t-sìl
> Is tha mi fhìn ag ionndrainn
>
> 'B fheàrr leam fhìn a bhi ruit pòsta
> Na cuid òir a' phrionnsa.
>
> 'B fheàrr leam do dhreach 's do phearsa
> Na Sasann le na h-ionntas

Mo cheist fear an t-siubhail aotrom
'S aotrom ceum an fhiùrain.

I am pining for the man who left on the grain ship.
I would rather be married to you than all the prince's gold.
I would rather have the beauty of your person than have England with all its riches.
My love the one who travels lightly, the handsome light-stepping youth.

It is said that initially the marriage went well and a son was born. At that time it was the practice in the islands that the children shared the parental bed; a practice Donald's wife frowned upon. Exasperated on one such night she exclaimed:

Nach uabhasach mar a dh' èirich dha na daoine bochda fhèin! Na droch chleachdannan a bh' aca.

Isn't it terrible what has become of the poor people - the bad habits they had!

With that, Donald snatched up the child and disappeared. It was said that Donald's conscience was troubled by his failure to honour the marriage contract with Catriona.

This version of Catriona's song was taken down from the singing of Donald MacNeil, Àrd Mòr, Bàgh a Tuath (Northbay), by the Irishman Colm O Lochlainn. On Donald's death in 1929, at the age of 24, climbing at Eas Conaill (Conal's Waterfall, now Powerscourt Waterfall) in County Wicklow, Colm had a book containing some 40 songs from Donald's repertoire published in Dublin.

Fèis Bharraigh (the Barra Festival), an annual event, was started in 1981 to sustain the musical tradition from which Flòraidh and many others sprang. This pioneering Fèis, a Gaelic arts tuition festival, established the model for more Fèisean around Scotland, each community-led and tailored to local needs. Currently, there are over 40 Fèisean being held annually.

Bhatarsaigh: *Vatersay*

South of Barra lies an archipelago of islands, The Barra Isles, also known as the Bishop's Isles since the time that King James VI transferred ownership of them to the Bishop of the Isles. All have been inhabited in the past but only Bhatarsaigh (Vatersay, ON, 'water island') now has a population.

In 1908, ten men from Barra and neighbouring Miughalaigh (Mingulay ON, perhaps 'main hill island') were brought before the Court of Session in Edinburgh on charges of breach of interdict and contempt of court. Their crime was to resist eviction from Vatersay which they had raided and on which they had constructed temporary huts and planted potatoes without seeking permission from the landowner, Lady Gordon Cathcart. The 'raiders' received a two-month prison sentence. The case caused such concern that the government purchased the island for crofting; in many ways, Vatersay was a microcosm of what was then happening across the Highlands and Islands as the demand for land became ever more pressing.

Nan Eachainn Fhionnlaigh (Nan, 'daughter of Hector, son of Finlay' or Nan MacKinnon) lived in Vatersay from 1902 to 1982. In 1931, the population of the island was 240 but, by the time of her death, it had fallen to about 100. She was a singer and storyteller with an inexhaustible memory for traditional folklore and songs. She was also the last surviving link with the songs and folklore of the nearby island of Mingulay, abandoned in 1912. Nan recorded over 600 songs and related over 1000 stories, anecdotes and proverbs to folklore collectors from the School of Scottish Studies. The stirring Clan MacNeil song 'Coisich a Rùin' ('Come on my Love') featured in her repertoire:

Ma thug Clann Nèill,
druim a' chuain orr',

Luchd nan ròiseal,
's nan long luatha,

's nam brataichean,
dearg is uaine,

’s nan claidheamhan,
geura, cruadhadh

nach laigh smal orr’,
anns na truaillean.

If the MacNeils have gone to sea, displaying their fast galleys, banners red and green, and swords sharp, steely, unblemished in their scabbards.

Located nineteen kilometres south of Barra, Mingulay, with some 55 hectares of arable and pasture land, is the next largest of the Bishop’s Islands. The islanders subsisted on fishing and farming but, as in St. Kilda, they were dependent on seabirds. Indeed, rent was payable to MacNeil in fachaich (‘fatlings’, shearwater chicks).

The ‘Mingulay Boat Song’ was written by Sir Hugh S. Roberton (1874-1952) in the 1930s. The melody is described in Roberton’s *Songs of the Isles* as a traditional Gaelic tune, probably titled ‘Lochaber’, indicating that the tune used for the song was that of ‘Òran na Comhachaig’ (‘The Song of the Owl’), a song from Brae Lochaber. Roberton’s song, however, describes fishermen sailing homeward to where their families wait:

Hill you ho, boys; let her go, boys;
Bring her head round, now all together.
Hill you ho, boys; let her go, boys;
Sailing home, home to Mingulay.

Although the fame of the song means that it is one of the few things now associated with the island, it was never sung by its residents, being composed after the island was abandoned. However, songs composed by or about residents of the island do survive. Niall Chaluim Dhòmhnaill or Niall Mac a’ Phì (Neil MacPhee) (1874-1929) belonged to a scholarly family and was described by Ben Buxton, author of *Mingulay: An Island and Its People*, as “a man of remarkable ability”. His ‘Òran do dh’ Eilean Mhiughalaigh’ (‘Song to the Isle of Mingulay’) recalled his former home:

’S tric a dh’èist mi gàir’ nan tonn
Ri cladach lom nan caolasan,
Is m’ aigne fhèin cho rèidh ri phong
’S mo chridhe trom a’ smaointinn air.
A liuthad car a chaidh don t-sruth
On chruthaicheadh an saoghal seo,
Air ais ’s air aghaidh gus an-diugh
’S fuaim a’ ghuth gun chaochladh air.

’S tric air feasgar Cèitein ciùin
’S gun leam ach speil de dh’fhaoileagan,
A shuidh mi greis gun mòran suim
Air binneag Druim na h-Aoineige.
An àm don ghrèin bhith dol sa chuan
Bu mhaiseach snuadh a h-aodainn leam,
’S ged a rinn i mìle cuairt
Cha tàinig tuar na h-aois oirre.

Leam bu mhiann bhith ’g amharc uam
Air madainn fhuaraidh fhaoilleachail,
A’ gabhail beachd air neart nan stuagh
Bu ghreannach gruamach caoir-ghealach.
A’ cur nan car dhiubh tè ma seach
Len cìrein geal nan laomanan,
A’ nighe cas nan creagan glas
’S a’ froiseadh às a’ mhaoraiche.

Often I listened to the clamour of the waves
Hitting the bare shore of the kyles,
My own spirit on good terms with its note
My heart sore thinking about it.
The many twists in the stream
Since this world was created
Backwards and forwards till today
But the noise of its voice unchanged.

Often on a calm May evening
Accompanied only by a flock of seagulls
I sat awhile, paying little interest,
On the height of Druim na h-Aoineige.
When the sun descended into the ocean
The colour of its face was beautiful
And although it had made a thousand circles
It showed no signs of age.

How I wished to look away out
On a cold January morning
Considering the strength of the waves
Irascible, moody, iridescent
Tumbling over, one by one
With their white crests flashing
Washing the feet of the grey rocks
Scattering shellfish of them.

A gradual exodus from Mingulay began in 1906 when three families 'raided' Vatersay, to be joined two years later by a further eight. In 1909, The Congested Districts Board purchased Vatersay for £6,250 and allotted crofts to the raiders. This persuaded the final six families to abandon Mingulay in 1912, leaving it as an island of only sheep and birds.

Caibideil 8: *Chapter 8*

An t-Eilean Sgitheanach: *The Isle of Skye*

An t-Eilean Sgitheanach (the Isle of Skye, or simply Skye) is the largest and northernmost island in the Inner Hebrides. Many fanciful suggestions have been offered for the meaning of the name Skye. The Celtic place-name scholar W. J. Watson was sufficiently concerned in the 1950s to write that:

> too often Gaelic words and phrases are mishandled, as would be the case with no other language.

For example, fossil bones were discovered in sediments near Elgol on Skye and were described in 2024 as *Ceoptera evansae*, a new genus and species of Middle Jurassic pterosaur. The announcement of its discovery explained that:

> the generic name, 'Ceoptera', combined the Gaelic word 'cheò'/ 'ceò' (pronounced 'ki-yo' – referencing Eilean a' Cheò [meaning 'Isle of Mist'], the common Gaelic name for the Isle of Skye – with the Latin word 'ptera', meaning 'wing'.

But the name Eilean a' Cheò ('island of mist') is a late, 19th-century romantic and poetic epithet for An t-Eilean Sgitheanach. The island's several peninsulas radiate from a mountainous hub dominated by An Cuiltheann (the Cuillins) and it is likely that this is the feature that gives the island its name, with early mariners likening the promontories to wings, the Gaelic for which is sgiath. Skye is the 'Winged Isle'.

Drochaid an Eilein Sgitheanaich: *The Skye Bridge*

Traditionally, the route from the mainland to Skye was the shortest sea crossing of around 500 metres across the narrow strait of Loch Alsh between the villages of Caol Loch Aillse (Kyle of Lochalsh, 'the strait of Spume Loch') on the mainland and Caol Àcain (Kyleakin, 'Acun's trait'). A ferry service operated here from around 1600 and, by 1971, the two 28-car ferries carried more than 300,000 vehicles each year. Slowly increasing prosperity in the islands and rapidly expanding summer tourist traffic caused queues for the ferries and ultimately the decision to construct a road bridge. This bridge, Drochaid an Eilein Sgitheanaich (the Skye Bridge), spans Loch Alsh, using Eilean Bàn ('fair island') as a stepping-stone. The bridge opened in 1995 and the ferry service ceased. Initially a toll bridge, it became toll-free in 2004, following a sustained campaign of opposition and protests. Such improved communications were one of the factors that saw the island's population (and that of Raasay) increase by 5% in the last decade to 10,450. Gaelic speakers amount to 25.9% of that number – 2670.

In the early 19th century, Lord MacDonald proposed the development of Kyleakin, to be re-christened New Liverpool, with plans for row upon row of tenement buildings. Although the project never came to fruition, the village consists of a long street of houses fronting the shore. A fairly recent book about Kyleakin stated:

> In 1263 anyone stationed here would have witnessed the great fleet of King Haakon making its way south to defend Scandinavian possessions on the western seaboard against the claims of the Scottish Crown.

However, the Rev. Lamont wrote in 1913 that this never happened. An examination of the sagas, he said, leads to the conclusion that Haakon's fleet sailed by the west of Skye and not through the Kyles. The interpretation of Kyleakin into 'Haakon's Strait' has led to this invention. Rev. Lamont believed that the name was the far more ancient Gaelic Acunn. And in corresponding symmetry, the southerly strait of Kylerhea commemorates Acunn's brother, Readha. The two brothers were members of Fionn's legendary band and reputedly both are buried in Glenelg at a place still called Iomair nam Fear Mòra ('plot of the big men'). The place-name expert, Iain Taylor, however, is of the view that this name refers to the current of the narrow channel.

Clann MhicFhionghain: *The MacKinnons*

To the south of Kyleakin is Caisteal Maol (Castle Moil, 'polled castle' i.e. towerless). With a commanding outlook of the narrows which separate Skye from the mainland, it was ideally situated to keep watch on passing shipping. What remains of the structure dates perhaps from the 15th century, but modern tradition states that there were much older fortifications on the site, originally built for a Norwegian princess nicknamed 'Saucy Mary' who charged a toll on any vessel using the narrow channel. A chain hung from the castle to the mainland prevented unpaid crossings. That tradition has been recently spiced up to say that Mary would also reward the payment of the toll by flashing her bare breasts. This modern invention springs from the medieval chain across the river Ouse in York and the adjacent pub known as 'Saucy Mary'.

Moil was a stronghold of Clann MhicFhionghain, the patronymic form of the Gaelic personal name Fingon ('fair born'). The MacKinnons moved the family seat probably from Dùn Ruingeil (Dun Ringill possibly 'fort at the rough ravine') to this castle, then called Dunakyn ('fort of Acunn'), possibly in the latter half of the 15th century. When an attempt was made in 1513 to restore the Lordship of the Isles under Sir Donald MacDonald of Lochalsh, the venue of the plot was Dunakyn, with no mention of Saucy Mary.

The A87 passes through Strath, land held by these MacKinnons:

An Srath Fhionghain gheal
'S an grinne beus gun smal;
An Srath is cruaidhe clach
'S an sgaitiche cù 'us bean.

The white Strath of MacKinnon of the most attractive quality without blemish. The Strath of the hardest rock and the most incisive dogs and women.

Along with many other clans who doggedly supported the Jacobite Risings, the MacKinnons suffered. Even when the cause was patently lost and Charles was a fugitive in Skye, the old MacKinnon chief did not desert his Prince. He was put on trial, with his life at stake, but was pardoned because of his old age. It is said that upon leaving the courtroom he was asked:

> "If King George were in your power, as you have been in his, what would you have done?"
>
> Mackinnon replied, "I would do to him, as he has this day done to me; I would send him back to his own country."

MacKinnon lands were confiscated and the nickname Clann Fhionghain nam Faochag ('Clan Mackinnon of whelks') implied their extreme poverty, being reduced to foraging the meanest of the shore's shellfish. Matters would improve later in the Spring:

> Air Là Fèill Pàdraig, mùinidh am bàirneach air an fhaochaig
>
> *On St Patrick's Day, the whelk goes out of season (literally, the limpet will urinate on the whelk).*

Apparently, as a small compensation for their self-sacrifice, it is claimed that it was from the Prince himself that the MacKinnons received the secret recipe for Drambuie liqueur. This is yet another example of Charles's supposed largesse.

In 1809, Lord Lyon, King of Arms, recognised William Alexander MacKinnon of Broadstairs, Kent, against other legitimate claimants, as MacKinnon of Strathaird and 33rd Chief of the Clan Mackinnon. This career politician was the eldest son of William MacKinnon of Antigua, a beneficiary of slavery. His 1846 *History of Civilisation*, an eight-volume account of human progress, decried slavery in Egypt, Greece and Rome but never mentioned slavery in the West Indies.

Some five kilometres west of the Skye Bridge is Ashaig. The name Ashaig, referring to a ferry crossing, denotes a much earlier use of the site. Here, there is also the old burial ground of Cladh Ashaig, by tradition connected with Maol Rubha (St. Maelrubha) (c.642-722). This was the ancient landing place of the saint. A sacred spring began to flow when the saint tore a small tree from the ground. Creag an Leabhair ('rock of the Book' i.e. the Bible), a rocky crag above the river, which he is said to have used as a pulpit, can still be seen. The saint's bell, which once hung from a tree and supposedly pealed of its own accord to summon the faithful, has been purloined.

The church at Ashaig was the first built in Strath and was one of the early Christian sanctuaries that afforded protection to a criminal who was allowed to remain there in safety until the anger of his enemies subsided. Such a man was called a cladhaire ('a churchyard dweller' or 'coward', denoting a man who hides from his enemies). St. Maelrubha is said to have made use of a rock to sail over from A' Chomraich ('the Sanctuary'), a name that derives from an area of inviolate ground which surrounded a monastery, its limits originally marked by crosses. By the end of the 7th century, Strath was Christianised and there were seven cilltean ('cells' or 'churches') and two teampaill ('temples' or 'churches') in the area. Kilbride and later Kilchrist were important but A' Chomraich (now simply Applecross) continued as the monastic headquarters.

St. Maelrubha is believed to have also occupied the small island of Pabaigh (Pabbay) opposite Ashaig, where there are the remains of a 13th-century chapel; evidently, the Norse were aware of its monastic community as the name Pabbay is derived from old Norse *papr* ('priest').

Lachlainn Mac Theàrlaich Òig: *Lachlan, son of young Charles*

One MacKinnon resident of Pabbay was Lachlann mac Theàrlaich Òig (Lachlan, 'son of young Charles'). He was born about 1665 in adjacent Scalpaigh (Scalpay, ON, 'ship island') where his father was the tacksman. Young Lachlan held Pabbay together with a portion of the adjacent mainland known as Ardnish, east of Broadford. Lachlan was a fine poet and one of the best known of his works is 'Latha Siubhal Slèibhe' ('A Day Crossing the Moor'). While he was relatively prosperous he was apparently on good terms with many of the Highland nobility but, on the death of some of his relatives, he found himself less well-off and realised that these nobles had been fair-weather friends.

One Christmas night, he visited Dunvegan Castle where the landed gentry had gathered, but he was refused entry to the place where he had once been so welcome. He left Dunvegan at once and set off for Strath. On the way he met, or thought he met, Compassion, Love and Generosity, exiles like himself from the courts of the nobles. They too were complaining bitterly about their banishment from places where they used to be in charge. Lachlan composed the song:

Marbhaisg ort, a mhulaid,
Nach do fhuirich thu nochd uam,
'S nach do leig thu cadal domh,
'S an oidhche fada, fuar;
Mas ann a dh' iarraidh cunntais orm,
A lunn thu air mo shuain,
Bheir mise greis an-dràsta dhut
Air àireamh na tha bhuat.

Latha 'siubhal slèibhe dhomh,
'S mi falbh leam fèin gu dlù,
A chuideachd anns an astar sin
Air gunna glaic is cù,
Gun thachair clann rium anns a' ghleann
A' gal gu fann chion iùil
Ar leam gur h-iad a b' àillidh dreach
A chunnacas riamh le m' shùil.

Woe betide you, sorrow, would that you had stayed away from me tonight and let me sleep as the night is long and cold. If the reason you've interrupted me is to ask me to account for myself I'll spend a while enumerating what's missing.

One day traversing the moor, I was walking along communing with myself with no companions on the way but a gun and a dog. In the glen, I came across children lost and sobbing helplessly. I admit that they were the most beautiful I had ever seen.

Another story about Lachlan concerns a wedding in Lochalsh. Traditionally a dronn was the bard's portion of mutton, the decorated rump of an ox or sheep. It was handed around and each person who received it was expected to produce a witty or ribald rhyme. Lachlan, on being offered this portion, and feeling that he had been regarded merely as a minor bard, composed such a scurrilous verse that he narrowly escaped with his life. This wedding custom, if not the murderous intentions, is still practised in the Faroe Islands, an indication, perhaps, of the strong Gaelic heritage of these isles. The poet died in 1734, aged 69 years, and was buried at Kilchrist in Strath.

Just beyond Breacais (Breakish, possibly 'speckled place'), there is a road leading off to the south, signposted to Armadale. The main road continues north-westwards towards An t-Àth Leathann (Broadford, ON, 'wide bay'). The Gaelic name is a more recent derivation and assumes that the *fjorðr* element meant a river crossing. Broadford today is a string of connected villages including one named Waterloo where veterans of the Napoleonic wars were allotted croft land. An inn was established here in the 17th century to provide for the needs of travellers crossing the river. By the late 19th century, Broadford Inn was being run by James Ross, who developed the recipe for Drambuie liqueur. Ross registered the name that means 'noble drink' as a trademark in 1893. Skye's second town, Broadford has a population of 1,106, of whom 151 speak Gaelic.

Uilleam Ros: *William Ross*

The poet Uilleam Ros (William Ross) (1762-1791) was born near Broadford, son of a pedlar from Skye. In 1786, Uilleam became a schoolmaster at Gairloch at the age of 24 and is known as 'The Gairloch Bard'. He carried out his teaching duties and also acted as catechist and precentor in the parish church. He had a fine voice and played flute and violin. William composed poems about his home area and its people but particularly about unrequited love. He had fallen in love with Mòr Ros (Marion Ross) in Stornoway and his rejection by her was said to have led to his early death. The eminent Gaelic scholar and poet Derick Thomson wrote:

> William Ross died in 1791, a long time after [Marion's marriage] to give credence that he died of love for her. Yet the legend has its own truth, for the ways in which his poetry differs from that of his fellow Gaelic poets of the eighteenth century. His personality seems the most vulnerable, and he wears his heart on his sleeve. This subjective element, and the conscious manipulation of it, was novel in the poetry of the century.

Ross succumbed to tuberculosis when he was 28 and is buried in the churchyard at Gairloch where a monument was erected in 1850. Oral versions of his poems were later collected by John MacKenzie and two volumes of his work were published. William Ross's poetry influenced the 20th-century Gaelic poet Somhairle MacLean, who considered his last song, 'Òran Eile air An Aobhar Cheudna' ('Another Song on the Same Subject'), as:

> one of the very greatest poems ever made in any language

in the British Isles:

Tha mise fo mhulad san àm
Chan òlar leam dram le sunnd
Tha durrag air ghur ann mo chàil
A dh'fhiosraich do chàch mo rùn;
Chan fhaic mi dol seachad air sràid
An cailin bu tlàithe sùil
'S e sin a leag m' aigne gu lar
Mar dhuilleach o bhàrr nan craobh.

Cha dùisgear leam ealaidh air àill',
Cha chuirear leam dàn air dòigh,
Cha togar leam fonn air clàr,
Cha chluinnear leam gàir nan òg,
Cha dìrich mi bealach nan àrd
Le suigeart mar bha mi 'n tòs
Ach triallam a chadal gu bràth
Do thalla nam bard nach beò.

I am sorrowful just now
I can't joyfully drink a dram
A maggot has hatched inside me
And has told my secret to others.
I don't see the girl of the bewitching eye
Passing on the street,
That's what has knocked my spirit to the ground
Like leaves from the top of a tree.

I'll not produce fine art
I'll not put a poem together
I'll not raise a tune on the harp
I'll not hear the laughter of youth;
I'll not climb the steep path
With the joy that I once had
But I'll journey, forever to sleep
In the hall of the dead bards.

In the 1880s, when ferrying Anne Campbell MacLeod to Coire Uisge (Loch Coruisk, 'cauldron of waters'), her rowers sang another of William Ross's love songs, 'Cuachag nan Craobh' ('Cuckoo in the Grove'). In composing his love poem, William undoubtedly made use of an existing tune but it was not, as MacLeod supposed, an iorram (boat song); the oarsmen had simply modified it to suit their stroke since they appreciated the lyrics so much. MacLeod set down what she remembered of the tune to use in a book she was to co-author with Sir Harold Boulton. Boulton judged the words of this song to be 'unworthy', so made a new set of verses:

"more in harmony with the plaintive tune".

This transmogrified William's work into *The Skye Boat Song*. Boulton's text gives an account of how Bonnie Prince Charlie, disguised as a serving maid, escaped in a small boat after the defeat of the 1745 Jacobite Rising, with the aid of Flora MacDonald. It is supposed that it describes Charles's flight from the mainland, but this is not quite correct. Charles left Benbecula to be rowed to Skye to avoid the tightening net of Government forces in the Western Isles. It has been observed that:

> as a piece of modern romantic literature with traditional links it succeeded perhaps too well, for soon people began 'remembering' they had learned the song in their childhood, and that the words were 'old Gaelic lines'.

On the road from Broadford to Elgol is Cill Chrìosd (Kilchrist, 'Christ Church'), the now roofless 17th-century parish church of Strath, built on an ancient site. It was used until 1840 when a new parish church was built in Broadford. Kilchrist was the Rev. Neil MacKinnon's principal church and, in 1625, he is said to have been the first minister on the island to dispense the sacrament according to the rites of the Protestant faith. While the religion "publicly taught within the realm of Scotland" was Presbyterianism, most, if not all, of the ministers of Skye belonged to the Episcopalian Church. It is said that MacKinnon always dressed in the kilt, and carried a sword even when he was officiating in the pulpit. Another of his churches was at Cill Ma Ruibhe (Kilmarie), dedicated to Maolrubha:

A choinnle Chill ma Ruighe
A Mhic ionmhuinn Fhionghuine
An talc tus catha da chuir
A mharcuigh Srath Shuairdail

Light of Kilmaree
Beloved son of Fingion
Strength at the onset of battle
O knight of Strath Swordale.

A further church at Cille Bhrìghde (Kilbride, 'church of St. Bride') seems to have been the original parish church, since the name Annat ('mother church') is associated with the site. The church stood near Clach na h-Annait ('stone of the mother church') and there is an adjacent well, Tobar na h-Annait ('well of the mother church'). The church was dedicated to Brìghde (St. Bride), meaning 'exalted one', a pre-Christian goddess and perhaps a continuation of the Indo-European goddess of the Dawn. She is associated with the Spring season; her feast day was 1st February, the day of the pagan festival Imbolc which marked the beginning of Spring and thus fertility. Brìghde was "the goddess whom poets adored" and she had two sisters: Brìghde the Healer and Brìghde the Smith. St. Bride shares many of the goddess's attributes:

Brìghde bhòidheach òigh nam mìle beus.

Beautiful Brìghde, maid of a thousand virtues.

The geologist Sir Archibald Geikie, writing, many years later, of Skye around the year 1852 recorded that:

> One of the most vivid recollections which I retain of Kilbride is that of the … clearance of the crofts of Suishnish … one afternoon … a strange wailing sound reached my ears at intervals on the breeze from the west … I could see a long and motley procession winding along the road that led north from Suishnish. It halted at … Kilbride, and there the lamentation became loud and long … the minister with his wife and daughters had come out to … bid them all farewell. …There were old men and women, too feeble to walk, who were placed in carts; the younger members of the community on foot were carrying their bundles of clothes and household effects, while the children, with looks of alarm, walked alongside. When they set forth once more, a cry of grief went up to heaven, the long plaintive wail, … was resumed, and when the last of the emigrants had disappeared behind the hill, the sound seemed to re-echo through the whole wide valley of Strath in one prolonged note of desolation.

The people were on their way to other townships or to be shipped overseas. Lord MacDonald's factor, Ballingall, claimed that eviction was an act of humanity since, with the new church in Broadford and the more convenient Kilchrist now disused, the parishioners had an additional eight kilometres to walk to church. Geikie wrote that he had:

> often wandered since then over the solitary ground of Suishnish. Not a soul is to be seen there now, but the greener patches of field and the crumbling walls mark where an active and happy community once lived.

Not a soul was to be seen because the sheep ranch, created from the two cleared communities, failed later that century and the tenancy was given up.

Ratharsair: *Raasay*

Returning to Broadford, the road north goes to Port Ruighe (Portree), the island's capital, through the Red Hills reaching the shores of Loch Sligeachan (Sligachan, 'place of shells'). Offshore at Sgonnsair (Sconser, meaning unclear) is Ratharsair (Raasay, 'roe deer island'). It measures 23 kilometres north to south, and five kilometres east to west. Traditionally the home of Clan MacSween, a name believed to derive from the Norse personal name, Svein, it became MacLeod territory from the 15th to the 19th century. A ferry runs from Sconser to Raasay.

Sea journeys then often led to drowning tragedies and an eminent victim was Iain Garbh ('rugged John'), 6th MacLeod of Raasay, who was drowned at Easter 1671 when his galley sank on the way home from a christening feast at the Lewis home of Coinneach Mòr ('big Kenneth'), 3rd Earl of Seaforth. It is said that one of his sisters composed a lament for him every Friday for a year after his death. In one of the surviving songs called 'Cumha Iain Ghairbh' she speaks of her anguish at his loss:

> Och nan och 's mi fo lèireadh
> mar a dh'èirich don ghaisgeach;
> chan eil sealgair na sìthne
> an-diugh am frìth nam beann casa.
> Bha mi uair nach do shaoil mi,
> ged is faoin bhith ga ràdh,
> gun rachadh do bhàthadh
> gu bràth air cuan farsaing.
> Fhad 's a sheasadh an stiùir dhith
> 's tu air cùl a buill bheairte,
> dh'aindeoin ànradh nan dùilean
> agus ùpraid na mara.
> Fhad 's a dh'fhanadh ri chèile
> a cuid dhealgan 's a h-acainn,
> is gum b' urrainn dhi gèilleadh
> do d' làimh threun air an aigeann.
> Ach b' i an doineann bha iargalt
> le gaoth à 'n iar-thuath 's cruaidh fhrasan:
> thog i a' mhuir na mill dhùbhghorm
> 's smuais i 'n iùbhrach na sadan.

I am so distressed about what has happened to the hero;
the hunter of venison is no longer in the steep hills of the deer forest.
Though it's foolish of me to say so, I once didn't believe that you would ever be drowned on a wide sea.
With you in charge of her tackle, while the helm survived,
regardless of the onslaught of the elements and the confusion of the sea.
While her pins and apparatus held she could respond to your brave hand.
But the storm was terrible with wind from the northwest and
heavy showers. It raised the sea into blue-black lumps and
smashed the ship into smithereens.

Subsequent chiefs of the MacLeods of Raasay supported the Jacobites in 1745 and, as a consequence, the original Raasay House and all dwellings were burnt down by government troops. Such was the scale of Government-sanctioned destruction and theft of property that the islanders were deliberately brought to the verge of famine.

In the 1760s, the MacLeod Chief in Raasay still maintained a piper in his retinue, one John MacKay who had been schooled in the MacCrimmon tradition. His son Angus went on to publish a collection of pibroch and became Queen Victoria's first personal piper.

In 1843, the last laird, John MacLeod, deep in debt, sold Raasay to George Rainy and emigrated to Tasmania. Rainy was a merchant and slave owner who used monies from the compensation paid to former slave-owners following the Slavery Abolition Act of 1833 to secure his 'Highland' estate. After the 1846 failure of the potato harvest, Rainy decided to convert as much arable land as possible to sheep farming. This required the removal of islanders and several townships were cleared, including Hallaig and Screapadal. Two boatloads of emigrants left for Australia in 1854, and another 160 followed in 1865. Rainy also banned marriages.

The estate was sold again in 1876 to Edward Wood, the 24-year-old heir to the Staffordshire Five Towns pottery fortune. But as conflicts between the laird and the islanders grew, he decided to turn Raasay over to sporting purposes. More people left.

The government purchased the island in 1922, but, in the 1960s, a Sussex doctor acquired part of it. His undue influence and lack of interest in the island's well-being earned him the nickname 'Dr No'. He sold it to the Highlands and Islands Development Board in 1979. A variety of developments, including the opening of Raasay House as a hotel and outdoor centre and the construction of a distillery, has helped to arrest the population decline which had seen a fall from over 900 in 1803 to 183 in 2022. A fifth speak Gaelic.

Somhairle MacGill-Eain: *Somhairle MacLean*

The poet Somhairle MacLean was born in Òsgaig (Oskaig, ON, 'strip of land at a water mouth') on the west coast of the island. Described by the Scottish Poetry Library as:

> one of the major Scottish poets of the modern era

he was credited, probably over so, by the Nobel Prize Laureate Seamus Heaney with saving Scottish Gaelic poetry. His writing has been said often to combine a traditional awareness with a modernist political outlook, in which Raasay and the areas around feature strongly. But, while his work dwells on the brutality of war, the Clearances and modern exploitation, he also writes about nature. Perhaps his most famous poem is 'Hallaig', focusing on the cleared village Halaig (ON, perhaps, 'high slope bay') on the east coast. Although the removal of people left an empty landscape populated only by their ghosts, nature repopulates the land:

> Tha iad fhathast ann a Halaig,
> Clann Ghill-Eain 's Clann MhicLeòid,
> na bh' ann ri linn Mhic Ghille Chaluim:
> chunnacas na mairbh beò.
>
> Na fir nan laighe air an lèanaig
> aig ceann gach taighe a bh' ann,
> na h-igheanan 'nan coille bheithe,
> dìreach an druim, crom an ceann.

Eadar an Leac is na Feàrnaibh
tha 'n rathad mòr fo chòinnich chiùin,
's na h-igheanan 'nam badan sàmhach
a' dol a Chlachan mar o thùs.

Agus a' tilleadh às a' Chlachan,
à Suidhisnis 's à tìr nam beò;
a chuile tè òg uallach
gun bhristeadh cridhe an sgeòil.

They are still in Hallaig
MacLeans and MacLeod
all who were there in the time of Mac Gille Chaluim:
the dead have been seen alive.

The men lying on the green
at the end of every house that was,
the girls a wood of birches
straight their backs, bent their heads.

Between the Leac and Fearns
the road is under mild moss
and the girls in silent bands
go to Clachan as in the beginning,

and return from Clachan
from Suisnish and the land of the living;
each one young and light-stepping,
without the heartbreak of the tale.

Sligeachan: *Sligachan*

Returning to Skye and continuing along the shores of Loch Sligeachan (Sligachan, or often now the ugly abbreviation 'Slig'), it is possible to see at low tide the remains of a well-preserved cairidh ('fish weir') used to catch the salmon that once swarmed in the loch, awaiting the right conditions to migrate up the Sligachan River. It no longer traps fish, the estate having breached its centre to preserve stocks for paying angling guests. Other estate improvements included a road linking Portree to the south end of the island which necessitated the construction of a bridge, designed by Thomas Telford, in the early 1820s. Its relatively recent date has not prevented it from becoming the scene of modern myths associated with the pools sculpted by the river beneath the arches of the bridge:

> The legend of Sligachan states that if you dip your face in the river water by the Sligachan Bridge, you will be granted eternal beauty … it is important that you wash your face the correct way … You must dip your face in the water, not bring the water up to your face … you must get on your hands and knees at the water's edge and fully submerge your face for seven seconds. Be warned, it is Scotland, the water is far from warm. Also, you cannot wipe the water off, you must allow your face to dry naturally. And that is how you gain eternal beauty from the faeries at the Old Sligachan Bridge on the Isle of Skye.

This is the junction of the roads to Portree and to Dunvegan, and the construction of the bridge made this a good spot to hold an annual cattle fair. Around 1830, a new hotel was built to cater for drovers and travellers but, with the increasing interest in climbing, it became a venue for mountaineers. As it is close to An Cuilitheann (the Cuillin Mountain), it provides a good viewpoint for seeing them, and many early climbers chose this as a spot to start ascents of the Cuillin.

Theories abound as to the meaning of the word Cuillin. It is suggested that it comes from the ON *kjölen* meaning 'ridges'. *Kjöllen* may also refer to the keel of a boat suggesting a similarity to the hull of an upturned ship. Others say the name is linked to Celtic mythology, the hills being the place where Cù Chulainn ('Culann's hound'), best described as a Gaelic mythological demigod, hunted. However, the two names have no etymological connection.

From Sligachan, the A82 proceeds across emptied moorland towards Portree. To the right of the road rise the flanks of Beinn Lì (Ben Lee, ON, 'slope hill'). The poet Ó Maoil Ciaráin lived perhaps in this locality, sometime in the 15th century. His 'Marbhna Fhearchoir Í Mhaoil Chiaráin' ('A Great Loss Has Been Brought On Me'), composed to lament the loss of his son, has been called one of the "masterpieces of medieval Gaelic poetry" and the poem's enduring influence made his name a byword for a father mourning for a son. His son Fearchar had left Scotland for a poetry tour in Ireland and was murdered there by Goill ('foreigners', meaning the English). The ancient poem survives thanks to its quality. It was considered of such a standard that it was included in *The Grammatical Tracts*, compilations by Irish bardic schools on the proper uses of grammar. Although the family was of Irish extraction, Fearachar was raised in Scotland. His father's lament commences:

Tugadh oirne easbhuidh mhór,
cneasghuin na coinnle rom chríon,
mo leanabh óm leas do ládh,
do beanadh mo lámh dheas díom.

Do folchadh gile a ghruadh mbreac,
budh buan ar mo chridhe a chnoc,
faríor nocha mhar mo mhac,
glan an tshlat do bhíodh fóm brot.

Mo chalann atá gan treóir,
atá mh'anam isan uaigh,
rem aonmhac ni fhoil mo shúil,
caolbhrat d' úir ghloin ar a ghruaidh.

A profound privation has befallen me,
my skin is withered by the candle's wound,
my child has been flung from my use
my right hand has been severed.

His glowing freckled cheeks are invisible,
its anguished kernel lives on in my heart,
I am wretched that my son is lifeless
shining shaft swathed within my cloak.

My body lacks all energy
my soul lies in the grave,
I will not set eyes on my only son,
a thin covering of fresh dirt on his cheek.

For 180 lines the father pours out his anguish and finally utters the words:

Nior ghabh dhíom an Coimdhe cead
fan ngníomh – mur do-roighne rug;
diomdhach mé don Righ do-rad,
mur do ghad dínn an té tug.

The Lord did not crave my consent
For the act - as He made so He has taken;
I am angry with the King who gave
For He has carried off the one He granted.

Blàr a' Chumhaing: *The Battle of the Braes*

Four hundred years later, Ben Lee's slopes were the reason the community defied authority in their attempts to regain access to land they depended upon for survival. The MacDonald estate decided to raise the rent levied on the people of Braes and, with their lease almost up, they agreed to pay the new rate. Despite this, their lease was not renewed. The crofters decided to withhold their rent until the matter was resolved, with some of them continuing to graze their sheep on the land at Ben Lee, despite it having been denied them. The estate tried to evict the crofters by using the law, but the attempt to clear the crofters off their land by the Sheriff's Officer from Portree was in vain: the people forced him to burn the summons papers. In response to this, 50 police were dispatched to Skye. When they reached Braes they were met with a hail of whatever missiles the crofters could find. Several people, including seventeen women, were arrested, and the men convicted and fined. Although only a small skirmish, the incident was widely reported and became known as the 'Battle of the Braes'.

The government, wearied by whingeing Highland proprietors and land reform agitation, set up a Commission under Lord Napier to investigate:

> … the conditions of the crofters and cottars in the Highlands ....
> and everything concerning them.

It had wide powers to call witnesses, demand any document and visit any place deemed necessary to obtain the fullest possible information. The Commissioners did so and presented their report in 1884. Although their recommendations were less radical than the reformers hoped, some of their demands were met. The government was slow to act and there was further trouble in Skye with gunships and marines sent to keep order. In 1886, the Crofters Holdings (Scotland) Act was passed and for the first time ever crofters had security of tenure which could be passed on to another family member. They had the right to compensation for any improvements they carried out and a Land Court was established to fix fair rents. A number of modifying acts have been passed since giving rise to a pithy definition of a croft as: 'a small piece of ground surrounded by legislation'.

The victory was celebrated in song by Màiri Mhòr nan Òran (Mary MacPherson, 'big Mary of the songs') (1821-1898). Born at Sgeubost (Skeabost, ON, 'Skidi's farm'), her wrongful conviction and imprisonment in Inverness spurred her to compose poetry. She moved to Glasgow in 1872 and subsequently qualified in nursing and obstetrics. She acquired a reputation for her songs and her championing of crofters in the increasingly heated debate over land rights. 'Òran Beinn Lì' ('Ben Lee Song') thanks those who fought for crofters' rights and secured access to the grazing on Ben Lee:

Thugaibh beannachd gu 'Pàrnell',
Thug a' bhuaidh air 'An t-Sàtan',
Air chor 's nach faicear gu bràth e
Tighinn air àrainn na tìr.

Nuair thàinig e chiad uair
'S lethcheud 'aingeal' fo riaghladh,
Chuir e còignear an iarainn
Ann an crìochan Beinn Lì.

'S na diùlnaich a b' uaisle,
'S nach robh riamh ann an tuasaid,
Chaidh na ruighich a shuaineadh
Gu cruaidh air an dùirn.

Chaidh an giùlan leis 'na h-aingle',
'S an glasadh an gainntir;
'S a dh'aindeoin cumhachd an nàimhdean,
'S leò am fonn is Beinn Lì.

'S na mnathan bu shuairce
'S bu mhodhaile gluasad,
Chaidh an claiginn a spuaiceadh
Ann am bruachan Beinn Lì.

My greetings to 'Parnell' who won a victory over 'Satan' so he won't ever be seen again coming near to this area.

When he came the first time, fifty 'angels' under his command, he clapped five in irons at the boundary of Ben Lee.

The bravest of men who were never in a fight, handcuffs were clasped harshly round their fists.

They were taken by the 'angels' and locked up in prison but despite the power of their enemies the land and Beinn Lì is theirs.

The kindly women, most polite in their doings, their skulls were broken on the slopes of Ben Lee.

The road leads eastwards to the fine natural harbour which is now Portree Bay, although it was once known as St. Columba's Loch. St. Columba visited Skye around 585 and is remembered in some five dedications in the north end of Skye. By the bay is the island's main town, Port Ruighe (Portree, 'slope harbour'), now thought of as King's Harbour, with the spelling altered to Port Rìgh. This name supposedly refers to an expedition around Scotland mounted by James V in 1540. The King is said to have landed at Creag a' Mhòr-shluaigh ('rock of the multitude') on the northern shore of Portree Bay. The arrival of his fleet is remembered in a Nicolson song:

Rìgh Seumas a còig 's a shluagh ann
Na cuairtearan glana suairce.

King James V and his host there
The well-mannered, elegant courtiers.

This armada was the last a reigning king conducted in an effort to 'daunt the Isles'; James died, probably of cholera, in 1542 and again regency (and anarchy) ensued. This period was one of immense difficulty for the state. The monarch was a female child; the year-old Mary and the other bulwark, the Catholic Church, had been near-fatally wounded by the theft of its revenues by the nobles. Half of the nation's best lands were legally owned by the Church but by now two-thirds of its institutions were in the hands of 'commendators', known as such since the property was entrusted to their 'care'. The institutionalised theft of this immense wealth was not reversed at The Reformation and so did not translate into adequate stipends for the clergy, nor care for the poor and infirm. Charles I's 1625 Act of Revocation targeted those church and royal lands illegally seized since 1540 in order to use some of the revenues to pay the clergy. This legitimate, if high-handed, act was seen by the noble squatters as an attack on their property rights and has been described as:

> the ground stone of all the mischief that followed after

i.e. The Bishops War and War of the Three Kingdoms. Charles ultimately lost his head, but the lands stayed where they were.

An Taobh Tuath: *Northern Skye*

Northern Skye comprises the four promontories of Tròndairnis (Trotternish, 'Thrond's ness' [with 'ness' denoting a promontory]), Bhatairnis (Waternish, 'water ness'), Diùranais (Durinish, 'deer ness'), and Minginis (Minginish, 'large ness'). The route around Trotternish is deiseal ('sunwise') from Portree and travelling northwest on the A87, bound for Uig and onto Kilmuir at the northern end of the peninsula. Of this part of Skye it is said:

Is olc a fhreagradh tu 'n iochdar Thròtairnis.
You wouldn't suit well in the lower end of Trotternish.

Trotternish's climate and soil are somewhat colder than in the rest of the island so that a delicate person might not do well there. This did not stop two centuries of feuding for its control.

At Ceann Sàil Eighre (Kensaleyre, 'head of the inlet at the beach') and Loch Snìothasort Beag (Snizort, 'snow fjord') is Carn Liath ('grey cairn'), a four-metre high chambered cairn. Its well-preserved state, surviving some 5000 years or so, is a testament to a belief in fairies and strict injunctions against tampering with their dwelling places. Further along the road is Snizort Parish Church, designed by James Gillespie Graham in 1800. Beyond again is Sòrn Choir Fhinn ('Fionn's kettle cradle'), a setting of three standing stones which were by tradition believed to be the tripod on which Fionn placed his kettle.

To the north is Cinnseaborg (Kingsburgh, perhaps from ON, 'king's castle'), the home of the tacksman Alasdair MacDonald, a factor for Lord MacDonald. It was to this house that MacDonald brought Bonnie Prince Charles and Flora MacDonald after they arrived by boat from Benbecula, on 29th June 1746.

Ùig (Uig, ON, *vík*, 'bay') has a population of about five hundred, strung around the wide sheltered sea loch of Uig Bay. Uig Tower, also known as Captain Fraser's Folly, is a 19th-century building, constructed to enhance the landscape but suggesting some other purpose. William Fraser became the owner of the Kilmuir Estate in 1855 and the tower was constructed around 1860 at the place where local tenants had to go to pay their rent to his factor. This resembled the tower erected in 1830 at Scolpaig, North Uist by the factor, Dr Alexander MacLeod, although this one was to provide employment as a means of famine relief.

Fraser cleared many tenants to create more profitable sheep ranches. In 1884, he attempted to evict a family at Garafad in Staffin during a rent strike. He called for help from the Government to break the strike, claiming that the local people had rebelled. In November of that year, a flotilla of naval ships transporting police and marines arrived in Uig Bay. However, the strike was not broken and the families remained in their homes.

The families at Garafad would probably have been aware of a ditty that was composed by a bard who had observed their technique for fertilising fields, whereby a creel of ashes and manure carried on their backs was struck smartly every so often, dislodging the contents on to the ground:

Am fasan a bh' ac' ann an Ùige
Chan fhaca mi riamh nam dhùthaichs';
Gabhail dhen bhat' air mo chùlaibh,
'S smùid air chliabh a' luathadh.

The fashion they had in Uig, I never saw in my country;
Striking at my back with a stick, with a stour from the ash creel so thick.

Fraser's tower was later turned into a family home but abandoned in the 1950s. Fraser himself was less fortunate with his own home. The large house he built for himself was washed away in a flood in 1877, an event seen by local people as divine retribution.

Nearby is a stone that was once known as the High Stone of Uig. The Brahan Seer ris purported to have said:

Olaidh am fitheach a shàth air bhàrr an làir air mullach clach àrd Ùige.

The raven will drink its fill of the ground on top of the high stone of Uig.

Ùr-sgeòil Shìthichean: *Fairy Fables*

The road into what is now known as the Fairy Glen starts opposite the tower. Fairy associations have very recently grown up in three specific locations in Skye: the Fairy Bridge, the Fairy Glen and the Fairy Pools. However, this specificity is bogus and fails to understand the Gaelic concept of the realm of the fairies. A leading academic has described the modern construct of the fairy world as an appropriately fictionalised setting for discussion of everyday moral dilemmas. In terms of 21st-century culture, they are TV soaps.

Three supernatural worlds were peopled by Fairies, Spirits and Witches. There were many forms of person in the fairy world, as well as animals such as the ùraisg, which had the qualities of man and spirit commingled, the each-uisge ('water horse') and the tarbh-uisge ('water bull'). Fairies and their fellow creatures inhabited a world below the earth and in lochs and streams. Prominent knolls and ancient monuments, brochs and burial cairns were their homes. They lived all over the underground world, so to identify specific localities is to diminish the force of nature the fairies represent. Further, each of these supposed locations has a Gaelic name which has no hint of fairy association. These are respectively: Beul-àtha nan Trì Allt ('ford of the three burns'), now Fairy Bridge, Baile nan Cnoc ('township of the knolls'), now Fairy Glen, and Coire na Creiche ('hollow of the raid'), now Fairy Pools.

The dominant modern narrative of the Fairy Pools obscures a local tradition of the culminating battle of Cogadh na Cailliche Càim ('war of the one-eyed woman'), fought in 1601 between the MacLeods and the MacDonalds. Donald Gorm Mòr MacDonald decided to end this internecine feud with a decisive battle. When Rory Mòr MacLeod was absent from the area, the MacDonalds launched a raid on northern Skye. The cattle seized were driven south to a traditional refuge for raiders, Coire na Creiche. Here the MacLeod forces, led by Rory's brother Alasdair, caught up with the MacDonalds. They joined battle late in the day and fighting continued well into the night. The MacLeods were utterly defeated, with the capture of Alasdair and some 30 of his kinsmen. Local people used to point out salient locations in the landscape where key events in the fight occurred. Now all that is referred to in the landscape is a series of pools and a recently concocted association with fairies.

Mogastad: *Monkstad*

North of Uig, opposite Lianacro (Linicro, ON, 'flax land'), is Mogastad (Monkstad, 'monk's town'), a settlement that has the epithet Mogastad nan Ròiseal ('Monkstadt of the high waves'). Following the Norse defeat, Arco Brannmhor, the last Viking, was, by tradition, holed up in the monastery on St. Columba's Island in what was formerly the loch of St. Columba. Ultimately, he was surprised and beheaded by the warrior MacSween. The main landscape feature is no longer the island monastery but the recently restored Monkstadt House, completed in 1741, and the new home of the MacDonald chief on his quitting Duntulm Castle. It remained the chief's residence perhaps until 1815 and is set above a sward of land reclaimed after the loch was drained in the six years following 1819. The drainage involved a good deal of hard labour but provided 230 acres of arable land whose fertility led to the saying:

Thug iad ort Mogastad a bhuain

They asked you to reap Monkstad

in other words, a never-ending task. The intense effort necessary to keep a mile of drain open proved too great and the land has partially reverted to swampy ground.

The Museum of Island Life at Kilmuir (Cille Mhòire, 'Mary's church') was opened to the public in 1965, utilising a cottage dating to the mid-19th century. This cottage is a good example of a typical Skye house of that time. By present-day standards, the old house was basic but adequate for its day, giving shelter and warmth to people who spent most of their time out of doors. James Boswell, in an account of his visit to Skye in 1773, describes a house in which they stayed in south Skye. He states:

> We had no rooms that we could command, for the good people here had no notion that a man could have any occasion but for a mere sleeping-place.

In Kilmuir cemetery, a memorial cross stands over Flora MacDonald's grave. She died in 1790 and according to tradition, she was buried in a shroud made from a bed sheet that covered Prince Charles on the night he spent at Kingsburgh. The epitaph reads:

> Her name will be mentioned in history and if courage and fidelity be virtues, mentioned with honour.

It was written by Samuel Johnson who met her during his tour of the Hebrides with James Boswell.

Dùn Thuilm (Duntulm, 'fort of the holm', perhaps referring to the adjacent off-shore island) is on the site of a fort known as Dùn Dhaibhidh ('David's fort'). The castle was built in the 14th and 15th centuries when the area was subject to feuds between the rival MacLeod and MacDonald clans. In 1498, the MacLeods, though not then in possession of Trotternish, were royally bound to maintain a birlinn of 26 oars and two of sixteen oars for naval service. By the early 17th century, the MacDonalds occupied the castle. In its heyday, this seat of lordship would have been the scene of much festivity, as the chiefs held court and feasted to the sound of music and song.

A poem by Iain Lom MacDhòmhnaill, addressed to Dòmhnall Gorm Òg (Sir Donald MacDonald or 'young dark-blue Donald') who succeeded his uncle Dòmhnall Gorm Mòr as 8th Chief of the MacDonalds of Sleat in 1617, captures the scene:

Thig loingeas le gaoith
Gu baile nan laoch
Ged bhitheadh na caoiltean garbh;

Gu talla nam pìos
Far am faramaich' fìon
Far am falaichear mìle crann.

Bidh cruit is clàrsaich
'S mnà uchd-àillidh
'N tùr nan tàileasg geàrr;

Foirm nam pìoban
'S orghain Lìteach
'S cùirn gan lìonadh àrd;

Cèir na drillsean
Rè fad oidhche
'G èisteachd strì nam bàrd;

Ruaig air dhìsnean
Fòirn air thìthibh
'S òr a sìos mar gheall.

A fleet will come with a fair wind to the home of the heroes,
though the straits be rough;
To the hall of the silver vessels, where wine is most merrily
dispensed, and where a thousand wagers are concealed.
There will be violins and harps and fair-bosomed women in the
tower of short chess-boards;
There can be heard the roar of pipes and Leith organs while
drinking horns are filled to the brim;

Wax ablaze throughout the entire night as men listen to the contest of the bards.
Lively dicing, chess-men arranged in order, and gold tabled as a stake.

Donald Gorm Mòr was clearly reluctant to give up these pleasures since one traditional explanation for the abandonment of Duntulm Castle was a result of his ghost frequently returning with two companions to help themselves to drink in the cellars, frightening the earthly inhabitants of the castle by their appearance and noise. Duntulm was vacated for a more comfortable house at Monkstadt, as we have seen.

Flòdaigearraidh: *Flodigarry*

To the east is the hotel at Flòdaigearraidh (Flodigarry, ON, 'wet meadow') and in its grounds is the home of Flora and Alan MacDonald who, upon their marriage in 1751, took the tack until 1759, when Alan succeeded his father at Kingsburgh. His nickname was Ailean nam Mìle Mart ('Alan of the thousand cattle') in recognition of his skill as a cattle drover, although this might be a playful allusion to the poetic epithet of a lover's 'thousand kisses'. Perhaps this has given rise to the tradition that it was Alan's great-grandfather Dòmhnall mac Iain 'ic Sheumais, the hero of the battle of Carinish, who was the first MacDonald to pioneer that trade.

Just beyond Flodigarry is Loch Sianta ('holy loch') and within three metres of the loch is one of fifteen named wells in the north of Trotternish and the most celebrated well in Skye, Tobar Loch Sianta. The *Old Statistical Account* (*OSA*) of 1792 describes the well as a bath made of stone. Offerings such as small rags, pins and coloured threads were left on a shelf made for the purpose in a wall of its enclosure. The water was regarded as very effective in treating eye conditions. It is celebrated in the rhyme:

Uisge tobar Teilebreac
Is duileasg à Loch Sianta
Faochagan à Rudha Dubh
Is saoidhean Theabraidh

Water of the well of Tellibreac,
And dulse from Loch Sianta
Buckies from the Black Point,
And saithe from Hebri.

Situated almost midpoint between the two settlements of Bhaltos (Valtos, ON, 'river mouth') and Cùl nan Cnoc (Culnaknock, 'back of the hills') is a memorial to the seven pupils of Valtos school who were killed in the First World War. It was erected in 1921 in front of their old school, which was itself demolished in the 1970s, leaving little evidence today that a school ever existed there. There is an earlier commemoration for them in a cumha ('lament') by Aonghas Stiùbhart (Angus Stewart) from Valtos, who wrote the song on his return to the area after the war. It evokes the desolation the war brought to the community and the poet:

Och, och a-nochd 's mi 'n Cùl nan Cnoc
Chan fhaigh mi fois no suaimhneas
'S gun fhios aig càch gu dè mo chàs.
Ged 's nàdarrach mo smuaintean.

'S cuimhne leam, 's gur geàrr an tìm
Bhon bha mi fèin gun ghruaimean
'S gun chùram nì air bith fon ghrèin
Mo laighe 's m' èirigh suaimhneach.

An còmhlan ciùin bu tric bha leam
Tha cuid san ùir nan suain dhiubh
'S chan fhaicear tuilleadh iadsan cruinn
An comunn grinn san Bhuailidh.

Tha cuid dhiubh sìnte thall san Fhraing
O 's ìosal clann nan uaislean
'S bidh sinne caoidh gu bràth na suinn
Thug saorsa dhuinn fon chruadal.

Tonight in Cùl nan Cnoc I can't get rest or peace. And no one else knows what's bothering me though my thoughts are quite natural.

I remember, and it's only a short time ago, when I was quite happy, with not a care in the world, contentedly sleeping and waking.

The even-tempered band who were often with me, some of them are sleeping in the ground and they won't be seen again together as a happy group in the Buaile.

Some are laid down over in France; how the children of the noble people have been laid low and we will lament forever the heroes who gave us freedom from adversity.

The work is one of over 200 known works composed across Gaelic Scotland in response to the Great War. 100 of these have been published in a handsome anthology, *Cuimhneachan* (2015) (Acair, Stornoway).

To the south of Culnaknock, the large car park is the starting point for the walk up to the area known as An Stòr (a term meaning 'great' from the ON, as in the Storebælt, 'great belt', the strait between the major islands of Zealand and Funen in Denmark). At 50 metres high, the most significant of several basalt pillars here is Bodach an Stòirr ('Old Man of Storr'). Bodach here is a euphemism for 'penis' and the older name was simply Bod an Stòirr.

At the Torabhaig (Torvaig, ON, 'bull's bay') campsite just outside Portree is a track leading east to the site of the former residence of Clann 'ic Neacail (Clan MacNicol, or Nicolson) of Sgoirebreac (Scorrybreck, 'speckled peak'). Tradition states that early in its history the clan held the Isle of Lewis as well as extensive territory on the north-western mainland. A 17th-century song commemorates the marriage of Malcolm Nicolson to Margaret, the sister of Iain Garbh Mac Ghille Chaluim, the Chief of the MacLeods in Raasay:

Ceud soraidh bhuam fhìn gu m' eòlas
Gu Sgoirebreac am bi chòisir,
Gu talla farsaing Chloinn Dòmhnaill,
Gu taigh mòr an ùrlair chòmhnaird
Far am faighte fìon ri òl ann
À cupannan donna bheòil bhòidhich;
Miosaran 's truinnsearan feòdair
'S amar bruithidh an eòrna,
Deoch cho làidir 's thig on Òlaind.

'S b' aithne dhomh fhìn beus bu dual dhut
'S beus dhe d' bheus bhith suirghe ghruagach
'S a' cur nan geall, leat bu bhuadhar.
'S gheibhte siud an taigh an uasail
Bhi 'g òl fìon à pìosan fuara
'N taigh mòr farsaing, 's ùrlar sguabte,
Ruighleadh ubhal sìos is suas air.

A hundred greetings from me to my familiar Sgoirebreac where the festive band would be, to the wide hall of MacDonald, to the great smooth-floored house where wine would be available to drink from brown fine rimmed-cups, pewter dishes and plates, and a vat for brewing barley, a drink as strong as any coming from Holland.

And I knew a custom you inherited and part of that was courting young women and betting successfully. And you'd find in the noble's house people drinking wine out of cold silver cups, in the great wide house with the swept floor; an apple would roll up and down on it.

Over the succeeding 800 years, the clan's possessions were reduced to the lands of Scorrybreck. Hence their contrasting epithets:

Far am bi fìdheall no pìob, bidh MacNeacail.

Nicolson will be wherever there is a fiddle or bagpipe.

Clann 'ic Neacail a' bhrochain thana, is an droch aran eòrna.

Nicolsons of thin porridge and bad barley bread.

The last chief sold the lands to the MacDonald estate and his two sons emigrated ultimately to Australia. Tormod (Norman), the younger of the brothers laments in song the fact that he has been banned from hunting in the Skye deer forests by order of his uncle, the factor for Lord MacDonald. Norman was drowned in Australia in 1841:

’S gann gun dìrich mi chaoidh
Dh’ ionnsaigh frìthean àird a’ mhonaidh
’S gann gun dìrich mi chaoidh.

’S mi bhith ’g amharc air na slèibhtean
Far am bi na fèidh a’ fuireach.

’S fhuair mi litir o na h-uaislean
Nach fhaodainn fhìn a dhol a mhonadh.

’S tha mo ghunna caol air meirgeadh
Cha tèid mi don t-seilg leis tuilleadh.

’S bidh mi nis a’ falbh na h-Innsean
’S chan fhaic mi mo nighneag tuilleadh.

I will climb no more to the wilds of the moorlands; I will climb no more.

Where I would be scanning the slopes where the deer live.

I received a letter from the authorities saying I must not go to the moorland.

My narrow gun has rusted, I can’t go hunting with it any more.

I’ll be leaving for the Indies and will no longer see my girlfriend.

Part of this area, overlooking the village of Portree, has been back in the hands of the Nicolsons since 1987. The land is now administered by Urras Clann MhicNeacail (The Nicolson Clan Trust), whose objectives are to ensure that the lands will be held in perpetuity for conservation, free public access and enjoyment.

Fèisean nan Gaidheal: *Festivals of the Gaels*

As the road sweeps around the north end of Portree Bay, the former jailhouse comes into view. The prison, built in 1800 by James Gillespie Graham, is now the offices of Fèisean nan Gaidheal, the organisation that supports the development of community-based Gaelic arts tuition festivals throughout Scotland. Fèis (plural Fèisean) is the word for a festival. Over the past 30 years the number of Fèisean has grown so that today there are 47, each one community-led and tailored to local needs. The skills taught at Fèisean are a valued aspect of the informal education of young people, as demonstrated by the level of volunteer commitment and parental support in local areas.

Dùthaich 'ic Leòid: *MacLeod Country*

Westwards beyond Portree, the junction of the A850 with the A87 at Borve allows travel to Waternish and the former church lands of the Cathedral of the Isles, along the clan boundary between the MacLeods and the MacDonalds, a zone often engulfed in conflict in the past. MacLeod territory starts across the Snizort River and, a little beyond at Skeabost, Eilean Chaluim Chille (St. Columba's Isle) sits in the river, about 400 metres from the mouth of the loch. Here are the remains of two churches and a number of post-medieval burial aisles. Evidence from a petition of 1433 in the papal archives shows that this was the seat of the bishops of Sodor from 1387 until about 1500 when it was superseded by Iona. The cathedral is a rectangular building, orientated east-west and measuring 23 metres by almost six metres, with a total area of nearly 122 square metres. The church is the largest in the Hebrides apart from Iona; plans and architectural features suggest a strong connection between St. Columba's Isle and Iona.

Across the river and just east of Skeabost House Hotel is the site of a 1539 battle between MacLeods and MacDonalds, known as Achadh na Fala ('field of blood'). There is a tradition that the heads of the slain accumulated at a prominent feature known as Coire nan Ceann ('the hollow of the heads').

A less gory and more fruitful feature here is the man-made structure on the northern shore of the sea loch, Cairidh Mòr Shniothasort ('great fish weir of Snizort').

In contrast to the more active techniques of deep-sea fishing, inshore waters lent themselves to passive trapping methods. The basic form of the cairidh ('weir') uses the natural mechanism of the tide. The weir is a fold of semi-circular form made on the seabed. These tidal traps, made of rough stone walling, wattle, stakes and perhaps combinations of these materials, are widely distributed around the Scottish coastline. When the sea flows in, the fish come over it and are left there once the tide recedes. They were in use within living memory to catch herring principally, a free resource until the estates broke them to prevent salmon, reserved for their paying guests, from being taken. 70 years ago, the great fish weir of Snizort was described as follows:

> ... this was the last working cairidh ... in Scotland ... everyone had a right to go to the cairidh to the point where I myself saw between 40 and 50 people fishing in it at the one time. Everyone had the right to choose which part of the cairidh he preferred ... the ones at the upper part would be in water up past their knees, those in the middle part would be under water up to their hips and those in the lower part up to their armpits in water and they had to stay put like this until the cairidh emptied, which would happen about two hours after the top of the wall first appeared. I heard old people say that they had seen as good as 300 cran of herring caught in the cairidh in one night. But in my day it was salmon that was most often caught in it; and 60 years ago no fewer than 40 salmon were caught in one tide. But some began to maintain that the salmon weren't able to climb up towards the river when they were killed in this way. For this reason the cairidh was knocked down and this ancient method of fishing brought to an end. This happened, ... in June of the year 1899.

Blàr Milleadh a Gàrraidh: *The Battle of the Spoiling of the Dyke*

At Ardmore in Waternish the church of Cille Chomain, now known as Trumpan Church, is adjacent to Millegearaidh, identified now as the site of Blàr Milleadh a' Ghàrraidh ('the Battle of the Spoiling of the Dyke'). In

October 2017, *The Scotsman* newspaper carried a feature entitled: 'Six of Scotland's bloodiest clan battles'. The article cited its pick of the most gory battles of Scotland's ancient past, where clansmen:

> were pitted against their rivals, the establishment – and even their own father – as they entered brutal survival mode.

Top of the list was the Battle of the Spoiling of the Dyke, where:

> the deep feud between the MacLeods of Waternish and the MacDonalds of Uist came to a cruel head in a church on Skye in 1578.

The gist of the tale was that the MacLeods were assembled for a service at Cill Chomain (Kilchoman, 'St. Coman's Church') or Tiumpan (Triumpan, 'one-sided hillock', also said to be named for its resemblance to a harp). Unfortunately for the congregation, tradition recounts that:

> … the MacDonalds, who had earlier landed in a fleet of eight ships at Ardmore Bay, surrounded the church and set it on fire. All the worshippers were burned alive apart from one young woman, who reportedly managed to escape by a window.

The MacLeods, alerted by the smoke and the fire, counter-attacked. Alexander Cameron wrote in his *The History and Traditions of Skye* (1892):

> Before the MacDonalds could regain their boats, which by the receding of the tide, were high and dry upon the rocks at Ardmore, they were attacked by the MacLeods. A desperate struggle ensued in which all the MacDonalds were slain. Their bodies were ranged in line alongside a turf dyke … and the dyke was tumbled over on the top of them – a quick but unfeeling form of burial.

So infamous is this event that it merits a mention in Ben Kieran's Blood *and Soil*: *A World History of Genocide and Extermination from Sparta to Darfur*. This officially undocumented skirmish might well have occurred sometime between 1570 and 1600. However, the standard accusation of sacrilegious church burning is only one of at least a dozen known examples. The "unfeeling burial" under a broken dyke is a misunderstanding; a recent anthology of Medieval Gaelic poetry explains that the notion of dyke-spoiling:

> ... is almost certainly folk etymology – an imagined explanation of a pre-existing Norse place-name, Millegearaidh, middle field and all is subsequent embroidery.

Of the actual skirmish itself, an anonymous, perhaps 17th-century song, has the lines:

Bha fir an sin
air dhroch càradh,
an druim fòdhpa,
's am buinn bhàn ris.
'S iomadh bean bhochd
bha gu cràiteach,
's i gun mhac ann,
's i gun bhràthair,
gun duine ann a
ghabhadh bàigh dhi.
'S mo mhallachd sin
aig Clann Raghnaill.

Men were there in a bad state,
Lying on their backs, their white soles showing.
Many poor women were deeply grieving,
Without a son, without a brother,
WIthout a man to show her affection
My curse is on Clan Ranald.

This is clearly a MacLeod composition. The fight was reputedly where A' Bhratach Shìth ('the fairy flag') of Dunvegan was last unfurled. This tattered silk flag is now in Caisteal Dhùn Bheagain (Dunvegan Castle), the ancestral home of the MacLeods. The flag is said to be the parting gift to a MacLeod chief from his fairy wife. It was probably woven in the Middle East and may be over 1,000 years old. The notion of donation by fairies of items ranging from flags, chanters and talismans, each with specific magical properties, was a relatively common trope.

Dunvegan's flag's power was to bring the clan victory in battle three times. At Blàr Milleadh a' Ghàrraidh its power made modest numbers of MacLeods appear, as the poet claimed, as numerous as blades of grass. Such war banners were a fundamental part of the battle array, as attested by the early Ossianic poem, 'The Banners of the Fian'. An evocation of their display was attempted in 1760 by James 'Ossian' Macpherson in his free translation of the original ballad:

> *Raise my standards on high, – spread them on Lena's wind, like the flames of a hundred hills. Let them sound on the winds of Erin and remind us of the fight. We reared the sunbeam of battle; the standard of the king. Each hero's soul exulted with joy, as, waving, it flew on the wind. It was studded with gold above, as the blue wide shell of the nightly sky. Each hero had his standard tool and each his gloomy men.*

The direct translation by Professor Donald Meek conveys far greater power and menace:

> Bu bhinn <sian[a]mhran) na sleagh
> agus monghar na míleadh,
> agus [s]rann bhratach sróill
> ag éirigh a madain ghaoithreóidh.
> Do thógamar Dealbh Ghréine
> bratach Finn mhóir na Féine
> <iomadh uair>chuir sí deannāl
> fa mhór Chanān Chinn tSléibhe.
> D[o] th[ógamarj an Aoincheannach Óir,
> b[ratach] Raighne go n-iomad slóigh,
> sróll lé goinfidhe cnrámh[a] is cinn,
> lē lēig[d]is fuil go faidhbrinn.

Sweet was the <whizzing> of the spears and the clamour of the warriors and the whirring of the satin banners, raisings in a morning of frosty wind. We raised Image of Sun, the banner of great Fionn of the Fian; <on many occasions> it caused a hot conflict around great Conán of Ceann Sléibhe. We raised the Single-Headed Golden One, the banner of Raighne with the numerous host – a satin banner by which bones and heads would be wounded, and by which they would cause blood to flow to the ankles.

This is the sort of effect the Fairy Flag was expected to have. The importance of flags and banners is clear from the story of the rescue of the Appin Standard at the battle of Culloden. Of the twelve banners of the Highland clans that were raised at Culloden, only the banner of the Appin Regiment came home again. The remaining eleven were publicly burned at the Mercat Cross in Edinburgh by the common hangman.

Alasdair Crotach: *Hump-backed Alasdair*

The main peaks in Duirinish, Healabhal Mhòr and Healabhal Bheag, are better known as MacLeod's Tables. Their distinctive plateau-ed shapes are visible throughout much of northwest Skye. The table-like form has attracted a tradition to the effect that Alasdair Crotach, 8th Chief of MacLeod, set out a feast on the top of one of these flat hills to win a wager with King James V. James was then attempting to control the chiefs and Alasdair's talent for diplomacy saved him and his MacLeod clan.

Alasdair undoubtedly had such skills, but the tale probably exaggerates these. A later chief, Iain Breac ('pock-marked John'), extended the castle and was the last chief to live there permanently with full courtly panoply including retaining the services of a highly trained classical poet, Ó Muirgheasáin; Ruaraidh MacMhurich, An Clàrsair Dall (Roderick Morrison, 'the Blind Harper'); a piper, the great Patrick Mòr MacCrimmon; and a 'fool' or jester, MacHandy.

The Blind Harper from Bragar, Lewis, who died about 1713, has been described as 'Scotland's last minstrel'. He underwent rigorous musical training in Ireland to prepare him for the life of a professional musician, still a prestigious career for those able to secure patrons among the landed aristocracy. Iain Breac of Dunvegan engaged him as his harper, though by now the relationship between chief and clan was changing, with the chiefs becoming more Anglicised and neglectful of their role as patrons of the arts and custodians of traditional culture.

Iain Breac did indeed have to spend periods in Edinburgh, partly through political pressure but also out of preference. On his death in 1693, his son Ruaraidh Òg ('Young Roderick'), was even less inclined to respect the traditional duties of a chief to his clan. In a stinging rebuke to him, the Clàrsair Dall's 'Òran do MhacLeòid Dhùin Bheagain' ('Song to MacLeod of Dunvegan') laments the passing of the old order and compares the new chief unfavourably to his father of whom he says:

chan fhàgadh e 'n Dùn gun cheòl

he'd never leave the castle devoid of music.

Màiri nighean Alasdair Ruaidh (Mary MacLeod), seen as one of the stalwarts of the new school of poetry that was emerging in the 17th century, and composing only a generation or so before Roderick's song, says of Iain's tenure:

Thoir an t-soiridh seo bhuam
Gu talla nan cuach
Far 'm bi tathaich nan truagh dàimheil;
Thun an taighe nach gann,
Fo an leathad ud thall,
Far bheil m' aighear 'us ceann mo mhànrain.

Bear this greeting from me
To the hall of the goblets,
Where the visit of the poor is welcome:
To the house without stint,
Under the slope yonder
Where resides my joy and the source of my melody.

Dà Thriath de Chlann 'ic Leòid: *Two Chiefs of Clan MacLeod*

In 2007, *The Herald* newspaper carried a piece which said that an Australian had claimed that he was the rightful chief of the Clan MacLeod. Guy MacLeod came forward after learning of the death of the 29th chief, John MacLeod. Leading clan genealogists had agreed that 54 year-old Guy had a claim, though none were convinced that he had the right to now become chief. His claim was based on being the direct male descendant of the 15th chief of MacLeod, Rory Mòr (Sir Roderick MacLeod) (1573-1626). The present chiefs are descended from Dame Flora MacLeod, the first female chief. The Australian claimant asked why John MacLeod was made chief when he had to change his name from Woolridge-Gordon to take on the job. Guy MacLeod asked:

> "How could John have been the chief of the MacLeods when he wasn't even a MacLeod?"

yet Dame Flora's descendants sit in Dunvegan.

The MacDonalds were not above a bit of re-christening either. In 1814, Colonel William Bosville left most of his fortune and estates to his nephew Godfrey MacDonald, provided he changed his surname to Bosville. However, when his elder brother Alexander died unmarried in 1824, Godfrey again changed his name to Bosville-MacDonald in order to become the 3rd Baron MacDonald. The Irish baronetcy suffered further contention later.

An Sruthan: *Struan*

It was perhaps of An Sruthan (Struan, 'stream'), south of Dunvegan, that the relief official James Chant said in early 1850 that:

> It is not too much to say that many of the swine in England are better fed and better housed than the poor of this island.

As Malcolm Grey's seminal work *The Highland Economy* explained, there was a despairing drift in search of land; perhaps the more serious result of eviction, bringing confusion and added difficulty for too many already crowded townships. It was remembered in one Skye township in 1884 that people from other townships began to crowd them until it was inhabited by 40 tenants. Originally there had been four. More obvious was the tendency of the rootless to collect in large groups – villages rather than townships composed of crofts. Here was the extremity of land poverty together with the lack of any alternative opportunity for livelihood. One historian coined the term "rural slum" to characterise such poverty and squalor. Grey himself stated baldly that the responsibility for such conditions lay in the population shift of the first decades of the 19th century, largely as a result of the onset of sheep farming. When the Potato Famine struck, the landed classes exploited their opportunity with great skill and, whenever possible, the very poorest were shaken out of the tenant structure and more reliable rent payers were retained. These policies simply exacerbated the sufferings of the poor and contributed to the persisting acute levels of destitution.

Geusto (Gesto, ON, 'goat inlet') beyond Struan, was the home of the cadet branch of the MacLeods of Gesto, many of whom served as senior soldiers chiefly in the service of the Netherlands. The most outstanding of them was Major-General Norman Macleod, whose son, Lieutenant-General Norman MacLeod, died in 1837 after a career in the Scots Brigade, also known as the Anglo-Dutch Brigade or the Anglo-Scots Brigade. This was an infantry brigade of the Dutch States Army. First formed in 1586, by the late 17th century it usually comprised six infantry regiments, three recruited primarily from Scotland and three from England.

Over the years, many ex-soldiers settled in the Netherlands, including Hugh Mackay, whose son, nephews and grandsons all served with the Brigade. This branch ultimately became chiefs of Clan Mackay and continues to hold the title of Lord Reay. Other less distinguished MacLeod descendants included Dutch Colonial Army Captain Rudolf MacLeod, who, in 1895, became the husband of Mata Hari who was executed for spying during the First World War.

Confusingly perhaps, there are two compilations of Gaelic music known as the *Gesto Collection.* The first of these was by Niel (sic) MacLeod, laird of Gesto, who, in 1828, published a book of transcriptions of the canntaireachd system from one of the last of the MacCrimmon pipers, Iain Dubh MacCrimmon. Just three years earlier, another MacCrimmon, Dòmhnall Ruadh ('red Donald'), died and with him much music. In the early 1770s, Donald had emigrated to North Carolina but returned in 1790 at the request of the Highland Society of London. In 1808, the Society proposed that a College of Piping be re-established at Fort Augustus, and that Donald should supervise instruction. Almost 200 years were to pass before the proposal saw the light of day and only then in Glasgow.

According to Sir Walter Scott's biographer J. G. Lockhart:

> MacLeod's hereditary piper is called MacCrimmon ... possessing about 200 tunes and pibrochs, most of which will probably die with him as he declines to have any of his sons instructed in the art.

Red Donald's decision not to pass his knowledge of piping on to his sons seems to be related to his dismay at the massive emigration from the MacLeod estates in the 1770s, in which he himself gave up his hereditary holding in Borreraig and sailed for North America.

The second *Gesto Collection* was by Dr Keith Norman MacDonald who was born in Sleat in 1834. From 1860, he worked as a medical doctor. He was appointed Civil Surgeon in Prome in Burma and became interested in the traditional medical knowledge of the Burmese people. In 1879, he published a still significant monograph, in part discussing ancient palm-leaf manuscripts and entitled *The Practice of Medicine Among the Burmese*.

In 1890, Keith Norman became the medical officer in Gesto Hospital and began work on the second *Gesto Collection* of Gaelic songs and puirt-à-beul ('mouth music'), interspersed with dance tunes for the fiddle, pipe tunes, and piano scores for all of the melodies. It seems that he intended to counter the ingrained Anglonormative perception of the Gael as an uncultured savage. Many of the puirt-à-beul that he included in the book are only to be found there; without his efforts our knowledge of this genre of traditional music would be diminished.

The crofting township of An Droighneach (Drynoch, 'thorn place') is where a side road leads into the peninsula of Minginis (Minginish, ON, 'main headland'), and the former lands of the MacLeods of Talaisgeir (Talisker, ON, 'sloping rock'). Johnson and Boswell visited Talisker's tacksman, Colonel John Macleod, 4th of Talisker, yet another officer in the Scots Brigade. In 1820, his grandson sold Talisker and emigrated to Tasmania with 36 members of the clan. Shortly afterwards, Hugh MacAskill took over the Talisker estate and completed the clearance process begun under his predecessor. Five years later, he founded the Talisker distillery, now owned by Diageo. Talisker was a favourite whisky of Robert Louis Stevenson. He wrote:

> The king o' drinks, as I conceive it, Talisker, Islay, or Glenlivet.

Continuing on eastward, the A863 road re-joins the A87 at Sligachan and its hotel. Aptly for this long-established watering hole, the name means 'small place of shells'. 'Shell' is a poetic epithet for a drinking vessel. An account of life at Dunvegan in the 1670s recounts that:

> When the chiefs returned home they summoned their friends and clients to a grand entertainment. After feasting, the old and young warriors sat down in order from the Chieftain, the harp was then touched, the song was raised and the Sliga-Créchin, slige chreachain, scallop-shell, or the drinking shell, went round.

This was the kind of occasion that the Clàrsair Dall often graced with music and song. Such events were not without their dangers as a witty, punning rhyme attests:

Bheir a-nall an t-slige chreachain
Oir 's ann aist' as blast' tha 'n dram
Gur math an t-àinm dhith creachan
Gur e an t-slige chreach a th' ann.

Bring over the scallop-shell
Since a dram tastes best from it
Ruination is the best name for it
For it is the shell of ruination.

Slèite: *Sleat*

At Skulamus (ON, 'Skali's moss'), the road goes south to the ferry terminal at Armadal (Armadale), a name thought to mean 'arm valley' and to refer to the bay. The Gaelic epithet Armadal nan Lùireach ('Armadale of the chain mail') suggests that the Gaels interpreted the Norse name as relating to armour. Armadale is in Slèite (Sleat, 'sloping moorland'), an ancient division that in 1463 was described as being a 'twenty-eight mark land', supplying one birlinn or galley for naval service to the Lords of the Isles.

Eilean Iarmain: *Isle Ornsay*

Eilean Iarmain or Eilean Dhiarmaid (Isle Ornsay, 'Diarmid's island') is thought to have been the site of an early religious community. The island itself shelters one of the best natural harbours in southern Skye and the MacDonald estate founded a village here in the early 19th century. Flora MacDonald was taken captive from here to the frigate *Unicorn* in 1746, before being sent to the Tower of London.

Isle Ornsay became an important fishing harbour, commercial centre and passenger ship stop. It was the base of operations of the late Sir Iain Noble. He began his career by establishing a merchant bank, Noble Grossart, in Edinburgh in 1969. When he was bought out, he used the proceeds to buy part of the MacDonald Estates on Skye, including 20,000 acres of land, most of which is on the Sleat peninsula. Sir Iain subsequently developed many business interests in Skye and elsewhere, including Hotel Eilean Iarmain and the whisky company Pràban na Linne. Although not a native Gaelic speaker, he spoke the language fluently and used his position as the landowner to support the language, introducing an employment policy of positive discrimination in favour of Gaelic speakers. He was directly responsible for the erection of the first Gaelic road signs in Scotland and he was also the founder of Sabhal Mòr Ostaig.

Dùn Sgàthaich: *Sgàthach's Fort*

Just before Teangue (ON, 'Tongue'), a side road leads to the west. This detour is worthwhile taking since at Tòcabhaig (Tokavaig, ON, 'Toki's bay') is Dùn Sgàthaich ('Sgàthach's fort'). It was here that Sgàthach the legendary sorceress lived, and taught young men martial arts. Sgàthach possessed a three-stringed magical harp, each named string of which was associated with a different outcome when tuned: Geantraighe (from gean, 'good cheerfulness', and traigh, 'strength') caused laughter and dancing; Gultraighe caused crying; Suantraighe caused heavy, balmy sleep. In addition to the training to arms, Sgàthach taught mutual friendship and fidelity. Cù Chulainn came here as a pupil and his name is more intimately associated with Dùn Sgàthaich than with any other place in Scotland.

Cù Chulainn: *Culann's Hound*

The physical remains of Dùn Sgàthaich possibly date from the 14th century, although on an earlier fortified site, and it was a stronghold of the MacLeods, held on their behalf by the MacAskills, before it became the principal seat of the MacDonalds of Skye, Clann Ùisdein, in the 15th century. The castle is now approached over a gully, bridged by two walls that flanked a drawbridge. But in the older fort of Sgàthach there was no such convenient access for the aspiring pupil, Cù Chulainn, whose strength was proverbial:

> Cho làidir ri Cù Chulainn
>
> *As strong as Cù Chulainn.*

The ancient Fingalian hero tale, 'The Ulster Saga', relates that when Cù Chulainn came here, Sgàthach denied him entry. It says that:

> When he came to the Bridge of the Leaps, beyond which was the country of Skatha, Cù Chuilinn found many sons of the princes of Ireland there. And among them was his friend Ferdia. But the Bridge of Leaps was very narrow and high, and it crossed a gorge where far below in the boiling sea ravenous monsters could be seen swimming. "Not one of us has crossed that bridge," said Ferdia, "for if a man step upon one end of it, the middle immediately rises up and flings him back and in leaping upon it he may miss his footing and fall into the sea where the sea-monsters are waiting for him." Three times Cù Chuilinn ran towards it and tried to leap upon the middle, but each time it flung him back. Finally, on the fourth leap, he landed in the centre of the bridge, and with one leap more he was across it,

and stood before the fortress. Sgàthach, impressed, accepted him as a pupil.

Cù Chulainn was a diligent scholar: He was known as Cù nan Cleas ('dog of tricks') and among his twenty-one geasan ('tricks' or 'devices') were the apple-feat, the edge-feat, the supine-feat, and the salmon leap. Cù Chulainn's 'salmon leap' has been described as an aggressive, highly effective combat strategy comparable to the aggressive jump of soccer players.

The hero fondly recalled his time here:

Deò-ghréine Dhùn Sgàthaich nan stuadh,
Ainnir bhràigh-gheal nan rosg mall,
Is e dh'fhàg mi 'n Innis an t-slòigh.

The sunbeam of Dùn Sgàthaich of waves,
White-bosomed fair of gentle eye,
Whom I left in the Isle of hosts.

Caisteal a' Chamais: *Knock Castle*

Immediately south of the turning to Dùn Sgàthaich is Caisteal a' Chamais (Castle Camus, 'bay castle'). It is usually referred to as Caisteal a' Chnuic (Knock Castle, 'knoll castle'), but has also had the colours ruadh ('ruddy') and ùaine ('green') applied to it. The visible ruin is medieval in date but likely to overlie an earlier Dùn Thorabhaig. It was a MacLeod castle in 1402 when William, 4th MacLeod chief, died here. In the following decades, the MacDonalds forced the MacLeods out. Dòmhnall Gorm Mòr MacDonald's possession of Sleat was confirmed in a charter of 1596, which stipulated that Castle Camus must be available as a residence for the king. The last reference to Knock as an occupied site dates to 1632.

As in the castles of Ashintully, Crathes, Ballindalloch, and Fyvie, it is claimed that the castle is haunted by a glaistig or 'Green Lady'; a ghost associated with the fortunes of the family who occupy the castle. The ghost will appear happy if good news is to come; if there is bad news she will weep. The castle is also said to have had a gruagach. Also known as a brùnaidh ('a brownie'), the gruagach was a household spirit that came out at night and performed various chores while the owners of the house slept. The human owners of the house were required to leave a bowl of milk or cream or some other offering for the gruagach which is described as easily offended; it would leave a home forever if it felt it had been insulted. Castle Camus's spirit is said to have had a particular concern with caring for livestock.

A' Chill Mhòr: *Kilmore*

A' Chill Mhòr (Kilmore, 'big church') is a site sacred since at least the 13th century when the first church was said to have been built by Crotach mac Gille Gorm ('hump-backed son of the blue servitor') who was a chief of the Logans of Druimdeurfait, Ross-shire, and a canon of Beauly Priory. This church is one of some dozen that have been said to have been burned along with their congregations. In this case, the culprits were a band of MacLeods who pursued MacIntyre fugitives to the church where they set the thatched roof alight and burnt them all to death. Wisely, as Ian Lom tells us, the 17th century successor building was slated:

Gu Eaglais Shlèite nan stuagh,
Chosd thu fèin ri' cur suas,
Ged nach d' fhuirich thu buan ri 'sgleutadh.

To the Church of Sleat with its gables,
Which you yourself paid to have erected
Though you did not survive to see its roof slated.

Sabhal Mòr Ostaig: *Great Steading of Ostaig*

To the south is Sabhal Mòr Ostaig ('great steading of Ostaig') (c.1840), one of the MacDonald farm squares. This agricultural building has been re-purposed as a Gaelic college; the vision of Sir Ian Noble. When Sir Iain bought the northern portion of the Sleat estate, his vision for his new acquisition was inspired by a visit he had made to the Faroe Islands in the 1960s. There he had been impressed by how the local linguistic and cultural renaissance had helped to create a correspondingly dynamic economic and creative revival.

Sir Iain was inspired to renovate Sabhal Mòr Ostaig, known locally as SMO, as a Gaelic cultural centre. Plans at first focused on the establishment of a Gaelic library that has become the largest public collection of Gaelic-related material in the Hebrides. From this kernel, a two-week summer course for Gaelic learners, attended by 22 students from Scotland and abroad, was held in September 1973 in association with An Comunn Gàidhealach.

Today, SMO is The National Centre for Gaelic Language and Culture and is an Academic Partner of the University of the Highlands and Islands. It is also home to several national projects, including Faclair na Gàidhlig (Dictionary of Scottish Gaelic), an inter-university initiative to produce a historical dictionary of Scottish Gaelic; Ainmean-àite na h-Alba (Gaelic Place-Names of Scotland), the national advisory partnership for Gaelic place-names in Scotland, and Tobar an Dualchais, Kist o Riches, an online resource dedicated to the preservation and promotion of Scotland's cultural heritage.

Somhairle MacLean wrote of SMO in his poem 'Gealach an Fhàis os Cionn Shlèite' ('Waxing Moon above Sleat'):

Dùn Sgàthaich 'na chàrnaich luim
's an Caisteal Uaine fo eidheann
is samhlaichean na falachd 's a' bhàis
a' tathaich am mùr marbha laga;
luibhean is blàthan an rùin
mu Shabhal Ostaig; agus solas,
deò-grèine dòchas nan Gàidheal,
mu ballachan ùra 's seana.
Mo dhùrachd gu robh math is buaidh
air obair luachmhòr an t-Sabhail.

Dunscaith a bare cairn of stones
And the Green Castle under ivy
and the ghosts of feuding and death
haunting their weak dead ramparts;

the herbs and flowers of aspirations
about Sabhal Ostaig; and a light,
sunbeam of the Gael's hope,
about its old and new walls.
May good fortune and success
be with the great work of the Sabhal.

Caisteal Armadail: *Armadale Castle*

Beyond is Armadale Castle, the former home of the MacDonalds. A mansion house was first built here around 1790 and, in 1815, a Scottish baronial mock castle was erected next to that house. This was the work of Alexander Wentworth MacDonald, 2nd Lord MacDonald (1773-1824) who established mills and lime kilns, churches and manses, piers, stores and inns across his estate. He initiated coal and marble mining and drainage and plantation schemes. He expended the bulk of his income on the improvement and embellishment of his estate and was left virtually bankrupt as his income, almost £29,000 by 1818, declined, mainly as a result of a failing kelp industry and poor rental returns. In 1798, he received permission from George III to raise a regiment, but his tenants were unwilling to join, and very considerable pressure was brought to bear upon them before the full complement of men was finally recruited.

When Alexander died unmarried in 1824, his younger brother Godfrey Bosville became the 3rd Baron MacDonald. He had served in the British Army prior to his succession and eventually rose to the rank of lieutenant-general. When Godfrey died in 1832 his eldest son, Alexander William, assumed the surname of Bosville and inherited the Thorpe and Gunthwaite estates in Yorkshire. However, as he was technically illegitimate in England, due to the legitimacy of an earlier Scottish marriage not being accepted, he did not succeed as 4th Baron of Sleat; this title fell to his younger brother, Godfrey William Wentworth Bosville-MacDonald.

Alexander William's grandson, Alexander Wentworth MacDonald-Bosville spent the last quarter of the 19th century trying to prove the legitimacy of the Scottish marriage and succeeded in having his grandfather retrospectively created the 19th chief, his father the 20th chief and he, himself, the 21st chief of Sleat. This unseated his cousin as 6th Lord Macdonald. In 1911, Alexander Wentworth Macdonald-Bosville travelled to Skye to take up residence at Armadale Castle.

At the same time, across in Kintail, the MacRaes were also scrapping as to who should hold the chieftainship. In the event, no one got the prize.

Vacated by the MacDonalds in 1925, Armadale Castle has fallen into ruin. The castle, gardens and the wider 20,000-acre estate, including a museum and the converted stables, are operated by Clan Donald Lands Trust. This charitable trust, established in 1971, was the brainchild of Ellice MacDonald (1913-2003) of Wilmington, Delaware and his wife Rosa, who used her considerable Du Pont fortune to support the Trust's purchase of lands that once formed part of the traditional lands of the Sleat MacDonalds.

In the grounds of the castle is Taigh-tasgaidh nan Eilean (Museum of the Islands). Although the primary seat of Clan Donald was at Finlaggan on Islay, this is the only place where you can discover the history of the Highlands and Islands through the Clan Donald story. The demise of the Clan Donald Lordship of the Isles was lamented by a late 15th-century MacMhuirich bard:

Ní h-éibhneas gan Chlainn Dòmhnaíll,
Ní comhnairt bheith 'na n-éagmhais;
an chlann dob fhèarr san gcruinne:
gur dhíobh gach duine céatach.

It is no joy without Clan Donald
It is no strength to be without them
The best race in the world
To them belongs every good man.

The road ultimately ends at Àrd Shlèite, now simply known as Aird. Its inhabitants were once known as Na Faoileagan ('the sea-gulls') from the saying:

Buntàta is faoileagan, biadh luchd na h-Àirde

Potatoes and seagulls, Aird folks' food.

Caibideil 9: *Chapter 9*

Na h-Eileanan Tarsainn: *The Small Isles*

To the south of the Sleat peninsula lies the small cluster of islands nowadays conveniently grouped as The Small Isles, a naming of recent origin. They are Canaidh (Canna), Rùm (Rum), Eige (Eigg) and Eilean nam Muc (Muck) and are now administered by the Highland Council authority. That they did have some coherence as a group in the past is recorded in the saying:

Nam bithinn-sa roinn an fhearainn
Bu libh Rùm is Eige 's Canaidh.

If I were the land dividing
You would have Rum and Eigg and Canna.

And since they are now treated as a group we shall deal with them in the same manner.

Gaelic applies the name Na h-Eileanan Tarsainn to them but, according to the scholar John Lorne Campbell, this was the 'sea-keening' name for Canna, as it was unlucky to utter the proper name while at sea. Other such names were: for Eigg, Eilean nam Ban Mòra ('island of the big women'); Rum had the title Rioghachd na Forraiste Fiadhaich ('kingdom of the wild forest'); and Muck was known as Tir Chrainne ('land of the sow').

Following the incursions of the Norse, by the 13th century, the islands were within the kingdom of Norway and part of the insular holdings of the MacRuaris. In 1248, Dugal MacRuari, a MacSorley, in other words, a descendent of Somerled, was in Bergen with his cousin, John MacDougall of Argyll. Both petitioned King Haakon IV for the title of King of the Northern Hebrides. John was successful but inherited an increasingly fraught position. One year later, Alexander II, seeking to reclaim the Hebrides, mounted a naval expedition to the west coast. The MacSorleys were now in a difficult place since they held their mainland estates from the King of Scotland but their islands from the King of Norway. Worse was to follow. In 1262 letters were sent to Norway complaining of Scots aggression, particularly in Skye. In response, Haakon's fleet arrived the following summer and Eric, a son of Dugal, was on board Haakon's flagship. But John of Argyll refused to help Haakon, preferring to lose his Hebridean dominions rather than larger estates on mainland Scotland. Dugal's brother, Alan, was active against the Scots, raiding far and wide after a part of the fleet was portaged from Loch Long over into Loch Lomond. Dugald's men acted as intermediaries in the negotiations with the Scots; those MacRuaris were bilingual.

In 1264, the Scots forced Angus of Islay and Magnus of Man to come to terms, but Dugald evidently maintained his island and mainland possessions. By 1292, the MacRuari estate included Garmoran, namely Moidart, Arisaig, Morar and Knoydart along with Eigg, Rum, Uist and Barra. Following the Wars of Independence and with the rise of Bruce's close ally, Angus of Islay, these MacRuari lands were incorporated, through marriage, into the Lordship of the Isles.

In the medieval period, and before the downfall of the Lordship, the island group seems to have continued to be shared between religious and secular powers. Ì Chaluim Cille ('St. Columba's Iona') held the islands of Canna and Muck, the latter apparently acting as a piggery for the monastery. Rum, with its herd of red deer, was a hunting ground for the Lordship. But gradually the ownership of the Bishopric of the Isles and the Abbey of Iona was eroded, reduced to nominal rents paid unwillingly by *de facto* occupiers whose successors became accepted popularly as the actual owners of the lands. *The Description of the Isles of Scotland*, c.1593, possibly an official military report for James VI, shows a complex pattern of ownership and possession, and we have already noted the later effect of the Act of Revocation, 1625.

Canaigh: *Canna*

Canaigh or Eilean Chanaigh (Canna, possibly ON for 'knee-shaped island') is the westernmost of the Small Isles. It is linked to the neighbouring island of Sanday. The island is seven kilometres long and one and a half kilometres wide. At the Reformation, Canna became a possession of the Bishop of the Isles, also known as the Bishop of Sodor (Sodor being the anglicisation of *Suðreyjar* or 'Southern Isles'). In 1561, the Bishop rented out the island to the Clanranald branch of the MacDonalds. Thomas Knox, the Bishop, sold Canna to the Earl of Argyll in 1627 and, although Clanranald held Canna, he was Argyll's vassal. This superiority lasted until Clanranald redeemed it in 1805.

The reputation of Dòmhnall Dubh na Cuthaige ('black Donald of the cuckoo'), the 13th chief of Clanranald who died on Canna in 1686, is not very good. He was born about 1625, fought with Montrose in the Civil War and married his first cousin Mòr, Marion MacLeod. Local tradition says that Marion was the Clanranald wife who was incarcerated in Còrr-dhùn (Coroghon, 'peculiar fort'), to prevent her from meeting a lover. An account of 1797 states:

> This castle was formerly used as a prison for the wife of MacDonald of Clanranald, to secure her from the addresses of MacNeil, an ancient laird of Barra. The lady, however, found means to affect her escape and join her lover for one night, having sewn together her blankets, she let herself down and fled.

In his 1690 Act of Settlement with the Scottish Kirk, William III granted the rents of the suppressed bishopric of Argyll and the Isles to the Synod of Argyll for the purpose of:

> erecting of English schools for rooting out the Irish language.

By 1698, the rents of the bishopric of Argyll and the Isles were financing 25 English schools, thirteen peripatetic schools and five grammar schools. The Act placed the financial burden of the schools upon the proprietors and their principal tenants. Opposition to this policy began to draw Highlanders together in support of the Jacobite cause. To counter this, in 1709, a number of subscribers in Edinburgh were incorporated under the title of The Society in Scotland for Propagating Christian Knowledge. It provided charity schools in the Highlands and Islands, supported by private subscriptions and interest payments from the Society's capital. These schools were to be manned by schoolmasters of proven loyalty to the State and they were to teach English, the Presbyterian Calvinist religion, Church music and arithmetic only. Most of the teachers were bilingual Gaels such as the poet Alasdair mac Mhaighstir Alasdair (Alasdair, 'son of Master Alasdair', Alexander MacDonald).

Clan Ranald tenants on Canna joined the Jacobites and suffered as a consequence. In April 1746, according to Alasdair's account, the ship *Baltimore* arrived and demanded meat; four days later, complaining that the meat was rotten, they slaughtered 60 cattle themselves. Twelve days later, *HMS Commodore* arrived and after receiving warnings about the lecherous intentions of the sailors, the women of Canna fled into the countryside until they were certain that the ship had departed.

In the spring of 1751, a book was published in Edinburgh bearing the title *Ais-Eiridh na Sean Chánoin Albannaich (The Resurrection of the Ancient Scottish Language).* Its author was Alasdair mac Mhaighstir Alasdair. His book contains 32 Gaelic poems and it was the first book of Gaelic poetry printed in Scotland and, for many years, the only one to be prepared for the press by its author. Hardly any Gaelic poets of the time could write their language and their poems were nearly always taken down from their recitation or oral tradition. Alasdair's book, like his own personality, is an unusual mixture of contradictions. He undoubtedly composed some of his poetry while Baillie of Canna. There is a strong local tradition that at least part of his famous epic 'Birlinn Chloinn Raghnaill' ('Clanranald's Galley') was composed in Canna, while he was lying under an upturned boat at the head of the harbour. Martin Martin in his *A Description of the Western Islands of Scotland* (1716) describes professional poets composing in the dark:

> They shut their Doors and Windows for a day's time, and lie on their backs, with a stone upon their Belly, and Plads about their Heads, and their Eyes being cover'd, they pump their Brains for Rhetorical Encomium or Panegyrick; and indeed they furnish such a Stile from this dark Cell, as is understood by very few.

Martin's comment on comprehension relates to the use of the high register form of Gaelic, understood by Gaeldom's elite from Caithness to Cork. Whether or not Alasdair used this method of composition, 'Birlinn Chloinn Raghnaill' combines the old with new imaginative power. The poem describes a working ship, its parts and its sixteen crewmen sailing from South Uist to Carrickfergus in Ireland. The last third of the poem is a vivid description of a ferocious storm that threatens to destroy the men and the ship but which they pass through only just making it to safe haven. The poem is almost 600 lines long and contains sixteen sections, interspersed with short expository passages. With the help of his friend, the Gaelic poet Somhairle MacLean, the poet Hugh MacDiarmid (1892-1978) produced a rendition of the Bìrlinn:

God bless the craft of Clanranald
When brangled first with brine,
Himself and his heroes hurling;
The pick of the human line!

MacDiarmid was not the only one to tackle such a colossal work but none can match the particularly fine modern rendering by Alan Riach. The birlinn sets out, men and oars straining:

Ràmhan mìn-lunnacha, dealbhach,
Socair, aotrom,
A ni 'n t-iomradh toirteil, calma
Bos-luath, caoir-gheal,

Chuireas an fhairge 'na sradaibh
Suas sna speuraibh,
'Na teine-sionnachain a' lasadh
Mar fhras èibhlean,

The oars smoothly handled,
each one in compulsion and balanced,
in tune, lightly carried, the weight of the water below
lifting the vessel and men of the crew,
rowing out in the night, for the tide -

The sea's phosphorescence
showers upwards in sparkles,
waves reach to stars in the sky
like fire, fall in embers, tumbling back down,
spindrift to black ocean's darkness to die -

The ship sails into a storm:

Ghrian a' faoisgneadh gu h-òr-bhuidh
As a mogal,
Chinn an speur gu dùldaidh, dòite,
Làn de dh' oglachd,

Dh' fhàs i tonn-ghorm, tiugh, tàrr-lachdann,
Odhar, iargalt,
Chinn gach dath bhiodh ann am breacan
Air an iarmailt:

Fadadh-cruaidh san àird-an-iar oirr',
Stoirm' na coltas,
'S neòil shiùbhlach aig gaoith gan riasladh,
Fuaradh-frois' oirr'.

Furnace-gold, hot-yellow, yolk-yellow, brass-brazen sun, burning
through fish nets of clouds, trellises meshed, burning them open,
emerges, and the clouds turn back, close in once again,
over all things, changing sky becomes ash, blackening and a blue
splash there, and then, thickening, bulging, effulging,
turning sick, pale, brown, beige, tawny, impending, bellying
down, and the fretwork rematches itself, closes in, hue
thick as tartan, dark weaves, flashes, and there high in the
west, a broken shaft, a dog-tooth of rainbow, colour stripes swelling,
a fang of sharp colour, clouds moving faster to cover it over, and the winds
pick up speed toss the clouds, as if showers of boulders,
grey fragments of stone, chips of earth, advancing in sky.

Its impact on the ocean is soon evident:

An fhairg' uile 's i na brochan
Strioplach, ruaimleach,
Le fuil 's le gaorr nam biast lorcach
'S droch dhath ruadh oir'

the sea, boiling porridge, all muddy and white,
all streaked in grey and bloodily red,
beaded and veined with magenta and puce

They survive the storm, and tattered sail lowered, they now row into a calm sea:

Rinn sinn an t-iomramh rèidh tulganach,
Gun dearmad:
'S ghabh sinn deagh longphort
aig barraibh Charraig Fhearghuis.

the rowing was rhythmic and even,
regular, regular, even and easeful,
carried us over the water,
and in to the harbour of Ireland,
round the point of Carrickfergus:

Safe haven.

John Lorne Campbell mentions that Alasdair's ghost has been seen in South Uist a number of times this century but those who have seen him claim it is not the poet but his brother, Angus, who was a tacksman in Uist.

The population of Canna given in the *OSA* in the 1790s was just 300. Within a generation, it rose to 400 to support kelp harvesting. That had become the main means of subsistence and, when the kelp price collapsed, destitution followed. In 1821, several of the inhabitants of Canna chose to escape their poverty by emigrating to Canada. Most of the remaining people were cleared to Sanday.

In 1827, D. M. Shaw, writing from Benbecula to Clanranald's legal agent in Edinburgh, said that the estimated population of Clanranald's estates including Eigg and Canna was 5,364, and he recommended deportation of 2000 from South Uist and Benbecula and another 200 from Sanday to Cape Breton at government expense – estimated at £2 a head. If possible, the estate should select the emigrants. Of Sanday, he wrote:

> The population of sand island of Canna is at least 200. The people neither fish nor do anything else. I cannot imagine how they live. They are most miserably poor. They make one year 9 tons and the next year 15 tons of kelp which I sell for them and credit them the price. This is all the rent they ever pay. Their whole efforts would not pay the fourth part of their arrears. The evil here arises entirely from excess of population. The people were sent to the island with a view to the fishing which however they never attended. They can contribute nothing towards payment of their fare to America.

D. M. Shaw seems to have been ignorant of a report on the local effects of the salt duties and its crude administration. It explained that:

> the poorer were totally deprived from ever having it in their power to obtain one bushel of salt, essential for preserving their catch and that the inhabitants of the islands and such parts of the coast as were remote from a customs house were in great measure excluded from any share in the fisheries.

To obtain salt, the Canna people had to sail to the distant Tobermory Salt Station in Mull and pay a tax of two shillings a bushel, a sum well beyond their reach. Little wonder that they never attended the fishing.

Reginald George MacDonald of Clanranald succeeded, aged six, in 1794, the first Clanranald chief to be educated at an English public school, Eton. But after coming of age in 1810, he started selling land to meet the expenses of the English social and political life in which he had become involved. In 1827, Donald MacNeill, the tenant of Canna, saw what was coming and bought the island for £9000. According to one report, the first thing MacNeill did was remove 200 inhabitants at his own expense and reorganise the remaining community, prohibiting squatting and subdivision of holdings. The 1851 census showed a halving of the population.

Donald MacNeill must have been in Canna in the summer of 1851 at the time of the great Clearance because there is a strong tradition that, as he was watching the people go, an old woman turned to him and said:

> Thig an latha fhathast gum fàg sibh Canaidh cho bochd rinn fhìn.
>
> *The day will come yet that you'll leave Canna as poor as ourselves.*

That was the case in 1881. News of the sale of Canna came to the islanders, not from MacNeill himself, but with a party of travellers who crossed over from Rum. A gentleman of the name of Thom, a Glasgow shipowner, had paid £13,000 for it. It is said that the price MacNeill got for the island was insufficient to meet all his debts, fulfilling the old woman's 1851 prophesy.

In 1938, Thom's family sought a sympathetic buyer, selling Canna to John Lorne Campbell, who organised the island as a farm and nature reserve. He lived there until his death in 1996. Canna House contains Campbell's important Gaelic and other archives which he donated with the islands to the National Trust for Scotland. His widow, Margaret Fay Shaw, remained at Canna House until her own death in 2004 at the age of 101. A renowned and important collector of Gaelic songs and folklore, she always said that her favourite song was 'An Gille Donn' ('The Brown-haired Lad'):

> Òigear nan rosg mìogach dh'fhàg m' inntinn trom
> 'S mise tha fo mhì-ghean mun ghille dhonn.
>
> 'S mise th' air mo sgaradh bho thoiseach an earraich
> Dhealaich uam mo leannan, maraiche nan tonn.
>
> Thug mi gaol a chràidh mi do sgiobair a' bhàta
> Gheibhinn cadal sàmhach leat air bhàrr nan tonn.
>
> 'S e 'n gaol a thug mi òg dhut a tha gam leònadh
> A chaoidh cha dìobair m' fheòil thu fhad 's is beò mo chom.

'S e bhith ort a' bruidhinn a-nochd a tha gun ruigheachd
Òigear a Chloinn Iain, dh' fhàg mo chridhe trom.

'S maraich' thu gu seòladh cho math 's a ghlac ròpa
Sealgair thu air mòintich 's leònadh tu 'n damh donn.

Dol staigh an Caol Cannach shèid e oirbh gu frasach
Thàinig fairge tarsainn 's bhuail e thu gu trom.

Thàinig air do chùlaibh na chuir anns a' ghrunnd thu
'S e dh' fhàg mise tùrsach mo rùn bhith tàmh fon tonn.

It's the young man of the sparkling eyes who has left my spirits low. I am sad about the brown-haired lad.

I am distraught since the beginning of spring. My sweetheart parted from me, mariner of the waves.

I gave love that caused me anguish to the skipper of the ship;
I would sleep peacefully with you on the crests of the waves.

It's the love I gave you when I was young that grieves me.
My flesh will never forsake you as long as my body lives.

Talking about you tonight disturbs me. Young man of Clan Iain who has left me heavy hearted.

You were a seaman as good as ever grasped a rope. You were a moorland hunter who could wound the brown stag.

Entering the Strait of Canna wind and rain hit you. A turbulent sea came over you and struck you a heavy blow.

From behind came what sent you to the sea floor. What has left me sorrowful is that my love lies beneath the waves.

Today the number of permanently inhabited houses in Canna is some twenty.

Eige: *Eigg*

Nearby Eige (Eigg, 'notched island') is nine kilometres long from north to south, and five kilometres east to west. With an area of 31 square kilometres, it is the second largest of the Small Isles after Rum. At one time the island's population numbered 500. Gaelic clings on. The sheltered nature of the island was known to fishermen who, in the event of storms, would recommend:

> Dèan Eige no Àrasaig dheth.
>
> *Head for Eigg or Arisaig.*

Saints such as Donan of Eigg and Maelrubha of Applecross were significant figures in the area's conversion to Christianity. Both St. Columba and St. Donan followed St. Martin of Tours in preaching self-imposed exile to missionaries who would wander to proclaim the Glory of God and to seek the peace of the resurrection in isolated places. There, after self-chastening, they would gather around them a muinntir ('family of monks') to create a self-supporting community preaching in the surrounding lands. The munntir in Eigg numbered 52 people according to the Irish annals.

Legend tells us that from her fort in Glenelg, the Queen of Moidart ordered her warrior women across to Eigg to massacre the monks. Donan and his monks were at Mass in the oratory on the 17th of April 617 and the saint begged the women to wait until they had finished. As they left the church all were beheaded, and their bodies then burnt. At midnight, lights appeared and voices were heard chanting Donan's death croon. Bewitched, the amazons found themselves compelled to follow lights leading towards Loch nam Ban Mòra ('loch of the big women') where their eyes finally rested upon a little island in the middle of the loch. One by one the women entered the loch and all drowned. From then on, the legend of the warrior women merged into the 'big woman' in the island tradition.

Cill Donain (Kildonan, 'church of the brown-haired one') was one of eleven churches or chapels where the saint's memory was revered. There were three St. Donans but, of these, Donan of Eigg held the chief place; he was styled:

> one of the most popular saints of Scotland.

Eigg came into the possession of Clanranald when it was granted to Roderick the son of Alan in return for the service of a ship of 26 oars, with its complement of men and provisions. When Dòmhnall Dubh ('black Donald') launched his bid to restore the Lordship of the Isles, Raghnall Bàn ('Ranald the fair'), Chief of Clanranald, refused to support him, so, in 1505, King James IV rewarded Ranald with the lairdship of Eigg and Arisaig. Later, in 1532, King James V provided a charter to Iain Mùideartaich (John of Moidart), confirming his position as laird of Eigg and Arisaig.

Ailean nan Creach ('Alan of the forays') the son and successor of John of Moidart, following his pact with the Devil, built the church of Kildonan as one of seven. If the tale is true, the date of the church must be before 1593, the year Alan died. Within, let into the east wall, is a tomb said to contain the remains of the prince of pipers, Raonull mac Ailein Òig (Ronald, 'son of young Alan'), the composer of some of the most celebrated pipe music in existence. He died in Eigg in 1645.

Uamh Fhraing ('St. Francis's Cave') commemorating St. Francis of Assisi, is on Eigg's coast. The entrance to the cave is narrow and is obscured by moss, undergrowth and a small waterfall. It is the site of the reputed Massacre of Eigg. *The Description* of 1593, mentioned earlier, contains an account of a massacre dated to 1577. According to Clanranald tradition, a group of MacLeods was being hosted in Eigg, but they became too forward towards local women. As a result, the local men rounded up the would-be lovers and cast them adrift in the Minch where they were ultimately rescued by other MacLeods. Seeking revenge, the MacLeods landed in Eigg in winter but were spotted by the islanders who hid in the cave.

After some five days of fruitless search, the MacLeods were on the point of leaving when they spotted an islander and followed his footprints in the snow back to the cave. The MacLeods piled flammable material at its entrance and set fire to it; the waterfall dampened the flames so that the cave filled with smoke, asphyxiating almost 400 people inside. Only one inhabitant of Eigg survived, an old woman who had not sought refuge in the cave.

John Lorne Campbell believed that the writer of *The Description* wanted to include the story as evidence of Highland barbarity and used it to cover up an incident of 1588/9. This was when Sir Lachlan MacLean was accused of having invaded The Small Isles with the aid of 100 Spaniards from a galleon that had limped into Tobermory harbour after the dispersal of the Spanish

Armada.The matter is made clearer by the report of Sir Lachlan MacLean's trial when the charges against him are more specific. In Campbell's view, Lachlan MacLean's real crime was the fact that he employed the Spaniards, then enemies of the King, in his feud against the MacDonalds, the King's subjects. But it seems that Sir Lachlan had some high-level protection. Found guilty of treason and murder, he was allowed to escape from Edinburgh Castle, and the only penalty he suffered was the forfeiture of his bail. As Campbell sensibly points out:

> The writer of the 1593 account of the Isles must have been perfectly well aware of all this, yet he says nothing about it, bringing in instead an incident said to have taken place on Eigg in 1577 … If the MacDonalds on Eigg had all been suffocated by the MacLeods in 1577, they would hardly have been available to be massacred by MacLean of Duart and his Spaniards in 1588.

The adjacent cave, Uamh a' Chràbhaidh ('cave of worship'), was used for religious services. To evade restrictions imposed by the government on Roman Catholic services, the inhabitants of Eigg began to hold services secretly in this large high-roofed cave. It was renamed 'Cathedral Cave' by Victorian visitors.

Eigg tenants also joined the 1745 Jacobite Rising and all the 38 surviving men who had taken part in the Rising were arrested by the navy and imprisoned in the Tower of London. Most died in squalid conditions, but the remaining sixteen were eventually sent to work in sugar cane plantations in Barbados.

A significant later 18th-century literary development was the publication of anthologies of vernacular Gaelic poetry. The first such anthology was *Comh-chruinneachaidh Orannaigh Gaidhealach* (1776), otherwise known as *The Eigg Collection*, compiled and published by Raghnall Dubh Dòmhnallach ('black Ranald MacDonald') (c.1728-c.1808), tacksman in Eigg and son of Alasdair mac Mhaighstir Alasdair. Ranald was influenced by the desire to gather Gaelic tradition in the wake of the Ossianic controversy, and the Eigg Collection provides some of the earliest printed versions of songs from oral tradition.

Iain Dubh mac Iain 'ic Ailein (John MacDonald), Raghnall Dubh's near contemporary and relative, appears to have belonged to the Morar branch of Clanranald. Described as a "competent poet" he is now best remembered for his witty description of the sharp-tongued women of Eigg and the troubles caused by their gossip in his poem 'Trod nam Ban Eigeach' ('Squabble of the Eigg Women'). It has been suggested that the popularity of love poetry in the late 17th century may well have given renewed impetus to the obscene and anti-female strain in poetry, in effect lampooning the romantic rhetoric. It is perhaps in that context that the song was composed:

Marbhphaisg air na mnathan feadhair
Nach gleadhadh an antlachd!
Tha mo chluasan air fàs bodhar
Le gleodhar an càinte;
Nis bho chaidh iad bho riaghailt
Leigeam srian len aimhleas,
'S tàirneamaid gu àite dìomhair
Bho mhìothlachd an cainnte.

A curse on the women of the fair who won't keep their discontent [quiet]. My ears have grown deaf with the babble of their scolding. Now since they've gone out of control, let me take the bridle from their mischief. Let's go to a secret place away from their offensive speech.

In 1817, with kelp rapidly increasing in price, the laird reduced the size of each tenancy to maximize his labour force. For example, the joint tenanted farm of Cleadale was re-arranged into 28 plots. The collapse in the price of kelp after the Napoleonic Wars led to similar patterns of destitution experienced in all the kelping areas. An Cachaleith Dearg ('the red gate'), a narrow pass at the top of the Laig cliffs, was where the cattle were taken to be bled for sustenance, a common practice in desperate times.

In 1827, Clanranald found a willing purchaser for the island, a Dr Hugh MacPherson. There is speculation that the money to buy Eigg might have come from India where Sir John MacPherson, his uncle, was said to have made his fortune as Governor-General and through his association with, and favours from, the Nawabs of the Carnatic Sultanate. After 800 years, Clanranald rule of Eigg came to an end.

In 1847, in the depths of the destitution caused by the failure of the potato crop, Dr MacPherson decided to evict his tenants and replace them with sheep. In 1853, all fourteen families in the village of Grùlainn (Grulin, 'stony field') were forced to leave Eigg. Brae was cleared in 1858. At the end of the century, in 1893, the MacPherson family sold the island to Lawrence Thompson.

In 1871, An t-Urr. Coinneach MacLeòid, Coinneach a' Mhaighistir (Rev. Kenneth MacLeod, 'Kenneth the schoolteacher's son'), was born in the schoolhouse at Sanna Beag ('little sand river'), the sixth child of Donald MacLeod, parish schoolmaster of the Small Isles. He served as minister in Colonsay from 1917 until 1923 and then in Gigha for the rest of his career. The poster boy of the Scottish literary world, he collaborated, between 1908 and 1929, with Marjorie Kennedy-Fraser on the four-volume *Songs of the Hebrides*. He took traditional material, freely modified it using his own imagination and rendered it in English. His work, including 'The Road to the Isles', composed to commemorate the Fallen of World War I, proved immensely popular.

MacLeod was the nephew of Janet MacLeod who came from a long line of Snizort tradition bearers. At the age of 80, she was able to give the folklorist Alexander Carmichael the best version he had ever heard of 'Seathan, Mac Rìgh Èireann' ('Seathan, Son of the King of Ireland'). She quoted two versions of a Gaelic proverb:

> Riaghladh goirid air an òir, ach riaghladh fada air an òran.

The variant was:

> Chan fhada thèid bonn òir ann an cuideachd, ach ruigidh
> òran math air làn cruinne de shluagh.

Both convey the same meaning:

> *A gold coin does not go far in company but a good song will*
> *suffice for a whole world of people.*

'Seathan' she called "the choice of waulking song" and her version comprised almost 200 lines. She regretted that she:

remembered but little of the song today compared with what I knew when no waulking was complete without me:

'S minig a chuala, 's nach do dh'innis e,
Gu robh mo leannan am Mighinis;
Nam biodh e 'n sin, 's fhad' o thigeadh e;
Chuireadh e bàta dha m' shireadh-sa,
'S chuirinn-sa long mhòr 'ga shireadh-san
Sgioba cliùiteach, ùrail, iriseal.

Nam faighte Seathan ri fhuasgladh,
Dh'fhàsadh an t-òr fo na bruachaibh,
Cha bhiodh gobhar an creig ghruamaich,
'S cha bhiodh lìon gun iasg an cuantan.

B' annsa Seathan air cùl tobhtaidh
Na bhith le mac rìgh air lobhtaidh,
Ged bhiodh aige leaba shocair,
'S stròl dhan t-sìoda bhith fo chasan,
'S cluasag dhan òr dhearg a' lasradh.

Tha Seathan an nochd 'na mharbhan,
Sgeul as ait le luchd a shealga
'S le mac caillich nan trì dealga,
Sgeul as olc le fearaibh Alba.

Woe to him who heard it but never reported it
that my darling was over in Minginish;
had he been there, he'd have come long ago;
he'd send a boat to come and look for me,
I'd send a ship to go and look for him
with a youthful crew, renowned and dutiful.

If Seathan could be released from bondage
gold would grow below the banks of the river,
there'd be no goats on gloomy clifftop,
nor net without fish in the ocean.

Better lying with Seathan behind a ruin
than be with a prince in an upper storey,
even though his were a soft mattress,
with a red gold gleaming pillow
and under his feet a strip of satin.

Tonight Seathan is a lifeless body,
tidings of joy for his pursuers,
and the son of the crone of the three needles,
an evil tale to the men of Scotland.

After being sold by Thompson in 1917, Eigg passed through various hands until it was purchased for £270,000 by Keith Schellenberg in the mid-1970s. Unlike his predecessors, Schellenberg had conservationist motives; he wished to restore listed buildings and preserve the natural environment. But relations with the local people soured. In 1994, Schellenberg sold Eigg to Marlin Eckhard, a German artist and, in 1997, the Isle of Eigg Heritage Trust persuaded Eckhard to sell the land to them. The ceremony to mark the handover took place a few weeks after the 1997 General Election and was attended by Scottish Office minister, Brian Wilson, a long-standing advocate of land reform. He used the occasion to announce the formation of a Community Land Unit to support further land buy-outs.

Between then and the 2011 census, the ordinarily resident population of Eigg rose from 65 to 83 as a result of young people moving to Eigg to set up business, as well as a handful of former residents returning to the island.

Rùm is Eilean nam Muc: *Rum and Muck*

Between Canna and the mainland is the island of Rùm (Rum, a pre-Gaelic name of unclear meaning). The spelling 'Rhum' is bogus. It was imposed on the Post Office and the Ordnance Survey in 1903 by the then proprietor, Sir George Bullough. Similarly, there was an attempt to turn the name Muck into 'Monk Isle' in the 18th century. The Laird did not like being known as MacLean of Muck.

In 1549, Rum was held by MacLean of Coll. The old hunting forest of the Lordship had disappeared and the population rose. The *OSA* of 1794 notes that the small native sheep of Rum had valuable wool which sold at the Redcastle market near Inverness for 14 shillings a stone, twice the usual price.

Protestantism in Rum was referred to by the Canna and Eigg people as Creideamh a' Bhata Bhuidhe ('religion of the yellow stick'). In the early 18th century Hector MacLean, the tacksman, had become a Protestant and wanted his tenants to follow suit, but they continued to attend Mass. One Sunday, he picked up a stick, knocked one of them on the head and drove the others to the Protestant church. The 152 inhabitants judged it prudent to convert.

Much of the same change and decline described in Canna happened in the other Small Isles. In 1790, 238 people left the Small Isles, mostly for America. Muck was cleared of half its people in 1828. Community life ended abruptly in Rum when it was cleared of almost all its population by 1828. Hugh Miller's comment in 1845 remains relevant:

> It would seem as if the depopulation of Rum had tended ... little ... to anyone's advantage. The single sheep-farmer who had occupied the holdings of so many ... had left the island: the proprietor ... seemed to have been as little fortunate as the tenant, for the island itself was in the market; and ... was on the eve of being purchased by some wealthy Englishman, who proposed converting it into a deer-forest. How strange a cycle! Uninhabited originally save by wild animals, it became ... a home of men ... They broke in from the waste the furrowed patches on the slopes of the valleys, they reared herds of cattle and flocks of sheep, their number increased to nearly five hundred souls ... Then came the change of system so general in the Highlands; and the island lost all its original inhabitants, on a wool and mutton speculation ... And now yet another change was on the eve of ensuing, and the island was to return to its original state, as a home of wild animals, where a few hunters from the mainland might enjoy the chase for a month or two every twelvemonth, but which could form no permanent place of human abode. Once more, a strange and surely most melancholy cycle!

Caibideil 10: *Chapter 10*

Iar-thuath na Gàidhealtachd: *The North West Highlands*

A century ago in all the areas west of Inverness, Gaelic was the predominant language. In the Kirkhill parish immediately to the west of Inverness, the 1881 census shows the number of Gaelic speakers was almost 900 out of a total population of 1480. By 1931, a fifth of the population were Gaelic speakers and by 1951 there were 113 out of a population of 1110 who spoke the language as their first tongue. The Highlands Council area saw a 1.4% increase in population between 2011 and 2022. But population change varied substantially between electoral wards across the council area. Ten of the 21 wards saw a decrease in their population. The largest decreases were in Inverness Millburn (down 8.2%) and Thurso and Northwest Caithness (down 7.0%).

Coinneach Odhar: *The Brahan Seer*

Caisteal Bhrathann (Brahan Castle, perhaps 'quern place') was once the home of Clan MacKenzie, commonly called the Lords of Kintail, after their original home. Their attachment to the place is recorded in the saying:

> Fhad 's a bhios monadh an Ceann-tàile, cha bhi
> MacCoinnich gun àl sa chrò.
>
> *For as long as there is moorland in Kintail, MacKenzie will have cattle in the fold.*

As the MacKenzie possessions increased, they built Brahan Castle, which remained their residence into the last century. The castle is intimately associated with Coinneach Odhar Fiosaiche ('sallow Kenneth of the second sight' or the Brahan Seer). He seems to have been a servant acquired along with the Isle of Lewis, as his birthplace was Baile na Cille (Balnakil) in Uig, Lewis.

In contrast to Lowland Presbyterian Scotland where over 4,500 mainly female victims burned or drowned, Gaelic-speaking Scotland had no formal tradition of persecution of witches. Yet one of the earliest witch-hunts took place in Easter Ross in 1578, when the sheriff of Cromarty authorised the arrest of six men and 26 women on charges of witchcraft. Among them was one Coinneach Odhar ('principal or leader of the art of magic'), probably the Brahan Seer of tradition and one of the best-known prophets in Scottish history. Tradition claims that he was executed at Gob na Cananaich (Chanonry Point) on the Black Isle and that, as he was being burnt in a barrel of pitch, he predicted all manner of physical deformities for the chiefs of Clan MacKenzie. He also claimed that the MacKenzies would lose Brahan and Kintail. A Matheson now resides in the former and much of the latter is owned by the National Trust for Scotland.

Some of Coinneach Odhar's prophecies have echoes elsewhere. For example, a prophecy ascribed to him says:

> Thig an latha 's an cuir peirceall na caora mòire an crann air an fharadh.
>
> *The day will come when the jawbone of the big sheep will put the plough on the hen-roost.*

This prophecy of the coming of the 'big sheep' is replicated in the reported words of the Glen Isla Seer:

> Tha an t-àm a' tighinn anns an toir fiacail na caorach coltair a' chroinn às an talamh an Ìle.
>
> *The time is coming when the sheep's tooth will take the coulter of the plough out of the ground in Islay.*

Both prophecies, although difficult to ascribe to anyone with certainty, demonstrate the widespread dislike of what, in 1947, the pioneering ecologist Frank Fraser Darling called the 'Coming of the Sheep':

> This colonisation was one of the epic events of Scottish history, though it is one not commonly referred to in history books.

Coinneach Odhar's name has acted like a magnet, drawing all sorts of alleged prophetic sayings to it and he still excites interest. In 1951, the folklorist Calum I. Maclean recorded from John MacDonald in Highbridge, Lochaber, a verse from the poem 'Am Bàs a Fhuair Coinneach Odhar' ('Coinneach Odhar's Death') composed by the Skye bard, Neil MacLeod:

'S ann anmoch feasgar Diciadain,
Nuair a bha 'ghrian a' dol fodha,
Mun bhliadhna sin seachd ceud deug, a
Rug an t-eug air Coinneach Odhar.
'S tha 'luath na cadal bhon tràth sin
Faisg air bràighe Allt an t-Sobhail,
Ann an clachan beàrnach frògach
Nach modha na crò nan gobhar.

It was late on a Wednesday afternoon as the sun was setting, about the year 1700, that death caught up with Coinneach Odhar. And his ashes are since then sleeping near the brae of Allt an t-Sobhail in a cemetery full of nooks and crannies that isn't any bigger than the goats' fold.

On a lighter note, a lullaby to one of the MacKenzie chiefs, 'Tàladh Choinnich Òig' ('Young Kenneth's Lullaby'), describes happier times for the MacKenzies:

A MhicCoinnich na biodh gruaim ort
Cha do ghlac do mhàthair buarach
No plaide bhàn air a h-uachdar
Ach sìoda dearg is sròl uaine.

A MhicCoinnich mhòir à Brathann
Mhic an t-seòid nach fhuiligeadh masladh.
Cheannaicheadh tu fìon dha t-eachaibh
'S cruidhean dhen òr a chur fon casan.

O son of Kenneth do not be sad. Your mother was never bound to do housework or have a white plaid around her shoulder but red silk and green satin.

O son of Kenneth, Laird of Brahan, son of the hero who never had to suffer shame. You would buy wine for your horses and you would put shoes of gold on their feet.

The Gaelic-speaking communities of the Brahan area were largely cleared. Writing in the 1880s, the Dingwall minister, Dr Kennedy, described how the owners of the land began to act as if they were also:

> owners of the people, and disposed to regard them as the vilest part of their estate. They treated them without respect to the requirements of righteousness or to the dictates of mercy ... families by hundreds were driven across the sea, or were gathered, as the sweepings of the hillsides, into wretched hamlets on the shore. By wholesale evictions wastes were formed for the red deer, that the gentry of the nineteenth-century might indulge in the sports of the savages of three centuries before.

Kennedy was minister of the town at the head of the Beauly Firth, now known as Dingwall (ON, 'thing' or 'meeting-place of the assembly'). Its naming as the place of such annual assemblies denotes the brief, high-water mark of the Earls of Orkney's efforts to gain the 'firthlands' of the east coast and access to the Great Glen. The Gaels call it Inbhir Pheofharain ('estuary of the River Peofhar', now Peffery, a pre-Gaelic name meaning 'bright') or Baile Chàil ('cabbage town'). Here, in the Mitchell Hill cemetery, is a tall memorial, erected in 1907, in honour of Eachann nan Cath ('Hector of the Battles').

Eachann nan Cath: *Hector of the Battles*

Eachann Gilleasbaig MacDhòmhnaill (Hector Archibald MacDonald) KCB, DSO (1853-1903) was also known as 'Fighting Mac'. A stonemason's son, he was a Gaelic speaker as were most people in the area at the time.

He enlisted in the Gordon Highlanders at seventeen, finishing his career as a Major General, a rare example of a soldier who rose through the ranks on merit alone. He distinguished himself in action with the Highland Brigade during the Boer War and became a national hero, knighted for his services. Posted to Ceylon (now Sri Lanka) as Commander-in-Chief of British forces, he faced accusations of homosexual acts with some local youth that led to his suicide in Paris in 1903. A Government Commission later concluded that:

> ... there is not the slightest particle of truth in foundation of any crime, and we find the late Sir Hector MacDonald has been cruelly assassinated by vile and slandering tongues.

The suicide of this popular war hero caused widespread shock. 80 years later it could still inspire poets. Iain Crichton Smith wrote his poem 'Eachann MacDhòmhnaill' ('Eachann nan Cath') in his memory:

Bha a' Ghàidhlig air do bhilean
anns na h-Innseachan, ann an Afraga
anns an Èipheit, anns a Sudan.
Chuir iad às dhut
Kitchener 's an còrr.
Ged a bha thu sabaid
le do chasan, le do dhùirn
bliadhnachan gun sguir
anns an teas uabhasach ud
ag èisteachd ris a Last Post
's air do bhroilleach
na meadailean a' losgadh.
Aon mhadainn ann am Paris
leugh thu am pàipear
a bha ag innse do sgrios.
Chuir thu an gunna ri do cheann.
Thug thu aon bhrag
's thuit an ìmpireachd air falbh.

Gaelic was on your lips
in the east, in Africa
in Egypt, in Sudan.
They destroyed you
Kitchener and the rest.
Although you fought
with your feet and your fists,
year upon year,
in that awful heat,
listening to the Last Post
with the medals on your chest
scorching.
One morning in Paris
you read the paper
that foretold your doom.
You put the gun to your head
and with that one shot the empire fell away.

Few musicians today playing the march tune 'Hector the Hero' by the fiddle composer, Scott Skinner, will be aware that it was composed in honour of Eachann nan Cath.

Cunndainn (Contin, 'confluence') is a name now applied to an extensive parish which extends from the village of Contin practically to the west coast. This might be the location of the tale of the burning of the Church of Cille Chrìosd (Kilchrist, 'Christ Church').

Sometime around 1485, Alan of Lundy led a party of Glengarry MacDonalds on a raid against the MacKenzies. Arriving on a Sunday morning, they saw that a number of local people had assembled in the Church of Kilchrist. The MacDonalds barred the doors and windows, set the thatched roof alight and ordered their pipers to accompany the screams of the dying within with appropriate music. The enraged MacKenzies counter-attacked with the result that none of the MacDonalds, save Alan, reached home alive. That, briefly, is the story. But is it true? This is one of at least a dozen such reported incidents, nearly all supposedly the work of the MacDonalds, a clan despised by the government; the alleged victims were vassals of the powerful House of Kintail, its chief a member of the Privy Council and sure to bring the atrocity before the Court. Retribution should thus have been swift. However, a search in court records for the corresponding Commission of Fire and Sword against the offending MacDonalds reveals no reference either to offence or retribution for this and other supposed church burnings.

Further west is Àicheallaidh (Achilty, possibly related to 'high'), once home to Murchadh Mòr ('big Murdo'), 5th Mackenzie of Achilty, who died around 1689. Murdo spent time in Lewis before 1670 as the factor to the Earls of Seaforth. A noted seaman, he became a cattle dealer, purchasing stock from the Lewis tenants for sale to the English market. On one trip South with a drove of cattle, he was forced to remain there for some time. To pass the time, he hired a horse-drawn buggy to take short excursions through the countryside and it was then that he composed a song called 'An Làir Dhonn' ('The Brown Mare') or 'Iorram na Sgiobaireachd' ('The Helmsman's Boat Song'). It recounts a voyage Murdo took home to Lewis, and describes the 'shaggy filly' as a poor substitute for his beloved boat:

Tha m' aigne fo ghruaim
's gun mi 'n caidreabh a' chuain;
cha chaidil mi uair air chòir.

Gur neo-shocrach mo cheum
air chapall na leum
cha fhreagrar leath' m' fheum le treòir.

Loth philleagach bhreun
fo phillean 's fo shrèin,
aon ghille na dèidh bu lòd.

Cha tugadh i ceum
ach duine 's i fhèin,
's gun cuireadh i feum air lòn.

Cha b' ionnan 's mo làir
air linne nam bàrc;
bhiodh gillean a ghnàth cur bhòd.

Chan iarradh i moll
no fodar no pronn,
ach sadadh nan tonn fo sròin.

My spirits are low without the companionship of the sea:
I can't sleep properly.

Unsteady my pace on the bounding mare, she doesn't answer
my needs at all.

Loathsome shaggy filly under pack-saddle and reins, capable
of carrying only one person.

She can carry only one man and herself, and she requires
feeding.

Not so my mare on the straits of the barques; your young men
were always waging stakes.

She wouldn't require chaff or fodder or oats but the tossing of
the waves under her bow.

The main water course at Contin (An t-Alltan Dubh, 'little black river') now known as The Blackwater, is celebrated in a song by Dòmhnall Friseal (Donald Fraser). He was born in the early 19th century in the area of Loch Bhraoin (Loch Broom), and he worked most of his life as a gamekeeper on a nearby estate. In the song, he gives his gun a personal name, just as the earlier nature poet Donnchadh Bàn had done before him. While Duncan's gun was Nic Còiseam ('Còiseam's daughter'), Donald called his Mòrag nighean Fhionnlaigh (Morag, 'Finlay's daughter'):

Tha 'n t-alltan dubh cho bagarrach,
'S e 'n dùil gun till e dhachaigh mi
Le thuraraich is le thartaraich,
Le bhagartaich 's le bhùraich.

Chì mi na daimh chràiceach thall
'S an lagan bheag sam b' àbhaist dhaibh;
'S nan tiginn uair mun tàinig mi
Cha bhiodh iad slàn sa chunntas.

Saoil thu Mhòrag nighinn Fhionnlaigh
An glèidh thu dhomh do ghealltanas,
Ma gheibh sinn thar an alltain seo
Nach toll thu fear den triùir ud?

The black stream is so menacing, intending to make me return home with its rattling and noisiness, its menaces and its roaring.

I see the antlered stags over in their usual little hollow, and had I come an hour earlier their numbers would not be the same.

Morag, Finlay's daughter, will you keep your promise to me, if we can get across this stream will you pierce one of these three?

At Garbh (Garve, 'rough place') is the junction of the A823 to Kyle of Lochalsh via Strath Brain ('valley of the River Bran'). Bran is an obsolete name for a raven. Westwards from here at Achadh na Sìne (Achnasheen, 'field of storms'), the rivers Bran and Carrann (Carron, 'rough water') meet. Here is the junction with the A890 and the road through Glen Conon to Lochcarron. The route passes from Inverness-shire into Wester Ross, an area with one of the lowest population densities in Europe, with just 1.6 people per km^2. The population in Ross and Cromarty declined by over a quarter between 1881 and 1926, a loss of over 20,000 people at a time when Scotland's population grew by over one-third.

The deserted village of Àirigh Neacaig (Arinackaig, possibly 'Nectan's shieling') is in Strath Carron. In 1679, this village was considered sufficiently important to be one of 28 in Lochalsh at which the Sheriff Officer from Tain read out a summons for Colin MacKenzie of Keppoch to answer charges at its Sheriff Court. The process took ten days. The OS map of 1882 shows that Àirigh Neacaig had 22 occupied houses or structures in use but, by 1961, the village had dwindled to only one structure. Clearance, along with failure to gain the modern amenities of power, water and a paved road, condemned it. Janetown would not have helped.

In what is now Lochcarron, a planned village was laid out around 1800 and named Janetown in honour of the wife of John MacKenzie of Applecross. It was formerly known as Tòrr nan Clàr ('hill of the flat slabs'). A local rhyme, ascribed to the Rev. Lachlan MacKenzie, refers to its change of name and its improved houses:

Faire faire, Tòrr nan Clàr!
Baile Sèine th' ort an-dràst',
Chan 'eil taigh air an teid fàd,
Nach bi simìlear air no dhà.

Alas alas, Tòrr nan Clàr!
You are currently called Janetown;
Every house burning peat,
Will have one or two chimneys.

Commenting in his work of 1956 *The Highland Economy, 1715-1850,* Malcolm Gray stated that as a result of the process of clearance:

> ... some settlements swelled from a few families to several hundred in the first half of the 19th century. One of such villages was Janetown, now Loch Carron, grown in the course of half a century from three or four families to almost 500 persons ... Such growth was the most dangerous in that it was not followed by any occupational diversification.

Disaster struck with the Potato Famine of 1846. By then, lots of land, each carrying the right to the grazing of two cows, were so subdivided that of 47 families, 25 had either one cow or none at all.

A' Chomraich: *Applecross*

The road junction to the Applecross peninsula is in Lochcarron. The name Applecross, from the Pictish name Aporcrosan ('confluence of the [river] Crossan'), is at least 1300 years old but is not used locally to refer to the 19th-century village which is called 'Shore Street,' or simply 'The Street'. Historically, St. Maelrubha had his monastery here and thus the area is known as A' Chomraich ('the Sanctuary').

Generally in the Highlands up to and after 1690, Episcopalianism, the theological doctrine of church government by bishops, was located in Perthshire, Ross-shire, Inverness-shire, Caithness and northern Argyll, while

Presbyterianism, government by church sessions, could be found in Argyll, Sutherland and Easter Ross. It is necessary therefore not to take entirely at face value the charges laid before a presbytery, heavily dominated by eastern Presbyterians, that met at Applecross on 5th September 1656, with the aim of rectifying a serious religious misdemeanour. The minute states that:

> They had ascertained that many of the inhabitants of the surrounding district had been in the habit of practising certain idolatries, and so late as the previous August had, on an island in Loch Maree, offered up a bull as sacrifice to 'Mourie' (conflated form of Maelrubha).

We learn the reason for the sacrifices from a subsequent entry in these records in 1678. Here it is stated that a sacrifice of a bull was offered for the:

> recovery of Christine MacKenzie, spouse of Hector MacKenzie of Mellon of Gairloch, by her husband, sons, and grandson.

The bull's flesh was then:

> assigned medicinally to Mourie's afflicted ones, viz., fatuous persons, on account, presumably, of its supposed magical properties.

The presbytery had also ascertained that in a wide area comprising the parishes of Applecross, Lochcarron, Lochalsh, Kintail, Contin, Fodderty, Gairloch and Lochbroom:

> the ignorant population were in the habit – among other idolatrous practices – of sacrificing bulls on Mourie's appropriate feast day (25th August), and of distributing the flesh.

At the 1921 census, nine out of ten locals in Applecross spoke Gaelic, making it the strongest mainland Gaelic-speaking area.

The coastal road north rejoins the main A896 at Sìldeag (Sheildaig, ON, 'herring bay'), another planned village founded in 1800, this time to train seamen for the war against Napoleon. When, in 1843, the Disruption of the

Church of Scotland came, 470 ministers and 800 congregations left to join the Free Church. In the years after this exodus, most of these congregations needed somewhere to hold services, and a wide range of temporary church accommodation was employed, such as a cottage in Berriedale, Caithness; a masonic lodge in Muthil, Perthshire; a malt barn in Fort Augustus; a distillery in Campbeltown; a barn in Creich and a storehouse in Resolis. Many congregations met in the open-air and tents were widely used, as were temporary wooden structures. In the parishes of Applecross and Shieldaig, the congregations met on the beach, with only the preacher having a tent for protection.

The A896 road through Glen Torridon (referring to a portage from Loch Torridon through the glen to Loch Maree) passes under the heights of Beinn Eighe to the north. This mountain name does not mean, as one recent authoritative book on the landscape had it, 'mountain above the wood', but 'file-shaped peak'. The full name for the rock outcrops forming the file is Bodaich Dubh Beinn Eighe ('old men of Ben Eighe'). Its extensive scree slopes gave rise to the rhyme:

> 'S i mo rùn Beinn Eighe
> Dh'fhalbhadh leam is dh'fhalbhainn leatha.
>
> *My love is Ben Eighe*
> *She with me and I with her would go.*

Ceann Loch Iubh: *Kinlochewe*

Ceann Loch Iubh (Kinlochewe, 'head of the yew loch') lies near the head of Loch Maree. St. Maelrubha founded a church on an island in the loch and has now given his name, in the contracted form of Maree, to both the island and the loch that was formerly known as Loch Ewe. Burial on the island required some effort but delivered both spiritual and secular status. More prosaically, it was claimed in 1750, utterly without substantiation, that wolves, when starving, raided churchyards and unearthed newly buried corpses. In Eadar Dhà Chaolas (Eddrachillis, 'between two straits') northwards on the road into Sutherland, it was asserted that the inhabitants had to transfer the burial of their dead to the adjacent Eilean Shannda (Handa, 'island of the sandy river') to avoid such depredations.

Of more importance, probably before the saint's arrival and long after, was the presence on the island of a holy well. It was one of over 600 sacred springs venerated before the Reformation but one particularly renowned for curing mental disorders. It has since lost its efficacy. About 1830, the first shepherd to a certain Mr Meyrick Bankes of Winstanley Hall, Lancashire and, by then, Letterewe Estate, had a sheepdog that went mad. He took the dog to Isle Maree and put him headlong in the well. The dog died the next day and the shepherd a week later. After that violation the well dried up.

Here also stands an oak tree, studded with nails and the many coins that have been driven into the tree as offerings from pilgrims. When Queen Victoria visited the island in 1877, she followed tradition, the belief being that if a silent wish was made by a person after having attached any metal article to the tree, that wish would be realised. The procedure has changed; once it was the well, not the tree, that possessed miraculous properties. Having drunk at the well, the pilgrim placed their thank you offering on the tree.

Calum a' Ghlinne ('Calum of the Glen' or Calum MacLean) was a native of Kinlochewe. As with so many of his contemporaries, Calum had been in the army and survived on a tiny pension. He had only one daughter, a beautiful girl who was yet unmarried due to her father's love of drink and consequent inability to provide a suitable dowry for her. Although he is apologising to her in his song 'Mo chailin dhonn òg' ('My young brown-haired girl'), he cannot promise that he will stop drinking:

> Ge mòr le càch na tha mi milleadh,
> Cha tugainn mo bhòid nach òlainn tuilleadh,
> 'S e gaol a bhith mòr tha m' fheòil a' sireadh –
> Tha 'n sgeul ud ri aithris air Calum a' Ghlinne.
> Mo chailin dhonn òg.
>
> *Although others think my spend is large, I couldn't promise that I wouldn't drink again. It's the love of feeling grand my flesh is seeking and that's the story told of Calum of the Glen. My young brown-haired girl.*

However, his daughter did eventually marry and was, by 1769, living with her husband in the parish of Contin. According to John MacKenzie the compiler of the important song collection, *Sàr Obair nam Bàrd Gàidhealach* (*The Beauties of Gaelic Poetry*), Calum's wife was an exceptionally patient woman. To illustrate, he recounts the story of a trip that Calum made to Dingwall to buy oatmeal. To paraphrase MacKenzie:

> … he naturally went into a public house to refresh himself. There he met a drover where they entered into familiar confab; gill (142 ml. of whisky) after gill was called until they got gloriously happy. Calum forgot his meal … and … they sat and drank until Calum placed his last sixpence on the table.
>
> After a pause, Calum said, "If I had more money, I would not go home for some time yet."
>
> "That's easily got," replied his crony. "I'll buy the grey horse from you."
>
> The animal speedily changed hands and gills continued to arrive. Again Calum exhausted his cash supplies.
>
> "I must go now!" he exclaimed.
>
> "You must," re-joined his friend, "but I cannot see for the life of me how you can face your wife."
>
> "My wife!" exclaimed the bard in astonishment. "Pshaw, man, she's the woman that never said worse to me than, 'Dia leat, a Chaluim!' ('God bless you, Calum!')"
>
> "I'll lay you a bet of the price of the horse that you will get an entirely different response," replied the drover.
>
> "Done!" said the bard. Away they went along with the landlord and two others to witness Calum's reception.
>
> He entered his home and as he approached he staggered … but his wife flung her arms about him, exclaiming, 'Dia leat, a Chaluim!'
>
> "Ah," replied Calum, "why speak thus softly to me? I have drunk my money and brought home no meal."
>
> "A heather bell for that!" said she. "We will soon get more money and meal too." "But," continued the poet, "I have also drunk the grey horse."

> "What matter, my love", re-joined his wife. "You yourself are still alive and never shall we want – never shall I murmur while my Calum is sound and hearty."

It was enough. The drover had to count out the money of the wager and, in a few hours, Mrs MacLean had the pleasure of celebrating her husband's return with the horse and the meal.

Am Pìobaire Dall: *The Blind Piper*

On the A832 north, some sixteen kilometres from Kinlochewe, there is a car park on the left. From the car park, there is a short path to the viewing point for the falls on Abhainn Garbhaig ('little rough stream'). They have been made more popular by being now named, sometime after 1905, for Queen Victoria, who visited them while making a 'pilgrimage' to St. Maelrubha's island on Loch Maree in 1877. They are also referred to as the Talladale Falls. Tealldhadal (Talladale, ON, 'ledge valley') was where John Mackay, the only son of Rory, piper to the Laird of Gairloch, was born in 1656. At seven, smallpox took his sight and he became known as Iain Dall ('blind John') or Am Pìobaire Dall ('the Blind Piper'). After his father's initial piping tuition, he was sent to the MacCrimmon school at Boreraig, Skye to finish his musical education.

There, the other pupils grew envious of John's superior skills. Once, as he and another pupil were playing the same tune alternately, MacCrimmon asked the other lad why he did not play like John. He replied that his fingers were sticky from having eaten skate. From this response came the taunt that northern pipers cast up to their rivals:

> Tha mheòirean as dèidh na sgait.
>
> *His fingers are after the skate.*

It is said that their envy drove the apprentices to remove John by throwing him over a precipice at Dùn Bhoraraig. Though he fell nearly eight metres, John miraculously landed on his feet and suffered no ill effects. The place is still called Leum an Doill ('the blind man's leap').

Such was his mastery of his craft that he was able to complete a tune left unfinished by an earlier student. John acknowledged the man's efforts by entitling it 'Lasan Phàdraig Chaogaich' ('A Flame of Wrath for Squinting Patrick'). In time he became a better composer than his teacher, which gave rise to the well-known proverb:

Chaidh fhoghlam os cionn MhicCruimein.

The pupil outstrips MacCrimmon (i.e. the teacher).

Iain Dall remained with MacCrimmon for seven years and, after his father's death, took the role of piper to the Laird of Gairloch, combining the offices of bard and piper. He died in 1754, aged 98. By then he had composed numerous pibrochs, strathspeys, reels, and jigs, including 'Cailleach a' Mhuilleir' ('The Miller's Wife') and 'Cailleach Liath Ratharsair' ('Grey Old Lady of Raasay), now usually known as Mrs MacLeod of Raasay.

In November 2010, after a 205-year stay in the Canadian Diaspora, his chanter was donated by members of the Nova Scotian Sinclairs to the collection at the National Piping Centre in Glasgow.

Geàrrloch: *Gairloch*

To the north is the community of Geàrrloch (Gairloch, 'Short Loch'), recorded in the following ditty:

Rathad mòr a Cheann Loch Iùbh,
Rathad ùr a Gheàrrloch;
Gabhaidh sinn an rathad mòr
Olc na math le càch e.

The high road to Kinlochewe,
The new road to Gairloch;
Regardless of what others say, we'll take
The high road to Gairloch.

In 1886, a local writer said that:

> These tourists, who thus professed to have 'seen Loch Maree', were a fair type of too many of those who rush through Gairloch, as if their sole object were to cover the most ground in the shortest possible time, and who thus fail to obtain any true perception of the belongings of the country, even of the scenery.

Plus ça change.

Near Gairloch Church of Scotland is a hollow in which open-air Free Church communion services were held immediately following the Disruption. The hollow is said to have been scooped out by the Fingalian hero, Fionn, as a bed where his white cow might calve. It is still called Leabaidh na Bà Bàine ('bed of the white cow'). It was said of the Fèinne:

> Na sia buadhan a bha cumail suas na Fèinne – Agh Fhinn, làmh Ghoill, bras-bhuillean Oscair, iomairt ealamh Oisein, ruith chruaidh Chaoilte agus suidheachadh Chonain air a' chath.
>
> *The six virtues that kept up the Fèinne – Fingal's fortune, Gaul's hand, Oscar's impetuous strokes, Ossian's deft play, Coilte's hard running and Conan's planning of the battle.*

The same advocate of slow tourism also wrote that many years before there had lived at Craig of Gairloch an old man named Alasdair mac Iain Mhic Fhearchair (Alasdair, 'son of John, son of Farquhar'). He was a man of great piety and respectability and he was one of 'Na Daoine' ('the men'). They were exceptionally righteous and learned men who acted as custodians and leaders of experiential religion and were highly esteemed by their Presbyterian congregations.

One morning, Alasdair went out to get bog fir for firewood. A tall fair-haired man, along with twelve companions all similarly dressed in belted plaids of MacKenzie tartan, suddenly appeared before him. The fair-haired one, who from his noble bearing was manifestly a chief, inquired:

"How fare the Gairloch family?"
Alastair replied, "They are well."

Then they departed. When they were leaving him, Alastair heard not the sound of their tread nor saw them make a step, but they passed away as if a gust of wind were bending down the tall grass on the hillside. To his dying day, he believed that he had had a vision of the great chief Hector Roy, founder of the Gairloch MacKenzie family with his bodyguard of twelve chosen heroes. None doubted him and similar manifestations have been recorded in other localities.

Gàradh Inbhir Iubh: *Inverewe Gardens*

In August 2015 the BBC genealogy series 'Who Do You Think You Are?' revealed that Donald Mackenzie, great-great-great-grandfather of celebrity chef Paul Hollywood, had been a crofter at Poll Iubh (Pollewe, 'pool on the Ewe River'). Sadly, there was no mention of a particular contemporary of Donald Mackenzie's, either in related internet pages or at the adjacent Inverewe Garden, where the man worked.

This notable garden was created in 1862 by Osgood Mackenzie on his 850 hectare estate. The man in question was Alasdair Camshron, Bàrd Thùrnaig (Alasdair Cameron, The Tournaig Bard) (1848-1933) who lived here all his life. His first school was a Gaelic medium one which was replaced about 1854 by a theoretically English medium Free Church school. Despite being in a class of 85, Alasdair made good progress with the help of a 'pupil teacher' whom he repaid by posting love letters for him at the Poolewe post office, four miles away. About 1867, he went to live and work as a shepherd for Osgood Mackenzie at Tùrnaig (Tournaig, 'rounded hillock'). It was MacKenzie who taught him English, giving him the run of his library and encouraging him to memorise and recite long pieces from the poets of the past. After ten years he became MacKenzie's sheep manager.

Cameron was a lifelong champion of Gaelic and a member of An Commun Gàidhealach, organisers of the Royal National Mod from its foundation in 1891. In 1926, his collected works appeared under the title *Am Bàrd*, consisting of five essays and 25 poems and songs. He died in 1933 and a cairn was erected to his memory at the southern corner of Inverewe Gardens in 1952. Perhaps his most popular song is 'Moladh Thùrnaig' ('In Praise of Tournaig'):

Tùrnaig aoibhinn, Tùrnaig àigh,
Tùrnaig shaoibhir, Tùrnaig làn,
Tùrnaig bheartach, 's pailte bàrr,
Tùrnaig chàiseach, ghrànach, throm.

Tha gach tlachd nad thaic air fàs,
Sliabh is srath is cladach sàil;
D' uillt de nèamhnaidibh cho làn,
Far an snàmh an dòbhran-donn.

Joyful Tùrnaig, blissful Tùrnaig, affluent Tùrnaig, complete Tùrnaig; rich Tùrnaig, plentiful of harvest, Tùrnaig of dairy produce, heavy with grain.

Every delight has grown near you, slope and strath and seashore; your streams where the brown otter swims so full of pearls.

At Am Fàn ('the slope') is the place now known as Allt Beithe (Aultbea, 'birch stream'), although strictly speaking that latter name refers only to the river running through the village. A branch road to the west leads on to Meallan Theàrlaich (Mellon Charles). The topographical feature 'meallan' here most probably refers to the mounded sand dunes fringing the shore. Meallan Theàrlaich is renowned for two accounts, one literary and the other gastronomic.

It is the birthplace of the author of *Sàr Obair nam Bàrd Gàidhealach (The Beauties of Gaelic Poetry)* published in 1841. The author, Iain Alasdair Òig MacCoinnich ('Young John Alasdair MacKenzie'), a farmer's son, was born in 1806. He was a printer to trade and worked at the *Inverness Courier* before being employed by the publishing arm of Glasgow University where he published books in Gaelic. But it was *Sàr Obair nam Bàird Gàidhealach* (*Beauties of Gaelic Poetry*) that gained him the reputation he holds today.

John MacKenzie wanted to give a context for his material and so this book was the first collection of Gaelic poetry and song to provide substantial biographical sketches of the poets. Each of the 32 sections contains a biographical account in English of the poet and at least one poem in Gaelic, gleaned from oral and other sources. 290 poems and songs and a wealth of additional information in English about the songs and their authors are contained in over 400 pages. Perhaps no other book has had such a profound effect on singers of Gaelic songs; his chronological arrangement of the songs by the author, together with generally good versions collected throughout the Highlands and Islands, makes *Sàr Obair* an important anthology.

MacKenzie's interests were wider than poetry, however, and he published a history of Prince Charles in 1844 and a series of witty and amusing articles, *A' Bheithir-Bheuma (Thunderbolt).* Always of a delicate constitution, he died at the early age of 32. Later the Gairloch community erected a monument to his memory. The inscription reads:

> Thogadh an càrn-cuimhne seo do dh'Iain MacCoinnich, de theaghlach Alastair Chaim Gheàrrloch, a thionail agus a chuir an òrdugh Sàr Obair nam Bàrd Gàidhealach, agus a sgrìobh, a thionail, a dheasaich, no a dh'eadar-theangaich deich air fhichead leabhar eile am measg iomadh cruaidh-chàs.
>
> *This monument was erected to John MacKenzie of the family of Alasdair Cam, Gairloch, who collected and prepared Sàr Obair nam Bàrd Gàidhealach, and wrote, collected, prepared or translated thirty other books in the midst of many difficulties.*

Today Aultbea is the production centre of Ritchies of Aultbea's marag dhubh ('black pudding'), a type of blood pudding. In the past, slaughtered beasts usually provided the ingredients for black pudding and drawing blood from living cattle was once universal in the Highlands. In the Gairloch area, it continued into the early 19th century. At the east end of The Glen, in the narrow pass about halfway between Gairloch and Poolewe, there is a flat moss called Blàr na Fala ('bog of blood'), because this was where the people took blood from their cattle. At Tournaig, also, there is a place where they bled the cattle landed there from Lewis.

Most traditional recipes involve stirring the fresh blood, adding suet and some form of rusk and a little seasoning, before filling the mixture into a casing and boiling it. Sheep intestines were formerly used but now synthetic cellulose skins and imported dried blood are used for the puddings.

The relatively limited range of ingredients and use of oats or barley to thicken and absorb the blood is typical of Scottish black pudding in comparison to Continental blood sausages. Black pudding recipes still show considerable variation across the country with many butchers having their own versions. Scotland's most famous, Stornoway black pudding, has been granted Protected Geographical Indicator of Origin status.

The coast road meets the A835 as this road goes down An Dìreadh Mòr (Braemore, 'great ascent'), and then along the shore of Loch Bhraoin (Loch Broom, 'loch of water') to Ulapul (Ullapool, ON, 'wolf or Ulli's farm'). The creation of this village was one of the projects of the British Fisheries Society. The Society established fishing stations on the north and west coasts from the Mull of Kintyre in the southwest to Duncansby in the northeast. Ullapool began promisingly but had not attracted much business before the herring deserted the west coast. Its fortunes did not revive until the 1840s.

Black cattle remained more dependable than the silver darlings – herring. Droving is remembered in 'Òran nan Dròbhairean' ('The Drovers' Song'), composed before 1831 by a Loch Broom drover, Murchadh Ruadh nam Bò, Murchadh MacCoinnich ('red Murdo of the Cattle', Murdo MacKenzie):

Siud far an robh na seòid –
Na dròbhairean nuair ghluaiseadh iad,
Na Bàideanaich bho sliabh gu tràigh
'S an Clàrca na dhuin-uasal' orr';
Bha MacPhàrlain is MacMhaoilein
'S Mac an t-Saoir à Ruadhain ann,
'S ma sheasas iad aig tòir na prìs
Chan fheàrr a' rìgh nan tuathanach.

'S bha iomadh glòir ann an Gleann Smeòil
Nuair thigeadh oirnn a' samhradh ann
A' ghrian mar òr dol sìos fo sgleò
Is ceòl an crò nan gamhnaichean
Bhiodh iomadh spòrs aig sean is òg
'S bu shòlasach bha 'n danns aca
Bhiodh iasg is feòil ri dìosgail bhòrd
Bha sùgh an eòrna 's branndaidh ann.

That was where the heroes were when the drovers moved on, the Badenoch men with cattle from slope to shore, Clerk, like a nobleman, leading. MacFarlane, MacMillan and MacIntyre from Ruthven were there. If they hold firm to their price the King will be no better off than the farmer.

It was always glorious in Glen Smeòil when summer came to us. The sun setting in a golden haze and music in the open shelter of yearling cattle. There would be much fun for both young and old and how happy their dancing! Fish and meat made the tables creak. There was whisky and brandy there.

Còigeach: *Coigeach*

The road now passes into the area of Assynt and, just beyond Drunrunie hunting lodge, is the junction with the road to Còigeach (Coigeach, 'place of fifths'). Division into fifths was common in Gaelic custom and here refers to the five townships of Achd an Dubh Àrd (Achduart, 'field of the black height'), Achd na Bhràighe (Achnabhraighe, 'field of the brae'), Achd an Inbhir (Acheninver, 'field of the river mouth'), Achd na h-Àird (Achnahaird, 'field of the promontory') and Achd Ille Bhuidhe (Achiltibuie, 'field of yellow-haired boy'). The most famous example Còig Còigeamh na h-Èireann ('five-fifths of Ireland'), gave rise to the saying:

> Tha còig còigeamh an Èireann agus tha còig còigeamh an Strath Èireann (Strathearn); ach 's feàrr aon chòigeamh na h-Èireann na còig còigeamh Strath Èireann.
>
> *There are five-fifths in Ireland and five-fifths in Strathearn; but one-fifth of Ireland is better than five-fifths of Strathearn.*

In the Disruption, most of the Còigeach Church of Scotland congregation of 1,500 left to join the Free Church, with only five parishioners remaining. Initially, the new church had nowhere to meet and further privation followed. In 1852-3, attempts were made to evict the crofting tenants here. However, the women disarmed twenty policemen and sheriff officers, burning their summonses. The Còigeach crofters held out for over two years and eventually, the estate gave up trying to resettle them, a rare victory for the people over the landlord.

The song 'Mo shoraidh leis a' Chòigich' ('My Farewell to Coigeach') was composed by Mordaidh Sheòrais MacIlleathainn (Murdo George MacLean), who was one of many Highland men who went to Montana, USA, to work as shepherds in the years before the First World War. He realised his dream of returning to marry and settle in Còigeach and his is one of the few preserved songs written in Gaelic in the American West:

> 'S ann tha mi 'n-diugh nam chìobair aig sàil nam beanntan mòr
> Far 'm bheil madadh-allaidh 's leòmhann is tìgearan gu leòr;
> Tha iad h-uile là mun cuairt dhomh 's mi buachailleachd mo spréidh
> 'S cha bhithinn fhèin glè shàbhailte gun mhusgaid bhith nam dhòrn.

> *Today I am a shepherd in the foothills of the great mountains where there are wolves and lions and tigers. They are around me every day as I tend to my flocks and I would be very unsafe without a musket in my fist.*

Asaint: *Assynt*

Asaint (Assynt, ON, 'ridge-end') was an area distinct from Sutherland from about the year 1314 when Torquil MacLeod of Lewis married the heiress of MacNicol of Assynt and became the lord of the district. For many years it was regarded as a province of Scotland in its own right, and it was later established as a civil parish. But with the introduction of counties it became part of the county of Sutherland. Parishes for administrative purposes were abolished in 1930 and then, in 1975, counties were replaced by a system of regional and district councils. However, the boundaries were retained for statistical as well as ceremonial purposes. The regions and districts were themselves replaced by unitary councils in 1996, and Assynt now forms a community within the Highland Council area.

This is also the limit of the area to the south once termed 'North Argyll' but now called Wester Ross. It acquired its earlier name because it was settled by missionaries from Dál Riata, based at the abbey of Applecross. When Fearchar mac an t-Sagart (Farquhar, 'son of the Abbot') became the Earl of Ross, the region of North Argyll started to acquire the name Wester Ross. Both names continued in use until the 15th century when Wester Ross became the exclusive term. The area has now acquired the general name 'Sutherland', while the Gaelic name is Cataibh ('place of the cat people').

To the Gaels, the ancient name 'Cataibh' continued to describe those former Pictish territories beyond the original Norse toehold in Caithness, much further to the east. To the Norse, the area to their west was known as the Dales. In Gaelic, this area is Dùthaich MhicAoidh ('MacKay Country') and it was only much later that the name Sutherland encompassed the county of the same name, following the consolidation of their extended territories by the Earls, Dukes and Duchesses of Sutherland. In other words, the name followed the family. To complicate matters, a distinction is to be made between the province of Strathnaver, which, at its widest extent, reached from the border with Caithness to the bounds of Assynt in the west, and the valley of the river Naver itself. The former is referred to as the Province of Strathnaver, while the latter is Strathnaver. But just when you thought that was all crystal clear, in 1629, Charles I fobbed off MacKay's just demands for payment by giving him the title of 'Lord Reay', the area of his then seat, the name deriving from 'rath' or 'fort'. Thereafter his lands were often called in English 'The Reay Country'.

A song composed in Assynt in 1912 by Alasdair MacLeòid (Alasdair MacLeod) links Canada and the village of An Cùl-cinn (Culkein, 'the common grazings'). We know little of MacLeod but he has left a fine description of the journey that so many Gaels made between the Clyde and North America in his song 'Cur Cùlaibh ri Asainte' ('Leaving Assynt Behind'):

Disathairne rinn sinn seòladh
Bhon Bhroomielaw 'n Glaschu
Measg treubhan dhe gach seòrsa
Air bòrd 'n "Southwark" Shasannach.

Dol seachad cùlaibh Èirinn
Bha muir is gaoth ri cathadh ann
'S na h-uile bha air bòrd
Gu tinn le cur na mara orr'.

Tha mi nochd gu tùrsach
Falbh air sràidean Chanada
Is caolas farsaing fuar
Eadar mi 's mo luaidh tha 'n Asainte.

It was on Saturday we sailed from the Broomielaw in Glasgow, among all sorts of people on board the English "Southwark".

Passing west of Ireland we were buffeted by seas and wind and everyone on board was seasick.

Tonight I am mournful wandering the streets of Canada, a wide, cold sea between me and my love in Assynt.

Five kilometres south of Kylesku and a ten kilometre walk eastwards across boggy ground from the road is Eas a' Chùil Àlainn ('waterfall of the beautiful tresses'). With a drop of 200 metres, it is the highest waterfall in the United Kingdom. No Gaelic song survives to extoll its virtues but northeast of it is Coire an Easain ('waterfall corrie') and its junction with Gleanna Gollaidh (Glen Golly, 'glen of the blind river'). This area is celebrated in the great pìobaireachd song, 'Cumha Choire an Easain' ('Lament of the Waterfall Corrie'), composed by Am Pìobaire Dall for Robert, chief of the MacKays, around 1690. The lament is in the form of a dialogue between Robert and the corrie:

'S mi 'g iarraidh gu Coir' an Easain
Far a tric a sgapadh fùdar
Far 'm biodh mìal-choin gan teirbeirt
Cur mac na h-èilde gu dhùbhlan.

I want to get to Coir' an Easain where gunpowder has often exploded, where greyhounds set forth, challenging the stag.

To which Coire an Easain replies to Robert:

'S e sin mise, Coir' an Easain
Tha mi 'm sheasamh mar a b' àbhaist
Ma tha thusa nad fhear ealadh
Cluinneamaid annas do làimhe.

That's who I am, Coir' an Easain, standing here as ever before.
If you are an expert let's hear your masterpiece.

The route crosses An Caolas Cumhang ('the narrow strait') which once had a ferry service, replaced by a bridge in 1984. It was only in 2019 that it was officially given its Gaelic name of Drochaid a' Chaolais Chumhaing ('narrow strait bridge'). Before that, it was known as The Kylesku Bridge.

In 1715, the Reay estate gave a 21 year lease of the salmon fishing to Peterhead merchants. For the inhabitants there were opportunities to supply the merchants and visiting busses (large fishing vessels) with fish, along with employment, gutting and packing. However, the odds were often stacked against the native fishermen. An official observer reported in 1785 that:

> the author ... has seen the crews of the busses from the Clyde, etc. attack the poor natives of the West Coast in their miserable canoes, drive them from their best fishing places, destroy their nets, cruelly maltreat them, and then let down their own tackling, in the places of which they had thus robbed the poor natives.

Views open up to the west of what is now known as Eddrachillis Bay, sited at the mouth of Loch a' Chàirn Bhàin (Loch Cairnbawn, 'loch of the white cairn'). This cairn was an especially important landmark in the vicinity since local tradition told of buried Viking treasure hidden within it. The peninsula to the north is, as the Gaelic says, Eadar Dà Chaolas ('between two kyles'), these being Kylesku and Laxford. The stretch of the sea beyond the loch's mouth gained its new, incongruous name, Eddrachillis Bay, sometime around 1900.

Dr MacIntosh MacKay (1793-1873) was born at Dubh Àrd ('dark height') on the shores of Eddrachillis Bay. In 1827, he was inducted as parish minister of Laggan. During his incumbency there he completed his work as editor of the Highland Society's Gaelic Dictionary, having based his work on material originally compiled by Ewen MacLachlan the renowned Lochaber scholar.

In this parish, as with others in this north-western corner of the Highlands, by the end of the 18th century, dire land pressure pertained. Many coastal settlements were overcrowded as a result of the displacement of population from the interior during the 'improvements' to the estate of the Countess of

Sutherland. In the early decades of the 19th century, the average croft here would support a family for only about eight months of the year, a deliberate estate policy. In Assynt, worse conditions prevailed; some 300 families were settled on the same number of arable acres, while in the peninsula of Eddrachillis the average acreage available was only slightly higher. In Tongue, to the north, each family there had the luxury of two and a half acres.

The land in the far north-west is called Am Parbh, now known by the map-makers' invention of Cape Wrath. The meaning is uncertain but seems to be Norse and to have the sense of 'turning', indicating its value to earlier seafarers navigating around the coast. In his *Voyage in the Lighthouse Yacht Nova Zembla*, Sir Walter Scott recounts a sea journey made from Leith in July 1814. On the 29th of August, he had reached this point and recounts:

> Lord Reay's estate, containing 150,000 square acres, ... was, before commencement of the last leases, rented at £1200 a year. It is now worth £5000, and Mr. Anderson says he may let it this ensuing year (when the leases expire) for about £15,000. But then he must resolve to part with his people, for these rents can only be given upon the supposition that sheep are generally to be introduced on the property. But ... Lord Reay must turn out several hundred families who have lived under him and his fathers for many generations, and the swords of whose fathers probably won the lands from which he is now expelling them. He is a good-natured man, I suppose, for Mr. Anderson says he is hesitating whether he shall not take a more moderate rise (£7000 or £8000), and keep his Highland tenantry.

Perhaps this is why it was said:

> Ma tha mise truagh, se mo thruaighe MacAoidh.
>
> *If I am in bad shape, I feel worse for MacKay.*

Yet their hospitality was renowned:

> A h-uile fear a thèid a dholaidh, gheibh e dolar o MacAoidh.
>
> *Every man who goes broke will get a dollar from MacKay.*

A subsequent author said that:

> it is perhaps fortunate for the name and honour of MacKay that he shortly afterwards disposed of these estates to the Earl of Sutherland, who ordered the great Sutherland clearance, of which so much has been written.

MacKay was not alone in selling up. In a study of the Highland Potato Famine, it is stated that, in 1846, of the 86 landowners in the famine-affected region, at least 62 were new purchasers who had not owned Highland property before 1800.

But the complete clearance of small tenants was not desirable as, given the economic imperatives of the time, it was lucrative for landlords to resettle the bulk of the population on the coast. There, they could work in the manpower-hungry kelp industry which by the start of the 19th century required 100,000 people across the Highlands. Holdings were deliberately made small so that the people would be forced by necessity to look for earnings from arduous, noxious kelping work or go fishing. The main areas of resettlement were around Scourie on the north shore of Loch Laxford, around Durness and on the coasts of Tongue and Farr. However, the prospective prosperity of the kelp and fishing industries proved ultimately illusory and landlords were faced with a 'redundant population'.

In 1835, James Loch, the Countess of Sutherland's factor in the area, was astonished to come across a crowd of 3,000 people on a rain-drenched hillside. They were there to hear the preaching of respected local divines, Na Daoine ('the men'). The social and psychological consequences of the collapse of the old order perhaps in some part accounts for the strength of evangelicalism in the 19th century Highlands. It gave people a sense of purpose and a way of coping with the profound changes and extreme poverty affecting them.

In 1843, in this area of the north coast, the Disruption left only twelve people attending the English services in the Church of Scotland. During the Clearances, many ministers' position on such 'improvement' was based on standard church doctrine, which then accepted Divine Will, no matter what degree of suffering this entailed. Given the church's uncritical stance on social issues, inaction by individual ministers in the face of such privation was not unusual. Nonetheless, the mass movement of congregations into the

Free Church during the Clearances was not solely a reaction to their ministers' inaction.

Dubhrinn (Durine, 'black headland') is the main village in Durness. A little over a kilometre from the village and sited at the western end of the bay at Baile na Cille (Balnakeil, 'church farm') is a religious settlement, founded in 722 by St. Maelrubha. The present ruined church building dates from 1619. Much is made in local tourism literature of the grave of Donuill Mac Morraichaidh (sic), Dòmhnall MacMhurchaidh ('Donald son of Murdo'). According to traditional tales, he raided from the east side of Loch Eriboll and was responsible for some eighteen murders. He paid Ùisdean Dubh MacAoidh ('black Hugh MacKay'), who was rebuilding the church, £1000 on condition he was buried in a specially built vault so that his enemies could not trample his grave.

Rob Donn MacAoidh: *Robert MacKay*

Between 2017 and 2019, the Strathnaver Museum and the Mackay Country Community Trust developed resources aimed at tourists, the Diaspora, and local residents that resulted in *Slighe Roib Dhuinn: Leabhar-iùil dhan àm a dh'fhalbh* (*Rob Donn's trail: a guide book to past times*), a bilingual 76-page guidebook containing the history and art connected to Rob Donn's poems. To my knowledge, it is perhaps the only community-wide interpretation project based on an individual Gaelic poet. A free map of the nine interpretive panels can be found at strathnavermuseun.org.uk.

Rob Donn MacAoidh ('brown-haired Robert MacKay') (1714-78) was a drover who spent most of his life in Strathmore, south of Loch Hope. Rob fulfilled the ancient function of the community bard, chronicling the wrenching changes that were then being inflicted on his community. Although best remembered now for his song in praise of Gleanna Gollaidh, it is only one of 225 of his works that survive, having been written down from the poet's own dictation. They are mostly on local themes, events and people in different strata of society from herd boys to chiefs. Witty and refreshingly frank, they point at the hypocrisy of landlordism and high society. Glen Golly, though, was clearly close to his heart:

Gleanna Gollaidh, Gleanna Gollaidh
Gleanna Gollaidh nan craobh;
Cò a chì e nach mol e,
Gleanna Gollaidh nan craobh.

Ri faicinn crìochan àrdain
Ga mo bhreugadh gu taobh,
'S ann a smuainich mi fanadh
An Gleanna Gollaidh nan craobh.

Chan àill leam bhur n-airgead;
'S ri bhur n-airm cha bhi mi;
Cha diùlt mi bhur drama,
Ach ri tuilleadh cha bhi.

Ged a gheibhinn gu m' ailghios
Ceann t-Sàile MhicAoidh,
'S mòr gum b' annsa leam fanadh
An Gleanna Gollaidh nan craobh.

Glen Golly, Glen Golly, Glen Golly of the trees;
Who could see it and fail to love it, Glen Golly of the trees.

Seeing regions of hauteur enticing me away
I considered I'd stay there in Glen Golly of the trees.

I don't desire your money and I'll never join your army;
I won't refuse your dram, but I'll do no more than that.

Though it might be my heart's desire to be in Kintail of MacKay,
More than that I'd much prefer to stay in Glen Golly of the trees.

Rob Donn's monument, erected in 1827 in the graveyard of the church at Balnakeil, is engraved with the following tribute in Gaelic, English, Latin, and Greek:

> This tomb was erected at the expense of a few of his countrymen.
> Ardent admirers of his native talent and extraordinary genius.

Two other men who also rest in Balnakeil are the brothers Joseph and Patrick MacDonald, important contributors to collections of Gaelic songs and pipe tunes. Joseph (1739-1763) wrote *Compleat Theory of the Scots Highland Bagpipe* during and after a long voyage to Calcutta in 1760. He led the way for men such as Angus MacKay (1813-1859), one of the four piping sons of Fear Eighre (Iain MacRuari of Eyre in Raasay), who compiled his own collection during the 1830s. In 1784, the other brother, Patrick, collaborated with John Ramsay of Ochtertyre on the production of *A Collection of Highland Vocal Airs*. In the introduction, he emphasised the process of collecting from living sources.

Further along the north coast is the district of Kintail, comprising the area on both sides of the Kyle of Tongue, and West Mòine, the lands on the east shore of Loch Eriboll. Tongue is the main village in a series of crofting townships here and it may be designated in three ways:

> firstly, the Gaelic Ceann Tàile (Kintail, 'bay head'); distinguishing it from another Kintail in a neighbouring county, it was called Cinn Tàile MhicAoidh ('MacKay's Kintail'); second, Kirkiboll (ON, 'church farm') and, third, Tonga (ON, 'Tongue') from the slip of land running into the sea.

Eòghainn MacDhonnchaidh: *Ewan Robertson*

It was in this Kintail that the poet of perhaps the finest protest song against clearance was born. The song in question is 'Mo Mhallachd aig na Caoraich Mhòr' ('My Curse on the Big Sheep') composed by Eòghainn MacDhonnchaidh (Ewan Robertson) around the time of the visit of the Napier Commission in 1883. The Commission was collecting evidence about the condition of the crofting communities and Ewan gave evidence before the Commissioners. Unfortunately, when he died in 1895, at the age of 53, the bulk of his writings were lost. However, this song survived to speak of the passage of 'trì fichead bliadhn'' (60 years) and the raw memories of the events of 1819-20 it describes:

Tha trì fichead bliadhn' is trì
On a dh'fhàg sinn Dùthaich MhicAoidh
Càit bheil gillean glan mo chrìdh',
'S na nighneagan cho bòidheach?

Bhain-Diùc Chataibh, bheil thu 'd shìth?
Càit bheil nis do ghùntan sìod'?
Do chùm iad thu bhon fhoill 's bhon fhrìd
Tha 'g itheamh measg nan clàraibh?

Shellair bhioraich tha san ùir,
Ma fhuair thu 'n gràs ris 'n robh do dhùil,
'N teine leis do chuir thu 'n tuath fo ruaig
Tha fuaim aig nis ri d' fheusaig.

Ceud Diùc Cataibh le chuid foill,
'S le chuid càirdeas do na Goill,
Gum b' ann an Iutharn 'n robh do shàil,
'S gum b' fheàrr leam Iùdas làmh rium.

Sixty-three years have passed since we left the MacKay Country. Where are my beloved fine lads and the beautiful girls?

Lady Sutherland, are you at peace? Where are your silk gowns now? Did they protect you from the worms and beasts eating among the planks?

Sharp Sellar now in the ground, if you got the grace you expected, the fire you used to evict the people is crackling at your beard.

Deceitful Duke of Sutherland with his relationship with the Lowlanders. I hope your heels are in hell; I would prefer Judas beside me.

The song is sung to the Gaelic tune 'Lord Balgownie's Favourite', an air that Robert Tannahill (1774-1810), the weaver-poet of Paisley, made popular in the Anglophone world by setting it to his poem 'Gloomy Winter's Noo

Awa'. It has received wider popularity with the screening of the film 'The Piano' where Michael Nyman set the words of Emily Dickinson's poem 'The Heart Asks Pleasure First' to the ancient tune.

Kintail remained the district's name until 1724 when the separate parish of Tongue was formed out of the original extensive parish of Durness. In the 1650s, there were no ministers in the parishes of Durness, Farr and Reay. To administer a large parish was particularly hard in the case of Durness. By the 1720s, there were already 2,500 people in the parish requiring instruction in doctrine, but though there were five places of public worship, both the minister and the people were, as the records state:

> ... under great hardships and inconveniences in travelling ... It being impracticable to travell on Horseback ... often endangers their lives ... and the Minister is frequently seven or eight weeks at once absent from his house on goeing about his ministeriall work, and not only many children dye in his absence without Baptisme, but people come to age, dye without haveing the benefite of a Minister to visite them when most earnest for the same.

Fearchar Lèigh: *Farquhar the Physician*

In Taobh Mhealanais (Melness, 'bentgrass headland'), local oral tradition identifies three localities that have associations with Fearchar Lèigh ('Farquhar the physician'). Tradition also maintains that Fearchar was a Beaton and that Fearchar's descendants became hereditary physicians to the Munros of Foulis. Patronage by the well-to-do meant that, in the Middle Ages, and especially in the hey day of the Lordship of the Isles in the mid-15th-century, native Gaelic-speaking doctors could afford the best of medical training, whether in Salerno, Montpellier, Bologna, Padua or Leiden. On returning home, they combined this professional education with their native lore, giving rise to a unique healing tradition. Although not all had the highest reputation:

> Gum bidheadhmaid air ar glèidheadh
> Bho lagh 's bho lighichean.
>
> *May we be preserved from lawyers and from doctors.*

There is no doubt that Fearchar of Melness was a member of that professional dynasty. He is named as *Ferchardus medicus* in the late 14th-century Exchequer Rolls for receiving gifts of money, presumably for services to the then King, Robert III. These skilled men also left a legacy of Gaelic medical manuscripts which form the bulk of the pre-18th-century Gaelic manuscripts in the National Library of Scotland. There are also records of Beaton doctors in Mull and South Uist. In the 1870s, Captain Thomas recorded that, in 1589, one of them, the:

> famous Doctor Beaton, of Mull, had the dubious fortune of being blown up when on board the Spanish ship *Florida*, in Tobermory, but escaped unhurt.

Dòmhnall MacLeòid is Fuadaichean Chataibh: *Donald MacLeod and the Sutherland Clearances*

Of the many novels that tell of the Clearances, the most widely cited are those called the 'Strathnaver novels'. *Butcher's Broom* by Neil M. Gunn (1934), *And the Cock Crew* by Fionn MacColla (1945), and *Consider the Lilies* by Iain Crichton Smith (1968) all use the Sutherland Estate's evictions in Strathnaver from 1814 onwards as the historical reference point of their narratives. The Sutherland Clearances, because of their scale, scope and swiftness, provoked strong reactions. Hundreds of families were cleared between 1807 and 1822. There were allegations of violence during the 1814 evictions but the subsequent trial for arson and culpable homicide of the factor, Patrick Sellar, led to his inevitable acquittal. These events are remembered in the Anglophone world mainly through the denunciations of a local commentator, Donald MacLeod, and the witness evidence collected by the Napier Commission in 1884.

Donald's recollections and writings are perhaps the most significant eyewitness accounts. The 1841 first edition of his *Gloomy Memories* was followed by a final, enlarged and improved edition, published in Toronto, Canada, in 1857. The book's full title is *Gloomy memories in the Highlands of Scotland: versus Mrs. Harriet Beecher Stowe's Sunny memories in (England) a foreign land, or A faithful picture of the extirpation of the Celtic race from the Highlands of Scotland.* The following extract shows MacLeod's purpose:

> I AM a native of Sutherlandshire, and remember when the inhabitants of that country lived comfortably and happily, when the mansions of proprietors … factors, magistrates, and ministers, were the seats of honour, truth, and good example ... But all this is changed … For five successive years … has scarcely anything been seen but removing the inhabitants in the most cruel and unfeeling manner, and burning the houses which they and their forefathers had occupied from time immemorial. The country was darkened by the smoke of the burnings, and the … children … of those who sustained the honour of the British name in many a bloody field … were ruined … dispersed, and compelled to seek an asylum across the Atlantic; while those who remained … became paupers, beggars – a disgrace to the nation whose freedom and honour many of them had maintained by their valour and cemented with their blood.

Macleod wrote as an eyewitness of the clearing of Rosal village. He described how:

> a dense cloud of smoke enveloped the whole country … [and the] … scene presented itself – all the houses in an extensive district in flames at once. I myself ascended a height about 11.00 in the evening and counted two hundred and fifty blazing houses, many of the owners of which I personally knew… The confrontation lasted six days ...

Although the people of Strathnaver had no answer to the then-accepted orthodoxy that 'improvement' was both morally and socially the correct thing to do, with the ends justifying the means, not all agreed. Hugh Rose, the laird of Aitnach, Easter Ross, had strong opinions against sheep farming which he first expressed in 1787. Although he advocated the introduction of new breeds of rams to improve the quality of the goat-like native sheep and their wool, he was scathing about the "kind of rage for sheep farming" which had:

> of late years prevailed in many parts of the Highlands of Scotland

and which was but:

> a mode for stretching and increasing rents; for the depopulation of a country can with no degree of propriety be term'd the improvement of it.

He warned of the precariousness of sheep farming, the problem of disease and the large amounts of capital required to establish a sheep farm. According to Rose, it was nothing but:

> mischief that may arise from this kind of speculation.

It has been calculated that in these Sutherland clearances, some 3,000 families were replaced by 29 tenants of huge sheep farms. When the poet Swinburne travelled through Strathnaver later in the century he wrote:

> Mile on mile on mile of desolation
> League on league on league without an end

Much mischief did indeed come of that desolation. The land is even emptier now and a recent Highland Council report warned that "severe population decline" is looming over Caithness and Sutherland, with the population of the former expected to fall by 18% and that of the latter to decline by 15% by 2040. The provision of life-line services for an ageing population has become increasingly problematic. Such is "desolation".

Yet its history remains contentious. Writing in 1992, the sociologist David McCrone said that interpreting Highland history:

> has become something of a cottage industry, with, broadly speaking, two opposing views: the orthodox one that … the Clearances of people from the land in the eighteenth (sic) century was economically necessary if somewhat socially unfortunate, and the radical stance that what happened in the last two hundred years was tantamount to class warfare in which people lost their birth-right.

It is telling that such an authoritative voice could dismiss the interpretation of Highland history as a "cottage industry" some twenty years after the publication of *The Making of the Crofting Community,* James Hunter's scholarly history of this contentious period. Matters have changed and there is now an ever-increasing volume of academic research. The Clearances, however, still divide. The journalist Brian Wilson wrote in *The Scotsman* in March 2018:

> Last week, three Scottish historians were assembled by Melvyn Bragg to discuss "The Highland Clearances" on Radio 4 [*In Our Time*] ... Since there was not a shred of variation in their interpretations, they can be quoted collectively as The Three Professors ... the voice of the Gael – whose language and culture were dispersed to the ends of the earth – was entirely missing. Not only missing but they were also heavily patronised. Words like "mythology", "exaggeration" and "romanticism" buzzed around the studio as The Three Professors ... achieved a consensus which added up to "not that big a deal, most of them went voluntarily, nobody really talked about it till the 1960s, get over it..." Their erudition was sprinkled with timeworn clichés ... "Unlike Ireland, the landlord is not seen as an alien" ... "the guilt of Presbyterianism" ... For anyone with an ear for this debate, it was like a time-warp with the clock turned back 40-odd years, as if James Hunter's landmark work, *The Making of the Crofting Community,* ... had never existed. Of course, The Three Professors are entitled to their opinion and their platform but it was scandalous that it went unchallenged.

To my knowledge, neither 'the Professors' nor the BBC responded.

And yet perhaps the most acute observation on the Sutherland clearances was made six decades ago; in his rigorously dispassionate account of the Highland economy in the 100 years between 1750 and 1850, Malcolm Gray said:

> But if Sutherland is notorious beyond other areas largely because of the violence arising from the accidents of personality, historical memory has not played false in selecting this to illustrate the process

> that was traversing the Highlands for so many years: from here were magnified all the ingredients, – the opposition of ideas as well as of interests – of the continuing clash of agrarian rationalization and tradition.

Gray is recognised by all serious writers as the single most authoritative source on the economic impact of the Clearances. However, rather than accept his view that Sutherland was the test case, many attempt to dismiss its relevance simply because it was exceptional in many aspects. Indeed some revisionism now seeks to suggest that an equally traumatic process was inflicted on Lowland Scotland a century earlier. The most recent scholarly exercise devoted grant funding for two researchers to scour the legal record, seeking evidence of Lowland distress occasioned by the earlier process; scant trace was found. It is a sad reflection of the status of Gaelic today that funding could be found for what was ultimately a futile exercise in comparative pain and yet none could be devoted to proofreading the Gaelic texts in the subsequent publication.

Strathnaver retains the power to move poets. Derick Thomson's 'Srath Nabhair' ('Strathnaver') is a fine example:

> A Shrath Nabhair 's a Shrath Chill Donnain,
> is beag an t-iongnadh ged a chinneadh am fraoch àlainn oirbh,
> a' falach nan lotan a dh'fhàg Pàdraig Sellar 's a sheòrsa,
> mar a chunnaic mi uair is uair boireannach cràbhaidh
> a dh'fhiosraich dòrainn an t-saoghail-sa
> is sìth Dhè na sùilean.
>
> *O Strathnaver and Strath of Kildonan,*
> *it is little wonder that the heather should bloom on your slopes,*
> *hiding the wounds that Patrick Sellar, and such as he, made*
> *just as time and time again I have seen a pious woman*
> *who has suffered the sorrow of this world,*
> *with the peace of God shining from her eyes.*

Caibideil 11: *Chapter 11*

Tuath air Inbhir Nis – An Ear: *North of Inverness – The East*

Just past a small marshy lochan, Loch Hollistan, which seems to derive its name from the personal name, Ùisdean (Hugh), the A836 crosses the boundary between Sutherland and Caithness. The Norse name 'Pettalands Fjord' for the Pentland Firth confirms the presence of an indigenous 'P-Celtic-speaking' group, now loosely known as 'Picts', prior to the arrival of both Norse and Gaelic speakers. The Norse initially applied the name Katanes (Caithness) to Duncansby Head, a name that acknowledges this as the promontory of the 'Catti' ('people of the cat'). The Catti seem to have inhabited an area roughly similar to modern Caithness and Sutherland. The lands south of the Ord of Caithness were later designated Sudrland (ON, 'southland'), being the southern part of Katanes. To the descendants of the incoming Gaelic speakers from the west, however, Cataibh refers to those former Pictish territories beyond the original Katanes, i.e. what is now termed Sutherland. On the other hand, to Gaels, the Caithness area, essentially the land south and east of Duncansby Head, is Gallaibh ('foreigners' land').

Along the coast is Thurso, the northernmost town on the British mainland. Originally, Thurso was known by the Pictish name Tarvodubron ('bull water'). Similarly Dunnet Head was Tarvedunum ('bull fort') and the town's name may have its roots there. Norse influence altered its name to Thjorsá, then Thorsá ('place on Thor's river'), based on the deity of Thor. The modern Gaelic name is Inbhir Theòrsa ('mouth of the River Thurso').

Thurso was a burgh of barony dating from 1633 and went through a number of guises until 1996 when independent local administration ceased and much of northern Scotland became a unitary council area. The town's Victorian Town Hall was surplus to requirements and became, in 2008, the venue of Caithness Horizons, now rebranded as the North Coast Visitor Centre. Described as "a superb modern museum", it was awarded a 5 Star Visitor Attraction rating by VisitScotland and it achieved Full Museum Accreditation.

'Gallaibh nan Gàidheal 's nan Gall':
'Caithness of the Gael and the Lowlander'

This fully accredited museum made no mention whatsoever of the Gaelic heritage of the western parts of Caithness. Instead, the Picts are placed centre stage along with the Vikings. This deliberate omission is consistent with an uncomfortable thread in Caithness life that decries the use of bi-lingual Gaelic and English road signs and has seen the efforts of Highland Council to recruit Gaelic-speaking teachers described as 'Nazi' by an elected councillor. Others holding similarly prominent public positions have denied that Gaelic ever existed in Caithness.

One authority has usefully set the record straight in a recent article, 'Gallaibh nan Gàidheal 's nan Gall' ('Caithness of the Gael and the Lowlander'). Examining a 1706 account of where Gaelic was preached within the bounds of the Presbytery of Caithness, it reveals the relative extent of Gaelic and English-speaking areas of Caithness. The report identified seven parishes where the Irish (Gaelic) language was used, viz. Thurso, Halkirk, Reay, Latheron, Farr, Wick (with the caveat that in Wick the people understood English also) and Durness. The population of the county was more evenly distributed then and the larger western parishes were not as sparsely populated as they are now. Unlike bilingual Wick, Thurso parish was populated mainly by monoglot Gaels. Another older statement suggests just where the linguistic boundary lay:

> [I]f ye suppose a Parallel to the hypotenuse drawn from Week (Wick) to Thurso, these on the Eastside of it speak most part English, and those on the West side Irish (Gaelic); and the ... Ministers ... preach to them in both languages.

In other words, the 'frontier' may have roughly followed the present-day railway line between the two towns, well within Caithness. That railway line reaches the second town in Caithness, Inbhir Ùige (Wick, 'mouth of the Wick river'). Ùig derives from ON, *vík,* meaning 'bay', as in the word 'Viking'. The British Fisheries Society completed the harbour here in 1811. With the rise in fisheries, the size of the town increased and Wick replaced Thurso as the centre of both shipping and trade in Caithness. By the late 19th century, the town was a magnet for seasonal fishermen and gutters from the Western Isles, particularly Lewis.

The herring boats followed the shoals around the coast of Britain and were followed by an army of curers, merchants, general hands and Clann-nighean an Sgadain ('herring lasses') who were an integral part of the fisheries. These women came from fishing villages all around mainland Scotland and from the islands. They began gutting and packing herring from the age of fifteen and travelled throughout the season, from Stornoway north to Lerwick and as far south as Yarmouth. It was estimated that 30,000 men and women took part in the annual migration from the Gaelic-speaking areas of the West. From Lewis alone, 5,000 were involved; about one in five of the island's population.

In his poem 'Clann-nighean an Sgadain' ('Herring Girls'), Derick Thomson wrote:

B' e bun-os-cionn na h-eachdraidh a dh'fhàg iad
'nan tràillean aig ciùrairean cutach,
thall 's a-bhos air Galldachd 's an Sasainn.
Bu shaillte an duais a thàrr iad
às na mìltean bharaillean ud,
gaoth na mara geur air an craiceann,
is eallach a' bhochdainn 'nan ciste,
is mara b' e an gàire
shaoileadh tu gu robh an teud briste.

Ach bha craiteachan uaille air an cridhe,
ga chumail fallain,
is bheireadh cutag an teanga
slisinn à fanaid nan Gall –
agus bha obair romhpa fhathast
nuair gheibheadh iad dhachaigh,
ged nach biodh maoin ac':
air oidhche robach gheamhraidh,
ma bha siud an dàn dhaibh,
dhèanadh iad daoine.

The topsy-turvy of history had made them
slaves to short-arsed curers,
here and there in the Lowlands, in England.
Salt the reward they won
from those thousands of barrels
the sea-wind sharp on their skins,
and the burden of poverty in their kists,
and were it not for their laughter
you might think the harp string was broken.

But there was a sprinkling of pride on their hearts,
keeping them sound
and their tongues' gutting-knife
would tear a strip from the Lowlanders' mockery –
and there was work awaiting them
when they got home,
though they had no wealth:
on a wild winter's night,
if that were their lot
they would make men.

Blàr Allt nam Mèirleach: *The Last Clan Battle*

On 13th July 1680, at Allt nam Mèirleach (Altimarlach, 'stream of the thieves'), so called, it is said, because of the plunder taken from the dead, a battle was fought between Sir John Campbell of Glenorchy and George Sinclair of Keiss over the ownership of the Girnigoe Estate. Sir John, whose friend General Hugh Mackay said of him that he was:

> as grave as a Spaniard, wise as a serpent, cunning as a fox and slippery as an eel,

laid claim to these Sinclair lands and, in 1677, was granted the title of the Earl of Caithness. George Sinclair, a close relative of the Sinclair earl, contested the claim and Campbell of Glenorchy obtained royal permission to invade Caithness.

Glenorchy augmented his clan forces with several companies of government troops and, on the 12th of July, took possession of the Hill of Yarrows with its commanding view of Wick. When a sudden mist came down, he decided to take the town by surprise. At Stirkoke and Altimarlach he split his forces, half of them being positioned on the slope by the river and the rest hidden in an adjacent gully. The alarm was raised and Sinclair's forces were deployed to meet the Argyllshire men, but were attacked both by the group on the slope and by a flanking attack from the gully. The Sinclairs were trapped against the Wick River, which is quite deep at this point, and many were drowned as they struggled to escape to the opposite bank. Of the 800 men on each side, some 300 Sinclairs died, the Campbells losing a mere handful. This battle is notable for being the last major clan battle in Scotland. On the way north, Glenorchy's piper, Fionnlagh Bàn MacÌomhair ('fair Finlay MacIver') composed two tunes. One is called 'Breadalbane Gathering' and the other is the popular, although perhaps not in Wick, 'The Campbells are Coming'.

Having failed to regain his inheritance by force, Sinclair of Keiss took to the law. Through the influence of the Duke of York, afterwards King James VII of Scotland, he became Earl of Caithness and his lands were restored in September 1681. Campbell of Glenorchy was made Earl of Breadalbane by way of compensation. He seems to have gained more, however, as the plunder taken away from Caithness gave rise to the phrase:

> Òr Ghallaibh air bòrd Bhealaich.
>
> *Caithness gold on the Taymouth table.*

The coastal A9 road from Wick reaches Dùn Bheithe (Dunbeath, 'fort of the birches') which was the early home of the author Neil Gunn (1891-1973). Many of his novels, including *Highland River* (1937) and *The Silver Darlings* (1941), are set in the area. His most memorable work, *Butcher's Broom* (1934), describes the Clearances. It is a powerful mix of social history, polemic and recreation of an isolated, traditional society. Gunn described his ambitions for the book:

> This novel deals with nothing less than the tragedy of a race. In its pages we see how death came to the Highlands of Scotland and swept the Gaelic civilization to hell; an ancient civilisation giving light and learning to the world while the Anglo-Saxon was yet a bloody barbarian.

Gunn has been criticised, without any proof offered, for a:

> superficial pandering to the void labelled 'Gaelic' in the minds of his readers.

While Gunn deeply regretted that he did not speak Gaelic, his profound knowledge of life in the glens inland from Machair Chataibh ('the coastal lands of Sutherland') was infinitely better than that of any other writer of his time or, indeed, of his critics. Of the three Strathnaver novels, *Butcher's Broom* is the most authentic in tone and expression.

Calum I. Maclean wrote in 1959 that these Clearances caused such resentment among the native population that the government was concerned by the failure of its recruiting campaigns in the Highlands during the Crimean War of 1856. He described how, without a single enlisted man on his estates, the Duke of Sutherland called a meeting of all the male inhabitants of the parishes. At the well-attended meeting at Dunrobin Castle he stressed the necessity of going to fight and offered every enlisted man a bounty of £6. For a long time, there was silence until an old man rose to speak quietly and deliberately. In MacLean's words, the old man said:

> I am sorry for the response your Grace's proposals are meeting here today … but there is a cause for it … Your … predecessors applied to our fathers for men … and our fathers responded to their call; they have made liberal promises which neither them nor you performed; we … estimate your promises … at the value of theirs … I do assure your Grace that … should the Czar of Russia take possession of Dunrobin Castle [we] could not expect worse treatment at his hands than we have experienced at the hands of your family for the last fifty years. You … have desolated the glens and straths … How could your Grace expect to find men where

> they are not, and the few of them which are to be found among the rubbish ... of the county have more sense than to be decoyed by chaff to the field of slaughter…

Brùra: *Brora*

Immediately north of where this meeting took place is Brùra (Brora, ON, 'river bridge'). It was once known as Inbhir Bhrùra ('estuary of the Brora River'), while the wider parish name is Claonadh (Clyne, 'inclining place'). The town had the epithet 'Brùra nam Maraichean' ('Brora of the mariners'*)*, perhaps as a result of its fine harbour. Brora had a herring curing industry dating back to 1595, using salt from saltpans that were heated by locally extracted coal. This community was described as a village of two halves: one half Gaelic and poorer, employed in fishing and living in the lower area; the upper half more prosperous and English-speaking.

A persistent theme in the Gaelic poetry of the late 18th and 19th centuries is the connection between the impact of clearance and the continuing availability of Highland recruits for the armed forces. In his 1844 poem 'Fàsachadh na Gàidhealtachd' ('The Depopulation of the Highlands'), the Brora poet Donald MacLeod laments the plight of his people. He is saddened by the state of the area, where heroes who once lived there have been replaced by pitiful shepherds:

> O Alba! mo lèir-chreach, do gharbh-chrìochan àlainn
> A dh'àraich na h-àrmainn bhi fàsachail, fuar;
> Na leòmhain dheas anmant' nach dealaicheadh rin càirdean
> Am borb-chath 's an àraich bu ràn-sgreadach fuaim;
> Bu mharbh-bhuilleach, garg-ghuthach, calgant an éirigh,
> Cuir dearg dhath air leargaibh a's balgan da 'n reubadh,
> Ach, O! mo sheachd thruaighean! Chaidh 'm fuadach do
>   chèin-thìr,
> 'S cha dh'fhuair sinn nan èirig ach cìobairean truagh.

O Scotland! My devastation, your beautiful rough bounds
That reared the heroes, are desolate and cold;
The skilful, courageous lions that would not abandon their friends
In the barbarous fight and most clamorous field of battle;
With death-striking blows, fierce-voiced and lively their rising,
Making the plains red and bellies being torn,
But, oh! My seven calamities! They were cleared to a foreign land,
And all we got in exchange were pitiful shepherds.

In one verse he wishes that Napoleon Bonaparte would come so that there might be the preposterous prospect of his being faced by a defence force of:

Cìobair a's fang-chù na'n deann, agus caor.

A shepherd and a fank-dog at speed, and sheep.

Dòrnach: *Dornoch*

The village immediately to the south is Dòrnach (Dornoch, 'pebbly place'), a name suggesting that the adjacent shore has pebbles the size of a dòrn ('fist'). The building of Dornoch Cathedral was started in 1223 and it was originally dedicated to St. Finbar. Burnt along with the Bishops Palace by the Master of Caithness and the MacKays in 1570, it was restored in the 1830s. Sixteen earls of Sutherland are buried there; also on display is the sarcophagus of Richard de Morovia who was a close relative of Hugh Freskin, the first Lord of Sutherland. Tradition says that around 1240 a party of Danes invaded and, in stemming their attack, Richard was killed. However, the arrival of superior forces routed the Danes. During the battle, the Danish leader was brained with the leg of a horse, an incident that accounts for the horseshoe on Dornoch's present coat of arms. In a totally cod etymology, the name Dornoch is said to come from dòrn-eich ('horse-blow'). Perhaps if the authorities had bothered to ask the some 40% of those in the town who spoke Gaelic at the time, the story would have been laughed out of court; the court in question being that of the Lord Lyon King of Arms. It accepted the invention and granted the coat of arms in 1929.

Dornoch seems to have had a thing about horseshoes. They feature in the accusations levelled against a Janet Horne in what has oddly been termed the 'pseudo-execution' of the last witch in the British Isles in June 1727. It seems that Janet's daughter had a deformity of her hands and feet. Neighbours accused Janet of having used her daughter as a pony to ride to the Devil, who had then shod the daughter. The trial was conducted very quickly; the sheriff judged both guilty and sentenced them to be burned. The daughter managed to escape, but Janet was stripped, smeared with tar, paraded through the town in a barrel and burned alive.

A near-contemporary writer simply noted that:

> there has been great noise of witchcraft in the parish of Loth, in Sutherland, by which the minister is said to have suffered.

The *OSA*, 1793, records that this minister was Robert Robertson, the first Presbyterian (i.e. non-Episcopalian) minister to be settled in the parish in 1718. The minister of Loth considered himself aggrieved by an odd old woman with a semi-paralysed daughter, and the matter was sorted out before a superstitious sheriff. Janet stood no chance, but beside the 17th tee of the golf course, a stone commemorates where she burnt. The sheriff was simply censured.

As Janet Horne was from the parish of Loth, eleven miles northeast of Golspie, she was almost certainly a Gaelic speaker since, even as late as 1891, half the population were recorded as having Gaelic as their first language. The same is true of Brora and Dornoch. By then a social divide was evident, with the language largely confined to the poor, particularly the fishing communities in these towns.

The Undiscovered Scotland website adds that Janet:

> provided 'proof' of her guilt by stumbling over a recitation in Gaelic of the Lord's Prayer during her trial.

It also includes the classic trope against the Highlander:

> Perhaps the real explanation lies more in the quality of the output of the local illicit still that week.

Sidera (now Cyderhall) just south of Dornoch and just east of A' Chlais Mhòr (Clashmore, 'the big ditch') is a name that records the burial mound of Sigurd Eysteinsson, Sigurd the Mighty, Earl of Orkney (c.875-892). He led the Viking incursion into the firthlands north of Inverness. At the height of his victorious campaign he was killed by the severed head of one his enemies, Máel Brìgte ('tonsured of St. Bride'), perhaps then *mórmaer* or provincial ruler of Moray. Sigurd strapped Máel Brìgte's head to his saddle as a trophy of conquest but, as he rode, Máel Brìgte's bucktooth cut into his leg. The wound became infected and Sigurd died. This traditional tale has been conflated with a broadly contemporary, historical figure since the Irish annals record the death, respectively in 1029 and 1032, of Máel Coluim and Gilla Comgain, sons of Máel Brigte. They probably died at the hands of the Norse Orcadians.

The Meikle ('big') Ferry is signposted at the north end of the bridge over the Dornoch Firth. This wide estuary and An Caol Catach (the Kyle of Sutherland) separates Sutherland from Ross-shire. Four rivers, including Abhainn Sin (Shin River), flow into the Kyle. Following that river course towards the interior, the road reaches the village of Luirg (Lairg or Shin). The river's name is probably connected to the word seann ('old').

Seumas MacMhathain: *Sir James Matheson*

Lairg was the birthplace of James Matheson, born in 1796, the undoubtedly Gaelic-speaking son of Captain Donald Matheson. In 1832, he and his partner William Jardine established Jardine Matheson and Co. For two centuries the company, known as The Firm, was the most important commercial enterprise in Hong Kong. It is today Jardine Matheson Holdings Limited. Both men were utterly committed to making money by either fair means or foul. One writer described them as "utter rascals" who:

> distinguished themselves by a ruthlessness bordering on infamy.

The partners wanted to expand their opium trade in China. When, in 1842, the Chinese attempted to suppress this illegal trade, they succeeded in persuading the British to wage war on China. A defeated China accepted the Treaty of Nanking which allowed Jardine Matheson and Co. to expand from Canton to Hong Kong and into mainland China. Continuing its rapidly expanding trade in smuggled opium, tea and cotton, Jardine Matheson diversified into other areas including insurance, shipping, and railways. When the partners eventually retired to British estates – Matheson to Lewis – their great fortunes had been derived principally from the opium trade.

Baile Dhubhthaich: *Tain*

On the south side of the Dornoch Bridge is Baile Dhubhthaich (Tain). It heads the list in a rhyme recording the main centres in the area:

Baile Dhubhthaich bhòidheach 's Dòrnach na gorta,
Sgiobal nan ùbhlan 's Bil an arain-choirc,
Earabol nan adagan,
Dùn Robain a' chàil,
Goillspidh nan sligean dubha 's Druim-ùidh an t-sàil

Bonnie Tain and hungry Dornoch,
Skibo for apples and Beil for oatcakes.
Eriboll for haddocks, Dunrobin for kail,
Golspie for black shells and Drumuie for brine.

All these places, except for Tain, are on the coast of Sutherland. Tain's English name derives from the nearby River Tain, from Indo-European, meaning 'flow'. The Gaelic name, Baile Dhubhthaich ('Duthac's town'), suggests a religious dedication, perhaps to Dubhthach, an 8th-century saint. He was one of the most loved of Scottish saints of the later Middle Ages and from the late 14th century until the Reformation, devotion to Dubhthach outstripped devotion to Andrew, Columba, Margaret and Mungo, or in other words, the whole hierarchy of Scottish sainthood. Tain was a significant sanctuary where people could claim the protection of the church and immunity from prosecution.

Not so for Alasdair Sgoilear ('Alasdair the scholar') whose fate has traditionally explained the loss of Tain's county town status to Dingwall. Alasdair, a renowned rogue, was brought to justice, and on being condemned to death, petitioned:

> Ma bheir sibh dhomh naoi leumannan agus naoi ceumannan, chan eil duine ann an Siorrachd Rois a bheireas orm.
>
> *If you give me (the feat) of the nine leaps and the nine steps, there is no one in Ross-shire who could catch me.*

The sheriff, unaware of the prowess of this 'Prodigious Leaper', declined the offer and hanged him. On hearing of Alasdair Sgoilear's fate, an enraged King deprived Tain of its status. The prodigious leaper is a common motif in the Aarne-Thompson-Uther Index (ATU Index) catalogue of international folktale types.

The status of Gaelic in Tain can be gauged by the fact that in 1750 Gaelic was preached every Sunday. The Burgh records contain a complaint brought in 1792 before the Sheriff by Alexander Fraser, kirk officer, against Rev. John Matheson and the session. The complaint was dismissed since the:

> libel was read before the session in English, but nine out of the ten elders did not know English.

Furthermore:

> the complainer had signed a confession, but he knows little English and did not know exactly what was in it.

The proportion of the general community that had no English would have been at least as high as that of the kirk session in question.

Gleann Mòr na Sìth?: *Glenmorangie?*

The Glenmorangie whisky distillery lies just to the north of Tain. It is currently owned by Louis Vuitton Moët Hennessy. In April 2013, *The Scotsman* newspaper reported that:

> Advertising watchdogs rejected a complaint disputing the accuracy of the whisky company's phrase, 'Glenmorangie – Gaelic for Glen of Tranquillity', which it has used for almost 10 years.

During the proceedings, the complainant said that his understanding was that the name Glenmorangie came from glen ('valley'), mòr ('big') and innse ('water meadow'). He said the company's commercials were misleading because they misrepresented the Gaelic language. The multi-national refuted the claim, its understanding being that the name was an English corruption of the Gaelic gleann mòr na sìth ('big glen of peace' or 'glen of tranquillity'). The company said it acknowledged the meaning of Glenmorangie depended on the perceived root of the word; it admitted that there was an academic argument over how various Scottish place names may have originated, but it believed the translation it had used was correct. The Advertising Standards Authority (ASA) consulted another language expert, who agreed that the complainant's translation was correct. But although the ASA said it acknowledged the complainant's translation, it believed that, because the company had taken care to research the origins of the name, it had good reason to use it.

Presumably the ASA felt that 'good reason' justified distortion. This is by no means an isolated case of embroidery by the multinationals who dominate the whisky industry. The meaning of the place name Glengoyne is obscure, but branding by the distillery suggests an association with wild geese. The Blair Atholl distillery in Pitlochry extolls the waters of its stream, the Aldour which has given the area and this distillery the name Otter Burn. Aldour is a shortening of the Gaelic Allt Odhar ('dun-coloured burn'), and not related to dòbhran ('otter'). Much the same distortion occurs in Speyside where Glenfiddich, we are told means 'glen of deer', when the name is more likely to refer to a wooded landscape, from Gaelic fiodh ('wood'). These 'translations' are symptomatic of a device used by distilleries and other companies by which they embroider relatively straightforward topographical descriptor names with additional romantic meanings. This practice has a long history. W. J. Watson said in 1922 that:

> in place-names, sanity and scholarship must conjoin; running after the bizarre or fanciful is fatal.

Unfortunately for the incurable romantics at Glenmorangie, while they might have sought to convey peace and serenity, their distillery's name translates somewhat less romantically as 'The Valley of the Big Haugh'.

Continuing south on the A9, Baile nan Gobhann (Balnagowan, 'smith's village') was once the seat of the Rosses of Balnagowan. Around 1610, James VI decided that when the number of MacGregor survivors fell to twelve, the Earl of Argyll was to be excused from maintaining a force to hunt them down and until then those that sheltered MacGregors should be fined a total of one-fifth of the value of their property. The Earl was given an opportunity to supplement his income by pocketing the lion's share of such fines. His scope was wide-ranging. A committee appointed for the purpose processed a list of over 100 persons, from Perth to Dingwall, who had been fined for harbouring MacGregors. George Ross of Balnagowan was fined the huge sum of £1,000. Clearly, George was a Gaelic-speaker who shared the Gaels' revulsion against the King's unwarranted vendetta against MacGregors. Thus fined punitively, when George died in 1615, his estate was bankrupted. The estate is now owned by the Al Fayed family, former owners of Harrods.

Sir Eachann Rothach: *Sir Hector Munro*

Nearer Dingwall, Taigh an Fhuamhair (Novar, 'giant's house') was rebuilt by Sir Hector Munro, on his return from India in 1765. The *Edinburgh Evening Courant* of June 1771 reported that an 'East Indian' slave called Caesar had escaped from Novar.

Hector Munro belonged to a renowned military dynasty, Clann an Rothaich (Munros), who were reputed to have had three generals, eight colonels, five lieutenant-colonels and 30 captains serving in the 17th-century Swedish armies of King Gustavus Adolphus. Hector had been a lieutenant in the Hanoverian army from about 1747 and was apparently tasked with the job of capturing Ewen 'Cluny' MacPherson for his part in the Jacobite Rising of 1745. Tradition has it that one day, Hector, with a party of soldiers, surrounded MacPherson's house in Badenoch. With no means of escape, 'Cluny' dressed himself as a groom and came forward to hold Munro's horse while they searched his house for him. On his return from the futile search, Hector is said to have handed the groom a shilling and then ridden off. Another version of the story is that Hector knew well enough who the groom was and winked at him as he threw him his fee. After nine years in hiding, MacPherson escaped to France in 1755.

In the 18th century, the Highlands became probably one of the most heavily militarily recruited places in the Western World. In local government, the influence of military men and half-pay officers was also increasing. Of the 83 registered freeholders in Elgin in 1786, seventeen held commissions in the army. Others, including Sir Hector held commissions in the East India Company. The contrast with other provincial towns such as Dundee, where in the 1770s not one of the fourteen town councillors was a military man, is striking. In the Highlands, almost a third of the electorate were military officers, outstripping the Lowlands, where the corresponding figure was just a tenth.

In 1760, Sir Hector secured a commission in the 89th (Highland) Regiment of Foot, a regiment raised in Aberdeenshire and Banffshire, at that time predominantly Gaelic-speaking areas, and with it was sent to India. His opportunity came in 1764, when he gained the important victory of Buxar despite odds of five to one. Soon after he was promoted to Lieutenant-Colonel and became the 9th Commander-in-Chief of India. This was a position with influence and opportunity for profit. As a letter in the Tain archive says:

> He (Hector) got £13,000 from the Nabobs and other officers, his relatives, £3000. In regard to money-getting and otherwise, the E.I.C. (East India Company) officers had been getting quite out of control. The restoration of that control was the object of Clive of India's mission.

When he returned to Novar in 1782, the local population was being cleared off the land, and Munro conceived the idea of building a monument as a scheme to give landless men some work. The resulting Fyrish Monument is on

Cnoc Faoighris (Fyrish Hill, meaning obscure), above Alness. It represents the Gate of Negapatam, a port of Madras, that Sir Hector captured in 1781. It was said that he had stones rolled down from the top of the hill to the bottom, so that hauling them up again extended the time spent on the works, and he duly paid the labourers for additional hours. He was remembered with affection by his fellow Gaels.

Moladh Chabar Fèidh: *In Praise of Stag's Antlers*

Alanais (Alness, 'Alan's place', Alan being the son of another village planner) is the site of events recorded in the song 'Moladh Chabar Fèidh' ('In Praise of Stag's Antlers'). The antlers are now the symbol of Ross-shire but, at the time the song was composed, Cabar Fèidh were the symbol of the MacKenzies and also their battle cry. It extolls Uilleam Dubh ('dark William'), 5th MacKenzie Earl of Seaforth:

Deoch slàinte chabar fèidh seo gur h-èibhinn 's gur
  h-aighearach;
Ge fada bho thìr fèin e, Mhic Dhè, greas ga fhearann e
Mo chrochadh is mo cheusadh is m' èideadh nar mhealladh mi
Mur ait leam thu bhith 'g èirigh le treun neart gach caraide.

Gur mise chunna sibh gu gunnach, ealamh, ullamh,
  acfhuinneach;
A' ruith nan Rothach 's math ur gnothach, thug sibh sothadh
maidne dhaibh,
O, cha deach Cataich air an tapadh, dh'fhàg an neart le eagal
  iad
Ri faicinn ceann an fhèidh ort nuair dh'èirich do chabar ort!

B' e 'n t-amadan Fear Fòghlais nuair thòisich e cogadh riut
Rothaich agus Ròsaich bu ghòrach na bodaich iad,
Frisealaich is Granndaich an campa cha stadadh iad,
'S thug Foirbeisich nan deann-ruith gu seann taigh Chùil
  Lodair orr'.

Theich 'ad uile is cha d'fhuirich an treas duine bh' acasan
An t-Iarla Catach ruith e dhachaigh, cha do las a dhagachan,
MacAoidh nan creach gun d' thàrr e às, 's ann dh'èigh e
'n t-each a b' aigeannach
Ri gabhail an ratreuta, nuair dh' èirich do chabar ort!

A toast to this Cabarfeidh, how delightful and how joyful; although far from his own land, Son of God, may he hurry to his country. May I be hanged and crucified and my clothing be disposed of if I fail to rejoice as you rise up with the support of brave friends.

I myself saw you armed with a gun, ready, prepared, equipped, chasing the Munros in great style, you gave them their morning rout. Sutherland men weren't heroic, their strength deserting them with fear on seeing the stag's head on you as your antlers were raised high!

What a fool was the Foulis man (Munro) when he began fighting with you. Munros and Rosses were stupid old men, Frasers and Grants wouldn't stay in camp, and the Forbeses fled to the old house of Culloden.

They all fled and not a third of their men remained. The Earl of Sutherland, he ran home without even firing his pistols; the plundering MacKay took off, he shouted for the most spirited horse to make the retreat when your antlers were raised!

The song has a complex history and has debated authorship. It is believed that it is a Ross-shire song and that the verses remembered today were composed by Tormod Bàn (Norman MacLeod) (c1670-c1757). It is about the 'Alness Affair' when, in October 1715, a Jacobite force of over 3,000 men under Seaforth's command dispersed a force of 1500 largely Gaelic speakers without firing a shot. Those who wisely fled from their out-manoeuvred position are listed in the song with great glee. The song is very popular, though perhaps not so among the clans who fled.

Balconie Castle was an ancient seat of the Earls of Ross. The Gaelic form of the name was given by W. J. Watson as bailcnidh, which he derived from bailc ('strong'). Thus Balconie's name would mean 'strong place', fitting for a major centre of lordship.

The tale of the Lady of Balconie is dated by the writer Hugh Miller to the early 17th century. She appears to have been a daughter of a Lord of Balconie and according to Miller:

> her nurse was a witch and secretly trained the girl in the black art.

It is said that visitors to the castle, expressing their scepticism at witchcraft, were startled when the young lady magically levitated the castle several feet into the air and, after some moments, deposited it safely back on its base. The tradition is that eventually The Lady was taken by the Devil himself at the Blackrock Gorge, where she still remains, chained in a cave and surrounded by fierce hounds.

The 1979 bridge over Caolas Chrombaidh (Kyle of Cromarty) takes the road over this estuary of the Moray Firth. The stretch of water derives its present name from the port, Cromarty ('little place of the bend'), where the estuary turns at the end of the peninsula to exit into the Moray Firth. The peninsula is known now as An t-Eilean Dubh ('the black island'), supposedly called such since, even at the time of the *OSA* (1790s), four-fifths of it was black moor – uncultivated moorland. However, the name is a contraction of Eilean Dhubhthaich ('Duthac's island'). This peninsula also had the names An Àird Mheadhanach ('the middle headland'), and Eadar Dhà Dhail ('between two valleys').

Fearann na Tòiseachd: *Ferintosh*

The A9 traverses the western end of the Black Isle through the parish of Urquhart which is almost contiguous with the barony of Ferintosh. In 1476, King James III granted to Donald, Thane of Cawdor, the liberties and privileges of a barony. The Gaelic tòiseach translates as 'thaneship'; thus the name Ferintosh refers to the land of the thane. In 1670, the Ferintosh estate was acquired by the Forbes of Culloden family. Nineteen years later it was sacked by the Jacobites. In compensation, Duncan Forbes of Culloden (1644-1704) secured the Crown privilege of distilling whisky, free of duty. The privilege was enjoyed by the Forbes family on their annual payment of about £500 and this lasted without interruption until 1786.

The privilege produced an immediate boom in the production of Ferintosh whisky and the name became synonymous with whisky. 'Duanag don Uisge-bheatha' ('Little Song to Whisky') by Ailean Dall MacDhùghaill ('Blind Alan MacDougall') (c.1750-1829) sets out its virtues:

Tha fàileadh gun fhòtas
Bho 'chneas Mhic an Tòisich
Chuireadh blàths ann am pòraibh
Là reòt' a's gaoth tuath.

O! siud i 'n deoch mhilis
Nach pilleamaid uainn,
Chuireadh blàths air gach cridhe,
Ge do bhitheadh iad fuar:
O! siud i 'n deoch mhilis
Nach pilleamaid uainn.

There's a flawless smell from Ferintosh whisky. It would warm your pores even in a freezing north wind.

Oh, that's the sweet drink we'd never send back. It'd warm every heart no matter how cold. Oh, that's the sweet drink we'd never send back.

He was born in Glencoe, where he worked as a tailor until he lost his sight. Thereafter he made a meagre living playing the fiddle at weddings and celebrations. About 1790, he and his family moved to Inverlochy and, with the help of another Lochaber poet, Ewan MacLachlan, his songs were published in 1798. From this point on, Alasdair Garbh (Alexander Ranaldson MacDonell of Glengarry) became his patron; in return, Alan wrote praise poems for the family.

Production at Ferintosh increased dramatically. In 1763, the output of whisky was 41,200 gallons but, by 1780, it had tripled. The population at Ferintosh grew. The *OSA* of 1792 reports that in the three-year period, 1737-39, the number of births was 29 but, by 1777-79, there were 83. By 1779, the population was 3,022 and it is estimated that over 1,000 people were involved in distilling whisky. Few men were left to cultivate the land.

In 1782, London papers carried a report that a large distillery, with an annual production of 10,000 gallons of spirits, was being constructed at Ferintosh. This was the last straw and there was an outcry from Lowland and English distillers against the flood of whisky produced in Ferintosh. In 1786, action was finally taken by the government and the privilege was withdrawn. Forbes of Culloden received a compensatory payment of £20,000. The demise of Ferintosh whisky was much lamented. Robert Burns in his poem 'Scotch Drink' (1786), devoted a verse to Ferintosh whisky, lamenting:

Thee Ferintosh! O sadly lost!
Scotland lament frae coast to coast!
Now colic grips, an' barkin' hoast
May kill us a';
For loyal Forbes' charter'd boast
Is taen awa'!

The large population at Ferintosh, uncompensated, was left without any means of supporting itself. All trace of what was once the largest concentration of distilleries in Scotland has all but vanished. There were 29 small distilleries in the Black Isle in the 18th century but, by the 1840s, all were gone. Legislation governing the production of whisky was complex and constantly changing and it was not always viable for Highland distillers to continue legal production. Legislative interference almost killed the legal industry and encouraged illicit production. The first twenty years of the 1800s saw the height of smuggling activity in the glens on the fringes of the Black Isle. The trade was often connived at by landowners, who saw it as a means of securing their rental payments. The law was flouted on a massive scale, with many legal distillers forced to close and, by 1821, there were only three left in Easter Ross. Finally, in 1823, with another overhaul of the legislation recognising the estate owners' interests, illicit distilling was doomed and legal distilleries could once more start production. The industry was saved in the nick of time and newly legal production centres in Speyside began to dominate the industry.

Eleven kilometres north of Inverness is the Tore roundabout, an intersection joining the A9 and the A832, next to the village from which it takes its name, An Todhar (Tore, 'the bleaching place'). Here finished linen fabric was once laid out to whiten in the sun. Some have mistakenly claimed that the name comes from the word for manure. At Tore is Cnoc an Acrais ('hunger hill') where Fèill Chnoc an Acrais ('hunger hill market') was once held.

The A9 reaches the Beauly Firth at North Kessock and completes the circuit of the north coast. Before the Kessock Bridge was erected in 1982 to carry traffic over the firth, Aiseag Cheasaig ('Kessock's ferry') plied between North and South Kessock. W. J. Watson states that the name of the ferry was "generally connected" with the 6th-century saint, Cessog (Kessock). If so, it makes the bridge over to Inverness the only one in Scotland to be named for a saint.

Caibideil 12: *Chapter 12*

A' Ghàidhealtachd, Deas air Inbhir Nis: *Highland Council Area, South of Inverness*

Cùil Lodair: *Culloden*

East of Inverness, at Cùl Lodair (Culloden, possibly 'the secluded spot at the shelving slope'), on the 16th of April 1746, the last battle on what is now British soil took place between the forces of Prince Charles Edward Stuart and those of the Hanoverian government commanded by his cousin the Duke of Cumberland. The two armies met on level, mainly boggy, terrain that gave Cumberland's larger, well-equipped, well-fed and well-rested force the advantage, robbing the Highlanders of the opportunity for the classic downhill charge. The battle lasted only an hour and the Jacobites were defeated, losing between 1,500 and 2,000 men killed or wounded, at the cost of about 250 government soldiers. Amid the carnage, MacDonald of Keppoch is said to have been struck down by a volley crying out:

> "Mo Dhia, an do thrèig clann mo chinnidh mi?"
>
> *"My God, have my clansmen deserted me?"*

The battle site is treated as a war grave by the National Trust for Scotland who have expended much effort in restoring the site to its approximate appearance on the day of the battle. In the 1880s, the local landowner, Forbes of Culloden, erected a memorial cairn and provided marker stones for the mass burial pits, noting the names of some of the clans in the Prince's army. The names he ascribed to the pits are conjecture. The mutilated corpses had been stripped of any clothing that might have provided an indication of their area of origin. The only honest markers are those that state 'mixed clans.'

Despite the Trust's worthy efforts to maintain a balanced narrative, a good deal of ink is spilt in mythologising the death of perhaps 2,000 men in a matter of an hour. One quite recent piece, published by the Trust itself, had the ranks of awaiting Hanoverian soldiers catching the sounds of the Highlanders conjuring up the spirits of their ancestors. While this practice was perhaps normal among Persian Zoroastrians, Gaelic Highlanders generally appealed to God. There is no reason to suppose that these hungry and exhausted men did not do the same while they waited for the Hanoverian bombardment. In any case, with an easterly wind in their faces, their enemy had no chance of hearing them and even had they done so, most could not have understood, as they had no Gaelic.

The wash of 19th-century Romanticism has softened the harshest of memories. That process was massively boosted by Jacobite songs that were then almost as well appreciated as love songs. John Stuart Blackie said that:

> These ballads have the double advantage of being at once real contemporary history and real popular poetry of the most classical type.

Blackie was expressing the opinion of most respected 19th-century poets and scholars that these works were created at the same time as the events they described. But that was not the case. Titles such as 'The Skye Boat Song', 'Ye Jacobites by Name',' Come o'er the Stream, Dear Charlie,' 'My Bonnie Moorhen' etc., were not in existence before 1780. They were mostly written by the likes of Robert Burns, James Hogg and Lady Nairne. Most of them purport to be contemporary with the events they describe, but they were fake and their authors knew it.

In contrast, the contemporary Gaelic literature of the time, mainly songs, has a rawness and expressive power lacking in the ballads. Among the finest poets who fought in the Jacobite ranks at Culloden was John Roy Stewart and his 'Òran Eile air Latha Chùil Lodair' ('Another Song on Culloden Day') gives an eye-witness account of the battle:

Air thùs an latha dol sìos,
Bha gaoth a' cathadh nan sian –
Às an adhar bha trian ar lèiridh.

Dh'fhàs an talamh cho trom,
Gach fraoch, fearann is fonn,
'S nach bu chothrom dhuinn lom an t-slèibhe.
Bha lasair-theine nan Gall

A' frasadh pheilear mur ceann –
Mhill siud eireachdas lann 's bu bheud e.

As the action opened and we charged, the wind drove snow at us; a third of our misery came from the sky.

The going grew grim, all heather, hummock and hag, and the exposed slope offered no help.

The Foreigners' musket balls raining round our heads tragically sullied the sheen of our swords.

John Roy does not acknowledge the presence of Gaels in the Government forces.

Another well-known Culloden song is a widow's lament. The consensus is that 'Mo Rùn Geal Òg' ('My Fair Young Love') was composed by Cairistiona NicFhearghais (Christina Ferguson) from Contin in Easter Ross who was married to William Chisholm from Strathglass who probably lost his life at Culloden:

Gura mis' th' air mo sgaradh,
'S ged a chanam, cha bhreug e:
Chaidh mo shùgradh gu sileadh
O nach pillear bhon eug thu;
Fear do chèille 's do thuigse
Cha robh furast' r'a fheutainn
'S cha do sheas an Cùil Lodair
Fear do choltais bu trèine,
Mo rùn geal òg.

'S ioma baintighearna phrìseil
Le 'n sìoda 's le 'n sròltaibh
Da 'n robh mise 'm chùis fharmaid
Chionns gun tairgeadh tu pòg dhomh;
Ged a bhithinn cho sealbhmhor
'S gum bu leam airgead Hanòbhair,
Bheirinn cnag anns na h-àithntean
Nan cumadh càch bhuam do phògan,
Mo rùn geal òg.

I have been torn in two, though I say it, it's true: instead of flirting I cry since death won't return you. A man of your sense and wisdom wasn't easily found; no one who stood at Culloden was as courageous as you, my bright young love.

Many affluent ladies with their silks and their satins were jealous of me for receiving your kisses; if I was so prosperous as to have Hanover's money, I'd still break the commandments if they stopped you from kissing me, my bright young love.

A little south of Culloden on the A9 to Perth is Deimhidh (Daviot, a Brythonic name cognate with the tribal name Demetae, known first from Roman writers). Alasdair Stiùbhart MacIlleathain (Alistair Stuart MacLean) (1922-1987), the son of a Church of Scotland minister, spent his childhood and youth in Daviot and learned English in school as his second language after Gaelic. MacLean wrote thrillers and adventure stories, including *The Guns of Navarone* and *Where Eagles Dare*. They were made into films and it is estimated that his books have sold over 150 million copies, making him one of the best-selling fiction authors of all time.

Close by is the small community of Dun Fhlicheadaidh (Dunlichity, 'fort of the wet place'). It was once claimed that:

> Fhad 's a bhios an t-allt aig Flicheadaidh a' ruith dhan taobh tuath, bith mallachd air Flicheadaidh.
>
> *As long as the Flichity stream runs northwards, Flichity will be cursed.*

William McGillivray was born here in 1764 and, aged twenty, he went to Canada to work for his uncle in the North West Company, trading in furs in Northern Canada. He succeeded his uncle as the last chief partner of the Company and he eventually owned substantial estates, both in Scotland and Canada. McGillivray has a mixed reputation, with one reviewer of a biography of him and his fellow traders, many also Gaelic speakers, saying:

> A more reprehensible lot could be hard to find in any nation's iconography. McGillivray owed his success to nepotism, the North West Company owed its success primarily to rum.

The land now opens out into the valley of Abhainn Spè (River Spey, meaning probably pre-Gaelic). The river appears in the saying:

> Spè, Dè agus Tatha, trì uisgeachan as motha fon adhar.
>
> *Spey, Dee and Tay, the three greatest rivers under the sun.*

The area is known as Bàideanach (Badenoch, 'drowned place'). The stem 'bad' is cognate with the English 'bath', perhaps describing the often inundated ground of the flood plain of the river Spey.

The river formed this broad strath between the mountain massif of the Monadh Liath ('the grey-blue mountain range') to the west and what are now known as the Cairngorms. The name 'Cairngorms' was first coined by non-Gaelic-speaking visitors around two hundred years ago to refer to the range of mountains that lie between Strathspey and Deeside. This unfortunate bundling of all the peaks into the name of only one peak in what is properly the Monadh Ruadh ('the red-brown mountain range') has destroyed the twinning and contrasting of the two mountain masses in the Gaelic imagination. These mountains form the heart of the Cairngorms National Park, correctly, Pàirc Nàiseanta a' Mhonaidh Ruaidh.

Writing in 1922 of his native area, the place name scholar Alexander McBain said that the OS maps for Badenoch contain about 1,400 names, a mere tenth of the names once used when the glens were filled with people. Most of these names are lost to us with the abandonment of the old system of crofting, summer migration to the hills and clearance of the population. This is a loss replicated across the Highlands.

Dòmhnall Bàn MacCruimein: *Fair-haired Donald MacCrimmon*

To the east of the road is Loch Muigh (Loch Moy, 'plain loch') and MacIntosh land, a clan loyal to the Jacobite cause. Lady Anne MacIntosh, wife of the chief, hosted the Prince at Moy Hall in early 1746. When the government commander, the Campbell Earl of Loudon, discovered this, he attempted a kidnapping raid. The result was Ruaig na Mòighe (Rout of Moy) when Louden's vastly superior force was tricked into flight by the subterfuge of the local smith and a few others who convinced the enemy that it was facing the entire Jacobite army. For the Gael, however, their amusement at the rout was tinged with sadness in that the piper of the MacLeod militia detachment in Loudon's forces, the famed Dòmhnall Bàn Mac Cruimein ('fair-haired Donald MacCrimmon'), was one of the few fatalities.

Donald MacCrimmon was hereditary piper to Clan MacLeod, part of the government militia force that marched on Aberdeen to seize the Jacobite, Lord Lewis Gordon. The force, however, was routed at Inverurie and Donald Bàn was taken prisoner. The next morning, contrary to custom, there was no pipe music in the Jacobite camp. When Lord Lewis enquired the reason, he was told that so long as MacCrimmon was a prisoner there would be no pipes played. Lord Lewis at once ordered that Donald should be set free. Not long afterwards, however, in the confusion of the rout, Donald was shot, probably by friendly fire.

After his death, his sister is believed to have written the words to the tune 'Cha till Mac Cruimein' ('MacCrimmon will never return'), believed to have been composed by Donald when he had a premonition of his impending death before he left Skye. The tune was frequently sung or played during the Clearances as emigrant ships carried Highlanders away from Scotland.

The adjacent location of Torr Darach (Tordarroch, 'oak hill') is associated with the seanfhacal (proverb):

> Chan ann a h-uile latha a bhios mòd àig Mac an Tòisich.
>
> *It is not every day that MacIntosh holds a court.*

It is said that the Earl of Moray summoned his MacIntosh vassals to meet him at Tordarroch, home of the Shaws since the 15th century. The Earl wanted to get his hands on Hector MacIntosh, the acting chief of Clan Chattan, who had led a raid on Moray's lands. He learned nothing, so he hanged eighteen MacIntoshes, as it is said:

> over the balks of the house where the court was held.

However, it seems more likely that the MacIntosh referred to here were not the Clan Chattan men, but one of the hereditary tòiseachs ('chamberlains') to the Earls of Perth. Tradition says that one of their number, in order to make himself famous and to suitably impress thieves in his custody, used to arrange for one to be hanged daily.

A little ditty from the early days of coaching outlines the progress made in a day's travel through the valley:

> Bracaist am Baile Chloichrigh, lòn an Dail na Ceàrdaich, dìnneir an Dail Chuinnidh is a' bhanais ann an Ràt.
>
> *Breakfast in Pitlochry, lunch in Dalnacardoch, dinner in Dalwhinnie and the wedding in Raitts.*

Raits is across the valley from Ruadhainn (Ruthven, 'red-brown place'), and the shell of the Barracks, sited on what seems to be a modified, natural mound. The Comyns or Cummings had a castle here but, after their conflict with Robert the Bruce, the stronghold became a royal possession. In 1689, the castle was burned during the first Jacobite rising by Iain Dubh nan Cath ('Black John of the Battles'), John Graham of Claverhouse, now better known as 'Bonnie Dundee'. The government bought the ruins in 1715 and had constructed the barracks by 1719. In the fifth, and final, Jacobite Rising, it was burned by the Prince's army as it marched north to Inverness before the Battle of Culloden in 1746.

An Dèidh Chùil Lodair: *Culloden's Aftermath*

It was here that, following Culloden, some 1,500 famished men of the Prince's army re-grouped, considering that bloody shambles as merely a temporary setback. The Prince sent them his infamous message to the effect that, since there was nothing he could do for them on this side of the water, he intended instantly to proceed to France, to:

> engage the court either to assist us effectually and powerfully or at least to procure you such terms as you could not obtain otherwise.

He obtained neither powerful assistance nor terms. Scandalously, Charles ordered the money he had sent to the men to buy desperately needed supplies be returned to him for his own personal use. Abandoned, the men dispersed to their homes and the nemesis that awaited them and their families. A fortunate few escaped to France.

After Culloden, the Gaels were at the mercy of a rattled and vengeful Hanoverian government. Over the coming months, 3,500 Jacobite combatants were rounded up and imprisoned; of these, 120, mainly clan leaders, were immediately executed; a further documented 90 died in prison; 1,000 were transported to the colonies; and 250 were 'banished'. A further 700 disappeared, their fate unknown, although probably most of them died in prison hulks on the Thames.

The general population also suffered horribly. Cumberland had already begun to ravage the estates of the Jacobite aristocracy during his march north, but what followed after Culloden was wider in scope and more ruthless in method. It was the systematic destruction of the basis of life in many communities that had been living, at the best of times, at the margins of survival. 'Rebels' found in arms were shot. Those that fled had their homes plundered and burned, their cattle driven away and their implements smashed.

In the 1995 publication *Bloody Culloden,* reference was made to a Gaelic song (published in 1825 in Stewart's *Sketches*) that "captured Jacobite anguish and loyalty". That author gave only one verse in translation which *Bloody Culloden*, evidently unaware of this eminent, anonymous song, quoted:

> They ravaged and burnt my country; they murdered my father, and carried off my brothers; they ruined my kindred, and broke the heart of my mother [a more truthful sense is 'stripped naked my mother']; but all, all could I bear without murmur if I saw my king restored in his own.

This song is 'Achadh nan Comhaichean' ('Field of the Covenant', a place-name in Lochaber):

> Mharbh iad m'athair, mharbh iad mo bhràithrean,
> Mhill iad mo chinneadh is chreach iad mo chàirdean
> Loisg iad mo dhùthaich is rùisg iad mo mhàthair
> 'S cha chluinnte mo mhulad nam buinnigeadh Teàrlach.

As one historian has put it:

> to describe Cumberland as arrogant and brutal is to differentiate him little from a very large proportion of the contemporary political and military elite of Hanoverian Britain. It is the indiscriminate and unintelligent nature of the savagery which he licensed which is so depressing.

Cumberland was not the first. The Comyn Lords of Badenoch also left a reputation for rapacity and cruelty behind them and their treachery has passed into a proverb:

> Fhad 's a bhitheas craobh sa choill, bithidh foill sna Cuimeinich.
>
> *While in the wood there is a tree, a Cumming will deceitful be.*

A desolate area to the east of the A9 road has had an evil reputation and a Cumming association among Gaels for many centuries. This is Gàdhaig nam Feadan Fiar (Gaick, 'cleft of the crooked streams'). As the saying goes:

> 'S mòr a b' fheàrr leam a bhith an Druim Uachdair na bhith ann an Gàdhaig nan creagan gruamach.
>
> *I'd much rather be in Drumochter than in Gaick of the gloomy crags.*

Gaick's ill repute is associated with a local curse:

> Dìol Bhaltair an Gàdhaig ort!
>
> *Walter's fate in Gaick to you*!

arising from Walter Comyn's death here in 1258. Walter, on his departure from his home in Ruthven, issued a bizarre order that all the women between fifteen and 30 years of age working the land at Ruthven should do so naked. Retribution was swift. On the high ground to the east on Allt a' Chaoirnich ('stream of rowans'), at a place known as Leum nam Fiann ('leap of the

Fenians'), his horse stumbled and Walter was unseated. His foot caught in the stirrup and he was dragged all the way back to Ruthven. When the horse arrived, all that remained of Walter was his foot in the stirrup. A search was made for his body and, when it was found, two eagles were tearing it apart. This track was later used as a cattle drovers' route, called Rathad nan Cuimeanach (Comyn's Road).

Seumas Bàn MacMhuirich: *James 'Ossian' Macpherson*

The area to the west was once known as Na Ràt ('the forts'), and the adjacent cleared village still bears the name The Raits. In 1790, a mansion was built nearby at Baile a' Bhile (Balavil, 'farm of the edge') on a site that was traditionally an ancient castle of Clan MacIntosh. However, its owner referred to the house as Belleville, a romantic French allusion.

So who was this rich builder? As one literary critic has said:

> In the early 1760s, probably the most controversial translation since Luther appeared in the form of the poems of Ossian.

The young translator, Seumas Bàn MacMhuirich (1736-1796), had collected Gaelic folk poetry in the Highlands, edited it and translated it into English in the form of lyrical poems and two epics. Born in adjacent Inbhir Tromaidh (Invertromie, 'confluence of the dwarf elder river'), James was working as a teacher in Edinburgh. It was as an initially reluctant translator of Ossianic bardic verse (after its purported third-century author, Ossian) that he gained renown, followed by controversy and considerable wealth.

Ceann a' Ghiùthsaich: *Kingussie*

The original village of Ceann a' Ghiùthsaich (Kingussie, 'head of the pine wood') was situated on the slopes by Ruthven Castle, but a new site across the valley was found for the improved village. *The New Statistical Account* (*NSA*) of 1835 states that:

> the language of the common people is Gaelic, but most of the young … understand English: among the better classes, the latter is preferred … it will cease to be a living language in this part of the country.

Although prophetic, the minister's calculations were too pessimistic; there were still Gaelic speakers here in the latter part of the 20th century. However, the author of the *NSA* entry was sympathetic towards the local population and unusually forthright about the causes of their impoverished condition:

> Still from the shortness of most of their leases, the non-residence of some of the proprietors, which drains the country of money, the still uncertain state of their crops … the common people continue in a very poor and uncomfortable state. The bravery of many of them has been well proved and they maintain a high reputation for hospitality and politeness. But these virtues are too often found in union with vices … quarrelling, intemperance, and an artfulness of address, are still features in their character.

One Kingussie resident was Dòmhnall Phàil ('Paul's Donald' or Donald Campbell) (1798-1875). Born at Dail na Spideil (Dalnaspidal, 'valley of the hospice'), he came to Badenoch as a shepherd about 1822. He lived at Gleann Gòineig (Glengoynack, possibly meaning 'wintry streamlet') for over 40 years, a place where according to local tradition the Devil would spend a few months each year, enjoying himself by pestering the stuirteagan ('black- headed gulls') that nested there.

Donald intended to emigrate to Australia with a group of the inhabitants of Inbhir Fhèisidh (Inver Feshie, 'confluence of the river of the boggy haugh') but remained in Badenoch. The departure of so many people from Kingussie on Latha Fèill Chaluim Cille (St. Columba's Feast-day), 9th June 1838, inspired his song 'Guma Slàn do na Fearaibh' ('Farewell to the Men'). The party had to walk to Oban where they took a ship to Glasgow and ultimately arrived in Sydney, Australia, on the 15th of September:

Nuair a dh'fhàgas sinn an t-àit' seo, cha chuir iad mòr-mhàl
oirnn
'S cha bhi an Fhèill Màrtainn cur nàire nar gruaidh.
Guma slàn do na fearaibh thèid thairis a' chuan.

Gum fàg sinn an tìr seo, cha chinnich aon nì ann
Tha 'm buntàt' air dol dhìth ann 's cha chinn iad le fuachd.
Guma slàn do na fearaibh thèid thairis a' chuan.

When we leave this country, we'll pay much less rent, and Martinmas won't bring shame to our cheeks. Farewell to the men who are going over the sea.

We'll leave this land where nothing will grow, the potatoes are ruined, and they won't sprout with the cold. Farewell to the men who are going over the sea.

Caibideil 13: *Chapter 13*

Moireibh, Obar Dheathain, Siorrachd Obar Dheathain, Aonghas is Baile Dhùn Dè: *Moray, Aberdeen City, Aberdeenshire, Angus and The City of Dundee*

Eastwards over the mountains of the Monadh Ruadh, now called the Cairngorms, lie the local authority areas of Moireibh (Moray), Obar Dheathain (Aberdeen City), Siorrachd Obar Dheathain (Aberdeenshire), Aonghas (Angus) and Baile Dhùn Dè (the City of Dundee). This area of five local councils straddles the northeast of Scotland and the great central massif of the Cairngorms and their fringing coastal plains. By far the largest in area is Siorrachd Obar Dheathain.

Siorrachd Obar Dheathain (Aberdeenshire, 'mouth of the River Don [a deity]') takes its name from the former County of Aberdeen, that had substantially different boundaries. The Aberdeenshire Council area includes the historic counties of Aberdeenshire (but not the City of Aberdeen); Cinn Chàrdainn (Kincardineshire, 'head of the copse'), also known as A' Mhaoirne (The Mearns, 'the stewartry'); and part of Banbh (Banff). Banbh, like Eilg, Èireann, and Fòtla, was a poetic name for Ireland.

One of Bartholomew's first thematic maps of 1895 shows the prevalence of Gaelic in Scotland with light pockets of Gaelic speakers in Aberdeenshire where it was spoken by between five percent and a quarter of the population. More specifically, in 1881, almost 20% of the population of the parish of Crathie and Braemar spoke Gaelic habitually. To the west of the river Quoich, the proportion was over two-thirds, and in the village of Inverey 87 out of the 104 residents spoke Gaelic. By then, substantial clearance of the population had taken place.

In 1726, Lord Grange, the younger brother of 'Bobbin Jock' of the '15. cleared Glen Lui of its people. Sir Robert Gordon created the Balmoral deer forest in 1833. Some of the worst clearances in Aberdeenshire occurred on the land owned by the Earl of Fife. When Glen Ey was cleared by him around 1840 to make way for a deer forest, an old woman reputedly cursed him and said he would never shoot another stag while she lived. He died suddenly at breakfast in 1847 when a fish bone caught in his throat. Queen Victoria leased the estate the following year. The last native speaker of Aberdeenshire Gaelic, Jean Bain, died in 1984.

Bàs Dhiarmaid: *The Death of Diarmaid*

Inland access from the South into Aberdeenshire is via Gleann Sìth (Glenshee, 'fairy glen'). At the head of the glen, the mountain Beinn Ghulbainn ('beak mountain') was the setting for a hunting party which proved fatal to Diarmad, one of the Fingalian heroes. Strangers here would have in the past been shown the den of the prey, a wild boar, a spring called Tobar nam Fiann ('well of the Fingalians') and a small lake called Loch an Tuirc ('boar's loch'). Here also was Diarmaid's grave in Tulach Dhiarmaid ('Diarmaid's hillock').

The alleged scene of the death of Diarmad is located in many places from Tiree to Sutherland. It was claimed to be in Easter Ross, Kintail, Brae Lochaber, Knapdale in Argyll and in Skye, but the strongest tradition remains here in Glen Shee. The tales all say that Fionn killed him because Grainne, his lover, had eloped with Diarmad. A successful hunt had killed a huge boar. Fionn, aware that the boar's hide hid a poisonous bristle, asked Diarmad to measure out the length of the slain beast by pacing along its back. Diarmad, walking with the grain of the bristle, safely completed the task but the implacable Fionn asked him to measure again, this time pacing against the grain of the hide. Inevitably, the poisonous bristle pierced the hero's only vulnerable part, his heel. As the boar's poison took effect, Diarmad pled in vain for a drink from Fionn's magic cup of healing. 'Bàs Dhiarmaid' ('The Death of Diarmaid') relates the tragic tale:

Èistibh beag mas àill leibh laoidh
Air a' chuideachd chaoimh so chuaidh,
Air Gràinne agus air Fionn fial
'S air mac O Duibhne nan sgeul truagh.
'N Gleann Sìth sin 's an gleann ra thaobh,
Far 'm bu bhinn guth fèidh is loin,
Far am minic an robh 'n Fhiann
An ear 's an iar an diaidh an con.

A Dhiarmaid na freagair an fhaghaid
'S na tadhail am fiadhach brèige;
Na rach teann air Fionn mac Cumhaill
O's cumhadh leis bhith gun chèile.
Thuit se an sin fo chreuchd,
Mac O Duibhne, ciabh nan cleachd,
Sàr mhac fulangach nam Fiann
Air an tulaich siar fa-dheas.

Listen a little while if you want to hear a lay about this kindly company now long gone, about Gràinne and the generous Fionn and about O Duibhne's son of the tragic tales. Yonder Glen Shee and the glen beside it, where the voice of stag and elk sounded sweet, where the Fèinn were ever hither and thither after their hounds.

Diarmaid, do not join the pursuit, do not take part in the false hunt; do not go near Fionn mac Cumhaill, since he finds it sad to be without a spouse. He fell there wounded, the curly-haired son of O Duibhne, the great long-suffering youth of the Fèinn, on that hillock to the south-west.

On the south side of the river Dee, some kilometres below Ballater stands the farmhouse of Baile Leitreach (Ballaterach, 'slope farm'), where George Gordon, Lord Byron:

roved as a young Highlander, o'er the dark heath.

In 1807, recalling those halcyon days, he wrote the poem 'Lachin y Gair', in essence about childhood, ancestry and sense of place. It contains the oft-quoted epithet, 'Brave Caledonia'. He begins his poem by contrasting the gentrified landscapes of southern England with the more rugged Highlands:

Away, ye gay landscapes, ye gardens of roses!
In you let the minions of luxury rove;
Restore to me the rocks, where the snow-flake reposes,

Though still they are sacred to freedom and love:
Yet, Caledonia, belov'd are thy mountains,
Round their white summits though elements war;
Though cataracts foam 'stead of smooth-flowing
fountains,
I sigh for the valley of dark Loch na Gar.

The name Lachin y Gair, now Lochnagar, probably comes from Lochan na Gàire ('little loch of the noisy sound'). This name seems to refer to the loch in the eastern corrie of Lochnagar. The mountain itself is Beinn nan Cìochan ('mountain of the breasts'). There are a few stories as to how the change of name came about, but the best is probably about the ghillie who was too embarrassed to tell Queen Victoria the real name of the mountain and instead referred to it by the loch's name, hence Lochnagar.

Bràigh Mhàrr is Baile Mhorail: *Braemar and Balmoral*

From Ballater, Braemar can be readily reached. Once known as Ceann na Drochaide (Kindrochit, 'bridge end'), the town has taken the wider area name of Bràigh Mhàrr ('upland of Marr') and the two town names, Achadh an Droighinn (Auchendryne, 'field with the thorn bush') on the west side of Clunie Water and The Castleton on the east side of the river, have disappeared. The Castleton was so named because it was reputed to contain the 11th-century ruins of a hunting lodge built for Malcolm Canmore. This land was originally held by the Farquharsons, once the keepers of the king's forests of Braemar, Cromar and Strathdee, but James Farquharson of Inverey sold that land along with Auchendryne to the 2nd Earl of Fife in 1798. The Farquharson's Invercauld Trust still owns 120,685 acres around Braemar.

Braemar is associated with a tradition of the killing of the last wolf in Scotland. It was shot either at Seann Bhaile (Shenval, 'old village'), near Braemar, or at Allt a' Mhadaidh-allaidh ('stream of the wolf') near Derry Lodge in the Forest of Mar. But there is also a story of Sliochd a' Mhadaidh-allaidh ('race of the wolf'). According to tradition, a child of a MacDonald widow from Braemar was snatched away by a wolf that then suckled the boy. The youth was returned to mankind and, as a writer, put it:

He took no offence at his re-establishment among the human race ... but he had a decided objection to return to his mother, choosing rather the society of a young damsel of his captor's family ... He reproached that mother in after-time thus:

A bhean ud anns a' bhaile thall,
Chuir coin a' bhaile air mo lorg
Ged do dh' òl mi bainne do chìche,
Is laigh mi naoi mìos nad bholg.

Wife of the farm yonder,
You put the dogs of the town on my track,
Though I drank the milk of your breast,
And lay nine months in your womb.

A report of about 1870 claims that there were three families in Braemar who traced descent from that character.

Staging a hunt was an ancient subterfuge for a military raid or for inciting rebellion. John Erskine, Earl of Mar (1675-1722), 'Bobbin' Jock', organised the last great timcheall ('tinchel'), known as the 'the Hunting of Mar', to disguise preparations for the 1715 Jacobite Rising. All the Jacobite leaders still loyal to the exiled Stewart kings met at Inbhir Call (Invercauld, 'hazel estuary') near Braemar, with 27 clan chiefs present. The plan and campaign logistics for the Rising were prepared under the pretence of "a Hunting in his own Country", as Mar referred to it. The standard of King James VIII, the 'Old Pretender', was raised on the Braes of Mar on 6th September and eventually, some 20,000 men joined Mar's forces.

The hunting method deployed in a tinchel consisted of a ring of beaters who surrounded a chosen area and gradually closed in on their quarry in specially constructed eilreigean (elricks, 'deer traps'). John Taylor, the self-styled 'Water Poet' who visited Mar in 1618, described the process as follows:

> The manner of hunting is this... [the hunters]... doe lie down on the ground till those foresaid scouts which are called the tinckhell doe bring down the deer.

Deerhounds were an indispensable part of the hunt and the best were described thus:

> Gnos mar chuaille,
> Cluas mar dhuilleach,
> Earball mu 'n speir,
> 'S an speir mar chorran.
>
> *Muzzle like club, ear like leaf, tail to the hough, and hough like sickle.*

After the 1715 Rising, the timcheall was banned. As Thomas Pennant explained some 60 years later:

> … hunting meetings, among the great men, were often the preludes to rebellion; for under that pretence they collected great bodies of men without suspicion, which at length occasioned an act of parlement (sic) prohibiting such dangerous assemblies.

John Brown (1826-1883), the Gaelic-speaking personal attendant and favourite of Queen Victoria, was born in Craichidh Àird (Crathienaird, 'high crathie', probably meaning 'shaking place'). He was appreciated by many, including the Queen, for his competence and companionship and resented by others for his influence and informal manner. Though he started work as a ghillie ('outdoor servant') at Balmoral Castle, he became a good friend to Queen Victoria. When he died at Windsor Castle in 1883, Victoria wrote to the poet Alfred Tennyson praising her faithful servant:

> He had no thought but for me, my welfare, my comfort, my safety, my happiness. Courageous, unselfish, totally disinterested, discreet to the highest degree, speaking the truth fearlessly and telling me what he thought and considered to be 'just and right,' without flattery and without saying what would be pleasing if he did not think it right … The comfort of my daily life is gone …

Balmoral is sited on Uisge Dhè (River Dee), a name recorded in the 2nd century AD in the work of Claudius Ptolemy, the Alexandrian geographer, as Deva, meaning Goddess, indicating a divine status for the river. There are several other rivers of the same name, with similar derivations, throughout Britain. A list of the genuinely old, pool-specific names on the River Dee divided the river into three sections.

In section one, from Braemar to Ballater, which was Gaelic-speaking until the 19th century, only one name in ten is English. Here, one of the largest pools in the river, Poll Mòrail ('majestic pool'), has given its name to the adjacent bank, now known as Balmoral.

In section two from Ballater to Aboyne, Gaelic-speaking until perhaps 1600, about half of the names are English, while in the third section, from Aboyne to Aberdeen, nine out of ten of the names are English.

An Còirneal Dubh: *The Black Colonel*

A legendary hero on Upper Deeside was An Còirneal Dubh ('the Black Colonel'), Iain MacFhearchair Inbhir Eidh (John Farquharson, 3rd of Inverey). This family were called Clann Mhic Sheumais, after Seumas (James), their founder. The Black Colonel is believed to have been born about 1642 and was known as 'black' because of his colouring, though the epithet could just as well have been applied to his tempestuous life.

He was involved in the Jacobite Rising of 1689 and had many narrow escapes from Government troops. Once his enemies burnt his castle but he escaped, stark naked, and with a mighty leap he and his horse cleared the swollen River Ey. The hump-backed bridge over the Ey where he jumped is known as Drochaid an Leum ('bridge of the leap'). 'Anna Bhuidh' Bhàn' ('Fair, Yellow-haired Anna') composed upon the death of his mistress, is the only poem attributed with certainty to the Black Colonel:

> Ochadan 's shiubhail Anna
> Dh'fhàg siud mise car tamaill fo bhròn;
> A-chaoidh cha tèid i às m'aire
> Gus am fàs mi buileach reòthta.

Nuair thig mi staigh an dùthaich
Bidh mo shùil air Ruigh' an t-Seilich
'S nuair thig mi staigh an dùthaich
Bidh mi 'g amharc an ùir sam beil i.

Nach truagh nach eil Mairead
Air charbad air a bheil Anna.

Alas Anna has died. That has left me sorrowful for a while.
She will never depart from my mind until I am frozen in death.

When I come in to the land my eye is always on Ruigh' an t-Seilich; when I come in by the land I always look at the earth where she is buried.

What a pity Mairead isn't on Anna's bier.

Apparently, Mairead was his wife.

John Farquharson, the parish minister of Strathglass was a grandnephew of the Black Colonel. Some years before the 1745 Rising, incensed by the treatment meted out by Simon Fraser of Lovat to one of his servants, Farquharson composed the poem 'A' Mhic Shimidh, mosgail à d' shuain' ('Lovat's Warning'). It contains the prophetic words:

'Mhic Shimidh, mosgail à d' shuain.
Èirich suas 'us cuimhnich d' olc,
Mar' rinn thu dò-bheart na' s leòr,
Tha deireadh do sgeòil a' teannadh ort

Tha fàidheachd a' tighinn gu teach.
Gun dèanar creach ort 'us tòir,
Gum faicear do cholann gun cheann.
'S gum bi do chlann mhaoth gun treòir.

Lovat, rise up from your sleep, rise up and remember your wickedness.
How you made more than enough mischief; the end of your tale is approaching you.

There is a prophecy coming to pass, that you will be plundered and pursued, that your body will be seen without its head and that your young children will be without guidance.

Simon Fraser was publicly beheaded on Tower Hill in London in 1747.

Iarla Mhàirr: *The Earl of Mar*

Northeast of the Braemar area and west of Alford (a tautological combination of 'ath' and 'ford', both meaning 'ford' in Gaelic and Scots respectively), on the river Don, is Ceann Droma (Kildrummy, 'at the ridge-end'). This area was Gaelic-speaking from c.800 to c.1600. The castle here was used by Gaelic-speaking nobles for most of its 500-year existence. At the beginning of the 15th century, it was the place of lordship of Alexander Stewart, the Earl of Mar. The mid-17th century *History of the MacDonalds*, written using Gaelic sources, contains an account of Mar's adventures following the Battle of Inverlochy in 1431, where he was defeated by Donald Balloch:

> The Earl of Mar was wounded in the thigh by an arrow and was in the hills for two nights, exhausted and hungry. At last, he met some women who had nothing to offer but barley meal. He accepted it gratefully and having no dish, removed his shoe, as a receptacle for the meal with water. He uttered the following proverb:

Is maith an còcaire an t-acras
Is mairg a ni tailceas air biadh;
Fuarag eòrna à sàil mo bhròige,
Biadh as fheàrr a fhuair mi riamh.

Hunger is a good cook,
Woe to him who scorns food;
Barley brose made in my shoe
Is the best food I ever got.

The earl reached the small hut of an Irishman, called Obirrin. According to custom he was received hospitably and his host cleaned and washed his wound. That night he could not sleep for the cold, so Obirrin warmed a cow's hide and wrapped it around the earl. The following day as he took his leave, the Earl of Mar told Obirrin that should matters get tricky for him he should go to Killdrummy Castle and ask for Alexander Stewart. If he did so, he would ensure that he would be rewarded for his kindness to him. This indeed happened and Obirrin went to Kildrummy and asked to speak to Alexander Stewart. The porter said he was a fool, but Obirrin continued to knock and the Earl of Mar heard the noise. He asked who was at the gate and the porter replied that there was a fool enquiring for Alexander Stewart. The Earl, recognising him, received him warmly and then composed to him the following verse:

> Ionmhuinn am firein tha muigh,
> O' Birinn as a' Bhriagaich;
> Bha mi oidhche ann a thigh
> Air mhóran bidh, ach beag aodaich.
>
> *Beloved the little person without,*
> *O' Byrne out from Briagach;*
> *I was a night in his house*
> *Of much food, but few clothes.*

Although there is some chronological uncertainty, Gaelic tradition correctly claims Alexander Stewart as a Gaelic speaker. His grandfather Robert II and his cousin Robert III would have been Gaelic speakers, since their lands of Carrick in Ayrshire, where they spent most of their time, were Gaelic-speaking. His father, Alasdair Mòr mac an Rìgh ('Great Alexander, son of the King'), was Earl of Buchan and the so-called 'Wolf of Badenoch' and his mother Mairead nic Eachainn (Margaret, 'daughter of Hector') spoke Gaelic.

Some 40 kilometres to the northeast of Kildrummy, and about twenty kilometres north of Aberdeen, is the Harlaw monument. This commemorates a nearby battle where the forces of Donald, Lord of the Isles, and the Earl of Mar fought each other to a standstill on 24th July 1411. Donald lost some 900 men, Mar a third fewer. Although there was no decisive victor, Mar claimed a strategic victory since it stopped Donald's campaign against the Earl's territory of Buchan. The event is known in Gaelic as Cath Gairbheach (Battle of the Garioch, 'place of roughness') and in English was often referred to as 'Red Harlaw', as a result of the terrible slaughter.

Brosnachadh-catha Chlann Dòmhnaill: *The Rallying Song of Clan Donald*

The Clan Donald bard Lachlann Mòr MacMhuirich (Great Lachlan MacVurich) is reputed to have composed 'Brosnachadh-catha Chlann Dòmhnaill' ('The Rallying Song of Clan Donald'). What makes this a remarkable composition is its format: each line contains two describing words, and each successive pair of lines begins with the same letter while remaining within the seven-syllable format of each line. Lachlann works through the entire Gaelic alphabet in sequence. The 'Brosnachadh' has several versions; here is an extract from the text, edited and translated by Derick Thomson:

A Chlanna Cuinn, cuimhnichibh
Cruas an àm na h-iorghaile:
Gu h-àirneach, gu h-arranta,
Gu h-athlamh, gu h-allanta,
Gu beòdha, gu barramhail,
Gu brìoghmhor, gu buan-fheargach,
Gu calma, gu curanta,
Gu cròdha, gu cath-bhuadhach,
Gu dùr is gu dàsannach,
Gu dian is gu deagh-fhulang ...

Children of Conn, recall now
Courage in time of combat:
Agile, ambitious,
Be bold, beautiful,
Brawny, belligerent,
Contumacious, courageous,
Clever, combative,
Deliberate, destructive,
Deadly, enduring,

It flows through all eighteen letters of the alphabet to reach the last letter 'u':

> Gu h-urlamh, gu h-ùr-mhaiseach …
>
> *Youthful and yearning …*

The 'Brosnachadh' may be the earliest metrical text in vernacular Gaelic as distinct from the formal literary language of Classical Gaelic, a claim Thomson was inclined to accept. However, it may just possibly be a later re-imagining, recalling the glory days of Clan Donald and the Lordship of the Isles.

Despite a century of determined efforts to the contrary, most historians still view the battle as an existential struggle for civilisation. As one has recently stated: the battle is still presented as:

> … a clash between the Celtic 'barbarity' of the Highlands and the Saxon 'civility' of the Lowlands. By sacrificing their lives to halt Donald of the Isles' Attila-like march into Aberdeenshire, the noble knights of the North-East not only prevented the sack of their burgh, but actually preserved Scottish civilisation from savage yet 'unknown' Highland 'terrors' which threatened to envelop the nation in darkness.

But the Earl of Mar was a cultured Gael and his opponent Donald, Lord of the Isles, the reputed Highland barbarian, was an undergraduate at Oxford University. This stereotyping is brought into stark relief when one considers that it was at the Abbey of Deer only 40 kilometres away to the northeast that a 10th-century Latin Gospel Book was written. With early 12th-century additions in Latin and Scottish Gaelic, these texts represent the earliest surviving written use of Gaelic in Scotland and are important for the light they shed on the development of Gaelic.

Sìleas na Ceapaich: *Cicily of Keppoch*

To the north and west is Baile Dhòrnaidh (Baldornie, 'farm of pebbly place'), the home of Sìleas na Ceapaich (Cicely MacDonald of Keppoch) (c.1660-c.1729). Her father, Gilleasbaig, was the 15th chief of the MacDonalds of Keppoch. Around 1685, she married Alexander Gordon of Camdell and moved to Baldornie. 23 poems composed by her or ascribed to her survive, including a number on the 1715 Jacobite Rising. In one song, 'Tha mi nam chadal, na dùisgibh mi' ('I am asleep, don't wake me'), her strong Jacobite sympathies are made clear:

'S e rìgh na muice
'S na Cuigse, Rìgh Deòrsa,
Is fada nur cadal gun dùsgadh sibh;
Mas tig oirnn an t-Samhainn,
Bidh amhach sna còrdaibh,
Is fada nur cadal gun dùsgadh sibh;
Nan èireadh sibh suas,
Ann an cruadal 's an duinealas,
Eadar ìslean is uaislean,
Thuath agus chumanta,
Sgiùrsadh sibh uaibh e,
Rìgh fuadain nach buineadh dhuinn,
Is dhèanainn an cadal gu sunndach leibh.

King George is the king of pigs and Whigs, you have been a long time asleep; before Hallowtide comes his neck will be in cords, you have been a long time asleep. If you were to rise up with courage and manliness, both nobles and vassals, tenantry and common folk, you would sweep him away from you, an alien king who doesn't belong to us, and I would joyfully join you in sleep.

Bràigh Aonghais: *Upland of Angus*

In 1515, William MacIntosh of MacIntosh was assassinated by his own clansmen, including John Roy MacLachlan, his near cousin. William's brother Lachlan sent a posse of twenty men in pursuit of the assassins. It traced the fugitives through Ross, Caithness, Strathnaver, Assynt, Lochalsh, Abertarff, Strathspey, Strathdee and to Glenesk, a distance of over 1,000 kilometres. In the valley of the River North Esk, one of the narrow glens on both sides of the Perthshire/Angus boundary, known as Bràigh Aonghais ('upland of Angus'), John Roy and his men were all killed. The pursuit described is in essence a circumnavigation of what was then Gaelic-speaking mainland Scotland.

The Braes of Angus, Glen Esk and Glen Isla were strongly Gaelic-speaking then, but the language was probably already in retreat by the end of the 18th century. In 1891, about one in five of the population still spoke Gaelic. A song ''S mòr mo mhulad' ('Great is my sorrow') composed by a Robertson and published in 1786 in an anthology compiled by John Gillies of Perth originates in Glen Isla, and is perhaps the most south-easterly Gaelic composition known. It seems that Robertson's sweetheart lived in Braemar and he had to make a long journey to meet her:

'S iom' oidhche anmoch a thug mo mheanma
Mi don ghleann ud thall.

Shnàmhainn thairis gun ràmh no darach,
Nam biodh mo leannan thall.

Sruth ga chaisid cha chùm air ais mi
Nam biodh mo leachd fo thuinn.

Shiùbhlainn giùthsaich ri oidhche dhùbh-dhoirch
Ge do bhiodh an driùchda trom.

Cha b' ann air mhèirle a bheirinn ionnsaigh
Ghlacainn mo ghràdh air làimh.

Many a night my imagination took me to yonder glen.

I would swim across without oar or ship if my love were over there.

The swiftest flowing current would not hold me back if my destination were under waves.

I would traverse pine forests in the blackest of nights even though the dew was heavy.

It wouldn't be as a thief that I would make the attempt. I would take my love by the hand.

The Admirable Crichton

Another 40 kilometres south, this time to the west, is Cluainidh (Clunie, 'meadow place') in Highland Perthshire, some seven kilometres west of Blàr Ghobharaidh (Blairgowrie, 'goat plain'). James Crichton, known as the Admirable Crichton, was born in 1560 and spent his childhood at Clunie Castle on an island in the Loch of Clunie. He was one of the most gifted individuals of the 16th century; a polymath, noted for his extraordinary accomplishments in languages, the arts and sciences. He was taught by the Gaelic scholar, politician and poet George Buchanan (1506-1582). By the age of twenty, Crichton was fluent in more than twelve languages, as well as being an accomplished horseman, fencer, singer, musician, orator and debater.

In a feat of intellectual bravura, he challenged the professors of the Collège de Navarre in Paris to pose any question on any science or liberal arts subject in Arabic, Dutch, English, French, Greek, Hebrew, Italian, Latin, Slavonic, Spanish, or Syriac. It is said that throughout the long day, the scholars failed to stump Crichton on any question they threw at him. Gaelic should be added to that list of languages, since it is inconceivable that James was not conversant with it, having been raised within a completely Gaelic area and taught by a native Gaelic-speaking tutor.

Blairgowrie still boasts Gaelic street names and a Gaelic choir.

Caibideil 14: *Chapter 14*

Peairt agus Ceann Rois, Siorrachdan Chlach Mhanainn agus Fiobha:

Perth and Kinross, Clackmannan and Fife

South of Kingussie the land rises to Druim Uachdair (Drumochter, 'ridge of the high ground') and the next major boundary, once the estate march between the great Badenoch and Atholl earldoms of the past. To the south is the unitary authority area of Peairt & Ceann Rois (Perth & Kinross). This boundary area was often referred to as Druim Uachdair nam Bò ('Drumochter of the cattle') and the road breasts the pass at 493 metres. A Panama-based firm, Compania Financiera Waterville, owns 22,869 hectares of Scotland, including Drumochter. Just 430 individuals own more than half of Scotland's non-public land. In Norway, seven times the size of Scotland, there are only 23 estates larger than 10,000 hectares. In Scotland, there is a gross i.e.144.

Most of the parishes in this area were part of the district commonly known as Garbh Chrìochan Pheairt ('rough bounds of Perthshire') or Highland Perthshire. Up to the Second World War, Gaelic held its ground here quite successfully. One reason for this may have been the insistence of the Duke of Atholl that the language was taught in his estate schools, in direct contrast to public education policy.

Rapidly losing height, the road enters the broad sweep of the valley cut by the river Garaidh (Garry, 'noisy one'). This is Blàr Athaill (Blair Atholl, 'plain of Atholl'). The name Athall derives from the Old Irish Ath-fhotla, or 'New Ireland', 'Fotla' being a traditional name for Ireland, although 'ford of Ireland' is also a suggested derivation. The debate as to which is truly correct does not diminish the bravura of the colonising Scots in naming this new-won land in memory of their Irish homeland.

As their minibus departs from Inverness, I have heard tourists being informed by their driver/guide that there was nothing to say about the stretch of land between that point and Perth, so they might as well sleep. They were also told that Atholl was the last point where they would see Gaelic names. Neither statement is true as will become clear.

Madaidhean-allaidh: *Wolves*

Wolves were once considered such a scourge that Donnchadh Reamhar ('fat Duncan') (born c.1275) founder of Clann Donnchaidh (Clan Robertson) was rewarded with land here after clearing the Plain of Atholl of them. It was said that wolves feasted on newly buried corpses they unearthed in graveyards. Here they once buried the dead in coffins made of flagstones to protect bodies from such depredations. People in other places had to bury their dead in burial islands. In *The Book of the Dean of Lismore* there is a plea to bring destruction to the menace of wolves, then plaguing the Highlands. Composed around 1450 by Giolla Críost Táilliúr (Gilchrist Taylor), it is entitled 'Beannuigh do Theaghlach, a Thríonóid' ('O Trinity, Bless your People'):

> Sgamhach conach aillse is acais
> ar lucht marbhtha na ngreagh nglas;
> Mac Dé le croidhe nau
> snoidheadh an chuain ainmheach as.
>
> *May murrain, rabies, cancer, poison strike the slaughterers of the grey herds; may God's son with new purpose lop away that misshapen brood.*

Documentary evidence shows that wolves survived until around 1680. But there are accounts, all largely similar, of the last wolf being shot some 70 years later in many areas, indicating myth rather than actual events. Several factors led to the wolf's extinction, including the loss of woodlands and a decrease in the red deer population. That decrease has been ruinously reversed; deer numbers are now probably ten times higher than they were in 1750. Environmentalists promote the wolf's return to control the deer and the serious detrimental impact of such numbers.

Diùc Athaill: *The Duke of Atholl*

The plain of Atholl is dominated by Caisteal Bhlàir (Blair Castle, 'castle of the plain'), originally a Comyn stronghold. The Murrays of Tullibardine gained the estate in 1629. The current Duke of Atholl is Bruce Murray, a cattle farmer in Australia, although trustees run the 50,231 hectare estate around Blair Castle. The Murrays' titles are well-known to all lovers of Gaelic choral singing since the coveted top prize at the annual Royal National Mod choral competitions is Sgiath MhicShimidh agus Mhorair Thulaich Bhàrdainn (the Lovat and Tullibardine Shield).

Blair Castle has strong associations with the exiled Stewarts' efforts to regain their throne. It was here in 1689 that the Jacobite leader, Ian Dubh nan Cath ('Dark John of the battles', John Graham of Claverhouse), died of his wounds. His breastplate, holed by a lead musket ball, is displayed at the castle. Tradition suggests supernatural involvement and the use of a silver ball to kill him. His remains are interred in St. Bride's, a church dedicated to the most important of all the Celtic Church's saints and the potent Celtic goddess, Brìghde. The church once served the original village but the inhabitants were cleared off the ground as part of 19th century improvements to the castle's designed landscape.

There are many examples of the divided loyalties of Scots in responding to Prince Charles' efforts in 1745 to restore the British throne to his father, titularly James the III, and this was spectacularly so in the Murray family. Lord George was commander of the Prince's army, while his brother William remained a resolute supporter of the Government, despite being besieged here by his brother's forces for seventeen days. The castle survived that siege and the attention of Cumberland's vengeful army, who spared it the usual torching meted out to the homes of those who were 'out' with the Prince.

In the post-1746 British state, the Gaelic aristocracy turned to soldiering. There was an unofficial competition between the ducal families of Atholl and Argyll for control of patronage in the developing British-Highland military system, a very lucrative business. Despite ducal enthusiasm, there was a history of anti-recruitment sentiment in Blair Atholl in the 1770s. The Duke's promise of land in return for military service was rejected by his tenants. It was stated that:

> perpetual possession of their lands … was promised them, if they would only raise a contingent equal to a man from each family. Some consented, but the majority, [chose] not to be dragged … into a war of which they knew neither the beginning nor the end.

Using violence, the Duke eventually raised the regiment but, when peace came, it is claimed that:

> the Duke, as if he had been a trafficker in slaves, was only prevented from selling them to the East India Company by the rising mutiny of the regiment.

Small wonder then that the Blair Atholl entry in the *OSA* of 1799 stated that the gentlemen were tall and handsome and fond of a military life, but the common people had learned to despise a soldier's pay and to hate a life of servitude. Many a would-be recruit took to the hills.

Gàidheil san Arm: *Gaels in the Armed Forces*

However, many Gaels did fight in America during the Seven Years' War of 1757 to 1763. Granted land for their services, their settlements formed a bridge for an influx of Highlanders from 1768 to the beginning of the American War of Independence. They tended to support the Crown rather than risk losing what they had just gained by loyal service. But they also expected to be rewarded accordingly. Life in the Highlands was becoming increasingly difficult; songs of this period complain that the nation needed the soldiers who now had no alternative save emigration.

One such Gaelic recruit was Adhamh MacFhearghais (Adam Ferguson), also known as Ferguson of Raith (1723-1816), a Scottish philosopher and historian of the Scottish Enlightenment. He was born at Lag an Ràtha (Logierait, 'hollow of the fort') and educated at the University of St Andrews. Being a Gaelic speaker, he was an obvious choice as deputy chaplain of the 42nd Regiment, The Black Watch. At dawn on 21st March 1801, Sir Ralph Abercrombie's army, including the 42nd, was close to Alexandria in Egypt when it was attacked by the French Armée d' Orient. For five hours, repeated French assaults were beaten back until they withdrew to Alexandria which subsequently surrendered. The contribution of Gaelic Highland soldiers to the victory in Egypt was recognised following the campaign.

Ferguson's successor as chaplain of the Black Watch, Reverend Seumas MacLagain (James McLagan) (1728-1805), composed a poem about the battle of Alexandria, 'Òran d' an Chath-bhuidhinn Rìoghail Ghàidhealaich' ('Song to the Royal Highland Regiment'). Here McLagan does more than simply repeat the allusions to the martial superiority of the Gaels that occur regularly in such poetry, but chose, as Sir Walter Scott did, to counter the distortions of John Pinkerton (1758-1826) who had sought to erase all Celtic elements from Scotland's history. In part, his work led to the Gothic versus Celtic debate raging at the time of the battle. Perhaps Pinkerton's most infamous characterisation of the Gaels was that they were:

> a dishonoured, timid, filthy, ignorant, and degraded race.

McLagan's stanza is a mild criticism of those 'Goths' denigrating the Gaels:

Ar gaisg do dhùisg dhuinn mi-rùn,
Nan Gotach fiata, searbh,
Seadh Iarmad Ghael, tha lìonmhor,
A' sàth na'r bian an calg.
Nis nì 'm bheil Got a sgrìobhas,
Nach bheil le miosgain garg,
Do nach sop-reic ar riabadh,
Thoirt fiach d' a fharuisg bhorb.

Our heroism awakened the ill-will
Of the wild, bitter Goths,
Indeed offspring of the Gaels, many are
The stabs in our hide with their spears.
Now there is not a Goth writing,
That is not bitter with malice,
Who would not make money out of our wounding,
To give value to their savage fakery.

Mairearead Ghriogarach: *Margaret MacGregor*

But poetry was not just the preserve of men as Mairearad Ghriogarach (Margaret MacGregor) (c.1750-c.1820) proved. Her songs were published as

Co-chruinneach dh'òrain thaghte Ghàeleach (*A Collection of Selected Gaelic Songs*) (1831). It contains 34 of her own compositions on a range of themes; poems about family members and family life give an insight into the late eighteenth-century Perthshire Gàidhealtachd, including the time she spent in school in Perth.

> Thug mi tamall an toiseach gun sprochd orm no sgìos,
> Rè an lath' ri fuaghail, gun smuaineach' air nì,
> Gus an cual' mi na dearcan bhith gan reic airson fiach,
> Ghrad-bhuail e m' bheachd-s' a Choir' a' Bhacaidh nam fiadh.
>
> 'S truagh gun bhith an Leitir Dhubh Lachlainn, 's ann a chaisginn mo mhiann,
> Gheibhte iomadach meas ann, gun neach a' farraid am prìs;
> Coir' gaolach mo chridhe am biodh iasg is sitheann gun dìth,
> Meadhg is bainne gun airceas, 's cha b' iad na drapagan tì.
>
> *For the first while, I was neither sad nor tired, sewing during the day, not thinking of anything, till I heard berries were being sold for a price, and I suddenly remembered Coir' a' Bhacaidh of the deer.*
>
> *It's so sad not being in Leitir Dhubh Lachlainn, that's where my desire would be met, many fruits could be got there without anyone asking their price; my beloved corrie where fish and venison are plentiful, whey and milk without scarcity rather than drops of tea.*

Beul-aithris Siorrachd Pheairt: *Perthshire Folklore*

An important effort to preserve Perthshire folklore was made by Lady Evelyn Stuart Murray (1868-1940), the youngest daughter of the 7th Duke of Atholl. Unusually for her time and position, Evelyn became a fluent Gaelic speaker and, during 1891, speedily collected 241 Gaelic tales and songs from local people. It has been written about her Gaelic folktale collection:

> it is the only one made by a woman, the only one to cover West Perthshire, the only one from which nothing was printed in the collector's lifetime and the only one which gives a proper idea of the richness and variety of the repertoire of both supernatural and historical legends, as well as longer folktales, to be found in one area.

There is uncertainty regarding her method of collection and her intentions for the materials. Although the Duke and his family had an enthusiasm for Gaelic on the estate, it appears that they thought that her activities were affecting her health and she was sent to convalesce in Switzerland. Her precocious and valuable initiative ceased, but fortunately, the family retained her manuscript and presented it to the School of Scottish Studies in 1958. In 2009, a book, *Tales from Highland Perthshire,* collected by Lady Evelyn, was published by the Scottish Gaelic Texts Society.

Coille Chnagaidh: *Killiecrankie*

Just south of Blair Castle, the river Garry cuts a deep defile through the hills. The area is known as Coille Cneaghaidh (Killiecrankie, possibly 'wood of the knobbly place', not, as is claimed by the NTS website, 'place of the woodpecker'). It was here that the opening salvos were fired in the ultimately futile Jacobite struggle that lasted from 1689 to 1746.

The Mull poet, Iain mac Ailein (John, 'Alan's son', John MacLean) (c.1655-1741) gives an account of the battle in a poem called 'Cath Raon Ruairidh' ('Battle of Rory's Portion') but in English, the Battle of Killiecrankie:

> Sgeula uam-sa mu Raon Ruairidh
> An robh na sluaigh a' còmhrag:
> Chuid as luaithe ghabh an ruaig dhiubh
> Bu daoine uaisle còir iad!
> Nan cùmte suas riu teine is luaidhe,
> Ris an d'fhuair iad fòghlam,
> 'S tearc a chruinnich riamh an uiread
> Gheibheadh turam beò dhiubh.

Air each glè-mhòr cruidheach ceumnach
Sleamhainn steudmhor mòdhar,
Cha bu lapach an aois macaibh
Ceannard feachd na Dreòllainn
Le bhuidheann threunfhear nach tais èirigh,
Ga robh cridhe treun mar leòmhann:
'S iad a dh'èigh an ciad ratreut
An dèidh luchd Beurla is cleòca.

I have reports about Killiecrankie where the forces were fighting; those that were soonest routed were the well-to-do nobles! If they had been provided with fire and lead in which they had been trained, rarely would there have gathered so many who would have received alive such honour.

On a great horse, shod and prancing, sleek, composed and stately, not puny for all his youthful years, the chief of the array of Mull men, with his troops of strongmen not slow in rising, whose hearts were mighty like lions: it is they who shouted the first pursuit after the men of English and cassocks.

Here the Jacobites ambushed the Government column with a Highland Charge as it marched northwards on the river bank. The Charge required them to rush at the enemy in an attempt to break their line of battle. Speed was essential, so they preferred to charge downhill and over firm ground; they removed their plaids for the same reason. Once within musket range, about 60 metres, they would shoot. Gun smoke from this mass discharge obscured their enemies' aim and the Highlanders avoided the enemy musket volley by crouching low to the ground immediately after firing. Then firearms were dropped and swords were drawn, the men making the final rush on the enemy line with a battle cry. This tactic gave the Jacobite forces a decisive victory over Government forces commanded by another Gaelic-speaking soldier, Seanailear Ùisdean MacAoidh Sgobharaidh (General Hugh MacKay of Scourie).

Associated with the battle is a widespread, though now little noticed, tradition of naming prominent chasms, particularly in Gaeldom, as a 'leap, a leum or a loup'. There are well over 130 locations across Scotland which have that place name element. This most publicised 'leap', The Soldier's Leap over the river Garry at Killiecrankie, is treated today as a unique historical event and it is also the site for essentialist tropes regarding the character of the Gaelic Highlander.

For example, one minibus driver/guide told his clients that the leap is seven metres wide and, although he expressed some doubts about it himself, he said that it was believable because:

> If I was being chased by a hundred ginger-haired, hairy Highlanders brandishing claymores, I would make that jump.

The welcometoscotland website, meanwhile, makes precise reference to a historical figure:

> It was here, after the Battle of Killiecrankie in 1689, that Donald MacBean, a soldier in the defeated government army, escaped his Jacobite pursuers by leaping across this 5.5m (18.5ft) rocky chasm,

while the mysteriousbritain website has an account which echoes the explanation of the guide quoted above in which:

> 'The Soldier's Leap' across the gorge is said to be where one of the government soldiers leapt to his escape … This is dubious, as the stretch is daunting to say the least, however, who knows what you can do with a horde of bloodthirsty Highlanders on your tail.

A tale in Gaelic about Killiecrankie has the fugitive, having leaped to safety, offering snuff to his pursuers. There are also echoes of Gaelic solidarity:

> At the Battle of Killiecrankie, a Highland soldier … leaped across the pass and when he had got to the other side he shouted to his pursuer: "Is gort a lean thu mi" *("You have followed me closely")*, to which the other, who turned out to be a Highlander, replied "Nan robh fios agam gu robh a' Ghàidhlig agad, cha do lean mi thu cho teann." *("If I had known that you spoke Gaelic, I would not have pursued you so hotly.")*

In an evident effort to elicit Royal sympathy, the informant added that:

> Queen Victoria ... was one day riding ... and W.D. was leading her pony. This was a man the Duke of Atholl kept as a kind of fool, but he was no fool, but awfully witty. Well, W. D. was telling Her Majesty every old story of interest about the place, and when he told her about the two Highland soldiers, she asked him what had made the man take such a dangerous leap ... to which he replied, "Because, your Majesty, they were going to shoot him." "A very good reason!" responded the Queen.

Baile Chloichrigh is Dùn Chailleann: *Pitlochry and Dunkeld*

The village name of Baile Chloichrigh (Pitlochry, 'village of stepping-stones') is of linguistic interest in that the English name has the older Pictish suffix *pett*, ('a land portion'). This area still had many Gaelic speakers in the 1881 census. Above the village at Maoilinn (Moulin, 'smooth, round hill'), is the site of what is reputedly the oldest church in Atholl, dedicated to St. Columba. At nearby Lag an Ràtha is where Alexander MacKenzie, the second prime minister of Canada, was born in 1822. He was the third of ten boys whose carpenter father died in 1836. MacKenzie was apprenticed at the age of thirteen as a stonemason to help support the family. He emigrated to Canada in 1842 to seek a better life.

The place name Dùn Chailleann (Dunkeld, 'fort of the Caledonians') records the ancient confederation of tribes that gave the later Roman Empire some trouble in the 3rd century AD – the Caledonii. They have given us Caledonia, the poetic name for Scotland used by Lord Byron and more recently in a folk song by singer and songwriter Dougie MacLean, a native of Dunblane, a little further to the south.

An earlier famous musician lived close to Dunkeld at Inbhir (Inver, 'river mouth'). Here was the home of Niall Gobha (Neil Gow) (1727-1807), a fiddler and composer. He started playing the fiddle at a young age but had to train as a weaver before he eventually gave up that trade to become a full-time musician. He was considered the best fiddle player in Perthshire, an area renowned for its musicians. It is said that, at age eighteen, he entered a competition being judged by John McCraw, a blind musician. John awarded him first prize and then claimed that he could detect Neil's style among 100 players. This remark came to the attention of the Duke of Atholl, who became Neil Gow's patron. Gow is credited with composing some 87 dance tunes, many forming the backbone of Scottish country dance music.

Peairt: *Perth*

The Gaelic name Peairt (Perth, 'copse') is from the older Brythonic word that the Romans modified to Bertha. This is the name of a new development to the west of the town, leapfrogging memory and erasing 1,500 years of Gaelic place-naming in favour of a Roman military designation that would have had the most ephemeral usage and connection to the place. Latin trumps Gaelic although it is dead and the latter most certainly is not. Gaelic was once very much alive in the town as the following saying attests:

> Trì iongantasan na h-Alba, drochaid Obar Pheallaidh, tobraichean Gleann Iucha is cluig Pheairt.
>
> *The three wonders of Scotland, Aberfeldy Bridge, the wells of Linlithgow and the bells of Perth.*

The terse official record for the year 1396 states that:

> ... on the 28th day of the month of September, at Perth, before Lord Robert King of Scotland ... there assembled for the purpose, since a firm peace could not be made 'twixt the two clans, to wit of Clanhay and Clanqwhwle, but slaughters and plunders were being committed daily on both sides, thirty of each side without armour of iron (mail) with axes, swords, and small knives, however, met by agreement, that one party might sweep away and destroy the other, and they engaged in combat. The whole party of Clanhay, except one, succumbed and died on the field, and of the other party, ten were left surviving.

This event is now known as the Battle of the North Inch of Perth. Although dubiety remains over the strange names of the combatants, they have been interpreted as Clan Cameron and the MacIntoshes of Clan Chattan. At the King's insistence, attempts had been made to get the two feuding clans to settle their differences amicably. This failed, however, and that led to the trial by combat. An amicable resolution of the clans' differences would have been a more sensible idea since they again fought each other at the Battle of Palm Sunday a few years later. This combat gave rise to the following saying:

Am fear nach cunntadh rium cha chunntainn ris.

I'll keep no reckoning with him that keeps no reckoning with me.

This was said by the Gobha Crom ('the hunched blacksmith'), Harry Wynd, at the fight on the Inch (Inch is the Anglicisation of innis, meaning 'haugh'). Having killed his man, Harry sat down to rest. The Clan Chattan chief came up and demanded the reason he was resting. Harry said he had fulfilled his bargain and earned his money.

"Him that serves me without counting his hours," said the chief, "I reward without reckoning wages."

The smith's riposte has led to the proverb:

Air a làimh fhèin, mar a bha 'n ceàrd sa chaonnaig.

For his own hand, as the smith was in the fight.

An Lia Fàil: *The Stone of Destiny*

Archaeological investigation suggests that Sgàin (Scone, possibly 'cleft'), a natural feature to the east, was a site of significance before 841 AD when Kenneth MacAlpin is supposed to have brought the Lia Fàil (the Stone of Destiny) here for use in coronations. The site itself was said to represent the voice of law and justice hence the saying:

Comhairle clag Sgàin, an rud nach buin dhut na buin dha.

Counsel of the bell of Scone, touch not what is not your own.

The stone is also known as the Coronation Stone in England. In 1296, Edward I purloined the Stone and had it incorporated into a specially designed coronation throne in Westminster Abbey. Doubt exists over that stone's authenticity, with claims that the monks hid the real stone and palmed Edward off with a substitute. It is also said that historic descriptions of a richly carved, dark stone do not match the present stone.

On Christmas Day 1950, four Glasgow University students removed the Stone from Westminster Abbey. The South Uist poet, Dòmhnall Ruadh Mac an t-Saoir, Bàrd Phàislig, (Donald MacIntyre, the Paisley Bard) wrote 'Òran na Cloiche' ('The Song of the Stone') to celebrate the event:

A' Chlach a chaidh a dhìth òirnn
air faighinn às an ìnean,
's gu deimhinne ma thill i
tha 'n nì sin gu math.

'S mo bheannachd air a' mhìlidh
a tharraing às a' chill i,
's a dh'aiseag, tha mi cinnteach,
i mìltean a-mach.

A' Chlach a bha sna linntean
a' fantainn aig ar sinnsreadh
bhon thàinig i dhan tìr seo
an tìm nam fear breac.

The Stone that was lost to us has been taken from their clutches and indeed it is back, that's a good thing.

My blessing on the heroes who dragged it from the church and transported it, I'm sure, many miles away.

The Stone that for centuries remained with our ancestors since it came to this land in the time of the speckled men.

Kay Matheson (1928-2013) from Inbhir Àsdail (Inverasdale, 'river mouth in the aspen valley') who became a teacher and Gaelic scholar, was one of the students involved in the removal of the Stone. It was ultimately recovered and was returned to Scotland in 1996 to Edinburgh Castle. It was used in Westminster for the coronation of King Charles III and, since March 2024, has been on permanent public display in Perth.

Siorrachdan Chlach Mhanainn agus Fìobha: *Clackmannan and Fife*

Travelling south from Perth, the next two local authority areas are Siorrachd Chlach Mhanainn agus Fìobha (Clackmannan and Fife).

The town of Dùn Phàrlain (Dunfermline), is a name thought to mean 'Pàrlan's Fort', though some claim it is the 'fort of the crooked burn'. The fort element refers to the castle in Pittencrieff Glen. The glen's name is an interesting compound of Pictish and Gaelic words. The prefix *pett* ('pit') was a Pictish land division, while the suffix is the Gaelic genitive chraoibh ('of the tree'). Evidently Gaelic as the naming language was extant in the area around 1050, although a 13th-century report indicates that its use was in decline.

Close by is Inbhir Chèitinn (Inverkeithing, possibly 'mouth of the wood river'). It was here that the Scots were defeated by Cromwellian forces in 1651. It was an even greater disaster for the Mull MacLeans. As they arrived on the battlefield, the Scottish right wing was already in retreat with the Cromwellians close behind them. Yet the MacLeans stood their ground. Enfiladed by cannon fire, trampled under horses' hooves and finally overcome by Cromwellian pike-men, they sold their lives dearly. It was during this battle that seven brothers died protecting their clan chief, each brother crying:

> "Fear eile airson Eachainn!"
>
> *"Another for Hector!"*

as they stepped forward. It became one of the Clan MacLean slogans. 750 men fell with few receiving quarter, the Cromwellians regarding Gaels as little more than vermin, and only 40 survivors eventually found their way back to Mull. Inverkeithing was as great a disaster for the MacLeans as Inverlochy had been six years earlier for the Argyllshire men. A generation later, many of the farms in Mull remained untenanted and the clan was so weakened by their sacrifice in defence of the nation that they were physically unable to defend themselves against the incessant pressure of the Duke of Argyll (to whom they owed a large sum of money). By 1685, the principal lands of Clan MacLean were in Campbell hands and Duart Castle was occupied by a detachment of regular government soldiers.

The elegy by Eachann Bacach MacIlleathainn ('lame Hector MacLean') to Sir Hector MacLean who fell at Inverkeithing contains the lines:

> Gur a h-iomadh laoch dòrn-gheal
> Chaidh an òrdugh mu d' bhrataich,
> Agus òganach sgiamhach
> Bha ga riasladh fo eachaibh.
> Agus spailp de dh'fhear-taighe
> Nach tug athadh dha phearsa,
> Toirt a chlaidheamh à duille
> Cheart cho guineach ri ealtainn.

> *Many fair-fisted heroes were arrayed around your flag, handsome youths who were mangled under horses and a spirited husband paying no attention to his looks unsheathing his razor-sharp sword.*

Some claim that the pipe tune 'Cumha Mhic an Tòisich' ('MacIntosh's Lament') commemorates these MacLeans, though the tune is the subject of much discussion. One hypothesis is that it commemorates Lachlann Beag, 14th Chief of MacIntosh, who was murdered by his half-brother's natural son in the 1520s. Another tradition tells that the chief's black stallion was cursed, leading to him being killed on his wedding day. His bride is said to have composed this lament:

> An leann thog iad gu d' bhanais
> Air t-fhalairidh bha e.
> Bha mi 'm bhrèidich 's 'm ghruagaich,

Am bhrèidich 's 'm ghruagaich,
Am bhrèidich 's 'm ghruagaich,
'S am bhanntraich san aon uair ud.

The beer arranged for your wedding was used at your funeral. I was a maiden, a married woman and a widow all at the same time.

Caibideil 15: *Chapter 15*

Lodainn an Iar agus Baile Dhùn Èideann: *West Lothian and The City of Edinburgh*

The great estuary of the Firth of Forth marks the next major boundary with the two authority areas of Lodainn an Iar agus Baile Dhùn Èideann (West Lothian and The City of Edinburgh) lying to the south.

The Queensferry Crossing bridges the estuary of Abhainn Foirthe (the Firth of Forth). The etymology of this name is obscure though perhaps deriving from an early Celtic descriptor, *vo-rit*, with an original sense of 'slow running'. It is known as the Abhainn Dubh ('black river') in its upper reaches. The island below the bridge crossing is Innis Garbh (Inchgarvie, 'rugged island'). On the south shore is the region of Machair Labhdaidh (Plain of Lothian).

Dùn Èideann: *Edinburgh*

Although less obvious in today's landscape, Gaelic and earlier P-Celtic tongues were heard around Edinburgh for many centuries. By the eighteenth century, the city's increasing population would have had many Gaelic-speaking Highlanders with one part of the city known as 'Little Ireland'. Leading institutions such as the University and the School of Scottish Studies the National Library of Scotland still draw many Gaels to the city.

The Romans knew the Castle Rock as Aluna ('rock place'), a name related to the Gaulish citadel Alesia, which contains the older Celtic word *al* (rock), as in the older name for Dumbarton, Alclud ('rock of Clyde'). But An t-Easbaig Sèon Carsuel (Bishop John Carswell) in 1565 wrote on the title-page of his book *Foirm na n-Urrnuidheadh* (*The Form of the Prayers*):

> Do bualadh gu a gcló i nDún Edin darab comh-ainm Dún Monaidh, a 24 là don Mhís Aipríl 1567 lé Roibeard Lekprevik.
>
> *Published in Edinburgh, sometimes known as Dùn Monaidh, on the 24 of April 1567 by Robert Lekprevik.*

Dùn Monaidh (possibly 'upland fort') was thus another name for Edinburgh. In all probability Dùn Monaidh was used loosely to denote the seat of the peripatetic Gaelic kings of Scotland, wherever it might be at any one time.

The 'Edin' in Edinburgh's name comes from Dùn Eidyn (meaning 'fort of Eidyn'), perhaps a territorial name of the Gododdin, originally the Votadini of Traprain Law, itself once known as Dun Pelder. It has been argued persuasively that the stem Eidyn refers to bulls. In the early Welsh poem *Y Gododdin*, there are likely associations with the Castle Rock. Mynyddog, king of the Gododdin of 'Eidyn's bright fortress', raised the war band that fought at the battle of Catraeth. The poem, in Old Welsh, is among the oldest surviving literature in the British Isles:

> Er pan want maws mur trin, er pan aeth daear ar Aneirin, nu neut ysgaras nat a Gododdin.
>
> *Since the gentle one, the wall of battle, was slain, since the earth covered Aneirin, poetry is now parted from the Gododdin.*

When the Gaels took over, they modified Eidyn to give the modern Gaelic form Dùn Èideann. It is not Dun Eodann ('fort on the slope face'), an error that has been around since 638 AD when the Irish chronicler Tigernach attempted some early place-name analysis. Also unlikely is the folk etymology connecting the name with a Mercian personal name, Eadwine (now Edwin), the King of Northumbria: he was killed in 633 AD before the Mercians made it here. Many areas of Edinburgh have Gaelic names, for example, Baile Àirneach (Balerno, 'sloe-tree farm') and Gilmerton ('Gille-Mhoire's farm'), that personal name indicating a devotee of the Virgin.

The Gaels have had an ambivalent relationship with Edinburgh, typified by the following verse in the waulking song, 'Iain Òg Mac Mhic Nèill' ('Young John, Son of MacNeil'):

> Chan e chreach mi –
> mo chùitear donn
> an làimh an Glaschu
> 's iad a ruitheadh
> chuir a Shasunn
> no Dhùn Èideann nan àrd fasan.

It is not that which destroyed me, [but] my noble courtier in captivity in Glasgow.
And them [?binding him] to send him to England or to Edinburgh of the high fashions.

In 1610, Donald MacDonald of Clanranald seized Iain, eldest son of Ruairidh an Tartair, the MacNeil chief, and sent him to Edinburgh where he soon died, one example of significant Gaelic personalities who were incarcerated in Edinburgh Castle from the 15th to the 18th centuries. According to tradition, his death led his foster mother to compose the above song.

In 1428, James I offered safe conduct to the leading men of the Gàidhealtachd to an audience at Inverness. He broke his word and either hanged or imprisoned around 50 of them. James IV, in July 1499, hanged the contender to the title of Lord of the Isles, John of Dunivaig, along with his three sons on one gallows at the Mercat Cross. In 1540, at Portree, James V netted more chiefs with the same dishonourable trick pioneered in 1428. On behalf of a now London-based James VI, Bishop Knox broke his holy oath to do the same thing at Aros in Mull in 1608. Some of those men ended up in Edinburgh Castle.

After the proscription of Clan MacGregor, many of the leading men of the clan were put to death in Edinburgh. Alasdair of Gleann Sreith (Glenstrae), the chief, and twelve leading MacGregors, were hanged in 1604. Alasdair was hanged a head higher to denote his status. It was also here that another MacGregor, Robin Òg, a son of Rob Roy, was hanged in 1754. Others sought redress and attended the Law Courts, with MacLeod of Assynt spending many years in litigation.

One visitor to Edinburgh, a MacLeod chief, was roundly criticised by An Clàrsair Dall (the Blind Harper) in 'Òran do MhacLeòid Dhùn Bheagain' ('Song to MacLeod of Dunvegan'), for wasting time and money there:

Thèid luach mairt no nas mò
'm paidhir stocainn den t-seòrsa 's feàrr,
is cha chunntar an còrr,
ducatùn air dà bhròig bhuinn àrd;
clachan criostail 's math snuadh
ann am bucaill mun cuairt gun smàl;
siod na gartain a suas
air dà thastan 's an luach 'nam bàrr.

Thig e mach às a' bhùth
leis an fhasan as ùir bho 'n Fhraing
's an t-aodach gasda bha 'n-dè
ma phearsa le spèis nach gann
thèid a shadadh an cùil –
"Is dona 'm fasan, chan fhiù e plang.
Air màl baile no dhà
glac am peana 's cuir làmh ri bann."

…

Thoir teachdaireachd uam
le deatam gu Ruaidhri òg,
agus innis da fèin
cuid d'a chunnart giodh e MacLeòid;
biodh e 'g amharc 'na dhèidh
air an Iain a dh'eug 's nach beò:
gum bu shaidhbhir a chliù,
is chan fhàgadh e 'n Dùn gun cheòl.

He'll pay the price of a cow – or more –
for a pair of the best stockings,
the change uncounted;
a ducaton for two high-soled shoes
with sparkling crystal gems set in immaculate buckles;
and for two shillings on go the garters
with their cost in their frills.

He'll emerge from the shop
with the latest fashion from France
and the grand clothes he sported
with pride yesterday
are tossed in a corner –
"They're not up-to-the-minute, not worth a plack.
On the strength of the rental value of a village or two,
take up the pen and sign a bond."

...

Take this message from me
to young Ruairi as quickly as you can,
and tell him, though he's a MacLeod, the danger he is in;
let him recollect the deceased Iain who is no more:
whose reputation was lavish,
he'd never leave the castle devoid of music.

The ducatùn ('ducaton'), mentioned in stanza one, a large, popular *negotiepenning* ('trade coin') was minted by the Dutch Republic in 1659 and contained 30.45 grams of fine silver while the lowly plang ('plack') in stanza two was a Scottish coin of the value of four Scots pence or, by 1707, one third of an English penny.

Such songs were usually composed for the approval of a diverse audience and the poet often kept references ambiguous and vague, but the Blind Harper's critique here was biting in the extreme. In his exasperation Ruaidhri Òg might well have quoted the proverb:

> Trì subhailcean a' bhàird: fios fithich gu ròic, cuireadh fial
> gu tàthadh rann, tart mòr gu òl a dhram.
>
> *The bard's three virtues are: a raven's foreknowledge of a feast,*
> *a generous invitation to compose verses and a mighty thirst for*
> *drinking his dram.*

Nonetheless, by the mid-18th century Gaelic harp music no longer sounded within Dunvegan Castle, now rented out to others.

Donnchadh Bàn, the poet of Ben Doran, lived off the High Street after he was given membership of the Edinburgh Town Guard from 1766 – in essence, a sinecure. His wife, Màiri Bhàn Òg ('fair young Mary'), had a drinks shop in the Lawnmarket and was apparently a skilled whisky distiller. Duncan landed in court on account of this, but he avoided punishment by claiming that he had drunk far more whisky than Mary had ever made. In his song, 'Màiri Bhàn Òg' ('Fair, Young Mary'), he adored her other attributes too:

A Mhàiri bhàn òg 's tu an òigh th' air m' aire
Rim bheò bhith far am bithinn fhìn
On fhuair mi ort còir cho mòr 's bu mhaith leam
Le pòsadh ceangailt' on chlèir,
Le cùmhnantan teann 's le banntaibh daingeann
Le snaim a dh'fhanas nach trèig.
'S e d' fhaotainn air làimh le gràdh gach caraid
Rinn slàinte mhaireann am chrè.

You, fair-haired young Mary, are the maiden on my mind, and I wish you to be with me all my life since I won a right to you, complete as I wanted, from the clergy, by nuptial ties; with stringent covenants and firmly fixed bonds, with a knot that will last and never yield; winning your hand, with all friends' good-will, has meant everlasting health in my heart.

An admirer of his poems, fascinated by Duncan's description of Mary, but disappointed by her actual appearance, hinted to the poet that she was not all that beautiful. The poet responded with the words:

Chan fhaca tusa i leis na sùilean agamsa.

You have not seen her with my eyes.

There was a tavern in Anchor Close off the High Street whose owner was very fond of the song 'Crodh Chailein' ('Crochallan', 'Colin's cattle'). The inn, with its drinking club, whose members named themselves the Crochallan Fencibles, a sardonic reference to the owner's beloved song, was a favourite of Robert Burns. Other Gaelic songs, for example 'An Gille Dubh Ciar Dubh' ('The Dark-haired Lad') and 'A' Bhanarach Dhonn a' Chruidh' ('The Brown-haired Dairymaid'), are known to have influenced Burns.

Pàrlamaid na h-Alba: *The Scottish Parliament*

Gaelic has played an important part in the work of Pàrlamaid na h-Alba (the Scottish Parliament) which opened in 1999. Gaelic's status in Scotland was formalised following the passing of the Gaelic Language (Scotland) Act in 2005. The Act established Bòrd na Gàidhlig as:

> … a body having functions exercisable with a view to securing the status of the Gaelic language as an official language of Scotland commanding equal respect to the English language, including the functions of preparing a national Gaelic language plan, of requiring certain public authorities to prepare and publish Gaelic language plans in connection with the exercise of their functions and to maintain and implement such plans, and of issuing guidance in relation to Gaelic education.

Turning back to Edinburgh Castle, the Royal Edinburgh Military Tattoo is performed annually in August on its esplanade by British, Commonwealth and international military bands and artistic performance teams. The first Tattoo of 1950 drew some 6,000 spectators. In 2018, 220,000 people watched the live performances, televised to 40 countries, allowing an estimated 100 to 300 million people to see the event. The Tattoo is suffused with images of Gaelic Scotland – kilts, tartan, bagpipes, massed pipe bands, kilted soldiers, whisky, a cuach (quaich), and a Gaelic toast for the lone piper.

Not all Edinburgh's military associations are as positive as the Tattoo. James Boswell wrote his journal, *Journal of a Tour to the Hebrides,* in 1786, thirteen years after his journey with Samuel Johnson through the Highlands and the Hebrides. In it he says that the 78th, Lord Seaforth's Highland Regiment, who had enlisted on condition that they were not sent out of the United Kingdom without their consent, mutinied in September 1778 on news of their posting overseas and camped on Arthur's Seat for three days and three nights, resisting all comers.

Boswell spares us the rest of the sorry tale. Among the 600 men encamped on Arthur's Seat were MacRaes from Kintail, thus giving the incident the name the Affair of the MacRaes, but they also included young men from Lewis who had enlisted to secure their parents' tenancies. Mistreatment by abusive officers, particularly George MacKenzie of Scatwell; poor rations; theft by officers of the levy money due them; arrears of pay; and ultimately false rumours that they were to be posted to the East Indies, forced the men's hands and they mutinied. In an unprecedented act, the authorities conceded to all their demands and the regiment was posted to the Channel Islands with a written assurance that it would not be posted to India. Two and half years later, that promise was broken and they were sent to Madras. By the time the regiment arrived 250 men were dead. On 13th June 1783, in a futile attack against a French fort at Cuddalore, British forces, the remnants of the 78th among them, suffered heavily with more than 900 killed or wounded. Despite assurances in Lord Seaforth's letter of service that the regiment would be disbanded in Ross-shire, its pitiful remains were disbanded in Madras, 10,000 sea miles from home. In the words of the poet Christopher MacRae, "only an odd one surviving of the hundred of us" ever returned to Kintail.

It is perhaps not surprising therefore that an anti-recruiting song is set in Edinburgh:

Latha dhomh 's mi sràidearachd
Gu h-àrd os cionn Dhùn Èideann
'S ann thachair orm an saighdear
Is dh'fhaighnich e mo sgeul dhomh.

'S thuirt e rium a liostaiginn
'S gun sheas mi greis 's gun dh'èist mi
Is thuirt e rium sa Ghàidhlig
'S i cheàird as fheàrr fon ghrèin i.

Is thug e dhan taigh-òsta mi
Oir dheònaich e bhith rèidh rium
Is chuir e bean na bainnse
Nam làimh am fianais cheudan.

Is chuir e bean na bainnse
Nam làimh am fianais cheudan.
Mo mhallachd aig an Fhrangach
Na champa chaoidh cha tèid mi.

One day out walking high above Edinburgh I met the soldier and he asked me about myself. He asked me if I would enlist and I stood for a while and listened. He said to me in Gaelic that it was the best profession under the sun.

He took me to the inn because he wished to befriend me and he placed the Queen's shilling in my hand witnessed by hundreds. My curses on the Frenchman, I will never go to his camp.

The cruel Colonel George MacKenzie of Scatwell died in his bed, aged 90.

Oilthigh Dhùn Èideann: *The University of Edinburgh*

Oilthigh Dhùn Èideann (the University of Edinburgh) was founded in 1582, the sixth oldest university in the English-speaking world. Gaelic only became a university subject of study 300 years later. The first Chair of Celtic in Scotland was established following a sustained campaign to raise funds for its endowment, spearheaded by John Stuart Blackie (1809-1895), Professor of Greek at the University.

Some years before 1882, Blackie was in Ceann Loch Lìobhainn (Kinlochleven, 'head of Loch of Leven'). There he had asked a local youth who was holding his horse what he called the animal. Perhaps expecting the Victorian equivalent of 'Dobbin', he was delighted when 'each' was the reply. '*Equus!*' was the Professor's delighted reaction, recognising instantly the Gaelic cognate for the Latin for 'horse'. That little spark fired his subsequent study of Gaelic. He championed the language and spoke of:

> ... its beauty, its poetic capabilities, its kinship to Sanskrit, Greek and Latin

all of which convinced him:

> ... of the recklessness of letting the language perish.

Almost single-handedly, he raised the £12,000 needed to endow the new Chair of Celtic at Edinburgh University. His death in 1895 was a day of national mourning.

Donald MacKinnon, the first professor of Celtic at Edinburgh, was born in 1839 in Cille Chatain (Kilchattan, 'St. Catan's Church') on the island of Colonsay. He was Professor of Celtic Languages, Literature, History and

Antiquities, and he made substantial contributions in each of the fields listed in his title. Today the Department of Celtic and Scottish Studies teaches Gaelic at all levels, covering modern and medieval language and literature, as well as wider aspects of Gaelic culture.

Sgoil Eòlais na h-Alba (the School of Scottish Studies) was founded at the University in 1951 to collect, preserve, research and publish material relating to the cultural traditions and folklore of Scotland. It holds an archive of some 33,000 recordings of traditional music, song, tales and other lore, many of which are now available online through the Tobar an Dualchais (Kist o Riches) website.

On 24th April 1567, the first book to be printed in either Scottish Gaelic or in Irish Gaelic was published in Edinburgh. This was *Foirm na n-Urrnuidheadh* (*The Form of the Prayers*), Bishop Sèon Carsuel's translation of John Knox's liturgy using Classical Common Gaelic. *Foirm na n-Urrnuidheadh* established the tradition of printed Gaelic, and also laid down a standard for Gaelic spelling. Carswell was very aware of the implications of the technological revolution of his own day and in his Epistle to the Reader he wrote:

> Acht atá ní cheana, is mór an leathtrom agus an uireasbhuidh atá riamh orainde, Gaoidhil Alban agus Eireand, tar an gcuid eile don domhan, gan ar gcanamhna Gaoidheilge do chur a gcló riamh mar atáid a gcanamhna agas a dteangtha féin a gcló ag gach uile chinél dhaoine oile sa domhan; agus atá uireasbhuidh is mó iná gach uireasbhuidh oraind, gan an Bíobla naomhtha do bheith a gcló Gaoidheilge againd, mar tá sé a gcló Laidne agus Bhérla, agas in gach teangaidh oile o sin amach, agus fós gan seanchus ar sean nó ar sindsear do bheith mar an gcédna a gcló againd riamh…

> *Great indeed is the disadvantage and want from which we, the Gaels of Scotland and Ireland, have ever suffered, beyond the rest of the world, in that our Gaelic language has never been printed as all other races of men in the world have their own languages and tongues in print; and we suffer from a greater want than any other in that we have not the Holy Bible printed in Gaelic as it has been printed in Latin and English, and in all other tongues besides, and likewise in that the history of our ancestors has never been printed…*

Many modern Gaelic poets were associated with Edinburgh. Milne's Bar in Rose Street in Edinburgh's New Town became a regular poets' meeting place in the 1950s and 60s. The back room was nicknamed 'Little Kremlin' and one visitor was the poet Somhairle MacLean. His poem 'Calbharaigh' ('Calvary') speaks of Edinburgh:

Chan eil mo shùil air Calbharaigh
no air Betlehem an àigh
ach air cùil ghrod an Glaschu
far bheil an lobhadh fàis,
agus air seòmar an Dùn Èideann,
seòmar bochdainn 's cràidh,
far a bheil an naoidhean creuchdach
ri aonagraich gu bhàs.

My eye is not on Calvary
nor on Bethlehem the Blessed,
but on a foul-smelling backland in Glasgow,
where life rots as it grows:
and on a room in Edinburgh
a room of poverty and pain,
where the diseased infant
writhes and wallows till death.

Some of the poets were left-leaning, and others were nationalists, including Deòrsa Mac Iain Dheòrsa (George Campbell Hay) (1915-1984). His poem 'Brònach Tadhal Dùn Monaidh' ('Sad to visit Dùn Monaidh [Edinburgh]') strongly expresses his sentiments:

Brònach tadhal Dùn Monaidh,
bail' a mhol na ceudan bàrd.
Nuair a chithear Dùn Monaidh
is deacair gun ochain a ràdh.

Seachd ceud is seachd agus mìle,
cunntas a mhill ar tlachd 's ar fois,
's a dh'fhàg sinn ris anns an ainbheach
air bheagan meanmhainn or toic.

Ge brònach tadhal Dùn Monaidh,
gheobh ar n-Alba saorsa fòs.
Brònach tadhal Dùn Monaidh
ach molar e fhathast gun bhròn.

It is sad to visit Dùn Monaidh, a town which hundreds of poets have praised. When one sees Dùn Monaidh, it is hard not to say alas.

Seven hundred and seven and a thousand was a reckoning that ruined our pleasure and our repose and left us exposed as bankrupts with little spirit after a wealth of it.

Although is sad to visit Dùn Monaidh, our Scotland will yet get freedom. It is sad to visit Dùn Monaidh but it will yet be praised without sadness.

Like some Gaels before and after him, one early visitor could not wait to shake the dust of the city from his feet. Gilleasbaig Ruadh Dòmhnallach ('red-haired Archibald MacDonald'), nicknamed An Ciaran Mabach ('the sallow stammerer'), a brother of Sir James MacDonald, Chief of Clan Donald, visited the city to get treatment for an injured leg. He was evidently staying near the Palace of Holyrood which, at the time of his visit around 1685, was undergoing renovation on behalf of James, Duke of York, for use as his private chapel. Gilleasbaig, as his poem 'B' annsa cadal air fraoch' ('I'd rather sleep on heather') makes clear, was disturbed by the early morning hammering of the carpenters:

Ge socrach mo leaba,
B' annsa cadal air fraoch,
Ann an lagan beag uaigneach
Is bad de luachair rim thaobh;
Nuair a dh'èirinn sa mhadainn,
Bhith siubhal ghlacagan caol
Na bhith triall chon na h-Abaid,
'G èisteachd glagraich nan saor.

Although my bed is comfortable I'd rather sleep on heather,
in a private little hollow, a tuft of rushes by my side; and when
I get up in the morning, I'd rather travel the narrow glens,
than head for the Abbey and hear the crashing of the joiners.

Dùn Èideann an-diugh: *Edinburgh Today*

Today's Gaelic community in Edinburgh is a vibrant and expanding one. It has secured improved educational opportunities for its Gaelic-speaking children and is fully integrated into the fabric of the city. The poetry of many accomplished poets continues to reflect its interests and concerns. 'An Tiona' ('The Tin') is a poem by one of this generation, lecturer and poet Pàdraig MacAoidh:

Nuair a bha mi sa bhun-sgoil
fhuair mi tiona sleamhainn tana
far an cuirinn m' fhaclan
sgriobhte air sgoltaidhean pàipeir.

Chan eil cuimhne agam air inneach
ach air cho doirbh 's a bha e fhosgladh
gun ainmearean 's gnìomhairean a' leum
a-mach às mar bhradain à lìon –

iorghail bhalbh mo chànain
a' snàmh gu sìorraidh gu dachaigh chaillte.
Nam cheann tha an tiona air meirgeadh,
's cha tèid fhosgladh gun bhristeadh saillte

When I was in primary school
I got myself this little flat tin
where I'd stash my words
writ on splinters of paper.

What I remember is not the design
but how difficult it was to open
without names and deeds leaping out
like salmon from a net –

the dumb babble of my languages
swimming forever towards their lost ground
the tin in my head rusting not to be opened
without breaking its crust of salt.

Caibideil 16: *Chapter 16*

Sruighlea is Siorrachd Dhùn Breatann an Ear: *Stirling and East Dumbartonshire*

Stirling's strategic location has been described rather dramatically as 'the Brooch of Scotland'; its ancient castle guards the only viable route north into the Highlands. The town is now the headquarters of the local authority area of Sruighlea (Stirling), but the authority's area extends well westwards to the boundary with Siorrachd Dhùn Breatann an Ear (East Dumbartonshire).

The route from Edinburgh westwards to Stirling and onwards to Crianlarich largely follows the Roman road, subsequently used, two millennia later, by the Hanoverian military road planners. It crosses a narrow waist of Scotland, little more than 65 kilometres wide, where the Romans sited their customs barrier, the Antonine Wall, in 143 AD.

Blàr Allt a' Bhonnaich: *The Battle of Bannockburn*

The road passes through the oxbows and loops of the sluggish Abhainn Foirthe (River Forth). To the west of Chartershall, the road crosses a small stream. Blink and you might miss it, but this is the most important stretch of water in Scottish history. It was here in 1314, in the stream's lower reaches, that the army of the English King Edward II was bogged down and destroyed, many of the invading force drowning in the muddy melee. Today the battle's name is rendered in Gaelic as Blàr Allt a' Bhonnaich (Bannockburn, 'Battle of the bannock stream'). This name has taken the English form of the Gaelic word bonnach ('scone'). All highly confusing, but in reality 'bannock 'seems to derive from an Old Welsh name for the escarpment of hills to the north where the Bannock Burn rises. The name is most likely bannauc ('abounding in peaks'). Inevitably, other interpretations exist.

Tradition relates that it was a flanking charge by 'the men of the isles' that finally broke English resolve. It is more than likely that the bulk of Robert the Bruce's men were Gaelic-speaking. Apart from pockets of English and

Flemish in the embryonic trading towns, the royal burghs, all the land from the Antonine Wall northwards was Gaelic-speaking in 1314. Despite their role in securing Scotland's freedom, "the Highlanders and people of the Islands" were described by John of Fordun, only one generation later, in 1363, as "a savage and untamed nation".

Sruighlea: *Stirling*

To get across yet another barrier, this time a boggy moss, travellers had to use either the Falls of Frew to the west or the bridge that spanned the river on the line of the Roman road to Perth. On a naturally strongly defensive site by the crossing, Stirling Castle held a key role as a stronghold. In Scotland's Wars of Independence, it was besieged eight times between 1296 and 1342. Perhaps as much ink has been spilt and nonsense said of the meaning of the name of Sruighlea (Stirling) as of anywhere. Since in 1891 almost four out of ten of the usually resident people in the small hamlets in the westernmost part of Stirlingshire still spoke Gaelic, it is reasonable to assume it is a name of Gaelic origin. It does not mean, as some suggest, 'striving', as a result of all the fighting around the place. Nor 'Melvin's hut'. The most sensible conclusion is that the name derives from the word for 'streams', an entirely logical naming, given the amount of water in the vicinity. Indeed the supernatural tale 'Mar a thogadh a' cheud chaisteal air Carraig Shruighlea' ('How the first castle was built on Stirling Rock') has the following rhyme:

Ma 's mise Tomas Sheochd,
Is mi a dhealbh an t-olc;
Tha thusa 'sin, a Shrutha-Shliabh,
Is tha mise gun d' fhiach an nochd.

If I am Thomas, son of Jock.
'Tis I devised the wicked plot.
There stands River Mount,
And for you, nought have I tonight.

hinting strongly that the original Gaelic-speaking community had a good understanding of the derivation of Stirling's name.

The actual castle itself most likely had its own name: we get a tantalising hint of this in the fact that one of the heralds of the Court of the Lord Lyon of Scotland is known as Snowdoun Herald of Arms in Ordinary. The ancient office was first mentioned in 1443 and the title is understood to derive from a part of Stirling Castle that bore the same name.

Na Tròisichan: *The Trossachs*

In the far west of the council area are Na Tròiseachan (The Trossachs), an area of lochs and valleys north and east of Glasgow that also straddles part of East Dunbartonshire. This was the first site of mass tourism in Scotland, thanks primarily to the popularity of Sir Walter Scott's 1810 narrative epic, *The Lady of the Lake,* that is largely set in this area. The Trossachs area remains popular with visitors.

The name Na Tròisichan ('the places lying athwart') applies to the hills dividing Loch Katrine from Loch Achray, which lie at a right angle to the glens containing the lochs. From the evidence in the *OSA* published between 1791 and 1799, Gaelic was still spoken in many villages and glens in this area. This was then the line of the 'language frontier' running approximately from the southern shore of Loch Lomond eastwards to Crieff, finally reaching the county boundary with Angus north of Blairgowrie. As a linguistic border area, the Trossachs were exposed to early English language infiltration from the Lowland districts to the south and east. The poet Alexander Campbell, a native of Strathyre, said in his *Journey from Edinburgh* (1802) that, while the customs of this region were still altogether Highland, the language spoken by most people was:

> a bad dialect of the ancient Celtic or Gaelic, greatly corrupted, and vulgar in point of pronunciation.

A common criticism of any dialect not familiar to the writer or speaker.

Baile Freòine: *Balfron*

Balfron is one of a string of villages on the route towards Stirling. The invented meaning of its name is a good illustration of the effect of Sir Walter Scott's writing on our landscape. An entry in a popular online encyclopaedia states:

> The name means 'village of mourning' in Gaelic … from a legend that the village was attacked by wolves, which stole children out of their homes. James B. Johnston, (1904) The Place Names of Stirlingshire has the following corroborative evidence: "Balfron. a. 1300 Bafrone … Prob. G. baill-a-bhroin, 'village of mourning'".

The source of all this speculation is probably the historical introduction to Scott's *Rob Roy* (1817) and his description of the Rout of Glen Fruin of 1603. Scott's heightened feeling for the subject made him romantically, but erroneously, state that the glen's name means 'sorrow'. Prosaically, the name Balfron is from Gaelic, Baile Freòine, and may possibly be connected with the river name in Glen Fruin which seems to stem from freòine ('fury'), referring to the river there.

Seòras Bochanan agus Raibeart Kirk: *George Buchanan and Robert Kirk*

On firmer ground, Balfron is the birthplace of Seòras Bochanan (George Buchanan (1506-1582)). Described as:

> the most profound intellectual 16th-century Scotland produced,

Buchanan was a polymath: Erasmian humanist, Calvinist, university professor, historian, playwright, political theorist, philologist, linguist and poet. Today, interest focuses on his theories of citizenship; yet, above all, he was a poet. Michel de Montaigne was Buchanan's pupil in Bordeaux in 1539 and classed him as one of the foremost Latin poets of his time. However, he was, first and foremost, a Gaelic speaker, if not an advocate of it; to him, Latin was the only tongue.

Buchanan was the strict tutor to the young James VI. He introduced Huguenot political theory into Scottish historiography, enabling him to construct a political argument for an ancient Scottish constitution in which the Gaelic monarchy was accountable to the political nation. His treatise of 1579, *De Jure Regni apud Scotos* (*A dialogue, concerning the due privilege of government in the kingdom of Scotland)* was intended to instil sound political principles into the mind of his royal pupil. Buchanan laid down the doctrine that the source of all political power is the people; that the king is bound by those conditions under which power was first committed to his hands and that it is lawful to resist, even to punish, tyrants. He famously described the King as "God's silly vessel". James was not amused with Buchanan's theories, and displeased authorities made persistent efforts to suppress the work. Condemned by Act of Parliament in 1584 and again in 1664, it was burned by Oxford University in 1683.

Also of great value is that Buchanan's *History* of 1582 clearly identified the Picts as a Celtic-speaking people. This did not prevent the next 400 years of bizarre musings about the "mystery" of the Pictish language.

These once populous surrounding valleys, such as Gleann Fhionglais (Glen Finlas, 'glen of the fair stream') described in 1804 by the writer James Hogg as 'excellent sheep-ranges', were cleared of their native Gaelic population to make way for large sheep ranches. The displaced remnants of those thriving communities created the congested village of Obair Phuill (Aberfoyle, 'mouth of the sluggish stream'), best known as the birthplace of Robert Kirk, the seventh and youngest son of James Kirk, minister of the parish. James was not a Gaelic speaker but his son Robert was a conscientious Gaelic and Biblical scholar, folklorist and translator. As the minister in Balquidder, in 1684, he prepared the Gaelic translation of 'Psalma Dhaibhidh am Meadrachd' ('The Metrical Psalms of David') for his own and other Gaelic congregations. Robert Kirk's Psalms have splendid lyrical verses:

> Is e Dia fhèin as buachaill dhomh,
> Cha bhi mi ann an dìth.
> Bheir e fa-near gun laighinn sios
> Air cluainean glas' le sìth:

Is fòs ri taobh nan aibhnichean
Thèid seachad sìos gu mall,
A ta e ga mo threòrachadh,
gun mìn rèidh anns gach ball.

The Lord is my shepherd, I lack nothing.
He makes me lie down in peace in green pastures:

He leads me beside with the waters, quietly flowing by
He guides me along the right paths for his name's sake.

Kirk is now best known for *The Secret Commonwealth of Elves, Fauns and Fairies*. Although he completed his work just before his death in 1692, it was not published until the early 19th century. *The Secret Commonwealth* is a systematic account of these denizens of the supernatural world along with extrasensory phenomena, including poltergeists, clairvoyance and doppelgangers. He provides what could be said to be a social and anthropological study of fairies: it is not a defence of their existence but a detailed description of them.

He also composed the secular 'Tionoil na nslòigh chum na seilig' ('Gathering of the host to the hunt'), a poem that celebrates a tinchel organised by the Marquis of Atholl, taking place over a week in August 1682.

The Latin epitaph on his monument at Aberfoyle Kirk simply reads:

Hic pultus Ill Evangelii Promulgator Accuratus et Linguae Hibernice Lumen M. Robertus Kirk Aberfoile Pastor Obit 14 Maii 1692 Aetat 48.

Here lies the accurate promulgator of the Gospels and luminary of the Hibernian (Gaelic) tongue, Mr. Robert Kirk, pastor of Aberfoyle, who died 14 May 1692, aged 48.

Calasraid: *Callander*

The next major settlement to the north is Calasraid (Callander, 'harbour street'), so named because the main street runs along the bank of the River Teith (meaning obscure). As with most areas in what is known as Garbh

Chrìochan Pheairt (Highland Perthshire), in the 19th century Callander was strongly Gaelic-speaking. The scholar, Michael Newton, amassed a collection of Gaelic materials from Highland Perthshire during the 1990s. He gathered so much material that he planned a five volume series covering the region. He managed to get the first volume, *Bho Chluaidh gu Calasraid (From the Clyde to Callander)*, published in 2010.

Dùghall Bochanan: *Dugald Buchanan*

The road northward from Callander to Loch Earn is by way of Srath Eadhair (Strathyre, 'strath of cornland'). The village of Stratheyre has the modern Gaelic name An t-Iomaire Riabhach ('the brindled ridge'). In the cemetery here is a monument to Dùghall Bochanan (Dugald Buchanan), one of the finest spiritual writers of Gaelic Scotland. Buchanan was born at Ardach (Ardoch, 'high place'), near Stratheyre, in 1716. He worked as a schoolmaster in Rannoch and was also a catechist, often preaching to meetings of over 500 people. When he died, in 1768, the men of Stratheyre arrived to take his body back to the Buchanan burial ground. The Rannoch people initially refused to allow this: Buchanan's work among them had been held in such high esteem that they wished him to remain in Rannoch. The two parties almost came to blows, but the Rannoch men eventually relented and he rests in Stratheyre.

His works were published in Edinburgh in 1863 as:

> Beatha agus iompachadh Dhùghaill Bochannain, a dh' eug ann an Ranach sa' bhliadhna 1768, … : maille r' a Laoidhean spioradail.
>
> *The life and conversion of Dugald Buchanan, who died at Rannach in 1768, ...: to which is annexed his Spiritual hymns.*

One of his poems is 'Fulangas Chrìosd' '(Christ's Passion'), in which he draws upon motifs in both English and Scots spiritual writings, rendering them in expressive Gaelic:

'S e fulangas mo Shlànaighear
A bhios mo dhàn a' luaidh,
Mòr-irioslachd an àrd-righ sin

Na bhreith 's na bhàs ro chruaidh;
'S e 'n t-iongantas bu mhìorbhailich
Chaidh innse riamh do shluagh,
An Dia bha ann o shìorraidheachd,
Bhi fàs 'na chìochran truagh.

The sufferings of my Saviour is the subject of my song, the great humility of that high king in his birth and his distressing death; it is the most amazing wonder that has ever been told to a people, the God who has been there for all eternity growing as a wretched infant.

The road from Lochearnhead climbs west to the head of Gleann Ogail (Glen Ogle, meaning unclear, but not 'pass of evil' as has been suggested as a result of its supposed resemblance to the Kyber Pass). It continues over the watershed, a route which was once known as Laraig Ìle (possibly 'pass of Isla'), and down to a junction with another road eastwards towards Loch Tayside. This junction is now called Lix Toll, 'toll' in memory of a 19th -century toll-house situated here. It is also the site of, perhaps, the best example of how misunderstanding the meaning of place names can lead to flights of fancy.

The name 'Lix' is often rendered as L(egio) IX, and it is thus claimed to commemorate the loss here of the Legio IX, the Ninth Legion of the Roman army. The story is essentially a conflation of the place name and the children's story *The Eagle of the Ninth*, a historical adventure novel written in 1954 by Rosemary Sutcliff. At that time, it was a widely accepted theory that this legion had been wiped out in Britain during the reign of Emperor Hadrian (117-138 AD). Scholarly opinion now disputes this since records indicate that detachments of the Ninth Legion were serving on the Rhine frontier later than 117 AD. However, the events have been the subject of film and have become firmly rooted in folklore. But what about the name 'Lix'? The name neatly and correctly describes the area as Lic, a place of flagstones.

Taobh Loch Tatha: *Loch Tayside*

To the east of Lix Toll is Loch Tay-side, lying within Perthshire. The loch receives its name from the great river that flows from its eastern end, Uisge Tatha, believed to be from the Indo-European root meaning 'flow', as seen in the river name, Tain, in Easter Ross. The might of the river is mentioned in the saying:

> Tatha mhòr nan tonn
> Bheir i scrìob lom air Peairt.
>
> *Great Tay of the waters*
> *will cut a swathe through Perth.*

The north side of the loch is known as Deasearach ('southerly area') while the south side of the loch is called Tuathearach ('northerly area'), the names reflecting the relative quantities of sun that each part receives. The lands were also known as the Barony of Lawers and were formerly part of the old Celtic Earldom of Atholl. Two great mountains dominate the north side of the loch, Beinn Labhair (Ben Lawers, 'speaking mountain'), named for the number of babbling brooks on its slopes, and Sìth Chailleann (Schiehallion, 'fairy hill of the Caledonians'). That the latter name references the native adversaries of the Romans is a remarkable and, by all accounts, genuine survival, although an earlier visitor was informed in 1772 that it meant 'constant storm', a meteorological condition from which it often suffers.

Most of this country was Gaelic-speaking for many centuries and, at the time of the *NSA* (1831-1845), the local minister of Fortingall, in the heart of this area, said:

> The Gaelic is the language of the natives. It is, however, losing ground, and losing its purity ... It is gratifying ... to the lover of Celtic literature, that so much has been done to rescue the language and insure its permanency and stability.

The efforts of collectors such as John Francis Campbell, stimulated by the interest in Macpherson's poems of Ossian, were by now well underway. "Permanency and stability" however was not assured. Still, in 2023, one elderly, native speaker of Perthshire Gaelic remained alive.

Cill Fhinn: *Killin*

The Rev. James Stewart who made the first Gaelic translation of the New Testament was minister at Cill Fhinn (Killin, 'white church'), to the east. This was only published in 1767. Killin, as was the case with many villages in the Highlands, grew rapidly in the 19th century, as successive numbers of dispossessed tenantry moved there, causing chronic overcrowding and severe poverty. Except for the natural kindliness of those who were better off, the impoverished and overcrowded population in the later 19th century could aptly be described by the saying:

Na biasta mòr ag itheadh nam biasta beag;
Na biasta beag a' dèanamh mar a dh' fhaodas iad.

The big beasts eating the wee beasts;
The wee beasts doing as best they can.

One Killin resident was Teàrlach Stiùbhart, Charles Stewart, who, in 1884, published *The Killin Collection of Gaelic Songs with Music and Translations,* recorded in the immediate area. From its contents, it is clear that Gaelic was then strong in the district. There are 33 songs ranging over themes of love, the Jacobites, the MacGregors, nature and Ossianic verse, including 'Bàs Osgar ('Death of Oscar'). Possibly the best-known song in the collection is 'Fàilte Bhraid-Albann' ('Welcome to Breadalbane') composed by a cobbler called Mac a' Mhaoilein (MacMillan). The story goes that he was ordered off the estate on account of his poaching activities. But the estate factor, Caimbeul Ach' Alladair (Campbell of Achalader), was so delighted with the song that he invited MacMillan to return. MacMillan refused:

Càit a bheil ann an Albainn
Àit' as fheàrr na Braid Albann mo rùin?
Tìr nan gaisgeach bha dìleas
A sheasadh na fìrinn 's a' chrùin;
Gheibht' ann cruinneagan bòidheach
A sheinneadh dhuinn òrain bha binn;
Tìr nan gillean bha àlainn,
'S lìonmhor filidh a chaidh àrach nad ghlinn.

Where is there in Scotland a place better than my beloved Breadalbane? Land of the loyal heroes who would defend truth and the crown. You would find beautiful maidens there who would sing melodious songs; land of the splendid men, many a poet was reared in your glens.

Also in the Killin collection is the 17th-century story of the creation of the tune 'Na Tulaichean' ('The Heights'). It recounts that Iain Dubh Geàrr Griogarach ('sharp dark John MacGregor') was at a fair in Killin when he was set upon by eight ruffians in Taigh na Sràide (Streethouse), the local inn. Being immensely strong and skilled with a sword, he either dispatched or wounded his assailants and managed to escape. He eventually reached Srath Spè (Strathspey), where he married Iseabail NicAnndra (Isobel, 'daughter of Andrew'). John then learned that a posse of thirteen men were hunting for him and he felt that he should make himself scarce, but Isobel persuaded him to stand and fight. They barricaded themselves in the barn, armed with a musket and a pistol. John fired on his assailants through holes in the wall while Isobel loaded the weapons for him. He succeeded in dispatching and then beheading them all. Following this thirsty work, Isobel gave John a drink of beer and together they composed 'Na Tulaichean' or, as it is now known, 'The Reel of Tulloch'.

Charles Stewart, the editor of the Killin Collection, was of the view that the tune was already an old one. In the final verse, reference is made to a MacAilpein (MacAlpine). Stewart says that these MacAlpines were renowned fiddlers in Killin and had been playing the tune for some 300 years:

Bho Thulaichean gu Bealaichean
'S bho Bhealaichean gu Tulaichean
'S mur faigh sinn leann 's na Tulaichean
Gun òl sinn uisge Bhealaichean.

Bu Ghriogarach dà-rìribh
À Ruadh-shruth an Gleann Lìobhann
A rinn an ceòl tha rìomhach
Ris an canar leinn "Na Tulaichean".

B' ann an Taigh na Sràide
A thug iad ionnsaigh bhàis air
'S mur biodh e ro làidir
Bha ochdnar nàmh ro mhurrach air.

From Tulaichean to Bealaichean, from Bealaichean to Tulaichean. If we don't get beer in Tulaichean we'll drink the water of Bealaichean.

It was indeed a MacGregor from Ruadh-shruth in Glen Lyon who composed the beautiful music which we call "Na Tulaichean".

It was at Taigh na Sràide that they made the deadly attack on him and had he not been so strong eight enemies would have done for him.

Gleann Lìomhann: *Glen Lyon*

Fionn mac Cumhaill, whose chief residence was An Dùn Geal ('the white fort'), had a close association with neighbouring Glen Lyon, once known as Cromghleann ('dark, bent glen'), as is recorded in the saying:

Bha dà chaisteal deug aig Fionn an Cromghleann dubh nan clach.

Fionn had twelve castles in the dark bent glen of stones.

A side road to the north, the B846, leads to the small village of Fartairchill (Fortingall, 'church at the foot of a steep slope'). By the village, there is a standing stone, one of a pair, known as Clach Taghairm nan Cat ('stone of the spiritual echo of the cats'), with an associated legend that at Hallowe'en wildcats formed a circle around it. But more baleful is that the stone must once have been the site of a 'taghairm' to achieve the 'spiritual echo'. It was a form of ailuromancy or divination using cats' movements, in this case roasting them on a spit, to predict future events.

It was at this church that one of the most significant collections of early Gaelic poetry was brought together by the compilers of *The Book of the Dean of Lismore* (1512-42). The collection takes its name from the title and office of James MacGregor who was Dean of Lismore, although resident in Fortingall. This manuscript was part of a haul of old writings that James 'Ossian' Macpherson collected on his research trip into the Highlands and Islands after the success of his first publication, *Fragments of Ancient Poetry,* in 1760. If Macpherson's credit is now sadly diminished by claims of forgery, Gaeldom is grateful to him for saving these valuable texts, though they proved somewhat difficult to read. Instead of the normal or traditional spelling, the writers adopted a style evidently based on contemporary Scots spelling. In addition to the letters of the Gaelic alphabet, they used k, q, v, w, and y as, for example, in skreive for sgrìobhadh ('writing'); skail for sgeal ('story'); rewve for riamh ('ever'); swille for suibhal ('travel') and wen for bhean ('wife').

The poetry in *The Book of the Dean of Lismore,* thus, has the appearance of Manx Gaelic. It was successfully translated by Eòghann MacLachlainn (Ewan MacLachlan) (1773-1822). The scale of the task is demonstrated in the following example of a poem written in this fashion by Fionnlagh, Am Bàrd Ruadh (Finlay, 'the red-haired Bard'), in the hopes of regaining the favour of the Eòin, the MacGregor chief who died in 1519:

Gaiwe reim chomre v cregar
failta rinni ra teacht it chenn
hugis lawe fane rair gin nani
a zraw clar si chri kaale.

Rendered in more conventional Gaelic orthography it reads:

Gabh rìm chomraigh, a Mheic Ghriogòir,
fàilte rinn rè teacht id cheann;
thugas làmh fà riar gan aighne,
a gtràth chliar' s a chraidhe cheall.

Receive and protect me MacGregor, greet me well as I come to you. I have decided to make peace without an advocate; you lover of poets, you darling of churches.

The glen was also the home of John Campbell of Glen Lyon, commander of the force responsible for the Glencoe Massacre.

An Ceannmhor (Kenmore, 'big-headed place') at the eastern end of Loch Tay, is a small planned village, with Taymouth Castle immediately to the east. The present castle dates from the 19th century built at a time when the Earls of Breadalbane were at their zenith, but this was the site of an older structure known as Caisteal a' Bhealaich (Balloch Castle, 'castle of the pass'). Originally a MacGregor stronghold, it fell into the hands of Cailean Liath ('grey Colin of Glenorchy'), and was one of the seven places he either embellished or erected in his lifetime. It was here, in 1570, that the feud between Colin Campbell and Griogair Ruadh ('red-haired Gregor', Chief of the MacGregors) culminated with the latter's death.

Mòr Chaimbeul: *Marion Campbell*

Mòr Chaimbeul, Mòr nighean Dhonnchaidh (Marion Campbell, 'daughter of Duncan') was the daughter of Duncan Campbell of Glen Lyon. While there was a fragile truce between the two feuding parties, she had married Griogair, but soon they were fugitives as the net closed in on her husband. He was captured in August 1569, and Grey Colin waited patiently until political events elsewhere, namely the killing of Regent Moray, the first head of government to be assassinated by a firearm, let him have his revenge. Marion is believed to have composed the song usually referred to today as 'Griogal Cridhe' ('Beloved Griogair') after Colin, her own cousin, personally beheaded Griogair on the 7th of April 1570:

Eudail mhòir a shluagh an domhain
Dhòirt iad d' fhuil an-dè
'S chuir iad do cheann air stob daraich
Tacan beag bhod chrè.

B' annsa bhith le Griogal Cridhe
Teàrnadh chruidh le gleann
Na le Baran mòr na Dalach
Sìoda geal mu m' cheann

Most beloved of all the people in the world, they spilt your blood yesterday. They set your head on an oak stake a little distance from your corpse.

I'd prefer to be with Gregor driving cattle to the glen than with the great baron of Dalach, white silk on my head.

Described by the poet Sorley MacLean as:

> Surely one of the greatest poems ever made in Britain

it is sometimes described as a lullaby that Mòr sang to her two sons, Alasdair Ruadh and Iain Dubh. Neither died peacefully in his bed. Iain fell in 1603 at the Battle of Glen Fruin and, in February the following year, Alasdair was hanged in Edinburgh as a result of the intrigues of another Campbell, Gilleasbaig (Archibald, 7th Earl of Argyll). MacGriogair à Ruadh-shruth (MacGregor of Roro) also joined Alasdair on the scaffold. His efforts to evade capture are recorded in another song, 'MacGriogair à Ruadh-shruth' ('MacGregor of Roro') that, along with Marion's lament for Griogor Ruadh and the song of Clan Gregor at Clachan Dìseart, form a group of songs, remarkable for their starkness, sincerity and beautiful melodies. MacGregor of Roro is told:

Nuair a thèid thu 'n taigh-òsta
Na òl ach an aon deoch
Gabh do dhrama nad sheasamh
Is bi freasdlach mud dhaoine.
Dèan am foghar don gheamhradh
'S dèan an samhradh don Fhaoilteach
Dèan do leaba sna cragaibh
Is na caidil ach aotrom.

When you go to the inn drink only one drink; drink your dram standing and pay attention to your people. Make autumn out of winter and summer from February, make your bed in the crags and sleep only lightly.

The song continues:

Though rare is the squirrel, a way can be found to capture it.
Noble as is the hawk, often it is caught by stealth.

Sound advice, as is the proverb:

Is e an suidhe docair san taigh-òst' as fheàrr.

The unstable seat in the inn is the best.

Obar Pheallaidh: *Aberfeldy*

To the east of Kenmore is Obar Pheallaidh (Aberfeldy). An online encyclopaedia says that the name stems from a combination of the Pictish *aber* ('the mouth of a river') with the Gaelic phellaidh, for the Christian missionary St. Paldoc. Quite why it was deemed necessary to create a fictitious association with a very obscure saint, if, indeed, the divine existed at all, is unknown. On the contrary, Peallaidh is perhaps the best-known of the Breadalbane 'ùruisgean'. According to Dwelly's dictionary, an ùruisg was:

> a being supposed to haunt lonely and sequestered places, a water god. The ùruisg had the qualities of man and spirit curiously commingled.

Peallaidh or to give him his full title, Peallaidh an Spùit ('Peallaidh of the spout') resided near the upper falls of the Aberfeldy burn in Moness and he had a companion, Brùnaidh an Easain ('Brownie of the small waterfall'), further down the stream and nearer the town. At least thirteen ùruisgean inhabited Breadalbane as the following rhyme demonstrates:

Peallaidh an Spùit is Brùnaidh an Easain
Babaidh an Lochain is Brùnaidh an Eilein
Padarlan à Feàrnan, Peadragan, Patragan

Triubhas-dubh à Fairtirchill, Fuath Coire Ghamhnain
Cas-luath Leitir, Amhlagan Dubh
Catan Ceann-liath, is Ùruisg Dubh Eas Amhlagan

Peallaidh of the Spout and Brownie of the Little Waterfall
Babaidh of the Lochan and Brownie of the Island
Padarlan of Fearnan, Peadragan, Patragan
Black-trews from Fortingall, the Spectre of Coire Ghamhnain
Swift-foot of Leitir, Black Amhlagan
Grey-headed Little Cat and the Black Urisk of Amhlagan Falls.

The town is also the spiritual home of Am Freiceadan Dubh (the Black Watch). In 1725, General George Wade was authorised to form six 'watch' companies from 'loyal' clans to patrol the Highlands, three from Clan Campbell, and one each from Clans Fraser, Munro and Grant. Their task was:

> disarming the Highlanders, preventing depredations, bringing criminals to justice, and hindering rebels and attainted persons from inhabiting that part of the kingdom.

Inevitably many theories abound as to why the epithet of 'black' may have arisen. Some aver that the name referred to the "black hearts" of the pro-government militia who had sided with the "enemies of true Highland spirit", or that it came from their preventing màl dubh ('black rent') – extortion payments to spare cattle from being lifted.

As usual in such matters, it is best to look at the facts; they were arrayed in standard government-issue plaids of the dark Clan Campbell tartan, in contrast to their red-coated regular soldiers. Once known as the 42nd (Royal Highland) Regiment of Foot (the Black Watch), it now bears the title of 3rd Battalion, Royal Regiment of Scotland. Although initially regarded with suspicion by both native and foreign observers, they were the nucleus of a force that became one of the most respected in the whole of the British army. This did not prevent one anonymous Englishman, observing them, probably in the 1730s, and being surprised:

> … to see these savages … at their several meals … mutter something in their own gibberish, by way, I suppose, of saying grace, as if they had been so many Christians.

Craoibh is Braco: *Crieff and Braco*

The small market town of Craoibh (Crieff, 'tree place') is the origin of the saying:

> Ag obair anns a' Chreig is a' loidseadh anns a' Chraoibh.
>
> *Working in the Craig ('rock') and lodging in Crieff ('tree').*

Up to the early 18th century, when it was superseded by Falkirk, Crieff was the centre for the seasonal cattle trade in Scotland.

In the Highlands, lacking extensive arable land, the rearing of cattle assumed prime importance. During the mild, rainy summers grass is abundant, but historically little hay was made to provide winter keep. The surplus stock had to be sold each autumn so that the breeding animals could be fed. The cattle destined for sale had first to be driven to the trysts or markets at Crieff, a relatively accessible meeting place for both the Highland livestock sellers and for the Lowland and English dealers. Some animals were sold for slaughter, whilst others went for fattening. The cattle markets usually took place over three days and were held three times a year, those at Falkirk for example on the second Tuesday of August and the second Mondays of September and October.

Rob Donn MacKay, the Sutherland bard, knew Crieff well and in 'Òran mar gu'm b'ann le dròbhair àraid d'a Leannan' ('Song composed as if by a drover to his Sweetheart') he sings of being at the tryst:

> Ged is socradh mo leabaidh,
> Chan e 'n codal bh' air m' ùidh,
> 'S tric mo smuaintean a' gluasad,
> Don taobh tuath leis a' ghaoith;
> 'S mòr a b'annsa bhith mar riut,

Ann an gleannan nan laogh
Na bhi cunntadh na Sàileach
Ann am pàirceachan Chraoibh.

Although my bed is comfortable I did not want to sleep. Often my thoughts steal to the north with the wind; How much better to be beside you in the little glen of the calves than to be counting the Sàl (Kintail) cattle in the parks of Crieff.

From Crieff, the B822 travels south to Braco. At Braco is the multi-phase Roman fort of Àrdach (Ardoch, 'high place'). The original name of the Roman camp was Cathair Mhaothail ('Muthil's fort'), Maothal being an ancient territorial name that still survives in the name of the town of Methil. In his poem 'Feòrag ghlas, tuath air Braco' ('Grey squirrel, north of Braco'), the poet Derick Thomson handles the complex cultural history of Scotland with humour. He strives to see that, as Gaelic culture has been overcome in many places, it had itself replaced other cultures in the past.

A' siubhal tron an dùthaich bhrèagh sin
chunna mi feòrag a' teicheadh bhon a' rathad:
tè ghlas a bh' ann, an treubh ùr tha sgaoileadh
tro dhùthaich nan Cruithneach...

S ann à Ameireagaidh a thàinig a sinnsreachd,
'S thuirt i rium, tha mi 'n dùil,
ged nach duirt mise guth,
'Carson nach tiginn a seo?
chaidh gu leòr dhe na daoin' agaibhse
a-null thugainne.'

bha mi a' smaoineachadh air na Cruithnich...
is beag a bha dhùil ac'
gun teicheadh an fheòrag ruadh
roimhn a' pheasan ghlas seo,
no gun cuireadh Gàidheil às dhan
a' chainnt acasan, 's gu fàsadh na Gàidheil fhèin
rudeigin Sagsanach.

Travelling through that bonny countryside
I saw a squirrel running away from the road:
a grey one, the new tribe colonising
the land of the Picts...

Her ancestors came from America,
and I think she said to me –
though I hadn't spoken
'Why shouldn't I come here?
Plenty of your people
went to our country.'

I kept thinking of the Picts...
they had no idea
that the red squirrel would retreat
at the coming of this grey pest
nor that the Gaels would eradicate
their language
and that the Gaels themselves would become
somewhat like the Saxons.

Sliabh an t-Siorraim: *Sherriffmuir*

South of Braco and close to Dùn Bhlathainn (Dunblane, 'fort of St. Blane') is Sliabh an t-Siorraim (Sherriffmuir), the site of the principal battle of the botched Jacobite Rising of 1715. The Jacobite leader, John Erskine, 'Bobbin Jock,' 11th Earl of Mar, did not lack men, but he lacked military competence. At Sherriffmuir on 13th November 1715, the Jacobites fielded approximately 9,000 men. Facing them was John Campbell, 2nd Duke of Argyll, commander of the government's forces in Scotland, with only some 3,400 troops. Neither commander managed matters competently and the two armies stumbled into each other almost by accident. Despite the exceptional bravery of his men and his superior numbers, Mar withdrew towards Perth, leaving the field to the government forces. This failure to defeat Argyll's army constituted a strategic defeat for the Jacobites, yet Jacobite supporters like the poet Silis na Ceapaich hoped for a further, more decisive battle. Her song 'Blàr Sliabh an t-Siorraim' claims:

> Dh'fhalbh a' chòir agus thàinig an t-eucoir:
> Amhairc fhèin air feum an t-sluaigh!
> Gu bheil Tòmas ag ràdh ann a fhàistneachd
> Gur h-iad na Gàidheil a bhuidhneas buaidh;
> Bidh fallas fala air gach mala
> A' cur a' chatha aig uisge Chluaidh;
> Nì Sasann strìochdadh ge mòr an t-inntleachd
> Aig iarraidh sìth air an rìgh tha uainn.
>
> *Justice has gone and injustice has come: look for yourself at the need of the people! Thomas says in his prophecy that it is the Gaels who will win the victory; every brow shall sweat blood, fighting the battle at the river Clyde; England shall submit, however great her cunning, seeking peace from the king who is away from us.*

This area was one of the ancient provinces of Scotland known as Srath Èireann (Strath Earn, 'strath of the river of Ireland') and it extends from Loch Earn in the west to the River Tay in the east. During James VI's efforts to extirpate the MacGregors, it was recorded, in March 1612, that some 240 persons were heavily fined in Dumbarton and Strathearn for having given shelter to them. It would seem that at that time the area was well within the Gaelic-speaking areas. Historian Ted Cowan said of this activity that:

> It has been calculated that in 1613-14 some nine hundred and twenty individuals were fined a total of £110,000. The vicious acquisitiveness of the Crown and Campbell partnership is without parallel in the annals of Scottish history. It was not to be forgotten or forgiven. Gilleasbuig Gruamach, (Archibald, Duke [sic] of Argyll) almost single-handedly created the reputation of the Campbells as one of the most hated, if most successful, clans in Scottish history.

Perhaps Gilleasbuig Gruamach's activities gave rise to the saying:

> Fhad's a bhios maide 's a' choille, cha bhi Caimbeulach gun fhoill.
>
> *For as long as there is a stick in the forest, there won't be a Campbell without treachery.*

Caibideil 17: *Chapter 17*

Siorrachdan Àir a Tuath, a Deas is an Ear:
North, South and East Ayrshire

To the southwest of Glasgow is the Clyde Valley area and on its adjacent coastline are the three local authority areas of Siorrachdan Àir a Tuath, a Deas is an Ear (North, South and East Ayrshire). This was the heart of the Cumbric or North Welsh-speaking kingdom of Strathclyde ('the strath of the River Clyde'). The area was absorbed into the Gaelic-speaking kingdom of Alba (Scotland) in 1018. There are traces of that older, linguistic heritage in names such as Àird Rosain (Ardrossan, 'point of the small promontory'), Dail Ruigh (Dalry, 'haugh at the slope'), Dunlop (possibly 'fort at the bend'), Cill Bhreannain (Kilbirnie, 'Church of St. Brendan'), Taobh a' Chaolais (East Kilbride, 'beside the sound'), Cille Bhrìghde an Iar (West Kilbride, 'St. Bride's Church, west), Cill Mheàrnaig (Kilmarnock, 'St. Ernoc's Church'), Cill Dingean (Kilwinning, 'St. Finian's Church'), An Leargaidh Ghallda (Largs, 'lowland sloping place') and, indeed, Ayr itself. The county's name is from Inbhir Àir, meaning the mouth of the River Ayr. By the early 16th century, Gaelic in the district had almost disappeared, with only small pockets in the hills.

Neil, Earl of Carraig (Carrick, 'rocky place'), died in 1256 and his daughter Marjorie, Countess of Carrick, married Robert Bruce, Lord of Annandale, who thus became Earl of Carrick. His grandson Robert, the future king, was born at Turnberry in 1274 and became Earl in 1292. He is generally understood to have been a Gaelic speaker. One historian puts it like this:

> ... Robert Bruce's upbringing was coloured by a mixture of traditions, of which the Gaelic tradition of Carrick and the west must have been one. In what is perhaps the earliest recorded appearance of the future king, we find him witnessing a deed of Alexander MacDonald of Islay in company with his father ...

The languages used at such a ceremony would probably have been Gaelic and Latin.

Bhaltair Ceannadach agus Raibeart Burns: *Walter Kennedy and Robert Burns*

Walter Kennedy (c.1455-c.1508) was a younger brother of the second Lord Kennedy of Dùn Iubhair (Dunure, 'yew tree fort') in South Ayrshire, which was then Gaelic-speaking. A graduate of the University of Glasgow, he held various ecclesiastical posts and had estates in both Carrick and Galloway. Although his surviving works are written in Middle Scots, we can assume from 'The Flyting of Dumbar and Kennedie' (c.1500), the earliest surviving example of the Scottish version of the 'flyting' genre in poetry, that he also composed Gaelic verse. In this poetic contest, poet, William Dunbar insults Kennedy's Carrick roots and associates him with 'Erschry'. By this time, the term 'Irish' in Scotland generally signified Gaelic:

> Sic eloquence as thay in Erschry use,
> In sic is sett thy thraward appetyte.
> Thow hes full littill feill of fair indyte.
> I tak on me, ane pair of Lowthiane hippis
> Sall fairar Inglis mak and mair perfyte
> Than thow can blabbar with thy Carrik lippis.

> *Such eloquence as they in Irishry [Gaeldom] use*
> *Is what defines your perverse taste.*
> *You have very small aptitude for good verse-making.*
> *I'll wager, a pair of Lothian hips*
> *Shall fairer English [Lowland Scots] make and more polished*
> *Than thou can blabber with thy Carrick lips.*

Cnoc Breac (Knockbrake, 'speckled hill'), Creag Dubh (Craigdow, 'black rock'), Creag Finn (Craigfin, 'fair rock') and Gleann Laoigh (Glenluie, 'calf glen') are all Gaelic place-names, suggesting the survival in the area of some Gaelic down to the mid-18th century. Robert Burns recalled a maternal rhyme:

> the old Highland one, Leiger m' chose – the only fragment remaining of the old words, is the chorus, still a favourite lullaby of my old mother, from whom I learned it:

Leiger m' chose, my bonie wee lass,
An leiger m' chose, my dearie;
A' the lee-lang winter night,
Leiger m' chose, my dearie.

'Leig air m' choise' means 'pee on my foot'.

Burns was also aware of a Gaelic superstition when he penned his poem 'Tam o' Shanter', where the witches cannot go beyond the keystone of the bridge:

Ludh an spioraid, dol timcheall na drochaid.
The way of the ghost, going round the bridge.

Arainn: *Arran*

Off the Ayrshire coast is Arainn (Arran), an island that has long been the playground of the wealthy. The meaning of Arainn is unclear but it is also known in Gaelic as Arainn nan Iomadh Aighean ('Arran of the many deer') since it featured under this title in a panegyric composed by tradition by Caoilte, companion of Ossian. This poem called 'Agallamh na Senorach' ('The Dialogue of the Ancients') first recorded in the 13th century, describes the island paradise:

Arran of the many stags
The sea strikes against her shoulders,
Companies of men can feed there,
Blue spears are reddened among her boulders.
Merry hinds are on her hills,
Juicy berries are there for food,
Refreshing water in her streams,
Nuts in plenty in the wood.

19th-century poets also extolled many of Arran's virtues:

Arainn bheag bhòidheach!
'S grinn do chleòca san t-samhradh,
Tha do bhruthain làn neòinein
'S do mhòinteach làn ceann-dubh.

Tha do bhric bhallach dhùbh-ghorm
Ri cùrsachd troimh d' aibhnean
'S a' chuthag rìomhach cuir smùid dith
A' tighinn an dlùths air a' bhealtainn.

Bonny little Arran! Beautiful your mantle in summer,
Your braes full of daisies and your moorlands of black-caps.

Your trout spotted and dark blue sporting briskly in your waters,
And the fine cuckoo calling loudly as May day approaches.

A native of the island, an Arainneach, might have the nickname Coinean Mòr ('big rabbit'), but the Gaelic dialect of Arran could be said to have died out when Donald Craig, the last speaker, died in the 1970s.

The island's main centre is Brodhaig (Brodick, ON *Breidvik*, 'broad bay'); the area around its royal castle, begun in the 1230s, was known as Tràigh a' Chaisteil ('castle shore'), while the site of the original village was near Cladach ('beach'). During the Cromwellian Protectorate, a garrison of English soldiers at Brodick Castle caused local resentment. There is a story of an attack on a Cromwellian foraging party halfway between Sannox (ON *Sandvik*, 'sandy bay') and Coire (Corrie, 'kettle-shaped hollow'). The site of the skirmish is said to be at Allt a' Chlaidhcimh ('sword burn'), with the last soldier killed at Clach a' Chath ('battle stone'). The name of this stone has now been translated back into Gaelic by some geological and mountaineering writers as Clach a' Chait ('stone of the cat').

Proceeding clockwise around the island from Brodick, the road reaches the sea again at Eilean Molaise ('St. Molaise's island'), now Lamlash. This was the island's holiest dedication to the saint now known as Molaise. He was born in 566 and, after 580, became a hermit in a cave on the island. Molaise was especially revered; when the Vikings arrived here they called Arran both Herrey or Hersey and Mallasey or Melansay, the latter derived from Eilean Molaise.

These Scandinavians provided many place names on the island: the glens of Ormidale (*Ormi-dalr,* meaning 'Ormi's dale'), Scorodale (*Skorri-dalr* named after Skorri, the giant) and Chalmadale ('Hjalamund's dale') preserve their personal names. The Norse occupation most likely saw the introduction of field names based on peighinn ('penny'). Arran rental place-names such as Dà Pheighinn (Dippen, twopenny land'), Peighinn Riabhach (Penrioch, 'speckled pennyland'), Penalister ('Alasdair's pennyland') and Peighinn a' Fleisdeir ('pennyland of the fletcher') record the old system.

Lying below the Iron Age fort of Tòrr an t-Seann Chaisteil ('height of the old castle') at Druim an Dùin (Drumadoun, 'ridge of the fort') is King's Cave, named for a spurious association with Robert the Bruce, although Bruce did draw his support from the wider area. King's Cave once had an association with the Fingalian hero, Fionn.

Somerled, Lord of the Isles, held Arran in the 13th century, with his son Angus receiving Arran when the patrimony was divided between the three sons. Following the power vacuum created by the Wars of Independence, his Clan Donald descendants had added the island to their maritime territories. However, despite their being a key ally of Bruce in his struggle for independence, by 1377, the Stewarts had pushed the MacDonalds out of Arran.

By 1503 the Hamiltons, close family members of the ruling Stewart dynasty, had become Earls of Arran. The Stewart family's grip on the island began to weaken when, in 1452, James III granted the castle at Loch Raonsa (Lochranza, ON 'rowan tree river') to Alexander Montgomery. The village itself is known as Ceann Loch (Kinloch, 'head of the loch'). The presence of Clan Donald in not far distant Kintyre spelt trouble. Dòmhnall Balloch (Donald Balloch), claimant to the Lordship of the Isles, stormed the island in 1544.

There were constant complaints from Highland parishes that communities suffered from too few ministers. By 1712, Lochranza, at last, had a "catechist and preacher of the Gospel", who had the tack of Coillemore, a little 'runrig' farm on the hill above the modern village. Here in the early 1760s, the woman Robert Burns called 'Highland Mary' served for a spell as servant to her uncle, the catechist Daniel Campbell.

According to one account, at that time there were almost 100 small runrig farms, comprising 1,110 families, but, by the early 19th century, "improvement" had begun and, in 1829, townships in the north of the island were cleared. Some families went to Canada to an area known as Megantic, around 60 kilometres from Quebec. Daniel MacMillan moved to Glasgow from Achadh Beag ('little field') above Coire. He and his brother founded MacMillan Publishers in 1843, and Daniel was the grandfather of Harold MacMillan who became Prime Minister in 1957.

A late 18th-century account said that estate pressure at that time was undermining the land allocation system of runrig, as tenants were now permanently allocated land holdings. The disadvantages of scattered individual plots being worked in competition instead of in harmony are obvious. Much of the ridicule of the ancient system was based on observations made at this time, and much came from clergymen with an academic interest in agriculture and a desire, in the days of patronage, to ingratiate themselves with potential patrons, the heritors.

Arran's adjacent island of Bòd (Bute, perhaps meaning 'fire') has a Gaelic heritage best remembered in a little ditty which attempts to be even-handed:

> Chan ann am Bòid uile a tha an t-olc, tha cuid dheth sa Chumaradh bheag làimh ris.
>
> *Not all the evil is in Bute, there is a bit in little Cumbrae beside it.*

Caibideil 18: *Chapter 18*

Gall-Ghàidhealaibh, Dùn Phris agus Eilean Mhanainn: *Galloway, Dumfries and The Isle of Man*

To the south of Ayrshire are Gall-Ghàidhealaibh (Galloway) and Dùn Phris (Dumfries). The place name Galloway is derived from the Gaelic Gall-Ghàidhealaibh ('amongst the Gall-Ghàidheil' or 'stranger-Gaels'). The specific identity of those to whom the term was applied is unknown, but the general view is that it referred to an ethnic or cultural identity such as the Strathclyde Britons or another related but distinct population. One theory is that it refers to a population of mixed Scandinavian and Gaelic ethnicities that may have inhabited Galloway in the Middle Ages.

It was said of the Loch Urr area that:

> The names of all the Places here, are Gaelic, which language was spoken in the remote parts of Galloway, so late as … 1672.

A possibly medieval Gaelic poem in five verses called 'Òran Bagraidh' was published in the book *From the Farthest Hebrides* (1978). 'Òran Bagraidh' (probably meaning 'threatening song') is much debated. Many parts of the song are unintelligible to modern Gaelic speakers, including academics and scholars. The song mentions Galloway place names in the Glenkens parishes. Its origins perhaps lie in a mid-15th-century legend set in either Threave or Douglas Castle, itself less than 28 kilometres from the Solway Firth and the English border, and concerning the execution of a local nobleman called MacLellan. Though uncertain, the story was widely believed. The traditional tale is that, having displeased the Black Douglas, this man was imprisoned. His uncle arrived with the King's order for MacLellan's release and was hospitably entertained to dinner by the Earl. While they sat over their wine, MacLellan was beheaded in the courtyard.

An eminent Gaelic scholar has written that:

> the poem seems to commemorate a violent event, and that a woman had a lot to do with it. It also laments the loss of beloved

territory in the hills. It is pervaded by sorrow and bitterness but shot through with occasional notes of defiance or threat.

He concludes that it is not possible to say that the poem is a wholly genuine late medieval work, nor is it possible to say that it is wholly fabricated. A tentative rendering commences:

Aoibhinn cumar an Eas Dhomhainn,
Aoibhinn Bealach crom nan Slògh,
Aoibhinn bruthaichean Beinn Beathach,
Aoibhinn 'n gleann san robh thu òg;
Trom dhomh madainn an aon latha,
Trom dhomh madainn a' Chrò Mhòir,
Nìorbh i èirig air an eislig
Caisteal Chaiseal ceilt' a' Chrò.

Pleasant is Cumar an Eas Dhomhainn,
Pleasant is crooked Bealach nan Slògh,
Pleasant are the braes of Benbeoch,
Pleasant is the glen in which you were young;
The morning of the one day has saddened me,
The morning of the Great Crò has saddened me,
No recompense for the funeral timbers
Is the castle of hidden Caiseal a' Chrò.

Eilean Mhanainn: *The Isle of Man*

Although not strictly within the scope of this survey, mention should be made of Gaelg/Gailck Vannin (Gaelic of the Isle of Mann, or Manx), closely related to Scottish Gaelic since the island was within the Scottish realm until it lost ownership in the Wars of Independence. English domination and the development of a separate orthography led it to diverge from the Scots and Irish Gaelic, while the 17th-century Lowland Scots' Plantation of Ulster and the extinction of Galloway Gaelic led to its geographic isolation. Yet in

1874 about a third of the population habitually spoke Manx (12,340 out of a population of 41,084). Although the last native speaker, Ned Maddrell, died in 1974, by then a scholarly revival had begun and teaching it in schools had started. The pupils may well learn the Manx proverb:

> Raad ta jees ta reih (roghainn), as raad ta troor ta teiy (taghadh).
>
> *Where two go there is choice, where three go there is picking.*

In Scottish Gaelic the sentiment is expressed thus:

> Cha 'n ionann iùl do dhithis, no slighe do thriùir.
>
> *Two men will take diverse roads, and three will go different ways.*

And indeed, it is now that we take our diverse roads.

> Beannachd leibh.
>
> *(Farewell).*

Fo-sgrìobhadh: *Postscript*

On the southern side of the Solway Firth, in Cumbria, formerly part of Scotland, is the church of Kirkbride, the Church of St. Bride, one of several Gaelic dedications located over the Border. On the north shore of the Firth is Elrig, its name deriving from the Gaelic word eilreig, meaning a trap into which deer were driven for the hunting pleasure of Gaelic nobility. This land was a Gaelic-speaking country and by the 10th century all the area to the North was increasingly dominated by its culture and by the Gaelic regal lordship of Alba, known in Latin as either *Albania* or *Scotia*, and in English as Scotland.

This short survey of Scotland has presented many places where the language and culture were dominant until the start of the 20th century. Against a background of language retreat, it remains a potent and vibrant presence in the North and the past four decades have seen increasingly significant attempts to raise the status of Gaelic, with campaigns to secure an adequate Gaelic presence in the media, to increase Gaelic medium education and secure Gaelic's status in law being partially successful. In Glasgow's West End, the first full Gaelic-medium school, despite newly expanded premises, and the creation of three additional schools in other areas, is oversubscribed. There have never been better opportunities for people to learn Gaelic. Nor for a very long time have there been so many good and gainful opportunities for those with Gaelic to use it.

Many Scots however have only a hazy understanding of their country's Gaelic legacy and one leading academic has pointed out that the 90% of schoolchildren who are ignorant about Gaelic might benefit from some classroom education. Such action has not taken place but it is hoped that this small contribution can in some little way address the reported "lack of basic knowledge", particularly as it pertains to Scotland's Gaelic places.

Taing: *Acknowledgements*

The book received generous funding from Urras Brosnachaidh na Gàidhlig, Urras an Eilein, Comhairle nan Leabhraichean, the Andrew Tannahill Fund, the McCaig Trust, the Gaelic Society of London and Foundation Scotland, without which it could never have been published and for which we are extremely grateful. The core of this book was work on a doctoral thesis supervised by my excellent supervisors Alison Phipps and Sheila Kidd. To them, I am immensely grateful.

Thanks are due to the manager, Angus Morrison, of Acair, the staff and colleagues in bringing it to press; I am thankful to Frances Murray, Greg Thomson and Margaret Ann Macleod for their careful copy-editing and typesetting. Dr John Gillies gave helpful advice about ways in which the text could be improved. My late brother Robbie supplied the geo-locations while my brother Cailean provided the maps.

I am grateful to the following authors, poets, or the publishers and relatives of the poets, for their exceptionally generous permission to include, without payment, material within copyright: Acair, Meg Bateman, David Beaman of *An Iodhlann*, Ellen L. Beard, Ronnie Black, Michel Byrne, Angus Campbell, Kenna Campbell, Mary Ann Campbell, Màiri Sine Campbell, Fr. Donald Cumming, David Currie of The Scottish Gaelic Texts Society, Alison Diack, Bill Innes, Cathlin Macaulay, Ruairidh MacIlleathain (Litir do Luchd-ionnsachaidh), Ruairidh Iain Maciver, Peter Mackay, Ishbel MacLean, Donald Meek, Margaret Mary Murray for the BBC, Michael Newton, Colm Ó Baoill, Alan Riach, Christine Rintoul of Comann Eachdraidh Uibhist a Tuath, Dòmhnall U. Stiùbhart, Taylor Strickland, Danny Thomson and Moray Watson. I am touched particularly by the generous support to this work given by Gavin MacDougall of Luath Press as well as Michael Schmidt and Alan Brenik of Carcanet Press.

For many of the poems, there exist excellent translations by other poets and I have used these where I can; otherwise, I have included translations by the Gaelic poets themselves where possible and appropriate. In a small number of cases, new versions are offered. Although I am well aware of the issues associated with self-translation, it was preferable to give a sense of the different ways in which Gaelic poetry can be, and has been, translated recently.

Coinneach Maclean, June 2025

Nota air Eadar-theangachadh Ainmean Àite:
Note on the Translation of Place-names

Almost a century ago, the Celtic scholar W. J. Watson pleaded that:

> in place-names, sanity and scholarship must conjoin; running after the bizarre or fanciful is fatal.

35 years later he was again sufficiently concerned to write that:

> too often Gaelic words and phrases are mishandled, as would be the case with no other language.

Sadly, little has changed over the years; many explanations remain fanciful and it has been claimed, for example, that the name Sròn an t-Sìthein (Strontian) has four meanings.

In such a field the best course of action is to cite a single authoritative source. Thus place-name explanation in this work is taken from Taylor I. (2011) *Place-names of Scotland*, Birlinn, Edinburgh. This book holds not only sage advice on meanings but has a wealth of additional, related information. In that publication, Strontian's entry is: Sròn an t-Sìthein, 'point of the fairy hill'.

In this publication, place names are handled in the following manner:

> Sròn an t-Sìthein (Strontian, 'point of the fairy hill').

Leabhar-chlàr Taghta: *Selected Bibliography*

To borrow a phrase from Newton that he himself had culled from elsewhere I have "stood on the shoulders of giants" in producing this work. The title of Marinell Ash's fine 1980 study on Sir Walter Scott's legacy, *The Strange Death of Scottish History*, barely raised an eyebrow. Scottish historians and those with a focus on Gaelic were only then getting into their stride. This book could not be possible without their efforts over the last half century and I am indebted to the deep scholarship of Meg Bateman, Ronnie Black, Hugh Cheape, Ted Cowan, Martin MacGregor, Rory MacIver, Wilson McLeod, Donald Meek, Michael Newton, Dòmhnall Uilleam Stiubhart and many others. The bibliography that follows is inevitably selective and is simply intended to provide access to texts which have informed my own interests. Dipping into any of those works will supply the reader with a treasure trove of texts and sources to deepen their knowledge of Scottish Gaelic culture and history.

BLACK, R. (2000) *An Tuil, The Flood: Anthology of 20th-Century Scottish Gaelic Verse* Polygon, Edinburgh

BLACK, R. (2001) *An Lasair, The Flame: An Anthology of Eighteenth-Century Gaelic Verse* Birlinn, Edinburgh

BROUN, D. and MACGREGOR, M. (Eds.) (2009) *Mìorun Mòr nan Gall, 'The great ill-will of the Lowlander'? Lowland Perceptions of the Highlands, Medieval and Modern* University of Glasgow, Glasgow

BROWNE, J. (1838) *History of the Highlands and of the Highland Clans A, Fullerton,* Glasgow

BRUFORD, A. and MACDONALD, D.A. (Eds.) (2003) *Scottish Traditional Tales* Birlinn, Edinburgh

CAMPBELL, J. L. (1933) *Highland Songs of the Forty-five* (ed.) John Grant, Edinburgh (Re-printed in 1984 by Scottish Gaelic Texts Society)

CHEAPE, H. (2008) *Bagpipes: A National Collection of a National Instrument* NMSE – Publishing Ltd, Edinburgh

DEVINE, T. M. (1994) *Clanship to Crofter's War The Social Transformation of the Scottish Highlands* Manchester University Press, Manchester

GILLIES, A.L. (2005) *Songs of Gaelic Scotland* Birlinn, Edinburgh

GRAY, M. (1959) *The Highland Economy 1730-1850* Oliver & Boyd, London

GREGORSON CAMPBELL J. (Ed) (2005) *The Celtic Otherworld* Ronald Black Birlinn, Edinburgh

GREGORY, D. (1836) *History of the Western Highland and Isles of Scotland* re-printed in 2009 by Erimitical Press, Vancouver

GUNN, M. (1938) *Butcher's Broom* Porpoise Press, Edinburgh

MACGREGOR, M. (2012) *Civilising Gaelic Scotland: the Scottish Isles and the Stewart Empire*. In: Ciardha, E.Ó. and Siochru, M.Ó. (Eds.) *The Plantation of Ulster: Ideology and Practice* Series: Studies in Early Modern Irish History Manchester University Press, Manchester

MACGREGOR, M. (1999) *"Surely one of the greatest poems ever made in Britain": the lament for Griogair Ruadh MacGregor of Glen Strae and its historical background* Cowan, E. J. and Gifford, D. (Eds.) *The Polar Twins* John Donald, Edinburgh

MACINNES, J. (2006) *Dùthchas Nan Gàidheal, Selected Essays* Newton, M. (Ed.), Birlinn, Edinburgh

MACKAY, P. and MACDONALD, J. (Eds.) (2020) *100 Dàn as Fheàrr leinn / 100 Favourite Gaelic Poems* Luath Press, Edinburgh

MACKILLOP, A. (2001) *More Fruitful Than The Soil, Army, Empire and the Scottish Highlands, 1715-1815* Birlinn, Edinburgh

MACLEAN, C. I. (1959) *The Highlands* 2006 edition Mainstream Publishing, Edinburgh

MCLEOD, W. & BATEMAN, M. (2007) *Duanaire na Sracaire, The Songbook of the Pillagers, Anthology of Medieval Gaelic Poetry* Birlinn, Edinburgh

MEEK, D.E. (2019) *Caran an-t-saoghail The Wiles of the World: An Anthology of Nineteenth-century Gaelic Verse* Birlinn, Edinburgh

MEEK, D.E. (Ed.) (1996) *Tuath is Tighearna: Tenants and Landlords* Scottish Academic Press Ltd, Edinburgh

NEWTON, M. (1999) *Bho Chluaidh gu Calasraid* Acair, Stornoway

NEWTON, M. (2009) *Warriors of the Word: The World of the Scottish Highlanders* Birlinn, Edinburgh

PITTOCK, M. (2010) *Plaiding the Invention Scotland* in *From Tartan to Tartanry; Scottish Culture, History and Myth* Brown, I. (Ed.) Edinburgh University Press, Edinburgh

ROSS, A. (2000) *The Folklore of the Scottish Highlands* Tempus, Stroud

STEVENSON, D. (2004) *The Hunt for Rob Roy, The Man and the Myths* Birlinn, Edinburgh

STEVENSON, D. (2014) *Highland Warrior, Alasdair MacColla and the Civil Wars* Birlinn, Edinburgh

STIÙBHART, D. U. (2005) *Rioghachd Nan Eilean – Kingdom of the Isles: Eachdraidh Nan Gàidheal 550-1550 – A History of the Gaels 550-1550* Clo Hallaig, Dunblane

TAYLOR, I. (2011) *Place-names of Scotland* Birlinn, Edinburgh

THOMSON, D. (1974) *An Introduction to Gaelic Poetry* Gollanz, London

WATSON, W.J. (1926) *The Celtic Placenames of Scotland,* London Reprinted in 1993 by Birlinn, Edinburgh

Tùsan nan Dàn is nan Òran: *Sources of Poems and Songs*

'A' Choille Ghruamach' (Òran do dh'Ameireaga) Iain MacIlleathain (John MacLean) in Watson, W. J. (ed.) (1918) *Bàrdachd Ghàidhlig 1550-1900* An Comunn Gàidhealach, Inverness

'Am Maraiche 's a Leannan' Màiri NicEalair (Mary MacKellar) in Sinclair, A. (ed.) (1879) *An t-Òranaiche (The Gaelic Songster)* Archibald Sinclair, Glasgow

'A Mhàiri Bhàn Òg' (Òran d' a chèile nuadh-phòsda) Donnchadh Bàn Mac an t-Saoir (Duncan MacIntyre) in MacLeod, A. (ed.) (1952) *The Songs of Duncan Ban MacIntyre* Oliver and Boyd for the Scottish Gaelic Texts Society, Edinburgh

'A Mhic Shimidh, mosgail à d' shuarn' Iain MacFhearchair (John Farquharson) in Diack, A. M. G. (1999) 'Gaelic verse from Aberdeenshire' Thesis, University of Aberdeen

'Anna Bhuidh' Bhàn' Anon. in Diack, A. M. G. (1999) 'Gaelic verse from Aberdeenshire' Thesis, University of Aberdeen

'An t-Alltan Dubh' Dòmhnall Friseal (Dònald Fraser) at https://www.bbc.co.uk/alba/oran/orain/an_t_alltan_dubh/

'An Tiona' Pàdraig MacAoidh (Peter Mackay) in Mackay, P. (2015) *Gu Leòr* Acair, Steòrnabhagh

'An t-Iorram Niseach' Anon at https://BBC Bliadhna nan Òran: An t-Iorram Niseach

'Alasdair à Gleanna Garadh' (Lament for Alasdair Dubh) Sìleas na Ceapaich (Sileas MacDonald) (1729) in Ó Baoill, C. (1972) *Poems and Songs by Sìleas MacDonald* Scottish Academic Press for the Scottish Gaelic Texts Society, Edinburgh

'Alasdair a laoigh mo chèile' (Òran do dh'Alasdair MacColla) Diorbhail Nic a' Bhriuthain (Dorothy Brown) in MacKenzie, J. (ed.) (1872) *Sàr-Obair nam Bàrd Gaelach* Edinburgh: MacLachlan and Stewart; Simpkin, Marshall, London

'A Mhic Iain 'ic Sheumais' A Mhuime NicCòiseam in MacDonald, A. and MacDonald, A. (eds.) (1911) *The MacDonald Collection of Gaelic Poetry* The Northern Counties Newspaper and Printing and Publishing Company, Inverness

Tùsan nan Dàn is nan Òran: *Sources of Poems and Songs*

'A' Mhisg' Iain Moireasdan (John Morrison) in Henderson, G. (ed.) (1896) *Dàin Iain Gobha (The Poems of John Morison)* Knox Press, Edinburgh

'An Eala Bhàn' Dòmhnall Dòmhnallach (Donald MacDonald) in MacAulay F. (ed.) (1995) *Dòmhnall Ruadh Choruna* Comann Eachdraidh Uibhist a Tuath, Lochmaddy

'An Gille Dubh-Dhonn' (Deoch-Slàinte nan Gillean, Òràin à Bàrraidh) in O' Lochlainn, C. (ed.) (1948) Fo Chomharda nan Trí Coinnlean, Baile Áth Cliath, Éirinn

'A nighean donn as grinne cruth' Eòghan MacColla (Evan McColl) in McColl, E. (1836) *Clàrsach nam Beann* Archibald Sinclair, Glasgow

'An Ataireachd Àrd' Dòmhnall MacÌomhair (Donald MacIver) in MacLeod, J.N. (ed.) (1998) *Bàrdachd Leòdhais* Acair, Stornoway

'Arainn bheag bhoidheach' in Currie, D., Balfour J.A. and MacKenzie, W. (eds.) (1982) *The Book of Arran* Kilbrannan Publishing Ltd, Isle of Arran

'Ar Gaisgich a Thuit sna Blàir' Iain Rothach (John Munro) in MacDonald, J., MacLeod, A., MacLeod D. J. (eds.) (2015) *Cuimhneachan, Bàrdachd a' Chiad Chogaidh* Acair, Stornoway

'An t-Sean-bhean' Dòmhnall MacAmhlaigh (Donald MacAulay) in MacAulay, D. (1967) *Seòbhrach às a' Chlaich* Gairm, Glasgow

'Banntrach Cogaidh' An t-Urr. Iain MacLeòid (Rev. John MacLeod) in MacDonald, J., MacLeod, A., MacLeod, D. J. (eds.) (2015) *Cuimhneachan, Bàrdachd a' Chiad Chogaidh* Acair, Stornoway

'Bàs Dhiarmaid' in Cooke, P., MacDonald, A., MacLeod, M. and Ó Baoill, C. (eds.) (2022) *The Eliza Ross Collection* Taigh nan Teud, Skye in association with the Musica Scotica Trust

'Bheir mise dhaibh banais am Bail' Ionar-aora' (Luinneag an Iasgair) Iain MacPhàidein (John MacFadyen) in MacFadyen, J. (1902) *Sgeulaiche nan Caol* Archd. Sinclair, Celtic Press, Glasgow

'B' e gairbhe na gaoithe' (Luinneag) Deòrsa Mac Iain Dheòrsa (George Campbell Hay) in Byrne, M. (ed.) (2000-3) *Collected Poems and Songs of George Campbell Hay* Edinburgh University Press, Edinburgh

'Birlinn Chloinn Raghnaill' Alasdair mac Mhaighstir Alasdair (Alexander MacDonald) in Riach, A. (2015) *The Birlinn of Clanranald* Kettillonia, Angus

'Birlinn Ghoraidh Chròbhain' Donnchadh MacIain (Duncan Johnstone) in Johnstone, D. (1938) *Crònan nan Tonn* Archd. Sinclair, Celtic Press, Glasgow

'Bothan Àirigh am Bràigh Raineach' Anon. MacKay, P. and MacDonald, J. (eds.) (2020) *100 Dàn as Fheàrr Leinn (100 Favourite Gaelic Poems)* Luath Press, Edinburgh

'Brònach Tadhal Dùn Monaidh' Deòrsa Mac Iain Dheòrsa (George Campbell Hay) in Byrne, M. (ed.) (2000-3) *Collected Poems and Songs of George Campbell Hay* Edinburgh University Press, Edinburgh

'Brostughadh-catha Chlann Dòmhnaill Latha Chatha Gharbhaich' Lachlann Mòr MacMhuirich (Lachlan MacVuirich) 'Aos-dàna Mhic Dhòmhnaill' ('MacDonald's High-poet') Thomson, D.S. (1968) Gairm pp 1512

'Bu mhiann leam am breacan tlàth' (Moladh rann do Shir Eachainn Mac Gilleain, Triath Dhubhairt) Anon. (1893) in Stewart, D. W. *Old and Rare Scottish Tartans* George P. Johnston, Edinburgh

'Bu bhinn <sian[a]mhran) na sleagh agus monghar na míleadh' in Meek, D. E. (1986) 'The Banners of the Fian in Gaelic Ballad tradition', *Cambridge Medieval Celtic Studies,* No 11, (pp 29-69), Cambridge

'Bu mhiann leam am breacan tlàth' (Moladh rann do Shir Eachainn Mac Gilleain, Triath Dhubhairt) Anon. in Stewart, D. W. (1893) *Old and Rare Scottish Tartans* George P. Johnston, Edinburgh

'Bùth Dhòmhnaill 'ic Leòid' Dòmhnall Mac an t-Saoir (Donald MacIntyre) in MacMillan, S. (ed.) (1968) *Sporan Dhòmhnaill – Gaelic Poems and Songs by the late Donald MacIntyre, The Paisley Bard* Oliver and Boyd for the Scottish Gaelic Texts Society, Edinburgh

'Calbharaigh' Somhairle MacGill-eain (Sorley MacLean) in Whyte, C. and Dymock. E. (eds.) (2011) *Caoir Gheal Leumraich (A White Leaping Flame)* Polygon, Edinburgh

Tùsan nan Dàn is nan Òran: *Sources of Poems and Songs*

'Cànan nan Gàidheal' Murchadh MacPhàrlain (Murdo MacFarlane) in Mhoireach, C. (ed.) (2022) *Doras gun Chlàimhean* Acair, Stornoway

'Ceud soraidh bhuam fhìn gu m' eòlas' ('Òran Mòr Sgoirebreac') Anon. in Maclean, A. (1993) *Some Nicolson Traditions, The Transactions of the Gaelic Society of Inverness Vol. LVII* Inverness

'Cha dìrich mi bruthach 's cha shiùbhail mi còmhnard' ('Fuirich a rìbhinn') Deòrsa Caimbeul (George Campbell) in Sinclair, A. (ed.) (1879) *An t-Òranaiche (The Gaelic Songster)* Archibald Sinclair, Glasgow

'Chan e chreach mi' (Iain Òg Mac Mhic Nèill) Anon. in Stiùbhart, D. U. Edinburgh University Library, Carmichael Watson MS 7 fo.14v published in Martin, P. (ed.) (2017) *Three Archipelagos: Perspectives on Early Modern Barra in Castles and Galleys* Islands Book Trust, Isle of Lewis

'Chan e dìreadh a' bhruthaich' Fearchar MacRath (Farquhar MacRae) in MacKay, P. and MacDonald, J. (eds) (2020) *100 Dàn as Fheàrr Leinn (100 Favourite Gaelic Poems*) Luath Press, Edinburgh

'Chì mi 'n Tìr' Seonaidh MacCumhais (John MacCuish) in Nic a' Ghobhainn, M. (ed.) (2014) *Bàrdachd na Hearadh* Harris Development Limited, Harris

'Clann-nighean an Sgadain' Ruaraidh MacThòmais (Derick Thomson) in Thomson, D. S. (1982) *Creachadh na Clàrsaich (Plundering the Harp)* Macdonald, Edinburgh

'Coinneach Odhar' Niall MacLeòid (Neil MacLeod) in Macleod, N. (1883) *Clàrsach an Doire* MacLachlan and Stewart, Edinburgh

'Coisich a rùin' Anon. in Craig, K. C. (ed.) (1949) *Òrain Luaidh Màiri Nighean Alasdair* Published for K.C. Craig by Alasdair Matheson & Co Ltd., Glasgow

'Cruachan Beann' Pàdraig Mac an t-Saoir (Peter MacIntyre) in *Mac Talla* 11: 20 (1902-03)

'Cumha Choire an Easain' Iain MacAoidh, Am Pìobaire Dall (John MacKay, The Blind Piper) MacKenzie (ed.) (1872) *Sàr-Obair nam Bàrd Gaelach* MacLachlan and Stewart, Edinburgh; Simpkin, Marshall, London

‘Cumha do dh’Aonghas ’ic Ailein’ Dòmhnall Mac a’ Ghobhainn (Donald Smith), MacKay, P. and MacDonald, Jo, (eds.) (2020) *100 Dàn as Fheàrr Leinn (100 Favourite Gaelic Poems)* Luath Press, Edinburgh

‘Cumha Hiortach’ Anon. in Stewart, A. and Stewart, D. (eds.) (1804) *Cochruinneacha Taoghta de Shaothair nam Bàrd Gaelach* Edinburgh

‘Cur cùlaibh ri Asainte’ Alasdair MacLeòid (Alasdair MacLeod) in Martin, R.(ed.) (2021) *The Coigach and Assynt Collection* Taigh nan Teud, Skye

‘Dh’fhalbh a’ chòir agus thàinig an eucoir’ (Latha Sliabh an t-Siorram 3) Sìleas na Ceapaich, (Cicily MacDonald of Keppoch) in Ó Baoill, C. (ed.) (1972) *Bàrdachd Shìlis na Ceapaich* Scottish Academic Press for The Scottish Gaelic Texts Society, Edinburgh

‘Deoch-slàinte Ailein Mhùideartaich’ (‘Tha tighinn fodham èirigh’) Iain mac Dhùghaill MacDhòmhnaill (John MacDonald) in Watson, W. J. (ed.) (1918) *Bàrdachd Ghàidhlig Gaelic Poetry 1550-1900* An Comunn Gàidhealach, Inverness

‘Deoch-slàinte nan Gillean’ Iain MacFhionghain (John MacKinnon) in Cameron, H. (1932) *Na Bàird Thirisdeach* The Tiree Association, The Observer Press, Stirling

‘Dòmhnall nan Dòmhnall’ in Mac-an-Roich, D. (ed.) (1848) *Òrain Ghàidhealach* Thornton and Collie, Edinburgh

‘Duanag don Uisge-bheatha’ Ailean Dall MacDhùghaill (Blind Allan MacDougall) in MacKenzie, J. (ed.) (1872) *Sàr-Obair nam Bàrd Gaelach* MacLachlan and Stewart; Edinburgh; Simpkin, Marshall, London

‘Ealaidh Ghaoil’ Eòghann MacLachlainn (Ewen MacLachlan) in Dòmhnallach, I. (ed.) (1937) *Ewen MacLachlan’s Gaelic Verse* University of Aberdeen, Aberdeen

‘Eachann MacDhòmhnaill’ (Eachann nan Cath) Iain Mac a’ Ghobhainn (Iain Crichton Smith) in Watson, M. (ed.) (2013) *Iain Mac a’ Ghobhainn A’ Bhàrdachd Ghàidhlig* Acair, Stornoway

‘Eilean Fraoich’ Uilleam MacCoinnich (William MacKenzie) in MacKenzie, W. (1936) *Cnoc Chùsbaig Òrain agus Dàin* Alex. MacLaren & Sons, Glasgow

Tùsan nan Dàn is nan Òran: *Sources of Poems and Songs*

'Eilean na h-Òige' Mgr Ailean Dòmhnallach (Father Allan MacDonald) in Watson, W. J. (ed.) (1918) *Bàrdachd Ghàidhlig Gaelic Poetry 1550-1900* An Comunn Gàidhealach, Inverness

'Fàgail Ghlaschu' Ruaraidh Caimbeul (Roderick Campbell) NicDhòmhnaill, J. and Chaimbeul, M. A. (eds.) (2015) *Bho Ghinealach gu Ginealach* Ceòlas Uibhist Earr, South Uist

'Fàilte Bhraid-Albann' Mac a'Mahaoilein, MacMillan, Stewart, C., *The Killin Collection of Gaelic Songs with Music and Translations* (Edinburgh 1884)

'Fàilte Thighearna Chluaidh' Iain MacDhùghaill (John MacDougall) in MacDhùghaill, I. (1870) *Gaisge nan Gàidheal, Òrain agus Dàin le Iain MacDhùghaill à Àird Ghobhar* J.E. and R. Inglis, Sandbank

'Fàsachadh na Gàidhealtachd' Dòmhnall MacLeòid (Donald MacLeod) in Maciver, R. I. (2018) 'The Gaelic Poet and the British military experience, 1756-1856' PhD thesis, Glasgow University, Glasgow

'Feasgar Foghair air Achadh Bhuana' Anon. in Sinton, T. (1906) *The Poetry of Badenoch* Northern Counties Publishing Company, Inverness

'Feòrag ghlas, tuath air Braco' Ruaraidh MacThòmais (Derick Thomson) in Thomson, D.S. (1995) *Meall Garbh (The Rugged Mountain)* Gairm, Glasgow

'Fios chun a' Bhàird' Uilleam MacDhùnlèibhe (William Livingstone) in Livingstone, W. (1882) *Duain is Òrain le Uilleam Mac Dhunleibhe* Archibald Sinclair, Glasgow

'Fhuaras mac mar an t-athair, math ar flathaibh ar n-eòlas' in Watson, W. J. (ed) (1937) *Scottish verse from the Book of the Dean of Lismore* Scottish Academic Press for The Scottish Gaelic Texts Society, Edinburgh

'Fulangas Chrìosd' Dùghall Bochanan (Dugald Buchanan) in Meek, D. E. (ed.) (2015) *Laoidhean Spioradail Dhùghaill Bhochanain* Comann Litreachas Gàidhlig na h-Alba, Glaschu

'Gabh rém chomraigh, a Mheic Ghriogair' Fionnlagh am Bàrd Ruadh (Finlay the Red Bard)

The Book of the Dean of Lismore in Watson, W. J. (ed.) (1937) *Scottish Verse from the Book of the Dean of Lismore* Oliver and Boyd for the Scottish Gaelic Texts Society, Edinburgh

'Gealach an Fhàis os Cionn Shlèite' Somhairle MacGill-eain (Sorley MacLean) in Whyte, C. and Dymock, E. (eds) (2011) *Caoir Gheal Leumraich (A White Leaping Flame)* Polygon, Edinburgh

'Ge socrach mo leaba' ('B'annsa cadal air fraoch') Gilleasbaig MacDhòmhnaill (Archibald MacDonald) in MacKenzie, J. (ed.) (1872) *Sàr-Obair nam Bàrd Gaelach* MacLachlan and Stewart; Edinburgh; Simpkin, Marshall, London

'Gleanna Gollaidh' Rob Donn MacAoidh (Robert MacKay) in Beard, E.L. (ed.) (2018) *100 Òran le Rob Donn MacAoidh* Taigh nan Teud, Skye

'Griogal Cridhe' (Cumha Ghriogair MhicGhriogair Ghlinn Sreith) Mòr Chaimbeul (Marion Campbell) in Watson, W. J. (ed.) (1918) *Bàrdachd Ghàidhlig* Gaelic Poetry 1550-1900 An Comann Gàidhealach, Inverness

'Guma Slàn do na Fearaibh' Dòmhnall Caimbeul (Donald Campbell) in Sinton, T. (ed.) (1906) *The Poetry of Badenoch* Northern Counties Publishing Company, Inverness

'Hallaig' Somhairle MacGill-eain (Sorley MacLean) in Whyte, C. and Dymock. E. (eds.) (2011) *Caoir Gheal Leumraich (A White Leaping Flame)* Polygon, Edinburgh

'Iain Ghlinne Cuaich' Anon. in MacKay, P. and MacDonald, J. (eds.) (2020) *100 Dàn as Fheàrr Leinn (100 Favourite Gaelic Poems)* Luath Press, Edinburgh

'Iorram na Sgiobaireachd' Murchadh Mòr MacCoinnich (Murdoch MacKenzie in Watson, W. J. (ed.) (1918) *Bàrdachd Ghàidhlig Gaelic Poetry 1550-1900* An Comunn Gàidhealach, Inverness

'Là Inbhir Lòchaidh' Iain Lom MacDhòmhnaill (John MacDonald) in MacKay, P. and MacDonald, J. (eds.) (2020) *100 Dàn as Fheàrr Leinn (100 Favourite Gaelic Poems)* Luath Press, Edinburgh

'Là Mille Gàrraidh' Anon. in Tolmie, F. (1911), *Journal of the Folk Song Society* (Vol.1 Part 3) pp 200-01, The Folk Song Society, London

Tùsan nan Dàn is nan Òran: *Sources of Poems and Songs*

'Latha 'siubhal slèibhe dhomh' (Òran do dhaoine uaisle an Eilein Sgiathanaich) Lachunn mac Theàrlaich Òig (Lachlan MacKinnon) in *Mac Talla* 10: 9 (1901-02) Jonathan MacKinnon, Cape Breton, Canada

'Latha dhomh 's mi sràidearachd (Gu h-àrd os cionn Dhùn Èideann) Anon. at https://www.tobarandualchais.co.uk/track/24744/l=g.

'Leanabh an àigh' Màiri NicDhòmhnaill (Mary MacDonald) *Mac Talla* 6: 18 (1897-98) Jonathan MacKinnon, Cape Breton, Canada

'Luinneag MhicLeòid' Màiri nighean Alasdair Ruaidh (Mary MacLeod) in Ó Baoill, C. (ed.) (2014) *Màiri nighean Alasdair Ruaidh – Song-maker of Skye and Berneray* Scottish Gaelic Texts Society, Glasgow

'MacGriogair à Ruadh-shruth' Anon. in Watson, W.J. (1918, reprinted 1976) Bàrdachd Ghàidhlig, An Comunn Gàidhealach, Inverness

'Mairg Thréigeas Inn, a Amhlaoíbh' Muireadhach Albannach O Dalaigh in O Cuív in Carney J. and Greene D. (eds.) (1968) *Celtic studies: Essays in Memory of Angus Matheson,* Routlege & Keegan Paul, London

'Mi 'm shuidhe an seo am ònar '(Clann Ghriogair air Fògradh) Anon. 16th in Watson, W.J. (ed.) (1918) *Bàrdachd Ghàidhlig Gaelic Poetry 1550-1900* (An Comunn Gàidhealach, Inverness

'Marbhna Fhearchair Í Mhaoil Chiarain' Ó Maoil Ciaráin in Breatnach, R.A. (1943) *Éigse* 3, pp.165-185 Am Baile Áth Cliath, Éirinn

'Mìle mallachd don òl' Dòmhnall Donn Bhoth Fhionntainn (Donald MacDonald of Bohuntine) in MacDonald, A. (1914) *Story and Song from Loch Ness-side* Northern Counties Newspaper and Print Company, Inverness

'Míolchoin gharga ar iallaibh órdha' (Lámh Aoinfhir Fhóirfeas i nÉirinn) Giolla Críost Brúilingeach in Watson, W. J. (ed.) (1937) *Scottish Verse from the Book of the Dean of Lismore* Oliver and Boyd for the Scottish Gaelic Texts Society, Edinburgh

'Mo chailin dhonn òg' Calum MacIllEathain (Malcolm MacLean) in MacKenzie, J. (ed.) (1872) *Sàr-Obair nam Bàrd Gaelach* MacLachlan and Stewart, Edinburgh; Simpkin, Marshall, London

'Mo Ghleannan Taobh Loch Lìobhann' Alasdair MacFhraing (Alasdair Rankine) in Campbell, B. (1987) *Òrain nan Gàidheal 2* Gairm, Glasgow

'Moladh Beinn Dòbhrain' Donnchadh Bàn Mac an t-Saoir (Duncan MacIntyre) in MacLeod, A. (ed.) (1952) *The Songs of Duncan Ban MacIntyre* Oliver and Boyd for the Scottish Gaelic Texts Society, Edinburgh (Translation Riach, A. (2013) *Praise of Ben Dorain* New Scottish Writing Poetry Pamphlet, Kettilonia, Angus

'Moladh Chabair Fèidh' Tormod Bàn MacLeòid (Norman MacLeod) or Murdoch Matheson in Watson, W.J. (1929-30) *An Gaidheal*, Vol. 25, An Comunn Gàidhealach Publications, Glasgow

'Moladh Deireannach' Iain Eairdsidh MacAsgaill (John Archie MacAskill) in Morrison A. (ed.) (1961) *An Ribheid Chiùil* printed for the editor by Learmonth, Stirling

'Moladh Thùrnaig' Alasdair Camshron (Alexander Cameron) in Moffat-Pender, I.M. (ed.) (1926) *Am bàrd: òrain, sgrìobhaidhean agus litrichean* Archibald Sinclair, The Celtic Press, Glasgow

'Mo shoraidh leis a' Chòigich' Murchadh MacIllEathain (Murdo MacLean) in Bryan, T. and V. (eds.) (1988) *Ullapool – Music of Lochbroom and Coigach* Drumrunie Press, Wester Ross

'Muile nam Fuar-bheann Mòr' Iain Dòmhnallach (John MacDonald) in Lobban, M.M. (2004) *Lachann Dubh a'Chrògain* The New Iona Press, Strathpeffer

'Murt na Ceapaich' Iain Lom MacDhòmhnaill (John MacDonald) in MacKenzie, A. M. (ed.) (1964) *Òrain Iain Luim, Songs of John MacDonald, Bard of Keppoch* Scottish Academic Press for the Scottish Gaelic Texts Society, Edinburgh

'Nam bithinn fhèin am shia bliadhn' deug' Anon. in MacMillan, S. (1971) *Bygone Lochaber* Printed for Private Circulation by K. & R. Davidson, Glasgow

'Ní h-Éibhneas gan Chlainn Domhnaill' Giolla Coluim Mac an Ollaimh in Watson, W. J. (ed.) (1918) *Bàrdachd Ghàidhlig Gaelic Poetry 1550-1900* An Comunn Gàidhealach, Inverness

'Na Tulaichean' in Sinclair, A. (ed.) (1879) *An t-Òranaiche (The Gaelic Songster)* Archibald Sinclair, Glasgow

Tùsan nan Dàn is nan Òran: *Sources of Poems and Songs*

'Och, och a-nochd 's mi 'n Cùl nan Cnoc' (Cumha) Aonghas Stiùbhart (Angus Stewart) in MacKenzie, W. (1934) *Old Skye Tales* MacLaren and Sons, Glasgow

'Och nan och 's mi fo lèireadh' (Cumha Iain Ghairbh) Piuthar Iain Ghairbh (Iain Garbh's sister at https://www.bbc.co.uk/alba/oran/orain/cumha_iain_gairbh/

'Òran Bagraidh' Anon. in Fergusson, D. A. (General Ed.), MacDhòmhnaill, A. I. (Gaelic Ed), Gillespie, J. F. (Music Ed) (1978) *From the Farthest Hebrides – Bho na h-Innse Gall as iomallaiche* MacMillan of Canada, Toronto

'Òran a' Pholitician' Ruaraidh "Ròideag" Caimbeul (Roderick Campbell) in NicDhòmhnaill, J. and Chaimbeul, M. A. (eds.) (2015) *Bho Ghinealach gu Ginealach* Ceòlas Uibhist Earr, South Uist

'Òran Beinn Lì' Màiri Mhòr nan Òran (Mary MacPherson) in Meek, D.E. (ed.) (1995) *Tuath is Tighearna (Tenants and Landlords)* Scottish Academic Press for The Scottish Gaelic Texts Society, Edinburgh

'Òran d' an Chath-bhuidhinn Rìoghail Ghàidhealaich' An t-Urr. Seumas MacLagain in Stewart, A. and Stewart, D. (eds.) (1804) *Cochruinneacha Taoghta de Shaothair nam Bàrd Gaeleach,* Charles Stuart, Edinburgh

'Òran do dh' Eilean Mhiughalaigh' Niall Mac a' Phì (Neil MacPhee) at https://www.feisean.org/fuaran/en/songs/oran-do-eilean- mhiughalaigh-en/

'Òran do MhacLeòid Dhùin Bheagain' Ruairidh MacMhuirich, An Clàrsair Dall (Roderick Morrison, The Blind Harper) in Matheson, W. (ed.) (1970) *The Blind Harper: An Clàrsair Dall* The Scottish Gaelic Texts Society, Edinburgh

'Òran don Phrionnsa' Alasdair MacDonald in Strickland, T. (2023) *Oran do'n Phroinnsa, Dastram Delirium, Selected poems of Alasdair mac Mhaighsir Alasdair)* Broken Sleep Books Ltd, Llandysul, Wales

'Òran do Shir Eachann' in Ó Baoill, C. (ed.) (1979) *Bàrdachd Chloinn Ghill-eathain, Eachan Bacach and other Maclean Bards* Scottish Academic Press for the Scottish Gaelic Texts Society, Edinburgh

‘Òran Eile air an Adhbhar Cheudna’ Uilleam Ros (William Ross) in MacKay, P. and MacDonald, J. (eds.) (2020) *100 Dàn as Fheàrr Leinn (100 Favourite Gaelic Poems)* Luath Press, Edinburgh

‘Òran Eile air Latha Chùil Lodair’ Iain Ruadh Stiùbhart (John Roy Stewart) in Campbell, J. L. (ed.) (1984) *Highland Songs of the Forty-Five* The Scottish Gaelic Texts Society, Edinburgh

‘Òran Ghlinne Chrò’ Gilleasbaig Mac an t-Saoir (Archibald Macintyre), in Black, R. (1974) Gairm 88, Am Foghar, pp 342-3

‘Òran mar gu’m b’ann le dròbhair àraid d’a Leannan’ Rob Donn MacAoidh (Robert MacKay) in Beard, E. L. (ed.) (2018) *100 Òran le Rob Donn MacAoidh* Taigh nan Teud, Skye

‘Òran Mhanitòba’ Iain MacIlleathain, Bàrd Thighearna Cholla (John MacLean, The Laird of Coll’s Bard) in Fèis Thiriodh (ed.) (2012) *Òrain an Eòrna – Traditional Gaelic Songs from Tiree* Fèis Thiriodh and An Iodhlann, Isle of Tiree

‘Òran na Cloiche’ Dòmhnall Mac an t-Saoir (Donald MacIntyre) in MacMillan, S. (ed.) (1968) *Sporan Dhòmhnaill – Gaelic Poems and Songs by the late Donald MacIntyre, The Paisley Bard* Oliver and Boyd for the Scottish Gaelic Texts Society, Edinburgh

‘Òran nam Prìosanach’ Iain MacIlleathain, Bàrd Baile Mhàrtainn (John MacLean, The Balemartin Bard) in Meek, D. E. (ed.) (1995) *Tuath is Tighearna (Tenants and Landlords*) Scottish Academic Press for The Scottish Gaelic Texts Society, Edinburgh

‘Òran nan Dròbhairean’ Murchadh MacCoinnich (Murdo MacKenzie) in MacAonghais I., Wilson G., Taylor, S.J. (1998) *Bho Dhròbhadh Gàidhealach gu Fàsaichean Astràilia* No. 19 Dornoch Studio, Dornoch

‘Òran nan Rocaidean’ Dòmhnall Mac an t-Saoir (Donald MacIntyre) in MacMillan, S. (ed.) (1968) *Sporan Dhòmhnaill – Gaelic Poems and Songs by the late Donald MacIntyre, The Paisley Bard* Oliver and Boyd for the Scottish Gaelic Texts Society, Edinburgh

‘Pìobaireachd Dhòmhnaill Dhuibh’ Anon. at http://www.celticlyricscorner.net/macaskill/piobaireachd.htm

Tùsan nan Dàn is nan Òran: *Sources of Poems and Songs*

‘’S ann aig Ceann Tràigh Ghruinneart’ Anon. at https://islayhistory.blogspot.com/2012/08/ceann-traigh-ghruinart.html

‘’S gann gun dìrich mi chaoidh’ Tormod MacNeacail (Norman Nicholson) in The Campbells of Greepe (2013) *Fonn* Acair, Stornoway

‘Seathan Mac Rìgh Èireann’ Anon. in Carmichael, A. (1954) *Carmina Gadelica, Vol V*, Oliver and Boyd, Edinburgh

‘Sgeula uam-sa mu Raon Ruairidh’ (Coille Chragaidh) Iain mac Ailein mhic Iain mhic Eoghainn (John MacLean) in Maclean, A. S. (1881) *Clàrsach na Coille* Alex MacLaren & Sons, Glasgow

‘’S gura mise tha gu h-uallach’ (Mo ghaol òigear a’ chuil duinn) Mòr NicIllÌosa (Marion Gillies) in MacDonald, A. and MacDonald, A. (eds.) (1911) *The MacDonald Collection of Gaelic Poetry* The Northern Counties Newspaper and Printing and Publishing Company, Inverness

‘Sìne Bhàn’ (Bruaillean cogaidh anns an tìr) Donnchadh MacIain (Duncan Johnstone) in Johnstone, D. (1938) *Crònan nan Tonn* Archd. Sinclair, Celtic Press, Glasgow

‘’S iom’ oidhche anmoch a thug mo mheanma’ (’S mòr mo mhulad) Robertson from Piteaghabhann in Thomson, D.S. (ed.) (1992) *The MacDiarmid MS Anthology* Published by Scottish Academic Press for the Scottish Gaelic Texts Society, Edinburgh

‘’S mise tha fo mhì-ghean mun ghille dhonn’ Anon. at https://www.bbc.co.uk/alba/oran/orain/an_gille_donn

MacDonald, A. and MacDonald, A. (eds.) (1911) *The MacDonald Collection of Gaelic Poetry* The Northern Counties Newspaper and Printing and Publishing Company, Inverness

‘’S nuair ràna mi ’n doras bha ’n glas air mo shròin’ Anon. Transcribed from the singing of Rona Lightfoot CD Eadarainn SKYECD28

‘Srath Nabhair’ Ruaraidh MacThòmais (Derick Thomson) in Thomson, D.S. (1982) *Creachadh na Clàrsaich (Plundering the Harp)* MacDonald, Edinburgh

‘Smeòrach Chlann Dòmhnaill’ Iain MacCodrum (John MacCodrum) in Matheson, W. (ed.) (1939) *The Songs of John McCodrum* Oliver & Boyd, Edinburgh

‘Soraidh Leibh is Oidhche Mhath Leibh’ Iain MacPhàidein (John MacFadyen) in MacFadyen, J. (1902) *Sgeulaiche nan Caol* Archd. Sinclair, Celtic Press, Glasgow

‘Tàladh Dhòmhnaill Ghuirm’ A Mhuime, (his Foster-mother) in Watson, W.J. (ed.) (1918) *Bàrdachd Ghàidhlig Gaelic Poetry 1550-1900* An Comunn Gàidhealach, Inverness

‘Tha do phearsa cuimir dealbhach’ nighean Tighearna Ghrannd (The Laird of Grant’s Daughter) in MacDonald, A. (1914) *Story and Song from Loch Ness-side* Northern Counties Newspaper and Print Company, Inverness

‘Tha mi nam chadal, na dùisgibh mi’ (Do dh’Arm Righ Sheumas) Sìleas na Ceapaich (Cicily MacDonald of Keppoch) in Ó Baoill, C. (ed.) (1972) *Bàrdachd Shìlis na Ceapaich and Berneray* Scottish Academic Press for The Scottish Gaelic Texts Society, Edinburgh

‘Tha mi sgìth ’n fhògar seo’ Iain MacRath (John MacRae) in Caimbeul, M. S. (ed.) (2020) *Iain mac Mhurchaidh, The Life and Work of John MacRae, Kintail and North Carolina* The Scottish Gaelic Texts Society, Glasgow

‘The Mingulay Boat Song’ Sir H. S. Roberton in Roberton, H. S. (1937) *Songs of the Isles* J. Curwen & Sons, London

Thig loingeas le gaoith’ (Òran do Dhòmhnall Gorm) Iain Lom MacDhòmhnaill (John MacDonald) in MacKenzie, A.M. (ed.) (1964) *Òrain Iain Luim, Songs of John MacDonald, Bard of Keppoch* Scottish Academic Press for the Scottish Gaelic Texts Society, Edinburgh

‘Thogail nam Bò’ Anon. in Newton, M. (1999) *Bho Chluaidh gu Calasraid (From Clyde to Callander)* Acair, Stornoway

‘Thug mi tamall an toiseach’ (Òran is i san sgoil am Peart) Mairearad Ghriogarach (Margaret MacGregor) in Byrne, M. (2007) *Mairearad Ghriogarach: sùil thòiseachail air bana-bhàrd air dìochuimhne* Scottish Gaelic Studies, Aberdeen University Press, Aberdeen

‘Trod nam Ban Eigeach’ Iain Dubh mac Iain mhic Ailein (John MacDonald) in Ó Baoill, C. (ed.) (1994) *Iain Dubh: òrain a rinn Iain Dubh mac Iain mhic Ailein* An Clò Gàidhealach, Aberdeen

Comharran-clèithe: *Grid-referenced Locations*

LOCATION	OS GRID REFERENCE
A	
Abbey of Deer	NJ 96855 48107
Aberfoyle	NN 52295 00986
Achdalieu	NN 05750 78450
Achilty Hotel	NH 45095 56658
Achnasheen	NH 16157 58480
Achnashellach	NH 00215 48183
Alan MacRanald's Leap	NH 45356 1 9271
Altimarlach	ND 33164 52568
Amhuinnsuidhe Castle	NB 04951 07806
Amity House	NB 42126 32735
Appin	NM 93653 46218
Applecross village	NG 71044 44463
Ardlui	NN 31759 15719
Ardmore	NG 22478 61224
Ardroil	NB 04406 32173
Arinachaig	NG 98505 4555
Armadale Castle	NG 64050 04650
Ashaig	NG 68718 24168
Aultbea	NG 87563 88916
B	
Balallan	NB 26065 19544
Balavil	NH 54350 53750
Balconie Castle	NH 61596 65727
Baldornie	NJ 42250 36950
Balfron	NS 54684 88690
Balivanich	NF 77723 55343
Ballachulish Village	NN 08543 58330
Ballantrushal	NB 37560 53779
Ballaterach	NO 42188 96020
Balloch	NS 39203 81888
Balmoral Forest	NO 25366 86902
Balnagowan Estates	NH76056 74948
Barra	NL 66600 98192
Barvas	NB 36102 49824
Battle of the Shirts	NN 28950 96750
Beauly Firth	NH 61299 47525
Ben Lee	NG 50211 33629
Ben Lomond	NN 36703 02866
Benbecula	NF 82526 53366

LOCATION	OS GRID REFERENCE
Blair Castle	NN 86554 66200
Borve Castle	NF 77337 50515
Bowmore	NR 31112 59733
Braemar	NO 15023 91408
Brahan Castle	NH 51687 54749
Breaclete	NB 15930 36771
Bridgend	NR 33538 62434
Broadford Hotel	NG 64041 23549
Brodick	NS 01455 36052
Brora	NC 90613 04023
Bunessan	NM 38458 21933
Butter Bridge	NN 23417 09514
C	
Caisteal Tioram	NM 66216 72430
Callander	NN 62846 07891
Canna	NG 27453 05493
Cape Wrath	NC 25968 74733
Carinish	NF 82071 60404
Carnasserie Castle	NM 83908 00848
Castle Camus	NG 67147 08714
Castle Moil	NG 75803 26347
Castle Rock	NT 25132 73501
Castle Toward	NS 11860 67860
Catlodge	NN 63755 93005
Chartershall	NS 79274 90319
Church of St. Fillan	NN 35791 28345
Cille Choirill	NN 30690 81204
Clach nan Tarbh	NN 32501 13676
Clachan, N. Uist	NF 81055 63895
Cladach, Brodick	NS 01176 37682
Clunie	NO 10950 43850
Cnap a' Chaolais, Ballachulish	NN 05172 59617
Coll	NM 20750 58450
Colonsay and Oronsay	NR 38165 93823
Commando Memorial	NN 20788 82369
Connel	NM 91123 34476
Contin	NH 45800 56127
Corpach	NN 09521 76848
Corrybeg	NM 99580 78858
Corrychoille	NN 25057 80616
Craignure	NM 71788 37150
Crathie	NO 26542 94950

LOCATION	OS GRID REFERENCE
Crianlarich	NN 38625 25335
Crieff	NN 86289 21296
Culloden	NH 74006 45000
Culnaknock	NG 51572 63085
D	
Dail Rìgh	NN 34250 29150
Dalilea	NM 73408 69320
Dalness	NN 14235 48305
Daviot	NH 72293 39344
Derry Lodge	NO 04134 93400
Dingwall	NH 55141 58730
Ditch of Blood	NF 8184160471
Drumnadrochit	NH 50825 30147
Drumochter	NN 63222 75638
Drynoch	NG 41150 31350
Duart	NM 74869 35316
Dùn Èistean	NB 53574 65040
Dun an Sticir	NF 89715 77675
Dun Nosebridge	NR 37150 60150
Dun Sgathaich	NG 59550 12050
Dunaverty Castle	NR 68815 07485
Dunbeath	ND 16050 29850
Dunblane	NN 78200 01275
Dunfermline	NT 08970 87449
Dunoon	NS 17295 77357
Duntrune	NR 79363 95576
Duntulm	NG 40992 74365
Dunvegan Castle	NG 24734 49116
Durine	NC 40198 67671
E	
Eas a' Chùil Àlainn	NC 28150 27850
Eigg	NM 47650 86850
Eilean Donan Castle	NG 88136 25858
Eilean Fraoch	NN 10866 25188
Eoropie	NB 51927 65153
Eriskay	NF 79529 11213
F	
Fionnphort	NM 30258 23279
Floddigarry Hotel	NG 46387 71918
Fort Augustus	NH 37946 09097
Fortingall	NN 74147 47000

LOCATION	OS GRID REFERENCE
G	
Gaick Lodge	NN 75761 84834
Gairloch Established Church	NG 80761 75609
Gartnaval	NS 55269 67879
Garve Hotel and An Goirtean	NH 39429 61730
Gesto	NG 35725 36633
Gigha	NR 64870 48852
Glen Croe	NN 24800 04493
Glen Esk	NO 52430 77356
Glen Gollaidh	NC 43581 41951
Glen Lyon	NN 72238 47617
Glenfinnan	NM 89750 80350
Govan	NS 54844 65341
Great Bernera	NB 18773 34789
Grisapoll	NM 18930 59132
Gruline	NM 54937 39841
H	
Harlaw	NJ 75144 24082
Highbridge	NN 20063 82118
Howmore	NF 75741 36437
I	
Inver	NO 01655 42235
Inverawe House	NN 02173 31591
Inverewe Botanical Garden	NG 86231 81622
Inverey	NO 08891 89226
Invergarry Castle	NH 31481 00632
Inverkeithing	NT 12956 82820
Inverness	NH 66642 45382
Inverlochy	NN 12039 75442
Inveruglas	NN 32270 09584
Isle Oronsay	NG 70117 12345
K	
Kenmore, Loch Fyne	NN 06481 01996
Kenmore, Loch Tay	NN 77350 45450
Kensaleyre	NG 41997 51401
Kilbride	NF 75182 14508
Kilbride, Skye	NG 58939 20240
Kilchorile	NN 30690 81204
Kildrummy	NJ 45488 16387
Kilmarie	NG 55356 17128

LOCATION	OS GRID REFERENCE
Kilmonivaig	NN 21283 81933
Kilmuir Cemetery	NG 39950 71850
Kilpatrick	NS 46669 72732
King's Cave	NR 88445 30925
Kingsburgh	NG 39431 55256
Kingussie	NH 75644 00509
Kinlochewe	NH 02721 62037
Kirkibost	NB 18778 34723
Kismul Castle	NL 66526 97948
Kyle of Cromarty	NH 58929 61299
Kyle of Lochalsh	NG 76112 27260
Kyleakin	NG 75268 26378
Kylesku Bridge	NC 22685 33817
L	
Laggan	NN 29338 97360
Lamlash	NS 03134 31617
Lettermore	NN 03135 59455
Leverburgh	NG 01725 86378
Lismore	NM 85196 40956
Lix Toll	NN 54770 30099
Loch Sianta	NG 47141 69938
Loch Urr	NX 76093 84566
Lochcarron Village	NG 90962 40112
Lochearnhead	NN 58866 23797
Lochmaddy	NF 91771 68892
Logierait	NN 96933 51972
Lòn na Fola	NH 47250 21950
M	
Macquarie Mausoleum	NM 54950 39850
Mallaig	NM 67570 97076
Mealfourvonie	NH 45705 22211
Mellon Charles	NG 84866 91191
Melness	NC 58128 60899
Milton	NF 74022 26921
Mitchell Hill Cemetery	NH 54920 58416
Monkstad	NG 37998 67506
Moy	NM 61743 24696
Mulhagery	NB 19364 11975
Mull	NM 52550 33079
Mullroy	NN 26922 81936

LOCATION	OS GRID REFERENCE
N	
New Achnacarry Castle	NN 17678 87966
North Inch of Perth	NO 11818 24231
Novar	NH 61412 67971
Nunton	NF 76640 53800
O	
Oban	NM 85950 29850
Old Inverlochy	NN 12039 75442
Our Lady of the Isles	NF 77635 40740
P	
Pennycross	NM 50707 26188
Perth	NO 11556 23479
Pitlochry	NN 93863 58204
Pollewe	NG 85718 80749
Portree Jailhouse	NG 48331 43452
R	
Raon Ruairidh	NN 91241 62925
Rodel	NG 04773 83184
Rum	NM 41156 99141
Ruthven Barracks	NN 76470 99750
S	
Sabhal Mòr Ostaig	NG 65517 06207
Salen	NM 57354 43104
Scalpay, Skye	NG 63077 28329
Scone	NO 13890 26230
Sconser	NG 52532 32245
Sheildaig	NG 80199 72694
Shenval	NJ 21542 29565
Sherrifmuir	NN 82894 02815
Shiel Bridge	NG 93549 18862
Siaba	NM 43822 19202
Signal Rock	NN 12126 56773
Site of the Battle of Glen Shiel	NG 99097 13381
Skeabost Island	NG 41812 48518
Sligachan Bridge	NG 48635 29841
Sligachan Hotel	NG 48542 29833
Snishival	NF 76765 34047
Snizort Parish Church	NG 42130 51726
South Queensferry	NT 12433 78201

LOCATION	OS GRID REFERENCE
Spean Bridge	NN 22194 81713
St. Moluag's Church	NB 51925 65155
Staffa	NM 32350 35550
Stornoway	NB 42476 32695
Storr	NG 50051 53982
Stratheyre	NN 56099 17192
Struan	NG 34261 38154
T	
Tain	NH 78065 82073
Tarbert, Loch Nevis	NM 79096 92414
Tarbet	NN 31610 04560
The Dark Flood	NM 90596 80814
The Museum of Island Life	NG 39530 71761
The Nunnery at Mealista	NA 99091 24056
Thurso	ND 11687 68450
Tiree	NL 98539 41175
Tongue	NG 66450 08950
Tordarroch	NH 67772 33434
Tore	NH 60267 52482
Torvaig campsite park	NG 49578 44931
Trinity Temple	NF 81563 60252
Tyndrum	NN 33009 30312
U	
Uig	NG 39626 64154
Uig Tower	NG 39545 63348
V	
Vatersay	NL 63208 94512
W	
Well of the Seven Heads	NN 30501 99147
Wick	ND 36236 50898

Clàr-amais: Index

Clàr-amais: Index

Clàr-amais: Index

Clàr-amais: Index

Clàr-amais: Index

Clàr-amais: Index

Clàr-amais: Index

Clàr-amais: Index

Clàr-amais: Index

Clàr-amais: Index

Clàr-amais: Index

Clàr-amais: Index

Riaghladair Carthannas na h-Alba
Carthannas Clàraichte/Registered Charity SC047866

Chuidich Comhairle nan Leabhraichean am foillsichear
le cosgaisean an leabhair.

Tha Acair a' faighinn taic bho Bhòrd na Gàidhlig.

First published in 2025 by Acair,
An Tosgan, Seaforth Road, Stornoway, Isle of Lewis, Scotland HS1 2SD

www.acairbooks.com info@acairbooks.com

Front cover illustration and design by Peter McDermott

The publishers are grateful for financial assistance towards publication of the book from the Gaelic Language Promotion Trust, Foundation Scotland, Urras an Eilein, the Andrew Tannahill Fund, the McCaig Trust and the Gaelic Society of London.

Typeset and designed in-house at Acair by Margaret A. MacLeod

A CIP catalogue record for this title is available from the British Library

Printed by Hussar Books, Poland

ISBN: 978-1-78907-169-6